Innovations in Group Facilitation:

Applications in Natural Settings

SCA Applied Communication Publication Program

Gary L. Kreps, Editor
Northern Illinois University

The SCA Program in Applied Communication supports the Speech Communication Association's mission of promoting the study, criticism, research, teaching, and application of artistic, humanistic, and scientific principles of communication. Specifically, the goal of this publication program is to develop an innovative, theoretically informed, and socially relevant body of scholarly works that examine a wide range of applied communication topics. Each publication clearly demonstrates the value of human communication in addressing serious social issues and challenges.

Editorial Board

Innovations in Group Facilitation:

Applications in Natural Settings

Edited by
Lawrence R. Frey
Loyola University Chicago

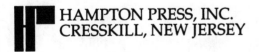 HAMPTON PRESS, INC.
CRESSKILL, NEW JERSEY

Copyright © 1995 by Hampton Press, Inc.

Printed in the United States of America

Library of Congress Cataloging-in-Publication Data

Innovations in group facilitation techniques : applications in natural
   settings / edited by Lawrence R. Frey.
      p.   cm. -- (SCA applied communication publication program)
   Includes bibliographical references and index.
   ISBN 1-881303-25-X. -- ISBN 1-881303-26-8 (pbk.)
   1. Group relations training. 2. Small groups. 3. Communication-
-Social aspects. I. Frey, Lawrence R. II. Series.
HM134.I56   1994   94-36275
302'.14--dc20-   CIP

Hampton Press, Inc.
23 Broadway
Cresskill, NJ 07626

CONTENTS

Foreword

Dennis S. Gouran
The Pennsylvania State University

In the nearly 60 years that have passed since Kurt Lewin attempted to adapt certain principles of the physical sciences to the study of small group behavior, research in the area has been marked by a series of ups and downs and assessments that have ranged from almost unbridled optimism about the future of inquiry to declarations of imminent demise. The chapters that follow would appear to suggest that in the 1990s the pendulum is swinging in the direction of hope and high expectations for a sustained period of applied work, through which groups can become more adept in the management of the organizational, institutional, and social problems currently affecting the human condition. In this respect, the volume extends the general line of work embodied in Hackman's (1990) recently published *Groups that Work (and Those that Don't): Creating Conditions for Effective Teamwork.*

To a large extent, the study of group process, from its inception, has been concerned with practical applications. Distinguishing current interest, however, is an expanded awareness of the importance of social context on the performance of groups and appreciation for variability in the methods appropriate to it. Historically, scholars have searched for general theories accounting for dynamics that, in fact, may well be peculiar to the specific sets of circumstances under which the members of groups deal with the issues and tasks confronting them. As a result, such perspectives as field theory, syntality theory, role theory, psychoanalytic theory, and even contingency theory have proved to have limited value both in unraveling the intricacies of interpersonal interaction in groups and in identifying the conditions under which desired outcomes are most likely.

The traditional logic governing the theory/practice relationships has been seductive and misleading. At its base is the notion that if we could somehow understand how groups function, then it would be a relatively simple matter to distinguish those that are effective from those that are not and then to take steps to assure that the essential conditions for effective performance are present. Hence, practice derives from theory and rigorous empirical tests of it. The chapters in this volume, on the whole, represent a significant departure from this logic.

Reflective of this departure is the concept of *facilitation*. The variety of tools and methods the contributors describe have in common an admittedly restricted utility. They are designed as aids to performance, not as governing mechanisms that determine ultimate success and failure. Although no method is completely free of underlying theoretical assumptions and premises, most of those examined here have not been direct outgrowths of formal theories of group process. If anything, these studies of facilitation methods will contribute to theory development and perspectives that are better focused and more directly relevant to specific types of task situations.

Further reflective of the departure from past logic are the focus on natural groups and the accompanying view that understanding group process as it functions in different social contexts requires the study of behavior with reference to the normal environments in which groups perform tasks and the specific objectives toward which their efforts are directed. Hence, the chapters comprising this volume report a series of case studies involving varied groups ranging from junior high school students who use tobacco to a Native American tribal council concerned with expanding participation in governance to teams attempting to implement organizational change. Within this frame of reference, theory is more likely to follow from careful and detailed observation than practice is to derive from theory.

The facilitation strategies and aids examined in these studies include the application of decision support systems to group decision-making and problem-solving tasks, refinements in conventional brainstorming and creative problem-solving techniques, focus groups as a source of information for generating and evaluating solutions to social problems, and "Interpretive Social Modelling" as a means of helping groups articulate and understand the problems and issues they seek to resolve. The assortment of facilitation methods is rich in potential and promise of possible extensions to the full range of task-oriented groups.

The authors of the individual chapters refrain from excessive claims about the virtues of the techniques and approaches they explicate because they are aware of the limitations of the means of group facilitation. However great the allure, novelty is not a guarantor of effectiveness. Group facilitation is clearly not a miracle cure for all that ails groups.

Rather, it is a family of tactics, strategies, and methods for converting group members' potential into maximum constructive action. Unfortunately, in everyday practice, the conversion is not uniformly successful. As is true of more traditional approaches to problem-solving and decision-making discussion, such as the method of reflective thinking, acceptance by group members, a willingness to conform to the requirements of the technique or strategy being employed, the ability to think intelligently, commitment to group goals, and a minimal level of skill in relating to others are crucial aspects of effective utilization. These are not especially easy requirements to satisfy.

An excellent example of how problematic participants can affect how successfully particular applications of a facilitation technique can be employed is the chapter by Poole, DeSanctis, Kirsch, and Jackson, who emphasize the importance of both understanding the purposes of group decision support systems and efforts to use them as intended as keys to optimum performance. They resist the temptation to excuse misapplication as anomalous and instead acknowledge the fact that mere availability of and exposure to technological aids are insufficient to assure their proper use.

Professor Frey and his associates should be commended for producing a volume worthy of the attention of serious students of group process and practitioners alike. The case studies reported not only illuminate applications of diverse approaches to group facilitation, but they also suggest possibilities for further research and scholarly inquiry. They additionally lay a substantial foundation for working with natural groups that, until recently, has been lacking in much so-called applied research. A great deal of the early work in this area consisted largely of consultants' "success" stories, with little hard, or even soft, evidence of how their initiatives in social and organizational settings actually played out.

There is, of course, much work to be done in the future on group facilitation. In addition to assessing the impact of problematic participants, there is the question of what constitutes an effective facilitative intervention. In some instances, the matter may be obvious, as in the case of a group attempting to identify means of improving morale in an organization. One might argue that the appropriate index of effectiveness would be implementation of a set of actions having that consequence and that are attributable directly to the intervention employed. Researchers must better address this issue and provide rationales for treating particular outcomes as indicative of the effectiveness of facilitation strategies and practices. Until this issue is addressed in a more concrete fashion, it will be difficult to determine the extent to which various approaches to facilitation result in both measurable and meaningful gains of the sort to which they are directed.

The fact that organizations and other types of social institutions are becoming more accessible to those doing applied research and that those in positions of authority are more receptive to innovation is a promising sign for sustained progress in determining what contributes to effective group performance and what poses obstacles to it. The conjunction of scholarly interest in groups and the real world problems that must be addressed by their members offers some exciting prospects both in respect to advancing knowledge and in contributing to society's material well-being. The chapters you are about to read represent important steps in these directions.

Acknowledgments

This text truly has been a group process and a group product. I have tried as an editor to facilitate the process, hopefully making it easier for these scholars-practitioners to accomplish the goals that they intended in their essays. My facilitator role was made easy by working with people who are both competent and extremely receptive to feedback. I want to thank each of the authors for making this project so enjoyable. The result is a group of essays that, although certainly not magical elixirs that will solve all the problems groups face, will, I hope, prove valuable to researchers, educators, practitioners, and, most important, group members. May all our group facilitation efforts be so easy and turn out so well.

About the Contributors

Ellen Bormann (B.A., Yale University) is Managing Director of Curtis-Bormann Associates, a communication consulting firm based in Minneapolis, MN. As a consultant, she has worked with such companies as Control Data, 3M, and the Minnesota Institute of Public Health, as well as various state and local governmental agencies.

Ernest G. Bormann is Professor in the Department of Speech-Communication at the University of Minnesota. Dr. Bormann is the author of numerous articles in such journals as *Today's Speech*, *Southern Communication Journal*, *Communication Studies*, *Journal of Broadcasting*, *Communication Monographs*, *Quarterly Journal of Speech*, *Communication Education*, and *Journal of Speech and Hearing Research*. He is author or coauthor of a number of books, including *Communication Theory, Small Group Communication: Theory and Practice* (3rd ed.), and *Effective Small Group Communication* (5th ed.). Professor Bormann is the recipient of the Outstanding Individual in Speech Communication in Minnesota Award of the Speech Association of Minnesota (1983), the Charles H. Woolbert Award for research projects that have stood the test of time of the Speech Communication Association (1983), the Outstanding Teacher Award of the College of Liberal Arts, University of Minnesota (1986), the B. Aubrey Fisher Mentoring Award of the International Communication Association (1988), the Distinguished Service Award of the Speech Communication Association (1990), and the Distinguished Scholar Award of the Speech Communication Association (1992).

Benjamin J. Broome (Ph.D., University of Kansas) is Associate Professor of Communication at George Mason University in Fairfax, VA, where he teaches courses in intercultural communication, group facilitation, and conflict management. He has designed

and conducted facilitated group sessions for a variety of organiza-
tions and community groups, including Ford Motor Company,
U.S. Department of Defense, National Marine Fisheries Services,
and several nonprofit groups. He has developed training programs
in interactive group design for the Defense Systems Management
College in Ft. Belvior, VA, and for the Instituto Technologico y de
Estudios Superiores de Monterrey in Mexico. He has worked with
several Native American Tribes, including the Winnebago in
Nebraska, the Menommine in Wisconsin, and the Comanche,
Apache, Cheyenne and Arapaho, and Pawnee Tribes in Oklahoma.
His work is published in several leading journals, including *Human
Communication Research, International Journal of Intercultural
Relations, Journal of Conflict Resolution, International Journal of
Conflict Management, Journal of Social Psychology, Management
Communication Quarterly, Communication Education,* and *Southern
Communication Journal.*

Joseph C. Chilberg (Ph.D., Ohio University) is Professor in the
Department of Communication at the State University of New
York at Fredonia, teaching courses in group and organizational
communication and training and development. His research and
consulting interests have focused on the role and process of group
facilitation and the use of interactive media in group and educational settings. He is a coauthor (with Arthur D. Jensen) of *Small
Group Communication: Theory and Application,* which includes a self-
facilitation manual for managing group projects.

John F. Cragan (Ph.D., University of Minnesota) is Professor in the
Department of Communication at Illinois State University. He
coauthored, with Donald C. Shields, his first published scholarly
article in 1970. His academic resume now includes 12 books, 34
articles, essays and book chapters, 70 convention papers, 48
applied communication research studies, 39 communication training programs, and 6 private, state, and federal grants.

Gerardine DeSanctis (Ph.D., Texas Tech University) is Professor in the
Information and Decision Sciences Department in the Carlson
School of Management at the University of Minnesota. Her research
interests include group decision support systems, impacts of computer graphics, methodology in information systems research, and
social theories of information systems. She has published extensively
in information systems, management, and communication journals,
and currently serves as an Associate Editor of *Organization Science.*
She is one of the developers of the Software Aided Meeting
Management (SAMM) group decision support system.

Patricia K. Felkins is Associate Professor of Communication at Loyola University Chicago, specializing in organizational communication, group process, and change consultation. For the past 12 years, Dr. Felkins has been a senior consultant with the B. J. Chakiris Corporation, working with management training, organizational development, and communication programs. Dr. Felkins is the coauthor of *Teamwork: Involving People in Quality and Productivity Improvement* (with Charles Aubrey); and *Change Management: A Model for Effective Organizational Performance* (with B. J. Chakiris and Ken N. Chakiris).

Lawrence R. Frey (Ph.D., University of Kansas) is Associate Professor of Communication at Loyola University Chicago. His primary areas of research and teaching are small group communication and communication research methods. He is the lead author of *Investigating Communication: An Introduction to Research Methods* and *Interpreting Communication Research: A Case Study Approach*, and is the editor of *Group Communication in Context: Studies of Natural Groups*. Dr. Frey has contributed chapters to a number of books and his articles have appeared in such journals as *Communication Monographs, Journal of Applied Communication Research, Communication Education*, and *Communication Studies*. In 1983, Dr. Frey was a recipient of Central States Communication Association's Outstanding Young Teacher Award.

Dennis S. Gouran (Ph.D., University of Iowa) is Professor and Head in the Department of Speech Communication at The Pennsylvania State University. Author of more than 100 books, articles, and reviews dealing with communication in groups, he is also past president of both the Central States Communication Association and the Speech Communication Association, as well as past editor of *Communication Studies* (formerly *Central States Speech Journal*). In 1992, he was named the first recipient of The Pennsylvania State University's Howard B. Palmer Faculty Mentoring Award and one of the first 10 Speech Communication Association's Distinguished Scholars. In 1993, he received Penn State University's Faculty Scholar's Medal for the Social and Behavioral Sciences.

Kathleen C. Harty is section chief of the Center for Nonsmoking and Health of the Minnesota Department of Health in Minneapolis, MN.

Michele Jackson (M.A., University of Minnesota) is a Ph.D. candidate at the University of Minnesota. Her dissertation research is a history of major examples of group communication technology, examining the relationship between designers' perspectives and technological development. Her areas of research include organizational communication, rationality in small groups, and communication technologies.

John (Sam) Keltner (Ph.D., Northwestern University) is an Emeritus Professor at Oregon State University, where he taught conflict management, mediation and arbitration, collective bargaining, and other related subjects for 25 years. He has extensive experience as a professional mediator, arbitrator, human relations and communication trainer, and educator. He is a principal of Consulting Associates, and founder of the Effective Communication Workshops, now in their 22nd year. He is a Charter member of the Society of Professionals in Dispute Resolution and former President of a newly organized Northwest chapter, a member of the Board of Directors of the Linn-Benton Mediation Project, and a trainer and member of the advisory committee for the Neighborhood Dispute Resolution Program in Benton County, OR. He is the author of *Mediation: Toward a Civilized System of Dispute Resolution* (1987), *The Management of Struggle: Elements of Dispute Resolution Through Negotiation, Mediation, and Arbitration* (1994), and other books and articles dealing with mediation, conflict, interpersonal communication, and human relations. He is also author and host of two videotape series depicting the nature and role of mediation in struggles between people and organizations.

Joann Keyton (Ph.D., The Ohio State University) is Associate Professor of Communication at The University of Memphis. Her research interests are organizational groups, flirting and sexual harassment in the workplace, and mentoring programs for females. She is on the editorial board of *Small Group Research*, and a certified SYMLOG practitioner.

Laurie Kirsch (Ph.D., University of Minnesota) is Assistant Professor in the Katz Graduate School of Business at the University of Pittsburgh. Her research interests include the management of information systems groups and activities in organizations and the impact of group decision support systems. She is active in information systems and management professional groups and has published in MIS Quarterly.

Gary L. Kreps (Ph.D., University of Southern California) is Professor of Communication Studies and a member of the Gerontology Faculty (Social Science Research Institute) at Northern Illinois University. He has published 15 books and more than 100 articles and chapters examining the role of communication in organizational life, health promotion, and education. Some of his most recent books include *Sexual Harassment: Communication Implications*

(1993), *Qualitative Research: Applications in Organizational Communication* (1993, with Sandra L. Herndon), and *Perspectives in Health Communication* (1993, with Barbara C. Thornton).

Bren Ortega Murphy (Ph.D., Northwestern University) is Associate Professor of Communication at Loyola University Chicago, where she teaches courses in persuasion, rhetorical criticism, gender, and ethics. She is a senior consultant with a major client service firm, focusing primarily on issues related to gender and facilitation techniques. Her research includes work on the relationship of media images and gender, media images and social movements, public discourse on gender issues, and women's education.

W. Barnett Pearce is Professor and Chair of the Department of Communication at Loyola University Chicago. Previous to this appointment, he taught at the Universities of Massachusetts, Kentucky, and North Dakota. His interests are sharply focused on "social constructionism" as a way of thinking about communication; his research wanders widely among the traditional "topics" within the discipline. He has contributed to many journals and anthologies; his books include *Reagan and American Public Discourse* (with Michael Weiler), *Culture, Politics and Research Programs: An International Assessment of Practical Problems in Field Research* (with Uma Narula); *Communication and the Human Condition; Development as Communication: A Perspective on India* (with Uma Narula); *Communication, Action, and Meaning: The Creation of Social Realities* (with Vernon Cronen); and *Communicating Personally* (with Charles Rossiter, Jr.).

Marshall Scott Poole (Ph.D., University of Wisconsin) is Professor of Speech-Communication at the University of Minnesota and Adjunct Professor in the Hubert H. Humphrey Institute for Public Policy. He has conducted research and published extensively on the topics of group communication, computer-mediated communication systems, conflict management, and organizational innovation. Scott is a principal co-investigator with the Minnesota Group Decision Support Systems Project and is co-developer of the Software Aided Meeting Management (SAMM) system.

David R. Seibold (Ph.D., Michigan State University) is Professor in the Department of Communication, University of California at Santa Barbara and has published more than 50 books, chapters, and articles. His current research interests include computer-augmented group decision making, influence strategies in the workplace, and organizational innovation processes (a recent article appeared in *Academy of Management*). He is also on the editorial board of *Management Communication Quarterly* and reviews regularly for *Administrative Science Quarterly*.

Donald C. Shields (Ph.D., University of Minnesota) is Associate Professor in the Department of Communication at the University of Missouri-St. Louis. He coauthored, with John F. Cragan, his first published article in 1970. His academic resume now includes 8 books, 42 articles, essays and book chapters, 35 convention papers, 40 applied communication research studies, 27 communication training programs, and 9 state, private, and federal grants.

Cynthia Stohl (Ph.D., Purdue University) is Professor of Communication at Purdue University. She has also taught at the University of Aarhus in Denmark and the University of Canterbury in Christchurch, New Zealand. Her research interests include communication networks, group communication, worker participation, and communication processes in international organizations. Her work has appeared in several books and journals, including *Communication Monographs, Human Communication Research, Management Communication Quarterly, Communication Yearbook,* and *Journal of Communication*.

INTRODUCTION

Applied Communication Research on Group Facilitation in Natural Settings

Lawrence R. Frey
Loyola University Chicago

From the quest for the Holy Grail to the alchemists' attempts to turn metal into gold, kings and queens and wizards and fools alike have searched throughout the ages for the magical elixirs that will cure their own and society's misfortunes. Today, the methods may be far less mystical and more scientific, but the search for such elixirs—from the antidote for AIDS to the production of fusion in the lab—goes on.

People currently see at least two general cures for what ails us in the modern age. The first is *education*, the belief that people can learn, usually with the help of others, how to help themselves. Education, especially in the United States, is seen as a great cure-all that miraculously will help people live a better life and make us equal in each other's eyes.

Nowhere is the value of education more apparent than in the communication discipline. Craig (1989) argues that communication is a "practical discipline" whose intellectual origins "can be found in work that attempts to systematize, evaluate critically, and improve public and private communicative practices" (p. 97). As Seibold (in press) explains, "Historically we have existed to help others speak more clearly, argue more persuasively, disseminate information more effectively, relate to others through talk more satisfactorily, and the like."

The second general cure is *research*, the systematic, step-by-step process of answering the questions we pose (Frey, Botan, Friedman, & Kreps, 1992). We have become a society that privileges the word "research" as a a "god term" that signifies an important, if not the most important, stamp of approval. Even the advertising industry is aware of the power of the appeal: "The latest research shows that . . . ."

The role of research, however, has expanded during the 20th century from focusing almost exclusively on the development, testing, clarification, and refinement of theory (basic research) to helping to solve "real-world" social problems (applied research). This concern for solving social problems has become an important basis for conducting communication research. As Cissna (1982) explains:

> Applied research sets out to contribute to knowledge by answering a real, pragmatic, social problem. Applied communication research involves such a question or problem of human communication or examines human communication in order to provide an answer or solution to the question or problem. The intent or goal of the inquiry (as manifest in the research report itself) is the hallmark of applied communication research. Applied communication research involves the development of knowledge regarding a real human communication problem or question. (Editorial statement)

Today, scholars study the practical significance, the applied value, of communication for solving many important social problems within a wide variety of contexts, from how to improve marital partners' communication to help stem the rising divorce rate to how to design communication campaigns to encourage people to practice safe sex in order to avoid the spread of AIDS and venereal diseases. Researchers, educators, and practitioners alike recognize the significant impact that messages can have, the value of educating people about how to design effective messages, and the importance of studying the message construction process.

Applied communication research, long considered the poor sister of basic communication research, has thus achieved a central place and status in the scholarship of the communication discipline. The Speech Communication Association's decision to launch the series for which this text is written, for example, attests to the acceptance and perceived importance of applied research within the communication discipline. Even Ellis (1982), who once called applied research "the shame of speech communication" for being "narrow, theoretically vacuous, without a research base, and, just as an aside, morally degenerate and politically naive" (p. 1), admitted recently that "applied research is crucial to the professional and intellectual development of communication" (1991, p. 121).

When these two elixirs—education and applied communication

research—are combined, there is a powerful potential for understanding how people can learn to use communication principles and practices to solve important social problems. Attempts to educate, however, need to be assessed in some way. We cannot just assume that instructing people about communication skills necessarily makes them better communicators in their interpersonal, group, and organizational lives; we need some evidence that instruction has, hopefully, some positive effects. The general purpose of this text is to do exactly that: to provide evidence of how instruction in communication can help solve important problems in the real world. The specific purpose of the text is to document the positive effects that facilitation of group communication has on solving some important problems that confront small groups.

GROUP FACILITATION

Nowhere is the need for applied communication research more important than in the study of small groups. Every segment of our society—from the largest multinational organization to the political workings of federal, state, city, and local governments to the smallest community action group to friendship groups to the nuclear and extended family—relies on groups to make important decisions, socialize members, satisfy emotional needs, and the like. Studies have shown that in the business world alone, managers spend 30-80% of their time in meetings (Mintzberg, 1973; Mosvick & Nelson, 1987), and Doyle and Strauss (1976) estimated that 11 million meetings take place every day in the United States. Seibold (1979) pointed out, in a rather scary prediction, that, "If we attend just four hours of work or civic meetings per week, we will have spent over 9000 hours in meetings during an average lifetime—more than one year of our life in meetings!" (p. 4).

When left on their own, however, groups often flounder and perform less effectively than possible. Indeed, the inefficiency of groups is the basis for an entire genre of jokes: "Committees are groups that keep minutes and waste hours," "A camel is a horse designed by a group," and "A meeting is a cul-de-sac down which promising young ideas are lured and quietly strangled." Joking aside, such inefficiency can have devastating consequences. Mosvick and Nelson (1987), for example, reported that inefficient group meetings resulted in losses of over $71 million per year for one company alone.

These problems lead many people to dread working in groups—Sorensen (1981) coined the term "grouphate" to describe this dread. The fact is, however, that working in groups is unavoidable. Lumsden and Lumsden (1993) respond to the oft-heard, "I'd really rather work alone . . .," with "Forget it, the twenty-first century works in groups" (p. 3). The reason for this is clear: In spite of the problems, group decision making *can* result in 40-50% increases in productivity over individual decision making ("The payoff from teams," 1989). The key word in that sentence, of course, is "can," and the reasons why this increase can occur have been noted by many researchers (see Davis, 1969; Hoffman, 1965; Maier, 1970; and Shaw, 1981) and were summarized recently by Poole (1991) as follows:

* Groups generally have greater knowledge than any individual.
* Groups have a diversity of perspectives on the situation, which results in better thinking. The greater the diversity (provided differences can be managed), the more effective the group.
* Group members can check each other's ideas.
* Merely being in the presence of others is psychologically arousing. This social facilitation effect stimulates greater effort by group members.
* Participation in group discussions often increases members' commitment to the decision.
* Bringing people with different points of view into contact will often surface conflicts which must be resolved for an effective and practical decision to emerge. (p. 67)

To achieve these benefits and prevent groups from floundering, individuals must first adopt more favorable attitudes about working in groups. Given that groups are here to stay, the adage, "Join them, don't fight them," certainly seems appropriate. Joining group work enthusiastically, however, does not mean accepting the floundering that often occurs. Groups also frequently need guidance and help in meeting the goals they set—they need *facilitation*.

The term *facilitation* is defined in the dictionary as "to make easier"; hence, *group facilitation* can be defined as any meeting technique, procedure, or practice that makes it easier for groups to interact and/or accomplish their goals. Meeting procedures are "sets of rules or guidelines which specify how a group should organize its process to achieve a particular goal" (Poole, 1992, p. 55). The goal may be to arrive at a high-quality policy decision or it may be to establish meaningful relationships that provide members with social support and emotional connections. The studies in this text look at five areas that are ripe for group facilitation: (a) promoting effective group problem solving and decision making; (b) encouraging constructive dialogue to resolve conflict and differences; (c) developing feedback techniques for empowering groups; (d) generating information in groups; and (e) building teams. Facilitation may also occur at the systemic level of the group itself, by getting groups, for example, to adopt particular discussion procedures, or it may focus on individuals, or even a single individual, within a group. Training individuals in effective group communication skills, for example, may reduce their grouphate (Sorensen, 1981). The techniques examined in this text focus mostly on group processes, but many can be used with individual group members, and one is intended to change the views of a single individual. Group facilitators can also focus on many aspects of individual and group behavior and can adopt a wide variety of theoretical perspectives to inform their facilitation efforts. Facilitators of therapy groups, for example, often use psychoanalytic procedures to promote members' self-awareness as well as personality and behavioral changes. This text focuses on techniques and accompanying theoretical perspectives that can be used to facilitate *group communication* for the purposes described. Finally, facilitation may occur because an outside consultant is asked to help a group, or as a result of members' attempts to help their group develop. In the former, facilitation typically takes the form of a technique that a consultant teaches a group to use, whereas in the latter, facilitation occurs whenever a member's behavior makes it easier for his or her group to move forward. The authors in this text are all consultants who were invited to work with groups, with the ultimate goal, in the cases of on-going groups, of getting the members themselves to adopt and use these techniques long after the consultants are gone. After all, one important sign of a consultant's success is that group members become competent at using the procedures and no longer need the consultant.

Over the years, there has been a tremendous growth in the sheer number of group communication facilitation techniques. Nutt (1984), for example, identified 47 different decision-making procedures (also see reviews of group facilitation techniques by Moore, 1987; and Poole, 1991). Some techniques—such as Robert's Rules of Order, assigning a devil's advocate, brainstorming, and focus groups—have become part of the general lexicon and part of group members' everyday facilitation toolbook, whereas others—such as the Delphi Method, the Nominal Group Technique, or Synectics—are understood and implemented primarily by experts who consult with groups.

There is also general agreement about why group facilitation procedures, in theory, should work. By focusing and guiding group members' communication and decision-making processes in a structured manner, they reduce the chances of engaging in faulty processes and harness the strengths of groups in at least nine ways:

1. Procedures coordinate members' thinking.
2. Procedures provide a set of objective ground rules.
3. Procedures protect groups against their own bad habits.
4. Procedures capitalize on the strengths of groups.

5. Procedures balance member participation.
6. Procedures surface and help manage conflicts.
7. Procedures give groups a sense of closure in their work.
8. Procedure make groups reflect on their meeting process.
9. Procedures empower groups. (Poole, 1991, pp. 75-80)

Although many group facilitation techniques are available and theoretical rationales for their success are apparent, there has not been a corresponding increase in research about the nature and effects of these techniques. Some texts offer general advice about using particular facilitation methods, but, as Gouran pointed out in the foreword, evidence traditionally has been in the form of consultants' "success" stories with little evidence offered for these claims. Research simply has lagged behind practical developments and advice giving.

This text seeks to narrow the gap between research and practice by documenting how a variety of facilitation techniques have been used with natural groups. Each of the authors has extensive experience as both a researcher and practitioner, and they bring these skills together in this text, showing us in case studies how they used a particular technique to facilitate group communication and make it easier for groups and, in the case of generating information from focus groups, researchers to accomplish their goals.

This chapter starts the process by introducing the reader to the study of group facilitation and pointing out some significant features of conducting research on such techniques in natural settings. To this end, the next section presents a brief history of research on group facilitation techniques. What emerges from this history is a clear need for research about the value of using these techniques with real-life groups. The chapter then introduces the case studies examined in this text and addresses some important issues that these and other applied researchers must confront when they study facilitation efforts in natural groups.

COMMUNICATION RESEARCH ON GROUP FACILITATION

Communication research on group facilitation seeks to understand how interventions that affect the communicative behavior of group members impacts group interaction, development, and goal attainment. For descriptive purposes, this research is divided into three time periods.

The Roots of Group Facilitation: 1890-1945

Scholarly interest in group facilitation can be traced back to the study of *social facilitation*, the influence of others in a group on individuals' behavior, at the turn of the 19th century (see Shaw, 1981). Triplett (1897), for example, assessed the effects of competition on individuals' behavior by studying the records that had been kept on three types of bicycle races: ones in which the riders rode by themselves, ones in which they were paced by a multicycle setting the pace, and ones in which they raced against several riders. The results showed that competition produced the fastest times, followed by paced races. Subsequent studies by Allport (1920), Pessin and Husband (1933), Travis (1925, 1928), and Weston and English (1926) found that the presence of others did produce social facilitation effects with respect to a wide range of behavior, although not always in the direction of better performance. The potential ability of groups to facilitate individuals' behavior, however, was firmly established by these early studies.

A second direction for early research *was demonstrating whether group discussion was superior when compared to individual problem solving* (usually questions of fact, although some information and evaluation tasks were studied as well). Research showed that groups usually were superior both qualitatively (i.e., better quality decisions) and quantitatively (i.e., faster decision making) than individuals working alone (e.g., Barton, 1926; Dashiell, 1935; Gurnee, 1937; Jenness, 1932; Marston, 1924; Shaw, 1932; Thorndike, 1938a, 1938b; Timmons, 1939; and Watson, 1928). Dickens and Heffernan's (1949) review of this literature concluded that, "After discussion, judgments tend to improve in accuracy and correctness" (p. 26). This improvement was shown to be due primarily to the effects that group discussion had on attitude change (Des Jarlais, 1943; and Simpson, 1938, 1939) and on thinking processes and argumentative reasoning (Miller, 1939).

A third group of forefathers adapted American philosopher John Dewey's work on human thought patterns to group discussion. Dewey (1910) proposed the *reflective thinking process*, a systematic cognitive pattern people use to solve complex problems that consists of five steps:

1. A felt difficulty.
2. Its location and definition.
3. Suggestion of possible solution.
4. Development by reasoning of the bearing of suggestions.
5. Further observation and experiment leading to its acceptance or rejection; that is, the conclusion of belief or disbelief. (p. 72)

Educators during the 1920s and 1930s saw Dewey's reflective thinking process as a model for democratic decision making and subsequently adapted and incorporated it into group discussion textbooks (e.g., Baird, 1927; Elliott, 1927; McBurney & Hance, 1939; and Sheffield, 1926).

McBurney and Hance (1939), for example, proposed the following five-step sequence that groups should follow to analyze a problem effectively:

1. Definition and delineation of the problem.
2. Analysis of the problem.
3. The suggestion of solutions.
4. Reasoned development of the proposed solutions.
5. Further verification.

Pedagogical writings about the facilitative effects of the reflective thinking pattern for organizing group discussion were prescriptive in nature; that is, educators simply asserted that groups should use this pattern to solve problems. Although Carr (1929) found that group discussion could be characterized qualitatively by the five reflective thinking steps, and Johnson (1943) developed an instrument for measuring the process, empirical research about the facilitative effects of reflective thinking did not occur until much later.

The Facilitative Effects of Communication: 1945-1970

The general study of small groups flourished between 1945-1970 due to both the promise of group research as a cure for war as well as the general increase in higher education and especially in the empirical social psychological fields (see Borgatta, 1960). Research about group communication and its facilitative effects also flourished.

The first line of inquiry concerned the effects of *communication networks,* "the arrangement (or pattern) of communication channels among the members of a group" (Shaw, 1981, p. 453). Researchers studied the effects of communication networks on a variety of outcomes—including leadership emergence, organizational development, member relations, and problem-solving efficiency—by imposing onto groups different communication structures (such as the wheel, circle, chain, or "Y") that restricted who could communicate with whom.

The results showed that the effects of communication networks on group problem-solving efficiency were moderated by the nature of the task: Decentralized networks were more effective for solving complex problems, whereas centralized networks were more effective for solving simple problems (e.g., Guetzkow & Simon, 1955; Hirota, 1953; Lanzetta & Robey, 1956a, 1956b; Lawson, 1964a, 1964b; Mulder, 1960; and Shaw, 1954a, 1954b). Research also showed that: (a) persons in more central network positions emerged as leaders more often than those in peripheral positions (e.g., Hirota, 1953; Leavitt, 1951; and Shaw, 1954b); (b) centralized communication networks led to centralized organizations in which information was fed to one central person who solved the problem, whereas unrestricted networks led to each-to-all organizational patterns in which all available information was transmitted to all group members, each of whom then solved the problem independently (e.g., Cohen, 1961, 1962; Guetzkow & Dill, 1957; Leavitt, 1951; Schein, 1958; Shaw, 1954b; and Shaw & Rothschild, 1956); and (c) group morale was greater in decentralized than centralized communication networks (Cohen, 1961, 1962; Lawson, 1965; Leavitt, 1951; Shaw, 1954b; and Shaw & Rothschild, 1956). This research thus showed the potential facilitative effects of communication networks, although the exact effects were dependent on the type of task groups confronted (see Hirokawa & Gouran, 1989).

A second line of research investigated the facilitative effects of *group leaders' communication*. Leadership theory during this era shifted from person-centered (trait theory) and context-centered (situational theory) approaches to foregrounding the effects of leaders' communicative behavior. Barnard (1938), for example, was one of the first to claim that communication was the most important skill needed for effective leadership. Lewin and his associates (e.g., Lewin & Lippitt, 1938; Lewin, Lippitt, & White, 1939; Lippitt, 1939, 1940; Lippitt & White, 1952; and White & Lippitt, 1960) argued for a style approach to leadership and tested it by experimentally exposing groups to three leadership styles (democratic, authoritarian, and laissez-faire) and then observing their effects on productivity and satisfaction. The results showed that authoritarian groups produced more, but this production tailored off when the leader left the room, whereas democratic groups produced at a consistently high rate and were far more satisfied and cohesive.

Other researchers investigated the relationship between communication and leadership emergence. Mortensen (1966), for example, showed that individuals who exercised substantial influence over group activities emerged as perceived group leaders over assigned leaders. Such research represented a functional approach to leadership, arguing that leadership results whenever members enact communicative behaviors that move a group forward. (Note the similarity between this definition of leadership and that advanced earlier regarding members' facilitative efforts within a group.) Scholars started pinpointing the specific communicative behaviors associated with different leadership styles. Blake and Mouton (1968, 1978, 1985), for example, devised a procedure for identifying different types of group leaders (bureaucrat, country-club manager, task master, compromiser, and ideal) by plotting members' behavior onto a grid with two axes: concern for people (socioemotional) and concern for production (task). Leadership during this era thus became associated with communicative behaviors that facilitate group interaction and task accomplishment.

An interesting offshoot of the study of the facilitative effects of leaders' communicative behaviors was the use of "metacommunication" principles (communication about communication) in laboratory training in group process. In June 1946, Lewin conducted a workshop designed to develop leaders' facilitative abilities by offering them opportunities to lead groups and then discussing with them the results of their efforts (see Benne, 1964). Members of these leaders' groups attended one of the processing sessions held for the leaders and began to comment on the comments that were made about them. These metacommunicative comments involved "the participants in the critical exploration of *their own process* in an intense, open, and confrontational way" (Keltner, 1989, p. 12). The value of this approach was apparent immediately to the organizers of these leadership seminars, and in 1947, they founded the National Training Laboratory in Bethel, ME with the purpose of using training groups (or "T-Groups," as they were called) to focus directly on group process. T-Groups later were adapted to focus on interpersonal communication for the purpose of promoting personal, interpersonal, and group growth (called "sensitivity groups" and "encounter groups"). The facilitative value of T-Groups and their derivatives has received a fair share of attention from researchers, with mixed results (see reviews by Blumberg & Golembiewski, 1976; Cooper, 1975; Cooper & Mangham, 1971; Golembiewski & Blumberg, 1977; and Lieberman, Yalom, & Miles, 1973).

The third line of communication research on group facilitation focused on *procedures for organizing group discussion*, mainly for the purpose of generating ideas. Merton (1946) and Merton, Fiske, and Kendall (1956), for example, used the focus group method as a way to study the persuasiveness of propaganda and as a means of increasing military morale. The focus group method "generally involves 8 to 12 individuals who discuss a particular topic under the direction of a moderator who promotes interaction and assures that the discussion remains on the topic of interest" (Stewart & Shamdasani, 1990, p. 10). The facilitative effects of this method, when compared to dyadic interviews, result from group members encouraging one another to share their views and ideas.

Osborn (1957) later proposed the "brainstorming" technique as a group discussion procedure for producing ideas. The technique was based on four simple rules:

1. Criticism is ruled out.
2. "Free-wheeling" is welcomed; the wilder the idea, the better.
3. Quantity is desired.
4. Combination and improvement of ideas through "piggybacking" are encouraged.

Subsequent research found that brainstorming groups did indeed produce more ideas than non-brainstorming groups (e.g., Bouchard, 1969; Brilhart & Jochem, 1964; Parloff & Handlon, 1964; and Weisskopf-Joelson & Eliseo, 1961). Lamm and Trommsdorff's (1973) review of the literature, however, suggested that although brainstorming groups did produce more ideas than non-brainstorming groups, individuals brainstorming alone actually produced more ideas than individuals brainstorming in groups, primarily because of the limited time available to group members to offer ideas and because there still was a fear of negative evaluation despite the attempt to rule out criticism.

Meanwhile, the effects of the reflective thinking pattern or variations of it were now being investigated empirically. Researchers showed that reflective thinking differentiated effective from ineffective group participants (Pyron, 1964; Pyron & Sharp, 1963) and led to higher quality group decisions (Sharp & Millikin, 1964), although some research did not show such advantages (e.g., Bayless, 1967; Brilhart, 1966; and Larson, 1969).

Communication as Group Facilitation—The Medium is the Message: 1970-1990

Contemporary scholars see communication not just as an act that someone does to another; more importantly, it is *the* process by which people attribute meaning, form relationships, make decisions, and so forth. Contemporary group research, therefore, has focused more and more on communication and its facilitation as *the* means for improving groups.

One important question concerns the effects of *group communication education* on group members, their interactions, and group outcomes. Research demonstrated that those who received training in group discussion (usually problem-solving or T-Group training) changed their attitudes and became more effective in interacting within groups. Larson and Gratz (1970), for example, showed that both problem-solving and T-Group training resulted in more open-mindedness and marked improvement in critical thinking ability, with increased problem-solving accuracy occurring only in the T-Groups, whereas Weaver (1971) showed that sensitivity training techniques served as catalysts for helping people relate better to others and for participating in structured, problem-solving group discussions. Other research showed that training in group problem solving did improve problem-solving proficiency (e.g., Dillon, Graham, & Aidells, 1972; Laughlin & Adamopoulous, 1980; and Laughlin & Jaccard, 1975). More recently, Firestien (1990) showed that groups trained in creative problem solving participated more, criticized ideas less, verbally supported ideas more, laughed more, smiled more, and generated more ideas than groups not trained in such techniques. These applied research results thus show the facilitative effect of group communication education.

The second line of research continues to explore the value of *discussion procedures* for generating ideas and making decisions. Philipsen, Mulac, and Dietrich (1979), for example, found that nominal groups (in which individuals work alone but their efforts are pooled as a group) produced fewer and lowerquality ideas than interacting groups, whereas Burleson, Levine, and Samter (1984) found that groups assigned to use an interacting decision procedure produced both better individual and group decisions than groups that employed either a staticized procedure that allowed no communication between group members or a nominal decision procedure that allowed only limited communication mediated by a leader-recorder or moderator. Nelson, Petelle, and Monroe (1974) found that brainstorming maximized both the quantity and quality of ideas generated, but Jablin (1981) actually found that significantly more ideas were produced in nominal brainstorming groups than in interacting brainstorming groups. Miner (1984) suggested that interaction is dysfunctional during the idea-generation phase of group decision making, but is facilitative during the evaluation and synthesis phases, whereas Hill (1982) argued that these differences could be accounted for by the type of task groups performed. Hirokawa (1985) found no differences in decision-making effectiveness between groups assigned to four discussion formats (reflective thinking, ideal-solution, single-question, and a free discussion format), whereas Jarboe (1988) found that groups assigned to use a nominal group technique produced more ideas for solutions than groups that used a reflective thinking technique. Hirokawa, Ice, and Cook (1988), however, did find that groups assigned to use a modified version of Dewey's "reflective thinking" process arrived at higher quality decisions than groups that used a low-structure process (those told only to base their "decision on a consideration of critical questions that need to be answered, and the critical information that needs to be taken into account, in order to produce a high quality recommendation" [pp. 221-222]). The results from these studies thus provide mixed evidence concerning the facilitative effects of group discussion procedures.

A third line of research concerns the facilitative value of *feedback* within small groups. Feedback provides important information about both group interaction and performance (see Ashford & Cummings, 1983; and Nadler, 1979), and research shows that feedback does increase group performance (e.g., Erez, 1977; and Nadler, 1979). Developing high-quality feedback processes within groups is thus crucial for effective task accomplishment. Leathers (1972), for example, showed that the quality of group feedback was related directly to the quality of the product in problem-solving groups, although Ogilvie and Haslett (1985) cautioned that different tasks probably require different types of feedback. Finally, research showed that observational schemes for coding group discourse can sometimes be used to provide facilitative feedback to groups. Boethius (1987) and Schantz (1986), for example, both used Bales and Cohen's (1979) SYMLOG (System for the Multiple Level Observation of Groups) observational scheme as an intervention tool to diagnose and treat threats to group unification and productivity.

The final line of research examines what *modalities of communication* best facilitate group interaction and performance (see Hirokawa & Gouran, 1989). Of particular interest are the new information technologies—such as teleconferencing, computer conferencing, and electronic meeting systems—because organizations are relying more and more on them for group meetings (see Hiltz & Turoff, 1978; Johansen, Vallee, & Spengler, 1979; Rice & Associates, 1984; and Short, Williams, & Christie, 1976). An electronic meeting system, for example, should increase the quality of group communication and decision making because it "enables all participants to work simultaneously, . . . provides equal opportunity for participants, . . . [and] permits the group to use a spectrum of structured and unstructured techniques and methods to perform the task" (Nunamaker, Dennis, Valacich, Vogel, & George, 1991, pp. 43-44). Researchers have found that in comparison to face-to-face groups, computer-mediated groups result in more even participation (Nunamaker et al., 1991; Pinsonneault & Kraemer, 1989), more process and initiation statements (Zigurs, Poole, & DeSanctis, 1988), arguments that are closer to the ideal type (Brashers, Adkins, & Meyers, 1994), and more ideas generated (Olaniran, Friedrich, & VanGundy, 1992; Pinsonneault & Kraemer, 1989). Hence, even though we are only beginning to understand the facilitative effects of such new technologies on groups, they promise to have wide-ranging effects.

STUDYING FACILITATION EFFORTS IN NATURAL GROUPS

The research reviewed above suggests that we know much about the facilitation of group communication and the results of such efforts. It is clear that both individual and group behavior *can be* influenced by discussion procedures, communication networks, members' communicative behavior, and communication modalities. Most important for the purposes of this text, facilitative interventions as educational efforts can prove successful.

When one looks closely at this literature, however, one must question the external validity of the conclusions drawn, primarily because of the type of people studied, the places where the research took place, the tasks assigned, and the lack of longitudinal research. Frey's (1988) review of the group communication studies published between 1980-1988 in journals sponsored by the international, national, and regional communication associations reports that 64% studied zero-history groups, 72% used students, 60% took place in a laboratory (50% of "field" research studied groups created for classroom purposes), and 72% observed a group only once (the average number of observations for groups studied more than once was only 2.75). The research on group facilitation reviewed above is even more telling. Every single study of group discussion procedures between 1970-1990, for example, studied student laboratory groups solving problems devised by the researcher.

The body of knowledge generated from these research studies is thus questionable, primarily because the ecological validity of these studies is suspect. Students simply are not as invested in laboratory groups as those working and living in groups in the real world, where the consequences for success and failure are usually very high; the tasks groups are asked to perform in the laboratory hardly mirror the important tasks that real groups must solve; and groups meeting only once in a laboratory or in a classroom setting hardly develop the intricate relational bonds and a sense of shared history that characterize on-going groups in the real world (see Frey, in press-a, in press-b).

In short, group analyses too often demonstrate what Farris (1981) calls a "social psychological error"—the tendency to explain groups from observations independent of their context. By treating groups as acontextual objects, researchers ignore the influence of the context, including the laboratory as a context, on group interactions and outcomes. Couch, Katovich, and Miller (1987) claim that this is fundamentally problematic, for "in our own everyday life, failure to pay attention to our surroundings is defined as a form of lunacy—autism" (p. 170).

There clearly is a need for additional verification of the findings regarding the use of group facilitation techniques. This is not simply another call for MRNTBD—"More research needs to be done" (Frey, Botan, Friedman, & Kreps, 1991). This is a particular call, the "call of the field," where the value of group facilitation techniques is tested with real groups in natural settings.

Real People Solving Real Problems: Overview of the Text

This text responds to this need by examining how a variety of group techniques have been employed to facilitate group interaction in natural groups. Each of the chapters explains a particular group facilitation technique, examines its use within a natural setting in a case study, and offers recommendations for using that technique with other natural groups.

As a set, the chapters examine a wide range of group facilitation techniques designed to accomplish a variety of group outcomes. These techniques and purposes include (listed in the order they appear in the text, with the author listed in parentheses):

- **Interactive Management (IM)** (Broome): A method for solving complex problem situations that uses: (a) Ideawriting—a technique for developing and discussing ideas; (b) Interpretive Structural Modeling (ISM)—a computer-assisted methodology to help groups identify the relationships among ideas and impose order on the complexity of the issue; and (c) Nominal Group Technique—a method for pooling ideas in times of uncertainty and disagreement.
- **Interaction Method (IM)** (Chilberg): A rule-based method for keeping a decision-making group on track during a meeting, including selecting the most appropriate practices to conduct meetings, allowing all members to participate in discussion, and reaching consensus about plans of action.
- **Intergroup Dialogue Forums** (Murphy): A method for promoting constructive dialogue and reducing negative perceptions between members of different groups within the same organization/culture.
- **Systemic, Social Constructionist Therapy** (Pearce): A group method, derived from social constructionist theory, for examining the way in which conversations reproduce conflicts and resolving such conflicts by changing the structure of those conversations.
- **Message Feedback** (Keltner): A reflective technique for replicating and returning the information contained in messages to the sender so that alterations in the message can be made by the originator.
- **SYMLOG (System for the Multiple Level Observation of Groups)** (Keyton): A quantitative group interaction observational scheme that can help a group reflect on its interaction in order to understand individual interactional differences and group interaction fields.
- **Focus Groups** (Kreps): A method for leading a group of respondents in a relatively open, yet structured, discussion for the purpose of generating ideas and revealing members' beliefs, attitudes, intentions, and behaviors.
- **Symbolic Convergence Theory (SCT-Based) Focus Groups** (Bormann, Bormann, & Harty; Cragan & Shields): A special kind of focus group interview technique informed by symbol-

ic convergence theory that is used to discover how attitudes, opinions, images, and feelings cluster into coherent rhetorical visions of experience.

- **Team-Building Techniques** (Felkins; Seibold): Methods designed to involve teams in planning, implementing, and monitoring organizational change at multiple levels (i.e., employee involvement groups and self-managed teams, organizational stimulations to develop teamwork, and collaborative inquiry in action-research groups).
- **Group Decision Support Systems (GDSS)** (Poole, DeSanctis, Kirsch, & Jackson): An electronic meeting system that combines communication and computer technologies (such as electronic messaging and teleconferencing) with decision support technologies (such as agenda setting) to facilitate decision making and related activities of work groups.

These group facilitation techniques are examined within diverse natural groups that are attempting to solve important problems. The problems and populations include (listed in the order they appear in the text, with the author listed in parentheses):

- Creating an action plan to promote greater participation in Comanche Tribal governance (Broome).
- Developing a new organization from scratch for the purpose of providing communication services to a university and the community at large (Chilberg).
- Increasing awareness, identifying issues, promoting constructive dialogue, and identifying solutions to gender issues in an international professional service firm concerned about the dearth of women in its upper management (Murphy).
- Developing and refining a new group facilitation process designed to resolve conflict through a simulation of a conflict involving attempts by a third world nation to develop a national policy about abused women (Pearce).
- Resolving disputes in arbitration between labor unions and management and in divorce and child custody mediation hearings (Keltner).
- Easing tensions within a functional work group composed of physicians, medical residents, and nursing staff (Keyton).
- Evaluating the performance and providing data for refining and improving the ability of an urban residential adolescent substance abuse rehabilitation center to meet the needs of community members; and refining the development and

implementation of health promotion media messages for preventing the spread of sexually transmitted diseases within a university community (Kreps).

- Discovering the rhetorical visions of teenage tobacco users for the purpose of constructing media campaigns to promote a tobacco-free lifestyle (Bormann, Bormann, & Harty).
- Assessing consumers' reactions to suggested improvements in a newspaper; developing meaningful fantasy themes for the opening arguments and legal case construction of a multimillion dollar suit from simulated juries composed of randomly selected community members; and assessing the law enforcement training provided to recent policy academy graduates (Cragan & Shields).
- Implementing collaborative inquiry in action research in a regional energy company moving from rapid expansion to a more stable, customer-based operating mode; providing simulations for leadership training for managers of a major retail organization; and introducing quality teams into a large financial institution (Felkins).
- Facilitating team process with a self-regulating team of employees managing a new-design plant (Seibold).
- Appropriating the features of a group decision support system by teams involved in an ongoing quality enhancement effort at a large service organization (Poole, DeSanctis, Kirsch, & Jackson).

The Paradox and Promise of Studying Real People Solving Real Problems

The studies presented in this text reveal both the promise of group facilitation techniques and the potential difficulties and tricky problems that researchers must negotiate when moving from the laboratory to the natural setting. This section examines some of the more salient issues that confront applied communication researchers working in the field, using some of these researchers' experiences (solicited through a series of questions) to illustrate these maneuverings. In the epilogue to this text, Stohl returns to many of these and other ethical issues and paradoxes in more detail.

The first issue concerns gaining access to the natural setting. Researchers cannot facilitate any group they wish; they must be invited to do so. Because the vast majority of applied communication research is client-based, researchers do not function autonomously within natural settings—they are guests who must be given permission to observe and facilitate group communicative behavior.

The researchers in this text gained access to the natural groups they studied in a variety of ways. Some, like Keltner and Kreps, own a consulting firm, whereas some, like Murphy, consult for client service firms, both of which afford numerous opportunities for gaining access to groups. Two of the researchers were asked by their university to consult with relevant groups: Chilberg was asked to serve as the advisor to the student organization he studied, whereas Kreps was contacted by the Department of Health Enhancement at his university to conduct the focus groups because of his expertise in the field of health communication. At other times, researchers simply luck out in gaining access. Poole and his associates had been developing a GDSS for some time and were presenting a description of the system at a GDSS Conference in Boston. The contact person at the IRS happened to be sitting in the room waiting for another presentation and heard their system described. It matched the needs of his quality program well, he thought, so he approached them about installing the system. They agreed to let the IRS have the system very cheaply and to program some parts of it to their satisfaction in return for being able to videotape sessions and give out questionnaires. In another interesting example, Keyton's significant other was a member of a group that needed help badly. She knew of the problems due to his frustration with the group and his need to sound off about it at home. She made the initial offer to facilitate the group to him, he took it to the group's leader, she and Keyton talked, and finally it was sold to the group. Getting access to natural groups thus happens in many ways, but sometimes it may be difficult, if not impossible, to obtain.

Once researchers have access, they often find that the natural setting impacts significantly on the design of their facilitation efforts and research. Sponsors of applied communication research often expect to participate in how communication problems are addressed by researchers (see Frey, O'Hair, & Kreps, 1990). Murphy, in her gender awareness workshops for a client service firm, is given a pre-packaged format to follow. There also are constraints operating in the field that often make it difficult or even prevent researchers from completing the research as designed. Kreps, for example, initially had problems recruiting parents of teenage substance abusers and potential abusers to the focus groups because of the perceived stigma these parents felt. Only after the Director of the Center wrote personal letters to these parents did some participate. In Keyton's study of hospital residents, the attending physicians denied her requests to participate in the study. This was unfortunate because, as the residents' immediate supervisors, their perceptions would have been very useful. Poole et al. experienced a slight problem with mortality, as groups dropped out of using the GDSS system over the 12-month course of their research project. There may also be time pressures impinging on researchers' goals and methods. Bormann et al. were handicapped by a lack of time, which was partially the result of the cumbersome red-tape involved in getting the official approval of the state health department and the state government after their immediate client decided to hire them. The result was that the advertising agency developing the commercial messages was rushed to complete its work before airtime and Bormann et al. could not have as great an impact on the scripts as they might have had with a better time frame within which to work. Compromises in research design and methods are thus part and parcel of conducting applied communication research in natural settings.

A third problem is getting groups to accept facilitation efforts. Many groups simply do not use effective meeting procedures in their daily interactions—which is why the facilitation is called for in the first place—and they resist attempts to incorporate them into their work habits, even during the facilitation process. Poole and DeSanctis (1990) once reported that 50% of the groups in their studies on procedure use did not follow the procedures faithfully. In Poole et al.'s study in this text, quite a few team members were resistant to the ongoing quality enhancement effort that was being implemented at their company, and these resistances may have carried over to this research study, leading some teams and members to never became fully proficient with the GDSS procedures.

Part of the difficulty may lie in how facilitators/researchers are viewed by group members. Members of groups within organizations, for example, may see a facilitator/researcher as a pawn of management and thus be wary. Bormann et al. report that the teenage participants in their focus groups on tobacco use were suspicious and skeptical at the beginning, seeing the meetings as efforts to get them to stop using tobacco. The facilitators, therefore, always started the focus group with comments and answers to questions to ally these suspicions. When it became clear that was not the purpose of the meeting and that the interviewers were asking for help and knowledge from the participants, the focus group members were more forthcoming. Seibold also found that it was crucial to develop good working relations with the team members of the new-design plant he studied in order to get them to trust him and his research procedures. Keyton's connections through her significant other with the group she studied also posed some initial difficulties, but these fears were dealt with by her insistence on not talking with her significant other about the project (in a way she would not talk to other group members about the project) once it started.

Being an outside, neutral facilitator, however, can sometimes be advantageous. Broome, for example, initially was concerned that his ethnicity might hamper his facilitation efforts with Comanche Tribal members. He found, however, that because he was not immersed in their cultural problems as an insider that he could concentrate on process concerns rather than on content concerns, which earned him the respect of Tribal members because that was precisely what they needed him to do.

Broome's work, as Stohl points out in the epilogue, also speaks to the need to match group facilitation efforts with members' needs, goals, and cultural values. Broome argues that the technique of Interactive Management was ideal for his work with Tribal members because it promotes collaborative group work that is compatible with the American Indian heritage. Murphy reports that she often throws out whole chunks of the pre-packaged workshop based on members' feelings about whether the material is useful to their situation. There is, for example, no need to discuss sexual harassment, certainly an important topic in principle for gender awareness workshops, if that is not an issue for the members of a particular group or organization.

One of the dangers in moving from the friendly confines of the academy to the field is bringing theories, facilitation techniques, and research designs wholecloth into the natural setting without accounting for the particular problems and characteristics evidenced in that setting. Kreps, Frey, and O'Hair (1991) argue that the best applied communication research is high on both theory and practice (thus debunking the traditional separation of basic or theory-driven research from applied or practical issue-driven research), which demands a match between researchers' theory, facilitation techniques, and research methods and participants' goals and needs. Virtually all the authors in this text worked from a solid theoretical ground that informed their facilitation practices and research efforts, but they also took great pains to adapt these to the demands of the natural group they studied. Clients do not care what works in theory or even what works for someone else; they want what will work for them!

Chilberg also points out that the issue of adopting a group facilitation technique does not rest solely with group members. As the advisor to a developing organization, he was often caught between two concerns: effective group facilitation and refraining from being overbearing in structuring the group interactions. He thus had to balance when to intervene and when to let the group members learn on their own how to use the procedures, even if this meant letting them get frustrated. If a central goal of facilitation is to get group members to adopt the procedures into their ongoing lives, then they must be given opportunities to fail. Facilitators cannot, therefore, just solve all of a group's problems for them. For learning to become permanent, it must be attributed to self, not to the guru-like qualities of a particular facilitator.

In the final analysis, there probably is bound to be some resistance to using group facilitation techniques. This resistance, moreover, should be seen as healthy and taken as a sign that the procedures are in fact working. Poole (1991) offers the following insightful explanation:

> In a nutshell, procedures improve group performance because they make groups uncomfortable. Procedures counteract sloppy thinking and ineffective work habits which are part and parcel of everyday group interaction. Because they go against the grain, procedures are "unnatural" and, hence, uncomfortable for groups. The central question, then, is how to get groups to take this bad-tasting medicine. (p. 66)

A fourth issue concerns ethical decisions that must be made in conducting research in natural settings. (See Stohl's epilogue for a discussion of the ethical dilemmas raised by the case studies in this text.) Although ethical decisions inform all types of research, they are particularly important in applied communication research with natural groups because researchers are "messing" with people's lives—they are impacting on how people make their living or lead their lives. If anything engenders this, it should not be done. That, of course, is easy to say, but often difficult to determine.

An issue such as confidentiality, for example, becomes even more important in the natural setting than in the laboratory. Kreps, in his study of parents of teenage substance abusers and potential abusers, had significant problems getting such lists because of confidentiality problems. Keyton reports that she was always being asked by residents how the chief resident rated them and always denied access to such ratings. The first few requests, she believes, were actually "tests" of her ethical standards and going against this promise would have doomed the study.

Another ethical concern has to do with whether researchers endorse the work that the client is doing and the researchers' ability to follow his or her ethical rules for conducting research. Bormann et al. assert that they found the goals and methods of the larger program—limiting the use of tobacco by teenagers in order to improve their health—one that they could ethically endorse. There are other potential clients, however, whose goals and methods would have caused them not to accept a contract (i.e., a very similar kind of study could be designed and implemented by a tobacco company to encourage teenagers to use tobacco). They also claim that they would never deceive research participants in order to manipulate variables. In their study, they were careful to explain what they were doing, honestly and in enough detail, so there were no surprises in how they conducted the group meetings.

There are also ethical concerns about reporting the findings from applied research, both to the members of the group studied and to people at large (i.e., members of the scholarly community). Because the information obtained from client-based applied research is proprietary, clients certainly have the right to control its flow, and researchers must decide whether they can respect their clients' decisions. Many organizations may wish to limit who sees the findings, including even denying access to members of the groups that were studied within the organization. Felkins thus insists on being able to feed back all data to the people in the teams she studies in in-depth debriefing sessions and will not contract with an organization unless this procedure is agreed on. Other times, organizations may refuse the right to publish the research for broader audiences. Pearce, for example, was asked not to use a case study of an actual group that had experienced the systemic social constructionist therapy, so he describes a simulation that the consulting group used on itself. Because the purpose of his chapter is to explain the development of this unique facilitation technique by a natural group (this consulting group), this restriction did not affect his research goals. Several of Murphy's clients are extremely cautious about anyone doing research on them, fearing that the data from the gender awareness workshops (such as information about discrimination) may be traced back and used against them in a lawsuit, which Murphy reports actually occurred in another company.

Many researchers value their clients' right to edit their reports and seek out such assistance. Poole et al.'s research partners have reviewed everything they have written because they regard getting such comments about their conclusions as important data in their own right. And, in the best of all possible worlds, clients too value the dissemination of research to broader audiences and become full-fledged partners in this endeavor, as in the case of Bormann et al. in which the principal client contact is a coauthor of the chapter.

A final ethical decision has to do with how committed researchers are to the groups and organizations they study with regard to helping them enact the changes they recommend and conducting follow-up research on such efforts. In contrast to the single observation of a zero-history group in the laboratory, applied communication research in the field most often demands longitudinal research, leading researchers to deep and meaningful relationships with their clients and the participants in their research. Many people, however, fear researchers who come in, diagnose problems, recommend solutions, and then depart, leaving the group to cope with what has been stirred up from the research. What are researchers' obligations and responsibilities to clients after they complete the facilitation and research? How can they be part of the solution and not part of the problem?

Fifth, researchers/consultants sometimes face the problem of getting a group or organization to accept and act on the results of their studies. Many organizations welcome such recommendations and incorporate them readily into their programs. Cragan and Shields' recommendations concerning the Sunday supplement magazine for the *St. Louis Dispatch*, for example, were endorsed enthusiastically and proved to be very successful. There may, however, be problems in getting the larger organization to accept the findings and recommendations. Broome reports that due to size restrictions, some members of the Tribal government could not participate in the group work. Because this group work is so unusual and has such power, people need to participate in order to see its benefits. Later, when he reported his findings to the Tribal government, he had to become a salesman as those who had not participated expressed grave concerns and perhaps never fully bought into it. Many organizations also may not be willing to enact the changes that the findings demand. Murphy reports that one of the biggest potential drawbacks to the gender awareness workshops is the participants' perception that they are ends in and of themselves and that management will not go any further in reducing gender inequality within the organization. Broome suspects that the participatory nature of the facilitation he used, although compatible with Tribal values, may have threatened some of the people in power, leading them to be wary of the research and the findings.

Facilitating groups in the natural setting and studying such efforts is certainly tricky business, demanding far more maneuvering and tightrope-walking skills than typically is needed in laboratory research. Applied communication research in the natural setting demands gaining access to a setting that may be difficult to obtain; often leads to negotiation and compromise in research design because of clients' needs; poses problems for facilitating groups because of real-life groups' hesitancy to adopt such procedures; requires sensitive understanding of the ethics of intruding into people's lives; and often produces confrontations with clients who may not be entirely receptive to the research findings and recommendations.

The paradox and promise of applied communication research in the natural setting are thus revealed: the difficulties experienced in conducting such research and the lack of control they engender, although seen from the perspective of laboratory researchers as problematic with regard to internal validity, are precisely what potentially can make applied communication research so powerful. The problems researchers face when studying real people solving real problems make applied communication research in natural settings difficult to do well, but when done well, it yields rich findings that can make a significant difference in people's—group members, clients, consultants, practitioners, educators, and scholars—lives. I hope that the chapters you are about to read reveal this promise.

PART I

Facilitation Techniques for Promoting Effective Group Problem Solving and Decision Making

Groups make important decisions every day that affect the lives of many. However, as noted in the introduction, groups often make less effective decisions than possible, and some of these miscalculations prove to be extremely costly.

One reason why groups make faulty decisions is because the members fail to discuss fully the nature of, and the solutions to, the complex problems they confront. Although some problems are relatively simple and are solved easily, others are more complex, demanding far more skills on the part of group participants. When groups confront complex problems, they often experience disorganization, become overloaded cognitively by the wealth of information available, and fail to identify either a range of acceptable solutions or the best possible solutions. Groups, therefore, often require facilitation to help members generate, clarify, structure, and record the variety of ideas necessary for addressing the complex problem situations they seek to manage.

In Chapter 1, Broome examines an approach to group work that was developed specifically for use with complex problem situations and that seeks to integrate behavioral and technical considerations in a computer-assisted system called *Interactive Management*. His case study is a specific application of Interactive Management with a complex social situation. Sessions are described that were conducted with the Comanche Tribe during March and May 1991. Sixteen group participants and a number of supportive observers worked together over two different three-day periods to design collectively a way to promote greater participation in Comanche Tribal governance. Based on the results from these planning sessions, the Comanche Tribe is now ready to take the next steps in overcoming barriers to community participation in Tribal governance. The results show how the process used in these sessions possesses several characteristics that can benefit efforts to conduct facilitated group work with a variety of complex problem situations.

A second reason why groups sometimes fail to make high-quality decisions is because they do not use effective operating procedures during their meetings. In particular, groups often have problems staying on track during a meeting, selecting the most appropriate ways to conduct meetings, getting all members to participate and share their expertise and views, and reaching consensus about plans of action.

In Chapter 2, Chilberg reviews the *Interaction Method,* a group facilitation technique that uses several rules and assigned roles to help prevent the occurrence of these key problems. After explaining this technique, Chilberg examines how it is used to guide the task group discussions of a newly formed organization and the consequences of not using it. Through observations of group sessions and interviews with the group leaders, the case study focuses on the sources of the gap between knowledge and practice of the facilitation rules and roles used by the task forces of this organization. The analysis reveals several fundamental issues relevant to the design and effective use of facilitation rules and roles—task complexity, task communication behaviors, and the role of procedures—and makes recommendations for adopting these and other facilitation practices.

1

The Role of Facilitated Group Process in Community-Based Planning and Design: Promoting Greater Participation in Comanche Tribal Governance*

Benjamin J. Broome
George Mason University

Decision makers today face a multitude of large-scale organizational and managerial problems that involve multiple parties, diverse interests, and often conflicting goals. For example, public officials are often called on to develop economic or political policy across national borders, organization heads must periodically institute large-scale organizational redesign, systems engineers regularly design sophisticated technical systems, and community leaders are frequently faced with formulating social programs that address deep-rooted conflicts. Often termed complex or "Class II" problems, these types of situations have been identified and defined by a number of scholars (e.g., Ackoff, 1979; Argyris, 1982; Cleveland, 1973; Kemeny, 1980; Rittel & Webber, 1974; Simon,

*The author would like to thank Ladonna Harris, President of Americans for Indian Opportunity and a member of the Comanche Tribe, for sponsoring the project described in this chapter and for inviting my participation as facilitator for these sessions.

1960). These situations are relatively "unprogrammable," in that past experience and existing solutions cannot be used as an accurate guide for dealing with the problem. Because dealing with tasks of this nature requires input from a variety of areas of expertise and demands reevaluation of the basic assumptions and variables underlying the situation, organizations are turning increasingly to problem-solving groups to grapple with these situations.

Researchers have identified several factors that affect the ability of small groups to develop quality solutions to complex problem situations. Two of the primary challenges confronting the management of group activity are to reduce or eliminate disorganization and to assist a group in handling large amounts of information. Research shows that most unassisted groups faced with complex tasks have significant periods of disorganized activity (Poole, 1983; 1985; Poole & Doelger, 1986; Poole & Roth, 1989). Similarly, as the task faced by groups becomes more complex, there is greater danger of cognitive overload (Miller, 1956; Simon, 1974), and groups need assistance in dealing with substantive, procedural, and relational problems (Hirokawa & Gouran, 1989), climate issues (Folger, Poole, & Stutman, 1993), and contextual influences (Friedman, 1989). Dealing with a complex situation thus requires use of a system that is capable of helping the group participants generate, clarify, structure, and record the variety of ideas necessary for addressing the problem situation they seek to manage.

Within the last 20 years a number of facilitation methods have been developed to help groups deal with various types of problem situations. Approaches such as Synetics (Prince, 1970) and the Interaction Method (see Chilberg, this volume; Doyle & Straus, 1976) are used widely for facilitating group problem solving. Each of these methods uses a professional group facilitator to foster creativity and move a group toward consensus. The professional facilitator brings an expertise about group dynamics, a status as an objective observer, and a set of skills not present in the group (Keltner, 1989). More recently, the availability of affordable and user-friendly technology has led to the development of several computer-based systems for assisting group decision making and problem solving (see reviews by Dennis, George, Giuseppe, Nunamaker, & Vogel, 1988; DeSanctis & Gallupe, 1985, 1987; Huber, 1984; Huseman & Miles, 1988; Johansen, 1988; Kraemer & King, 1988; McDonald, 1990; Nunamaker, Dennis, Valacich, Vogel, & George, 1991; and Pinsonneault & Kraemer, 1989). Facilities for supporting group work with computer assistance have been built at schools such as the University of Arizona, University of Minnesota, and SUNY-Albany, as well as at numerous corporate sites including IBM and Xerox Corporation. Whereas approaches such as Synetics and the Interaction

Method grew out of research in the social sciences, the computer-assisted approaches are based in management information systems and information technology. The former have made little use of the new technologies that might assist groups in managing information, whereas the latter have failed to pay sufficient attention to the behavioral aspects of group interaction (Broome & Chen, 1992). More importantly, none of these approaches were developed initially to address complex problems.

One approach to group work that was developed specifically for use with complex problem situations and that seeks to integrate the behavioral and technical considerations is a system developed by Warfield (1976, 1990) called *Interactive Management* (IM). Group facilitation in IM is based on: (a) responding to the demands of complexity (Cleveland, 1973; Deal & Kennedy, 1982); (b) employing a functional problem-solving sequence (Simon, 1969); (c) honoring design laws concerning variety, parsimony and saliency (Ashby, 1958; Boulding, 1966; Miller, 1956); (d) drawing role distinctions among context, content, and process (Warfield, 1986); (e) balancing behavioral and technical demands of group work (Broome & Chen, 1992); (f) employing criterion-selected consensus methodologies (Warfield, 1982b), and (g) implementing a designed problem-solving environment (Broome & Keever, 1989). IM has been applied in a variety of situations to accomplish many different goals, such as developing space-based lasers (Christakis, 1985), assisting city councils in making budget cuts (Coke & Moore, 1981), developing instructional units (Sato, 1979), designing a national agenda for pediatric nursing (Feeg, 1988), developing computer-based information systems for organizations (Keever, 1989), improving the U.S. Department of Defense acquisition process (Alberts, 1992), promoting world peace (Christakis, 1987), and developing new automotive design processes (Staley, & Broome, 1993).

The purpose of this chapter is to describe a specific application of IM with a complex social situation. Sessions are described that were conducted with the Comanche Tribe[1] during March and May 1991. The Comanche Tribe (see Wallace & Hoebel, 1986) is located in Southwest Oklahoma, and the members of this Tribe face economic[2] and social[3] situations similar to other groups of Native Americans in the United States. The planning sessions described in this chapter took place as a follow-up to similar sessions that had been held just over one year earlier (February 1990) in the same location. Those earlier sessions addressed the major issues that faced the Comanche during the coming decade and identified options for addressing those issues. A theme that was reflected in much of the group's discussion was the need for greater community participation in Tribal governance. Sixteen group participants and a number of supportive observers worked together over two different three-day periods to collectively design a way to promote greater participation in Comanche Tribal governance. The participants and observers represented the various communities that make up the Comanche Tribe, as well as members of the Comanche Business Committee, which is the primary governing body of the Tribe.[4]

PROCESS AND METHODOLOGIES

The IM process generally moves through three structured phases: (a) definition of the problem; (b) design of alternatives; and (c) selection of the preferred alternative(s). The approach assigns to participants all responsibility for contributing ideas, and the group sessions are managed by a trained facilitator. Methodologies for generating, clarifying, structuring, interpreting, and amending ideas are selected to match the phase of group interaction and the requirements of the situation. Computer assistance is used with many of the methodologies (see below). Finally, the sessions always take place in a specially arranged physical environment that provides a comfortable working space for participants and sufficient display space for ideas and structures.[5]

Three of the group methodologies typically used with IM are: Nominal Group Technique (NGT) (Delbeq, Van De Ven, & Gustafson, 1975); Ideawriting (Warfield, 1990); and Interpretive Structural Modeling (ISM) (Janes, 1988; Warfield, 1982a). NGT allows individual ideas to be pooled effectively and is used in situations in which uncertainty and disagreements exist about the nature of possible ideas. NGT involves five steps: (a) presentation of a triggering question to the participants; (b) silent generation of ideas in writing by each participant working alone; (c) serial recording of ideas by the facilitator on butcher-block paper in front of the group, and then posting of the filled butcher-block paper on walls surrounding the group; (d) serial discussion of the listed ideas by the participants for clarification of their meaning; and (e) selection by the participants of the more important items through a voting process.

Ideawriting is a method for developing ideas in a small group and allowing the members to explore the meaning of these ideas through open discussion. Ideawriting involves six steps: (a) formation of several small groups of 3-6 persons each; (b) presentation of a triggering question to the participants; (c) silent generation of ideas in writing by each participant working alone; (d) exchange of written sheets of ideas among group members, with opportunity for individuals to add ideas as they read others' papers; (e) group discussion and clarification of unique ideas; and (f) a report by each small group that explains the ideas generated in the group.

ISM is a computer-assisted methodology that helps a group identify the relationships among ideas and impose order on the complexity of the issue. The ISM software utilizes mathematical algorithms that minimize the number of queries necessary for exploring relationships among a set of ideas (see Janes, 1988). ISM can be used to develop several types of maps, including *influence structures* ("supports," "aggravates"), *priority structures* ("is more important than," "should be learned before") and *categorizations of ideas* ("belongs in the same category with"). The functions of ISM are: (a) *interpretive*—the group judges where and how items are related; (b) *structural*—an overall structure is extracted from a complex set of items on the basis of the relationships among items; and (c) *modeling*—the specific relationships among items and the overall structure is portrayed in graphic form (Moore, 1987).

The five steps of ISM include:

1. Identification and clarification of a list of ideas (using NGT or Ideawriting);
2. Identification and clarification of a "relational question" for exploring relationships among ideas (e.g., "Does idea A support idea B?"; "Is idea A of higher priority than B?"; "Does idea A belong in the same category with idea B?");
3. Development of a structural map by using the relational question to explore connections between pairs of ideas (see below);
4. Display and discussion of the map by the group; and
5. Amendment to the map by the group, if needed.

In Step 3, group participants view questions (that are generated by the ISM software) projected on a computer screen in front of the room. The questions take the following form:

> "Does:
> A
> relate in X manner to:
> B
> ?"

"A" and "B" are pairs of ideas from the list developed by the participants in Step 1 of ISM and the relationship "X" is the statement identified in Step 2. The group engages in a discussion managed by the facilitator about this relational question, and a vote is taken to determine the group's judgment about the relationship. A "yes" vote is entered in the ISM software by the computer operator if a majority of the participants see a significant relationship between the pairs of ideas; otherwise, a "no" vote is entered. Another pair of ideas is then projected to the participants, another discussion is held, and a vote is taken. This process is continued until the relationships between all necessary pairs of ideas have been explored. The ISM software then displays a structural map showing the result of the group's judgments.

The length of time required to complete discussion of all necessary pairs of ideas depends on the total number of ideas in the set, but generally the process requires between 3 to 8 hours of group deliberation. The number of necessary queries also depends on the total number of ideas in the set, but generally the ISM software is able to infer approximately 80% of the judgments involved in relating the complete set of ideas. The ISM software makes these inferences based on a set of mathematical algorithms developed by Warfield (1976).

In the IM design sessions with the Comanche Tribe, these methodologies were used with the group participants to address the following objectives:

1. To identify the major barriers to community participation in Comanche Tribal governance;
2. To organize these barriers into an "influence map" that represents relationships among these barriers;
3. To propose options and initiatives for resolving the system of barriers displayed in the influence map;
4. To organize these options and initiatives into categories that are useful for designing a strategy for action;
5. To sequence these categories for the purpose of making choices; and
6. To make selections from categories to build an alternative plan of action.

Phase 1: Identifying and Structuring Barriers to Participation in Tribal Governance

In order to develop a deeper understanding of the situation, the participants were first asked to identify barriers that inhibit community participation. During the first phase of the design sessions, two consensus methodologies were used. First, NGT was used to help participants identify, clarify, and discuss issues that have a negative impact on community participation. The following triggering question was used for the idea-generation session:

> "What are the barriers to greater community participation in Comanche Tribal governance?"

In responding to this triggering question, participants were asked to focus on the *undesirable* aspects of the situation and to avoid solution statements. Participants were also asked to use the following phrases as guides for writing their statements:

Conflict between . . .	Inadequate . . .
Demand for . . .	Interference from . . .
Demise of . . .	Lack of . . .
Dilemma of . . .	Loss of . . .
Existence of . . .	Refusal to . . .
Failure to . . .	Shortage of . . .
Hostility towards . . .	Unwillingness to . . .
Inability to . . .	

Following the fourth step of the NGT, in which the group discussed the list of ideas in order to clarify their meaning, participants were asked to select a subset of these barriers to structure during the ISM session. In order to determine this subset, each participant indicated the five barriers he or she considered to be of greater importance, relative to the other barriers, and ranked these from 1 (more important) to 5 (less important). These selections were collected from the participants and summarized. ISM, which asks group participants to make collective judgments about the relationship between paired items, was then used to structure this subset of barriers according to the following relational question:

> "In promoting greater community participation in Comanche Tribal governance, does:
>
> A
>
> significantly aggravate:
>
> B
>
> ?"

The "aggravate" relationship examines the negative influence that problems have on each other, and it can be interpreted as "makes worse," "increases the severity of," "exacerbates," "makes it more difficult to resolve," or "magnifies the effects of." The structuring process allowed the participants to produce an *influence map*, which showed the group's consensus on how the more important barriers negatively influence each other. In this case, the influence map represents the "problematique" faced by the Tribe. Following the display of this structure, the participants engaged in a discussion of the map.

Phase 2: Identifying and Structuring Options for Promoting Greater Participation

With the structure of barriers to community participation as a foundation, the participants next identified options for dealing with the barriers. By identifying these options based on the problematique faced by the Tribe, participants could be more confident that they were addressing the deeper issues and not just the symptoms of the problem situation.

During Phase 2, the Ideawriting and ISM methodologies were used, this time to generate and structure options for addressing the situation. The following triggering question was used for the Ideawriting:

> "What are the options for addressing the barriers to community participation in Tribal governance that are displayed in the influence map?"

In responding to the triggering question, participants were asked to focus on possibilities (activities and initiatives) that, when selected, would contribute to achieving the Tribe's goals. Participants were also asked to use the following action verbs as guides for phrasing their statements:

Adopt . . .   Establish . . .
Build . . .   Identify . . .
Change . . .   Increase . . .
Conduct . . .   Plan . . .
Decrease . . .   Prohibit . . .
Develop . . .   Promote . . .

Disseminate . . .	Provide . . .
Emphasize . . .	Research . . .
Encourage . . .	Support . . .

Following the clarification of these options, participants organized the options into similarity groupings. Using ISM, participants were asked to make judgments about whether pairs of options should be grouped together. The following relational question was used during the ISM structuring session:

> "In promoting greater community participation in Comanche Tribal governance, does option:
>
> A
>
> belong in the same category with option:
>
> B
>
> ?"

The relationship indicated by the phrase "belong in the same category with" can be interpreted as "share significant elements in common with." An initial subset of those selected by participants as the most important ideas were structured using the computer. The results from structuring this subset were displayed on the wall and discussed by the participants, with titles given to those categories that were clearly defined. After participants expressed satisfaction with the preliminary field, the remainder of the ideas were placed in the categories without computer assistance, under the process guidance of the facilitator. Participants then gave titles to all categories that were still without a name. The titles from the categories were then sequenced according to the order in which participants felt it was most appropriate to make choices from the field. Category titles were used as input for an ISM using the following relational question:

> "In promoting greater community participation in Comanche Tribal governance, should selections be made from category:
>
> A
>
> before (or at the same time) as selections are made from category:
>
> B
>
> ?"

The relationship indicated by the phrase "selections should be made before" can be interpreted to mean that "choices made from one category will inform or influence choices to be made in another category." If participants felt there was sufficient reason to consider one category before another, then that category was placed earlier in the field. If participants judged it as important to consider two or more categories simultaneously, these categories were placed next to each other in the field. The resulting structure is called an "Options Field" because it presents a menu of options from which selections can be made for implementation. The Options Field serves as the basis for the next phase of the design, in which participants engaged in making choices.

Phase 3: Developing an Options Profile

An influence map of barriers to participation and an ordered grouping of options for addressing the situation provided a basis for designing a program to improve the situation. An "Options Profile" is developed by asking participants to consider category-by-category the total set of available options in the Options Field, beginning with the category lying at the beginning of the field, and to select from each category those options (if any) that should be implemented within a specified time frame. Although a number of different "profiles" might be developed, the participants proposed initially a set of options that might be started immediately and on which significant progress could be demonstrated during the coming year. The result is a set of initiatives that should be considered for immediate implementation by the Tribe. Additional actions can be added to the field as new ideas are developed and as conditions change. Similarly, additional profiles can be developed for other time frames. The following question was used to guide the selection process:

> "Which are the options that should be
> selected from category
> X
> for implementation by the Tribe during the
> next six months to one year?"

The items selected through this systematic discussion resulted in an alternative "Options Profile" that could serve as a plan for starting work on promoting greater participation in Tribal governance.

RESULTS

Barriers to Participation in Tribal Governance

The idea set built by the group during Phase 1 consisted of 64 problem statements (see Table 1.1). Problems included *attitudes*, (e.g., a "feeling that I cannot make a difference"), *social problems*, (e.g., the "influx of drug and alcohol abuse"), *communication difficulties*, (e.g., "no communication mechanisms in place to pass on information"), *structural barriers*, (e.g., an "inappropriate form of government laid out in the constitution"), *educational deficiencies*, (e.g., a "lack of knowledge about Tribal issues"), and others. Using the voting process described earlier, participants selected 18 of these barriers as being of "greater relative importance," and these ideas were structured during the ISM session.

The influence structure resulting from the ISM is portrayed in Figure 1.1. The barriers are displayed from left to right, with the problems having the most influence shown on the left side of the map. Those items marked with a bullet and grouped within a single box are part of a "cycle," that is, they are mutually aggravating. Several "walks" can be taken by following various "paths" that exist in the map. To walk a path, start on the left side of the map and follow the arrows that represent the line of influence. For example, one walk starts with item 14, "inappropriate form of government," and continues with the cycle that includes items 15, 52, 7, and 58, all of which are concerned with the relationship between leadership and the Comanche people, which influences item 62, a "lack of understanding of the constitution," which then influences the cycle that includes items 2, 3, 4, and 10, all of which are concerned with interpersonal relations and conflict, which in turn influences item 1, "feeling that I cannot make a difference." The negative influence exerted by those problems on the left are *propagating* in nature; that is, their aggravation propagates along the path from item to item, making the impact of the items on the left greater than it might otherwise appear. By starting with an item on the left side of the map and following its path of influence, one can understand the difficulties brought about by that item. Similarly, by starting with an item on the right side of the map and walking back to the left, one can understand the pressures that may make it difficult to resolve a particular problem.

The following general statements can be made in interpreting Figure 1.1:

1. The three problems that are perceived to be *exerting* the greatest degree of negative influence for the Comanche are:
    *   Inappropriate form of government (Item 14)

Table 1.1. List of Barriers to Community Participation in Comanche Tribal Governance*

1. Feeling that I cannot make a difference
2. Factionalism
3. Existence of a great deal of apathy on the part of the membership
4. Jealousy and rivalry among the Tribal members
5. Lack of direct response from Comanche Business Council
6. Wrong attitude among the Tribal members about getting involved
7. Lack of leadership togetherness
8. Indifference about what is happening in Tribal governance
9. Lack of interest by the adult members of the Tribe
10. Lack of involvement form the community in Tribal administration.
12. Too much dependency on Tribal government
13. Reluctance to face possibility that ideas will be criticized
14. Inappropriate form of government as laid out in the Tribal constitution
15. Lack of communication mechanisms to pass on information from Tribal government to the community
16. Lack of knowledge of Comanche heritage in younger generation
17. Lack of adequate involvement by Tribal members with today's problems of drugs and alcohol
18. Lack of check and balance system in Tribal government
19. Influx of drug and alcohol use within the Tribal leadership and the staff
20. Attitude of "give me" instead of "what can I do?"
21. Living too far away to use the Tribal complex
22. Lack of an out-reach group
23. Lack of proper representation in the Tribal government
24. Lack of convenient ways to get involved
25. Unwillingness to change anything
26. Failure of membership to respond to invitations to attend meetings
27. Failure of elders to accept their responsibility to share their knowledge and abilities with the younger generation
28. Conflict between traditional and contemporary self-values among younger people
29. Attitude of "my community doesn't get any benefits"
30. Lack of a positive attitude
31. Greediness
32. Lack of a place to come together
33. Loss of identity as a Comanche
34. Lack of knowledge about Tribal issues
35. Lack of responsiveness by Tribal staff
36. Failure to enforce the constitution
37. Indifference by Comanche Business Council to do what the Tribal Council approves
38. Inability to network by Tribal staff
39. A spirit of defeat that exists

Table 1.1. List of Barriers to Community Participation in Comanche Tribal Governance* (cont.)

among the Tribal members

40. Lack of professionalism
41. Lack of jobs
42. Lack of a sense of Tribalness
43. Lack of communication in not knowing our Comanche language
44. Lack of farsightedness by elected officials
45. Failure of elected officials to carry through with their promises
46. Inadequate planning for economic development
47. Lack of positive participation skills
48. Failure to recognize and value life experiences of community members
49. Lack of drug and alcohol counselors
50. Failure to utilize those who have "been down the road" with drugs and alcohol
51. Too much authority by Comanche Business Council
52. Lack of accountability by leadership
53. Failure of Comanche Business

Council to give respect to Tribal members' views
54. Failure to change the way housing authority operates
55. Failure of knowledgeable Tribal members to share their expertise with leadership
56. Requirement that governance conform to outside powers
57. Lack of knowledge by Tribal members
58. Lack of system for interrelationship between leadership and Tribal members
59. Lack of knowledge about process for individuals to place items on agenda
60. Use of closed-door meetings on issues that concern the Tribe
61. Forced geographic dispersion of Tribal members
62. Lack of understanding of constitution by Tribal members
63. Lack of understanding of housing authority by Tribal members.
64. Lack of control over amount of housing payments

*Slight changes have been made in the original wording of some statements in the table in order to better communicate the meaning of the statement to the reader.

- Lack of communication between leadership and Tribal members (cycle of Items 15, 52, 7, and 58)
- Inadequate leadership (Item 45)

Each of these problems lie to the far left of the influence structure without being influenced significantly by the other problems in the structure; however, they influence negatively a large percentage of the total problem set. Failure to address adequately these three problems will make it

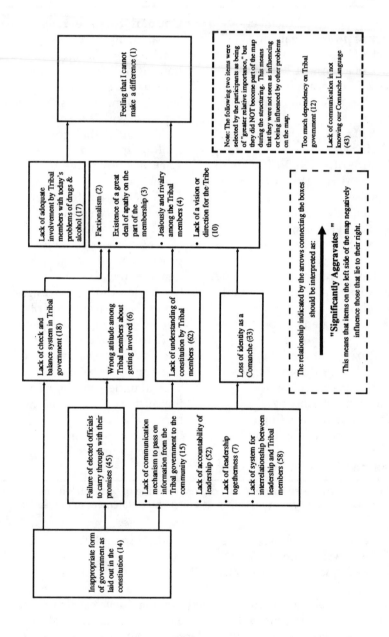

Figure 1.1. Influence Map of Major Barriers to Community Participation in Comanche Tribal Governance

very difficult to deal with the overall Tribal situation during the next decade.

2. The problems that are receiving the most "pressure" from the other problems on the map are:
- Failure to get involved (Items 1 and 3)
- Conflict between Tribal members (Items 2 and 4)

It is likely to be very difficult to address these two problems without first addressing those problems that lie to their left. This would remove some of the pressure on them and would make it more likely that the investment of resources in their solution would pay off. Although it is very difficult to address these two problems directly, addressing those problems that are impacting them negatively sometimes results in the resolution of problems such as these that lie on the right side of the map.

Options for Overcoming Barriers

The idea set built by the group during Phase 2 consisted of 99 ideas. The group organized the options into 10 categories and gave headings to these categories. These categories were then ordered according to the sequence in which the group perceived it was most appropriate to make choices from the categories. The participants selected a total of 29 options that should be implemented as part of a short-term plan. Figure 1.2 displays the Options Profile developed by the participants. The Options Profile includes the total set of 99 ideas, the 10 categories with their headings, the choice-making sequence, and the selections of options that make up the short-term plan. These options range from relatively straightforward tasks, such as encouraging people to "read the constitution" (Item 1) or "posting the Tribal agenda" (Item 58), to tasks involving a great deal of coordination, such as "developing a community-based vision statement" (Item 38) or "forming a committee to get feedback on constitution" (Item 5). With the exception of Items 90 and 91 in Category D, the items represent specific options that realistically can be accomplished or on which significant progress can be made within a one-year time period.

DISCUSSION

Implications for the Tribe

The IM process contributed significantly toward addressing the primary topic of the sessions, to promote greater community involvement in

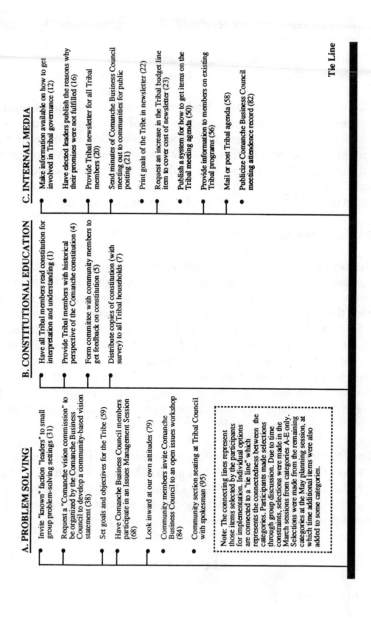

Figure 1.2. Options Profile for Promoting Greater Community Participation in Comanche Tribal Governance

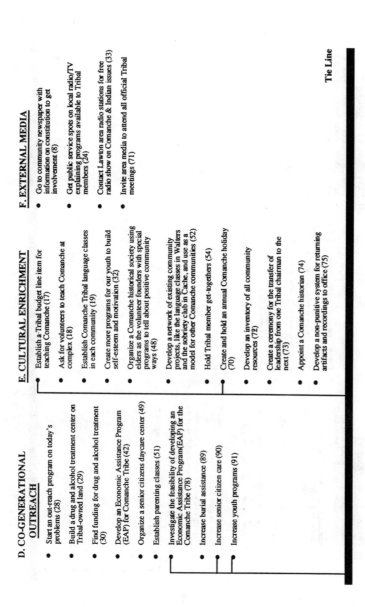

D. CO-GENERATIONAL OUTREACH

- Start an out-reach program on today's problems (28)
- Build a drug and alcohol treatment center on Tribal-owned land (29)
- Find funding for drug and alcohol treatment (30)
- Develop an Economic Assistance Program (EAP) for Comanche Tribe (42)
- Organize a senior citizens daycare center (49)
- Establish parenting classes (51)
- Investigate the feasibility of developing an Economic Assistance Program(EAP) for the Comanche Tribe (78)
- Increase burial assistance (89)
- Increase senior citizen care (90)
- Increase youth programs (91)

E. CULTURAL ENRICHMENT

- Establish a Tribal budget line item for teaching Comanche (17)
- Ask for volunteers to teach Comanche at complex (18)
- Establish Comanche Tribal language classes in each community (19)
- Create more programs for our youth to build self-esteem and motivation (32)
- Organize a Comanche historical society using elders as the volunteer founders with special programs to tell about positive community ways (48)
- Develop a network of existing community projects, like the language classes in Walters and the sobriety club in Cache, and use as a model for other Comanche communities (52)
- Hold Tribal member get-togethers (54)
- Create and hold an annual Comanche holiday (70)
- Develop an inventory of all community resources (72)
- Create a ceremony for the transfer of leadership from one Tribal chairman to the next (73)
- Appoint a Comanche historian (74)
- Develop a non-punitive system for returning artifacts and recordings to office (75)

F. EXTERNAL MEDIA

- Go to community newspaper with information on constitution to get involvement (8)
- Get public service spots on local radio/TV explaining programs available to Tribal members (24)
- Contact Lawton area radio stations for free radio show on Comanche & Indian issues (33)
- Invite area media to attend all official Tribal meetings (71)

Tie Line

Figure 1.2. Options Profile for Promoting Greater Community Participation in Comanche Tribal Governance (cont.)

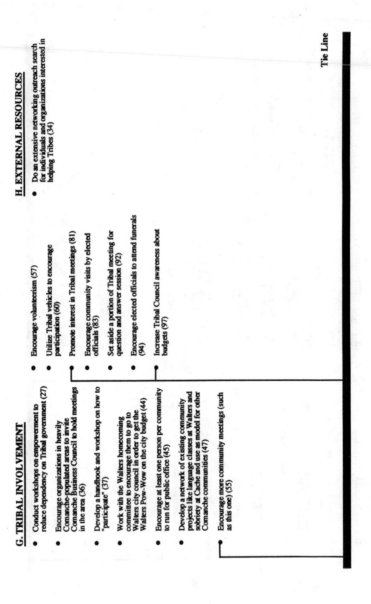

G. TRIBAL INVOLVEMENT

- Conduct workshops on empowerment to reduce dependency on Tribal government (27)
- Encourage organizations in heavily Comanche-populated areas to invite Comanche Business Council to hold meetings in the area (36)
- Develop a handbook and workshop on how to "participate" (37)
- Work with the Walters homecoming committee to encourage them to go to Walters city council in order to get the Walters Pow-Wow on the city budget (44)
- Encourage at least one person per community to run for public office (45)
- Develop a network of existing community projects like language classes at Walters and sobriety at Cache and use as model for other Comanche communities (47)
- Encourage more community meetings (such as this one) (55)

- Encourage volunteerism (57)
- Utilize Tribal vehicles to encourage participation (60)
- Promote interest in Tribal meetings (81)
- Encourage community visits by elected officials (83)
- Set aside a portion of Tribal meeting for question and answer session (92)
- Encourage elected officials to attend funerals (94)
- Increase Tribal Council awareness about budgets (97)

H. EXTERNAL RESOURCES

- Do an extensive networking outreach search for individuals and organizations interested in helping Tribes (34)

Tie Line

Figure 1.2. Options Profile for Promoting Greater Community Participation in Comanche Tribal Governance (cont.)

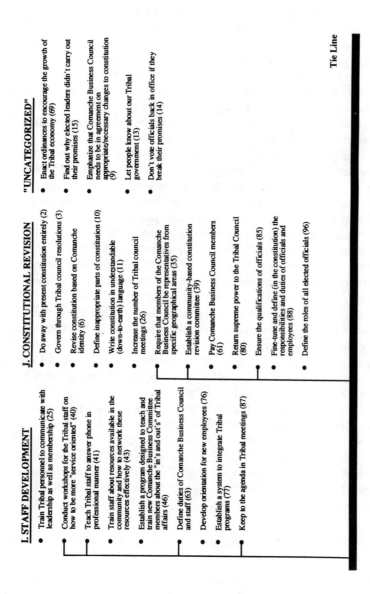

I. STAFF DEVELOPMENT

- Train Tribal personnel to communicate with leadership as well as membership (25)
- Conduct workshops for the Tribal staff on how to be more "service oriented" (40)
- Teach Tribal staff to answer phone in professional manner (41)
- Train staff about resources available in the community and how to network these resources effectively (43)
- Establish a program designed to teach and train new Comanche Business Committee members about the "in's and out's" of Tribal affairs (46)
- Define duties of Comanche Business Council and staff (63)
- Develop orientation for new employees (76)
- Establish a system to integrate Tribal programs (77)
- Keep to the agenda in Tribal meetings (87)

J. CONSTITUTIONAL REVISION

- Do away with present constitution entirely (2)
- Govern through Tribal council resolutions (3)
- Revise constitution based on Comanche identity (6)
- Define inappropriate parts of constitution (10)
- Write constitution in understandable (down-to-earth) language (11)
- Increase the number of Tribal council meetings (26)
- Require that members of the Comanche Business Council be representatives from specific geographical areas (35)
- Establish a community-based constitution revision committee (39)
- Pay Comanche Business Council members (61)
- Return supreme power to the Tribal Council (80)
- Ensure the qualifications of officials (85)
- Fine-tune and define (in the constitution) the responsibilities and duties of officials and employees (88)
- Define the roles of all elected officials (96)

"UNCATEGORIZED"

- Enact ordinances to encourage the growth of the Tribal economy (69)
- Find out why elected leaders didn't carry out their promises (15)
- Emphasize that Comanche Business Council needs to be in agreement on appropriate/necessary changes to constitution (9)
- Let people know about our Tribal government (13)
- Don't vote officials back in office if they break their promises (14)

Tie Line

Figure 1.2. Options Profile for Promoting Greater Community Participation in Comanche Tribal Governance (cont.)

Comanche Tribal governance. The item that lies to the far right-hand side of Figure 1, and which receives pressure from all the remaining items on the influence map, is the "feeling that I cannot make a difference" (Item 1). These sessions were designed, in part, to help restore the confidence and ability of community members of the Comanche Tribe to have an impact on the Tribe's future. The sessions described in this chapter represent one step in accomplishing that goal.

At the end of the sessions, participants commented on the significance of the work that had been accomplished, and many expressed excitement and hope and a strong appreciation for the opportunity to participate in designing the future of the Comanche Tribe.[6] The products produced during the planning sessions should also provide the Tribe's leadership with a better understanding of the current situation and a clear plan for moving forward during the next several months. The map displayed in Figure 1 shows the system of problems that confronts the Tribe and the potential influence of these problems on each other and on the overall situation. It shows that the starting points for many of the Tribe's difficulties are an inappropriate form of government and the existence of communication difficulties between the Tribal leadership and the Tribal members. Until these problems are addressed directly, little progress can be made in dealing with problems such as "factionalism," "apathy," and "jealously/rivalry," or in improving the overall Tribal situation.

Based on the results from these planning sessions, the Comanche Tribe is now ready to take the next steps in overcoming barriers to community participation in Tribal governance. The Options Profile (Figure 2) developed by participants identifies several areas in which work should start immediately. Of particular importance are the areas of Problem Solving (A) and Tribal Involvement (D). The options selected from these two categories call for small group problem-solving meetings, development of goals and objectives for the Tribe (a "vision statement"), planning sessions for the Comanche Business Committee, and community meetings to deal with various issues. The people of the Comanche Tribe have spoken through these sessions, and now the task is to keep these words alive by working toward improving the situation of the Comanche people.

Implications for Facilitated Group Planning and Design

The process used in these sessions possesses several characteristics that can benefit efforts to conduct facilitated group work with complex problem situations. First, the process promotes *disciplined dialogue* between the participants in the facilitated sessions. Rather than allowing outgoing individuals to dominate the discussion, every person is given an opportunity to contribute ideas and opinions. Instead of constant interruptions, individuals are allowed to finish their thoughts before others speak. In place of the theme-switching that characterizes many groups, discussions stay on track and participants have a chance to build on others' thoughts. Second, the process promotes *learning through iteration*. Ideas that are proposed during the early phases of the process are next clarified, then related to one another, and used as building blocks for later phases. In this way, learning occurs at a gradual, deliberate pace, with constant opportunities for revision and reinforcement. Third, the process emphasizes the *integrated nature of outcomes*. Ideas that are proposed by participants are always discussed in light of the total set of ideas, and the process directly engages the participants in exploring the links between ideas. Participants learn about the systems nature of the problems they are facing, and they develop a holistic picture of potential solutions.

The methodologies used in these sessions also exhibit properties that can enhance the facilitation of group work. The influence structuring work conducted with ISM is essentially an activity in *mapping perceptions* of the group. Participants are given the opportunity to explore connections and links between ideas that would have gone undetected without such structuring work. ISM provides participants with useful insights into the relationships between ideas, and it leaves them with a product that can guide their thinking as they design potential solutions.

The Options Field and Options Profile products, in particular, have several characteristics that strengthen group problem-solving efforts. First, the Options Field contains a *dynamic set of ideas* to be considered for implementation. The initial idea set can grow larger as new situations are encountered and as new individuals are brought into the planning process. Second, the list of ideas is *organized into meaningful categories* that reflect the uniqueness of the problem situation. Rather than relying on pre-established categories that may not apply to the current situation, participants consider the commonality between ideas and generate titles that reflect the thread of meaning running throughout the items in each category. Third, the overall set of categories represents a *systemic whole* in which the selection of any single option is always made in light of the total set of ideas available. Fourth, the progression of the categories represents an *ordered sequence* from which informed selections are made. By considering categories in the proposed sequence, the choices that participants make from later categories are informed by those choices made already in previous categories. Fifth, the Options Field supports the *creative process* of identifying options. Although ideas vary widely in their scope and feasibility, they all represent potential contributions to improving the situation. Because the appearance of an option in the Field represents only a possibility and not a final decision, ideas are included without the concern for feasibility or realism that often stifles creativity. Sixth, the Options Field *supports full participation* in the planning process. Every individual's ideas can be included in the field for consideration by the community. Seventh, the use of both the Options Field and Options Profile allows for better *tracking of the decision-making process*, because the Profile displays both the options selected for implementation and the options that were not selected. Those involved directly in constructing the plan, as well as those not involved directly, can better understand the rationale for selecting a particular option because the other options that were considered simultaneously are also available for review. Eighth, the Options Profile represents an *alternative plan for action* that can be considered along with other alternatives developed by different groups or by the same group at a different time. The availability of alternatives allows for consideration of a wide range of optional plans before choosing a final plan, and it also allows for different plans to be developed for different scenarios. For example, two different plans, a short-term six-month plan and a longer-term 10-year plan, can be developed using the same Options Field. Finally, the plan that results for any scenario can be *modified easily* as conditions change and as the completion of some options results in new needs or possibly decreases the necessity of performing other actions that might have been selected initially.

Recommendations for Further Applications

Although Interactive Management sessions have been conducted in a wide variety of naturalistic settings, its use with Native American Tribes represents a unique application. Even though there are cultural considerations in applying group facilitation methods in Native American communities, the use of IM appears to be congruent with several aspects of Native American culture (see Broome & Christakis, 1988). The holistic approach of IM, its process orientation, and its ability to create a collaborative problem-solving environment are all compatible with Native American heritage. Thus, IM is potentially a valuable method that Tribes can use to confront the contemporary problems they face.

One of the most serious problems confronting many Tribes is internal conflict. In some cases, the discord has become so serious that Tribal governments have been completely paralyzed by their inability to develop consensus. Tribes are looking for ways to gain input from members and to promote greater participation in Tribal affairs. Based on the success of applications such as the one described in this chapter, it appears that facilitated group meetings, when based on principles such as those guiding the IM process, offer the potential for transforming the current situation. This is supported by other work that has been conducted with Native American Tribes. In addition to the application described in this chapter, IM sessions have been held with the Winnebago (see Broome & Cromer, 1990), Porch Creek, Menominee, Cheyenne/Arapaho, Apache, and Pawnee Tribes.[7] Work is also continuing with the Comanche Tribe.[8]

The internal conflicts confronting Tribal governments are also characteristic of many other social groups across the United States and around the world. Communities, organizations, and special interest groups are looking for ways to build consensus and manage conflict. There is a tremendous need for methods that help diverse individuals develop relational empathy (Broome, 1993). The shelves of most organizations are filled with volumes of organizational analyses, mission statements, organizational redesigns, and long-range plans that are of little use simply because they were produced by an outside consultant who sought "input" primarily through questionnaires and/or interviews. Such documents are rarely understood and seldom accepted by the members of the organization and thus are of use primarily to the consultant who produced them. These organizations need to conduct their planning and design through meaningful group work that is based on sound behavioral and technical principles. The IM process utilized in the Comanche sessions represents over 25 years of development, and it has been tested with hundreds of groups. It is one of the few facilitated group processes that originally was designed explicitly for complex situations. Perhaps by using a facilitated group process such as IM that is capable of dealing with complex problem situations, planning documents will stay off the shelf and become living pages in the growth and development of organizations.

NOTES

[1]The Comanche people called themselves *Nununuh,* meaning "The People." Early French and American explorers knew the Comanches by their Siouan name, Padouca. The Spanish actually gave the Comanche their present name, using a word that comes from the Ute term *Komántica,* which refers to "enemy" or, more accurately, to "anyone who wants to fight me all the time." In the mid-19th century, the population of the Comanche Tribe was estimated to be 20,000 people and consisted of several bands, ranging in number from 50 to 3,500. The territory of the Comanche ranged over the southern plains from what is today Kansas to central Texas. The Tribe moved to this area from the Rocky Mountains around the year 1700. They were members of the Shoshonean group that included the Shoshone, Ute, Paiute, and

Bannock Tribes, who still live in or near the Rocky Mountain range. The
Comanche were the most skilled horsemen (and horsewomen) in the
West, and they were famous for their courage in battle. By the 1850s, the
Comanche had been at war with the Spaniards in Mexico for almost two
centuries and with the Texans for 40 years. The Comanche made a number of treaties with the U.S. government between 1834 and 1875, including the Medicine Lodge Treaty of 1867, under which the Comanches and
their Kiowa and Apache allies were assigned a nearly 3 million acre tract
of land in southwest Oklahoma. This tract was later reduced significantly by the Jerome Agreements of 1892 and 1906, which allotted 160 acres
to each individual Comanche. The Comanche Tribe today consists of
8,690 people, with the majority of the population below the age of 40.
Tribal members must be direct descendants from an original allottee and
must possess 25% Comanche Indian blood. Approximately 4,500
Comanche live in southwest Oklahoma, and there are sizable concentra-
tions of Comanche in Texas and California. There remains approximately 132,000 acres of allotment land still held in trust.

[2]The total Tribal budget is over $3 million (in FY 90 it was $3,111,438).
Sources of funds for the Tribal budget include the Bureau of Indian
Affairs, U.S. Department of Education, U.S. Department of Labor, U.S.
Department of Health & Human Services, and Tribal operations such as
a bingo operation. The Tribe operates several social service programs
(including a jobs program, a family violence program, aid to the elderly,
and burial assistance), the Indian Child Welfare Program (offering counseling, crisis intervention, and recruitment of foster homes), the New
Pathways Program (a halfway house), a higher education program,
adult vocational training, the Carl Perkins Program (providing vocation-
al-technical training), a library project (with an emphasis on cultural and
historical texts), a food distribution program (providing USDA com-
modities), the Home Improvement Program (HIP), the Job Training
Partnership Act (JTPA) Program, a Senior Citizens Center, the
Community Health Representative (CHR) Program, a nonemergency
transport system, and a substance abuse program. The Tribe has joint
ownership, with the Kiowas and the Apaches, of two businesses, The
Native Sun Water Park and KCA Apparel (a clothing manufacturer). At
present, the Tribe operates no business by itself.

[3]In some ways, the Comanche are more fortunate than many Tribes.
Although education generally is one of the primary problems faced by
Tribes in the United States, Bill Southard, a member of the Comanche
Tribe, cited a recent report that showed the high school graduation rate
and the college attendance rate of the Comanche are well above the
national average and are the highest of any Indian tribe in the United
States (personal communication).

[4]The governing body of the Comanche is the Tribal Council, which consists of all Tribal members 18 years of age or older. There are approximately 6,100 eligible voters. The Tribal Council elects seven members to staggered terms on the Comanche Business Committee (CBC), including a Chairman, Vice-Chairman, and Secretary/Treasurer. These officers also serve as officers of the Tribal Council. Terms of office are 3 years, and an individual may serve only two consecutive terms. After a gap of 3 years, an individual may run again for office. Nominations for the three officer and four member positions are made at the annual Tribal Council meeting in April. All members of the Tribal Council are eligible to vote in a primary and, if necessary, in a runoff election held in late spring or early summer. There are six polling sites, and absentee ballots are available on request for those Tribal members living outside the tribal area.

[5]Ideally, IM sessions take place in a special room that has been designed for this type of work. A number of such rooms have been built, including those at George Mason University in Fairfax, VA, City University of London, Defense Systems Management College at Ft. Belvoir in northern Virginia, Southwest Fisheries Research Center in La Jolla, CA, and the University of Sao Paulo, Brazil. The primary features of the room are: support for the physical comfort of the participants during long working days; ample and flexible tabletop working space; adequate wall space for manual posting of butcher-block paper, display of graphical representations of structures produced by the group, and projection of computer output; and facilities for computer support of sessions and production of intermediate results. Many sessions, including the work described in this chapter, have been conducted outside specially built rooms. However, in all cases, special care is taken prior to the sessions to select an appropriate room and to set it up as closely as possible according to the requirements outlined above.

[6]The following are representative comments from the participants:

> I really feel honored to be here because these are the concerns that I've had for a long time and they're not even voiced by most of us because you're not always able to say something for fear of stepping on someone's toe or saying something that's not reflecting something that you really feel, and someone misinterprets what you say a lot of times. And I just really appreciate being able to deal with these things. I just feel the oneness that I've always wanted to feel about my culture.

> I've learned more about the way things are in the last few days, and I understand more about the way things work now. This is a very exciting time because we have the opportunity with this group to turn the corner and head things in a different way. While it'll take a lot of work and a lot of time, if we use the right effort and perspec-

tive we have the chance to make things a lot better for the Tribe.

I think this is the right road, the right attitude, and I like the mix we have here.

I've always known a lot of these problems and I've always been the loud mouth about saying what was wrong with our Tribe, but I never was able to see it in this perspective and the system that's working here. I know it's going to work for us.

I have always felt like somehow, some way, the Tribe needs something to give its membership some type of input such as this. I really didn't understand what we were starting last year but as I got into it and as we finished it, I was hoping that it was the vehicle we were looking for to get the Tribal members involved enough to do the things that we needed to do. I think that we will develop a system that will not only work for the Tribe through the year 2000 but will help us get there and be successful.

[7]Much of this work has been sponsored through Americans for Indian Opportunity (AIO) in Washington, DC (Ladonna Harris, President), and through Oklahomans for Indian Opportunity in Norman, OK (Iola Hayden, Director).

[8]At the time of this writing, additional sessions have been conducted to create the "Vision Statement" advocated by the participants (see Figure 2). Grant proposals have also been written to obtain funding for conducting sessions to revise the constitution, another option selected by the participants and represented on the Options Profile.

2

The Interaction Method: A Case Study in Using Group Facilitation Rules and Roles*

Joseph C. Chilberg
SUNY-Fredonia

The use of facilitative practices by manufacturing and service organizations that emphasize group-centered work is increasing the need for empirical-based knowledge on the efficacy of group facilitation practices in natural settings. That most research on group facilitation has been conducted using experimental groups in laboratory settings raises questions of application to groups in natural settings. Furthermore, group communication research has focused largely on theoretical questions about the efficacy of communication practices to decision making and problem solving. There is, however, little research that actually examines the efficacy of communication practices to the *meeting* as a unit of analysis. The group meeting is the largest unit of analysis in group communication, and the main types of meeting tasks are making decisions and solving problems (Chilberg, 1989). These two tasks are comprised of episodes, activities, and acts that represent the subunits of analysis within a meeting. Group meetings, however, often do not run as smoothly as planned. Steiner (1972) argues that "a group's actual productivity is equal to its potential productivity minus losses due to faulty processes" (p. 9). These faulty processes usually have to do with the fundamental

*Special thanks to the chairs of the ACA Coordinating Committee, Elizabeth Allen and Amy Geragosian, for their insightful contributions to the case study data and analysis. They reinforced my faith in applied education.

problems of keeping a decision-making group on track during a meeting, selecting the most appropriate practices to conduct meeting tasks, allowing all members to participate in discussion, and reaching consensus about plans of action.

This chapter examines a group facilitation technique, called the *Interaction Method (IM)*, that is designed to solve these specific problems. The Interaction Method first is described, and its use in a natural setting is then examined. Concluding remarks focus on the implications of this case study for the adoption and use of IM and examine promising directions for future research on group facilitation practices.

THE INTERACTION METHOD

The Interaction Method (Doyle & Straus, 1976) was designed to facilitate task group meetings. After observing numerous decision-making groups, the authors identified several fundamental problems that occur during meetings that undermine group productivity. They then designed several rules and roles to prevent the occurrence of these key problems. The IM prescribes four field-tested rules, a third-party neutral process facilitator, and a recorder role to prevent common dysfunctional meeting practices. The rules are the Focus Rule, Tool Rule, Consensus Rule, and No Attack Rule (Jensen & Chilberg, 1991). In addition, it is recommended that the group produce a Group Memory by recording the meeting proceedings visibly before the members on large sheets of paper to track and record the group's progress.

The *Focus Rule* is intended to overcome the problem of the wandering discussion by requiring a group to identify its agenda and the results desired from each agenda item prior to discussion. Each agenda item is to be stated in a results-oriented form (e.g., identify criteria for choosing an organization's logo). This rule provides the group with a specific direction for discussion and a basis for determining whether discussion is appropriate to the selected focus. The Focus Rule can enhance group productivity by establishing outcomes and keeping members on track which, in turn, contributes to member satisfaction and cohesion by reducing the frustration created by tangential communication and allowing the group to complete its tasks.

The *Tool Rule* addresses the common problem of applying an inappropriate methodology to address a given focus; that is, using the wrong tool for the job. Once group members have a clear task focus, they need to determine the method that best fits the focus. For example, if the focus is to generate a list of criteria to consider in developing an organization's logo, the use of Brainstorming would be superior to open discussion in terms of quantity and quality of ideas (VanGundy, 1984).

The Tool Rule obviously requires the successful use of the Focus Rule in that a clear focus provides the necessary direction for selecting an appropriate tool among the available options that will contribute to increasing productivity. Additionally, consideration of members' characteristics (e.g., introverted, reticent, etc.) and the relational dynamics of the group (e.g., tension, conflict, apathy, etc.) can aid in selecting tools that reinforce relational development and maintenance. For example, a group that is experiencing member reticence or apathy could use the Round Robin technique, which allows each member to take a turn to contribute to the discussion focus without interruption. The Round Robin technique can increase participation and contributions, and promote member ownership of a meeting.

The *Consensus Rule* deals with the problem of relying on only a few group members to make group decisions. It is used to avoid the domination of decisions by one or a few members, and, consequently, to promote participation by all members, thus affirming members' ownership of the meeting. This rule requires that all members accept all group decisions before finalizing them. All focus, tool, and substantive decisions are to be reached *consensually* unless agreed to otherwise (e.g., the members agree to use a voting procedure).

Whereas the Focus and Tool Rules are used in a temporal sequence, the Consensus Rule operates in tandem with both of them. This rule encourages the "assembly effect" whereby, through member participation and shared ownership of decisions, the group will outperform its most expert member or the mere addition of members' knowledge (Brilhart & Galanes, 1989).

The *No Attack Rule* is meant to prevent the negative evaluation of a member and its consequences by requiring members to evaluate ideas, not members. This rule is intended to prevent communication behaviors that undermine group morale and cohesion and to focus attention on the substance of discussion. The rule operates at *all* times during the meeting in an effort to reduce the incidence of defensive communication that can lead to hostility, withdrawal, and generally the reduction of members' satisfaction with the group. The rule thus emphasizes the task at hand by reinforcing the evaluation of ideas, which, in turn, promotes group productivity.

The *Group Memory* is recommended as a means of recording the proceedings of meetings. The common record is structured by the foci and selected tools of each meeting and displayed as the meeting progresses. This procedure frees members from taking notes, allows members to focus on the immediate discussion, and provides a shared reference and an immediate check on what took place during the group discussion. The Group Memory also reinforces the Focus and Tool Rules in that each focus is written down and the selected tool organizes the recording of the discussion in terms of the steps, episodes, or sequences of the tool procedures and requisite communication behaviors. For example, Brainstorming demands three distinct steps that require a specific type of communicative act(s) per step: idea generation through information sharing; clarification through question and answer; and selection through evaluation.

The IM also prescribes role specializations during meetings as a way to ensure the effective application of the rules. The roles of facilitator and recorder relieve the assigned leader and members from the responsibility of implementing and monitoring the rules so that they can direct their attention to the substantive matters of the meeting. Ideally, the facilitator and recorder should be from outside the group and neutral about the group's task to prevent their involvement in the content of the meeting and the decisions made, and to avoid members' perceptions of procedural power plays that can occur easily when members or chairs perform facilitative roles (Doyle & Straus, 1976; Keltner, 1989). It is, however, the job of all members to keep the facilitator and recorder on track should they overstep the boundaries of their roles. In the absence of a trained third-party facilitator and recorder, the leader and members are responsible for enacting the process roles and rules.

THE APPLIED COMMUNICATION ASSOCIATION COORDINATING COMMITTEE

The Applied Communication Association (ACA) was formed during spring 1989 to provide communication majors at the State University of New York College at Fredonia with an opportunity to apply and develop curriculum-based skills. The ACA's mission is to provide members with knowledge and experience in the application of communication theory and practice in professional settings and social contexts. The mission was to be fulfilled through the presentation of speakers and workshops and the delivery of communication services to the Communication Department and the community at large. The organization was a zero-history group, with much to do in setting up its operational structure and procedures beyond its governance by-laws. The officers had to construct the organization before it could develop effective communication activities and services. This development of an organization from scratch provided numerous opportunities to apply course-based knowledge and communication practices. After all, "Communication is the process of organizing" (Johnson, 1977, p. 3).

The Coordinating Committee (CC) of the ACA is comprised of four officers and an advisor who are responsible for developing the organization and coordinating members' activities. The CC is responsible for planning the general membership meetings, coordinating internal and external communication, and initiating and coordinating organizational development tasks and communication service projects. The duties of the officers include serving as the facilitator and coordinator for teams related to each officer's functional area: Resource Development, Public Relations, Activities and Projects, and Finance. Each officer is responsible for helping his or her functional team members develop procedures for routine tasks (e.g., the PR team advertises meetings and activities) and identifying and implementing developmental and service projects. The teams were also implemented to create a context for applying communication principles and increasing opportunities for participation and involvement by the members. Officers were expected to be process facilitators during meetings, coordinators between meetings, and to avoid taking on team tasks.

The club advisor plays the role of participant-observer. In this particular case, he contributes ideas, makes procedural recommendations, provides resources, and participates in committee decision making. His main duty is to help the organization develop communication practices to achieve its mission. The advisor discovered, however, that he had to avoid being perceived as directive to prevent alienating officers and taking over the committee. He detected resentment from the organization's first set of officers toward his efforts to influence the task priorities and meeting practices. Even though others have found that undergraduate communication clubs need directive advising (e.g., Litterst & Ross, 1989), such a style may breed resentment and alienation. If the group members' maturity level is low to moderate (i.e., low technical knowledge and skills coupled with moderate task motivation), a "selling" style is more appropriate (Hersey & Blanchard, 1975). The advisor and chairs thus need to encourage the application of course knowledge and practices without undermining members' participation and ownership of the committee, meeting practices, and decisions.

Although the CC existed within a college setting, this group was not a classroom group. It was a volunteer organization comprised of members with common interests and shared goals. As in most organizations, in which small task groups are the major means by which decisions are made, all of ACA's decisions are made in the group meetings of the Coordinating Committee, the teams, and the general membership. The CC thus provided an opportunity to observe the application of the Interaction Method in a natural setting.

Training in the Interaction Method

Half of the officers, including the chairs of the ACA, took a group communication course prior to taking office. The guiding principle of the course was that theory and technique should inform group communication processes and practices. Instruction thus focused on the functional implications of theory and practice to task group processes. The process function of communication was then linked to the task and relational functions of communication. The relationship of process to task productivity and relational maintenance established a basis for judging the efficacy and appropriateness of the specific techniques covered in the textbook for the course. Students were then introduced to specific techniques in terms of their task and relational advantages and disadvantages. This framework provided a cognitive structure for matching types of task and relational needs with specific techniques to fulfill them. Students were instructed on the use of the rules and roles of the Interaction Method to manage the overall meeting process, and they experienced them through numerous exercises and demonstrations. The ACA chairs who took the group communication course were able to apply some of the practices learned in the group course to facilitate the Coordinating Committee's meetings. At the same time, there were several key practices relevant to effective and efficient group communication that were applied inconsistently or virtually ignored. In effect, there was a gap between knowledge and practice. An assessment by the advisor based on the CC's practices was planned to uncover the source of this gap.

I took a particular interest in the ACA's meetings because I was the advisor to this organization, the instructor of the group course, and had co-authored the textbook for the course (Jensen & Chilberg, 1991). The text included two chapters on skills and techniques for conducting meetings and making effective decisions, as well as a special section, titled "The Group Project Facilitator," that was designed to aid groups in the application of effective meeting and decision-making practices. Finally, although I had limited opportunities to observe the use of skills and techniques in the class project groups, I did observe directly the ACA officers' application of group communication practices during the Coordinating Committee meetings.

ASSESSING THE USE OF THE INTERACTION METHOD
BY THE COORDINATING COMMITTEE

The assessment of the CC's use of the group facilitation rules began with a review of three semesters of the group's agenda and minutes for each meeting for signs of a lack of facilitation practices and completion of meeting tasks. This review was a useful source of information on process problems because the committee had adopted the practice of evaluating the strengths and weaknesses of their meetings and recording these evaluations in the minutes. The second source of assessment information was derived from interviews I conducted with the recent and past CC chairs. The following interview questions were provided to the chairs a week prior to a telephone interview: a) What rules/roles were used and how were they adopted?; b) How consistent was each rule used and to what effect?; c) What were sources of difficulty in implementing rules/roles?; and d) What were the consequences of the level of use of the rules/roles? Third, a source of assessment information was derived from observations made by me as the advisor of the committee over the period of time under review.

Meeting Agenda and Minutes

The CC agenda and minutes were available for 22 of the 26 meetings held over a 15-month period. The minutes of 18 of these meetings included end-of-meeting evaluations. The evaluations were reviewed to identify statements concerned with process-related issues. The evaluations provided indicators of members' cognizance of meeting rules and recurring meeting problems.

Table 2.1 indicates that the CC members were aware they had difficulty maintaining the focus of discussion during their meetings. Other evidence of the need for the Focus Rule was found in the format of written agenda items and in the generalized phrasing of minutes of the meeting. Specifically, the Focus Rule requires agenda items to be stated in a results-oriented manner and that agenda item results be reported in terms of the outcome of the agenda item. These requirements, however, were not being met consistently by the CC. Instead of phrasing an agenda item in a results-oriented form (e.g., generating ideas to increase member participation in the ACA), it would be stated in a general topical form (e.g., member participation problem). Of the 22 meeting documents, 3 meetings had all statements in the focus rule format, 10 had most, 7 had some, and 2 had none. Although the minutes indicated the use of the Focus Rule, actually staying on focus during a meeting was less consistent. Members noted that their involvement and participation during the meeting were strong and that they experienced supportive and cooperative communication. There was, however, recognition of difficulty in completing the planned agenda. The absence of frequent mention of meeting productivity coupled with frequent recognition of the supportive/cooperative climate may be indicative of more success in the relational than task dimensions of the group communication process.

Table 2.1. CC Meeting Process Evaluation Issues

ISSUE	MEETINGS ($n = 18$)
Well focused/better focusing	4
Need more focus	13
Productive (informative/achievement)	4
Positive climate/cooperative	12
Strong participation/involvement	7
Agenda not completed	3*

* Tabling of business concerned with organizational development tasks is not reflected in total.

Interview Data Results

The answers to each interview question were content analyzed by me for themes and patterns. My teacher role did not appear to hinder candid responses by the student chairs, because work in the CC involved regular evaluation of the members' and my meeting behavior as the advisor. Additionally, the chairs' interest in applied communication contributed to their willingness to provide thoughtful and candid answers to the interview questions. The analysis of the answers on rule use, consistency of rule use, and how the rules were adopted were virtually identical across interviewees.

What rules were used and how were they adopted?

None of the rules and roles of the IM were adopted formally; that is, there was no discussion or written documents indicating the acceptance and manner of rule use. At the same time, there was recognition and use of the rules throughout the CC's meetings. The rules were adopted informally, largely through their initiation and use by the chair and advisor. The Focus Rule, Tool Rule, and Group Memory, however, were used inconsistently depending on the situation, whereas the Consensus and No Attack Rules were evidenced consistently in the chairs' and members' meeting behaviors.

The Focus Rule was demonstrated through the wording of agenda item statements and requests to return to or establish a focus during the meeting. The rule was first initiated by the chair through the agenda for the meeting and then reinforced by the advisor during officer reports by indicating when officers got off focus. Most of the agenda items across all the meetings were phrased, explicitly or implicitly, as specific goals. The outcomes for more complex agenda items that involved several subfocuses were, however, less clear. Sometimes the subfocuses were listed, typically in topical form, but not in a form that indicated the desired result. The second way the focus rule was evidenced was when discussion became unclear or went off on a tangent. In these instances, the rule was used either by the chair to raise a question that signalled a need to bring the discussion back to the initial focus, or the advisor or a member would indicate that the group needed focus or were off on a tangent. Two frequent occurrences of losing discussion focus were during officer reports and when the business of the meeting involved a new and complex task (i.e., the task involved several unrecognized subfocuses).

Officer reports would get sidetracked into task discussions when some issue, task, or duty raised in the report was related to another officer's duties, triggering a tangential discussion. The relevance of the tangential discussion to the member initiating it usually was clear to all, but was not appropriate to an officer's report per se as it raised old or new business for deliberation during the report. It was very easy to get sidetracked during reports because of the numerous cross-functional tasks involving two or more officers. Thus, reports would slide into decision-making discussions and peripheral matters as each member reported his or her business. That the discussion was relevant to the group's business encouraged members to participate in decision-making communication at a time when information sharing was the task at hand.

This tendency to lose focus during officers' reports became a problem in two respects. First, it took time away from the planned agenda because new agenda items were interjected surreptitiously into the meeting through the officers' reports. These informally added agenda items frequently led to rushing through or not finishing the planned meeting agenda. Second, it led to spontaneous decision-making practices that undermined careful information gathering, analysis, and evaluation. The CC members agreed finally to keep reports on focus by only permitting questions of clarification or contributions of additional information relevant to the report topics. Any additional business or needed decision triggered by discussion would be covered during a later agenda item or added to the meeting agenda.

The other common situation that led to Focus Rule violations occurred during a new complex task that required three or more subfocuses to be completed. There were two types of problems evident in this situation: the breadth of the focus task and focus specificity. The breadth problem occurred even when the task was stated in a results-oriented form, and the discussion would take several substantively different directions until it became clear that it was unproductive and that members had become frustrated. This problem was due in part to the unanticipated and unrecognized subfocuses that led to the perception of tangential communication. In actuality, the discussion was focused, but the focus was too broad and needed to be narrowed. Losing focus occurred even when the chair identified subtopics of a complex task in an attempt to structure discussion. These attempts, however, led to a lack of focus specificity as the focus was a topic, not a specific results-oriented statement. The ambiguity of topical agenda items seemed to increase off-focus discussion. The difficulty of staying on focus could be attributed to working on the complex task as if it were a single task, working on too complex a task at one time, and/or not articulating tasks in terms of specific results-oriented statements.

The issue of keeping focus was addressed more consistently as the CC developed over time and situations occurred in which management of discussion was needed. However, the Focus Rule was not adopted formally; that is, there was no agreement or formal procedures to establish the Focus Rule as part of the operating procedures for meetings. The CC members did not agree to establish collectively the foci in outcome-oriented form for each meeting, to determine the order of foci, and to maintain the focus of discussion at a given time. When the Focus Rule was used in part or whole, it was situational (e.g., when what the group was trying to accomplish became unclear or when the rule was established formally to guide officer reports) or used inconsistently (e.g., agenda items or their outcome not phrased in result-oriented form).

When asked about the effect or utility of the Focus Rule when it was used, both chairs acknowledged that it sharpened the focus of discussion, reduced tangential communication, saved time, helped reveal complex tasks, and contributed to critical task analysis and decision making. Additionally, the chairs believed that identifying and keeping focus increased task productivity and a sense of task achievement by the group members.

With the exception of using the Round Robin procedure for conducting officer reports, tools (techniques) were used situationally. The advisor would suggest the use of Brainstorming or Ideawriting for an idea-generating task or Ranking to organize or reduce decision choices. Otherwise, the majority of the meetings were characterized by open discussion. Because the Tool Rule was based on the identification of the focus, it was not adopted per se by this group. That is, the members simply did not decide formally on the appropriate tool for a given focus prior to conducting it.

The chairs identified two positive effects of the CC's limited use of tools. First, using the tools enhanced the quality of task performance and the outcomes. Second, the Tool Rule increased members' awareness of the relationship of the tools to the tasks. Additionally, the use of tools contributed to the applied mission of the organization by developing the officers' cognizance of and competence using techniques learned in the group communication course in order to improve group process. This latter point became important when the organization adopted the use of functional teams that were facilitated by the officers.

The Consensus Rule and No Attack Rule, although never adopted formally, were operative consistently during group meetings. The chairs always checked with the members on all task and process decisions and, with the exception of one incident, members did not judge each other negatively. The use of these two rules is more likely due to the social emphasis of the college culture, in which the importance of getting along and avoiding confrontation shape members' task communication behavior. Furthermore, the chairs' concern with group development, shared decision making, member satisfaction, and developing members' confidence in the chairs' role performance motivated them to check consistently for member consensus.

Both chairs found that soliciting group consensus encouraged and acknowledged the importance of member involvement, increased the pool of ideas, helped test decisions, increased support for decisions, and reduced the domination of decisions by the chair or advisor. Overall, seeking consensus confirmed the decision-making role of members and increased their sense of group ownership.

The chairs believed that the lack of personal attacks had several positive effects. Most noteworthy was the emphasis on evaluating ideas, not people. Members focused on evaluating ideas and decisions and were able to accept ideational evaluation without taking it as a personal attack. It is likely that the value of "getting along" contributed to the lack of attacking communication behaviors. At the same time, the members appeared to have internalized the proactive element of the No Attack Rule in that they would evaluate ideas or situations, not the person. For example, one officer had clearly been remiss in performing his responsibilities, largely due to a lack of coordination. The members did not blame him but focused instead on solving the problematic situation. One chair thought that the formal adoption of the No Attack Rule would be useful in reinforcing the evaluation of ideas, encouraging constructive task behaviors, and establishing the norms and bases for interventions when personal attacks occurred.

The Group Memory was also not used to record and display meeting proceedings. Instead, the minutes of each meeting recorded by the CC secretary was the method used for keeping business meeting records. With few exceptions, the recording of the minutes visually before the group occurred when the committee engaged in or reviewed the results of an idea-generating task using Brainstorming. Recording the discussion visually before the group was initiated typically by the advisor. When used, however, the Group Memory did have noticeable value. It contributed to effective task performance by providing a shared reference and record of the meeting, required articulating and reinforced maintaining the focus, and contributed to establishing variety and separation between ideas and choices. The advisor noted that if the group used the Group Memory throughout the meeting consistently it would reinforce the use of other adopted rules (e.g., Focus and Tool Rules) and provide a shared map of the whole meeting for reference which would be approved as the meeting proceeded. On the relational side, the display of a member's contributions could validate that member's idea and enhance his or her self-concept, which can promote personal satisfaction, involvement, and partnership with other members.

There was no designation of specialized meeting process roles beyond the traditional chair and secretary duties. There was also no designated process facilitator. The advisor, and to a lesser extent the chairs, performed some process functions informally by either identifying and/or advocating the order of business, or recommending and leading the group in the use of a tool for conducting a task. The chairs would solicit members' consensus when the meeting agenda required prioritizing business due to time constraints or when tasks needed immediate attention. On a few occasions, members initiated process behaviors by bringing discussion back on focus. Generally, the process role, when initiated, was shared informally but initiated largely by the advisor and chairs. The members left process matters to the chairs, which limited opportunities for developing their process facilitation awareness and skills.

What contributed to difficulties in initiating the rules?

The chairs identified numerous sources of difficulty in initiating the rules both formally and informally. The difficulties were reviewed by the interviewer and categorized into the following six themes:

1. Lack of common knowledge and ability to apply rules.
2. Members' resistance and dissatisfaction with highly structured meetings (e.g., too much like classes and too work-oriented and serious).
3. Lacked procedures to operationalize rules.
4. Inconsistent use and modeling of rules.
5. Nonroutine, complex tasks.
6. Lacked value for and motivation to implement facilitation practices.

That all of the CC officers did not complete the group communication course during their term of office and that the committee did not provide instruction on the rules and roles of the Interaction Method were the most telling sources of difficulty. Even members who possessed such knowledge were not readily able or willing to advocate the adoption of the rules or initiate them situationally. This difficulty in initiating rules and roles was related to the second difficulty, resistance and dissatisfaction with highly structured meetings. Basically, the advisor and the chairs did not advocate the formal adoption of the rules as a way of building the membership of the organization and encouraging members to run for office. It was clear from experience and comments made between meetings that some officers did not like highly structured meetings that resembled the group communication course. No one felt comfortable advocating the adoption of the rules in view of the ACA's efforts to build and maintain membership in a young organization and enhance members' interest in running for office. This situation compromised the organization's mission of applying what was learned in courses and served to undermine the instruction of members who were unfamiliar with the rules.

These two difficulties precluded the development of needed procedures to operationalize the rules. Although situational application of the rules occurred, it was inconsistent. The inconsistency of application led to inconsistent modeling which further served to discourage the use of the rules and hindered learning through example.

As noted earlier, nonroutine tasks that were complex were a major reason why the group lost focus during the discussions. This loss of focus was due largely to treating a complex task as if it were simple. When this occurred, the broad-based discussion led eventually to a recognition that there were specific subtasks that needed to have their own focus. At the same time, the realization that there were subfocuses within a complex task was an opportunity to advocate identifying all relevant focuses and working on them one at a time. The realization that a task was complex reinforced the application and situational use of the Focus Rule.

The lack of value and motivation to implement meeting procedures by some members hindered other members or the advisor from advocating the adoption of formal meeting rules. Additionally, the adoption of the IM would have been a task in its own right. The demands of school and employment, coupled with the CC's volume of organizational development tasks, posed a challenge to the officers' motivation to work on adopting the IM rules. The committee's job of developing the organization, coupled with its responsibility for initiating service projects, was demanding and, at times, overwhelming. The task overload was a main reason for proposing and using functional teams comprised of an officer and general members to perform routine tasks, develop the infrastructure of the organization, and initiate communication service projects. Nonetheless, the lack of value toward facilitation practices and the volume of the CC's tasks did not encourage the additional work involved in adopting the meeting rules. At the same time, the group needed to consider the long-term payoffs that the short-term efforts of adopting facilitative practices could provide.

What were the consequences of the level of use of rules?

The chairs identified numerous consequences of the level of use of the rules and roles. The consequences were of two types: those that were perceived to have occurred and those that could occur if the rules were adopted formally. All of the consequences, however, were reflected in five themes: (a) efficiency loss; (b) effectiveness loss/gain; (c) participation loss/gain; (d) relational development or maintenance loss/gain; and (e) obstacles to the implementation of the rules.

The efficiency losses were attributed mainly to not establishing a clear results-oriented focus or not maintaining focus. The chairs believed that these problems contributed to inefficient use of time, not completing the meeting agenda, and sidetracking the group from the immediate task. They thought that the consistent application of the Focus Rule would improve the use of the groups' meeting time.

The effectiveness losses were attributed to not adopting the Focus and Tool Rules. The main losses occurred in the quality of task performance. The chairs believed that complex tasks or those requiring careful analysis would have benefited from the use of the rules. Specifically, using the Focus Rule would have encouraged the analysis of complex tasks prior to working on them, whereas using the Tool Rule would have helped the group to identify techniques appropriate to the subtasks of a complex task.

Another source of effectiveness loss occurred with the use of the Consensus Rule. One chair believed that although the Consensus Rule was operative during meetings, agreement at times seemed feigned or uncritical. She noted that there was a lot of agreement and few objections or criticisms. Although the rule did not cause this situation, it could contribute to ineffective task performance and decisions if members were not willing or able to voice criticisms or concerns. Ideally, the Consensus Rule should draw out members' points of view and encourage decision testing that can increase the quality of the decisions. Seeking consensus on critical decisions may demand a more engaging procedure that requires members to voice their position and reasons rather than merely asking if there is agreement. The chairs thought they encouraged participation and involvement by not advocating the formal use of the rules. This is not to say that using the rules would decrease participation in and of itself but that the members would have been dissatisfied with the restrictions and demands imposed by a formally structured process. The chairs feared confronting members over the use of the rules and expressed even greater fear of creating dissatisfaction that could lead to losing present or future officers in an organization struggling to develop and maintain itself. At the same time, the loss of focus contributed to losing members' attention. Not considering the use of an appropriate tool for the task and relational situation that confronted the group was thought to hinder broader participation and allowed more vocal members to dominate discussion. The chairs speculated that the use of the Group Memory as well as a formally structured meeting process could reduce spontaneity. It is likely that instituting the rules to structure the meeting process formally could reduce spontaneity initially, but once operational they would only limit off-focus spontaneity.

The chairs believed that the use of the rules would contribute to relational development and maintenance. The rules provide a way of managing various sources of task ineffectiveness and inefficiency that frustrate individual and collective satisfaction with the group. A chair conjectured that bringing a member back to focus could be perceived as disconfirming, although there was no indication of this from incidents in which it occurred when all members understood the rule and its purpose.

The obstacles to implementing the rules were attributed largely to the lack of commitment to formal adoption, lack of knowledge, and inconsistent modeling of the rules. Additionally, members did not develop the process facilitation awareness and skills needed to use the rules and roles. This latter problem not only hindered the initiation of rules but proved to be problematic for officers when facilitating the functional teams. The lack of experience with process facilitation in the CC meetings carried over to facilitating the functional teams whose members had less knowledge, experience, and understanding of group process than the CC members.

The PR team illustrates how the lack of knowledge and experience with the rules hindered the officers' ability to perform the role of process facilitator. The CC's secretary role included facilitating the PR team meetings. One of the tasks of the PR team was to propose and make a banner for the organization. After several weeks, however, the team had not come up with a proposal. The advisor offered to observe the PR team meeting to determine what was hindering the team's productivity. The team members assembled for the meeting and were sitting in a haphazard fashion. Specifically, the members were seated such that they could not all see each others' and especially the facilitator's face. The members had no common visual focus. The banner task included a discussion on the type of material to use, the colors of the banner, the organization's colors, the size and shape, the layout, and the wording of the banner. This discussion proceeded to move back and forth across these topics depending on who spoke. Numerous ideas were presented for all the topics, but none were developed nor were any decisions finalized before the focus shifted to another topic. It was clear that the team was working on a complex task and that several subfocuses needed to be identified, ordered, and treated one at a time. Additionally, there was no place to visualize issues that needed diagrams or examples. A task involving visual decisions obviously would benefit from access to materials to visualize choices (i.e., size, shape, and layout). The meeting ended with no clear achievement, a frustrated facilitator, and disenchanted members.

The advisor met with the secretary/facilitator to review her observations, and a plan of action was developed to manage the three problems. The recommendations required creating a common focus using the Focus Rule, using an appropriate tool for each focus involving idea generating, and using a Group Memory procedure.

The plan required her to seat the team members in a semi-circle before a large writing surface (e.g., chalk board or easel with wall space) to establish a common focus and to draw attention. She would present the team with the subfocuses visually in result-oriented terms of the banner task in a logical order; banner content before layout, size before layout, and so on. This discussion procedure would be followed by a review of the Focus Rule that would guide the discussion of each task. Because each of the focuses required some initial idea generating, Brainstorming was recommended to achieve this activity. Because the club used electronic mail and the team was pressed for time, Ideawriting over electronic-mail was suggested for generating ideas between meetings.

The secretary/facilitator planned the next PR team meeting based on these recommendations. Her E-mail to the advisor on the results read: "The meeting . . . went well—for once. I used the board during the meeting and it went much, much better! I felt so much more organized and in charge, and, believe it or not, everyone participated."

Based on observations as the advisor and the perceptions of the chairs, adopting the rules and developing officers' as well as members' ability to perform the facilitator role would be advantageous to the organization. These rules and roles would first contribute to the mission of the organization to apply what has been learned in classes. Second, they would enhance the effectiveness and efficiency of the CC and team meetings. Finally, the opportunity for members to develop effective facilitation skills for group meetings would allow them to apply such skills to other groups in civic and professional settings.

DISCUSSION AND RECOMMENDATIONS

The CC embraced the rules that emphasize the maintenance function of group communication through the consistent use of the Consensus and No Attack Rules. At the same time, the inconsistent use of the Focus and Tool Rules, the Group Memory, and the facilitation role reflected a deemphasis of the task function. This deemphasis of the task-oriented rules per se was perceived to reduce the efficiency and effectiveness of the group meetings. Furthermore, the chairs and advisor believed that using the rules would further the CC's ability to improve task performance and the quality of group decisions. Additionally, having members share in and take ownership of the decisions about group processes by using the rules would help facilitate the activities of the meetings and develop members' group process awareness and skills. A review of selected group communication research about the relationship of task complexity, task communication behaviors, and decision-making procedures to effective small group meetings will further explain the observations of the chair and advisor and help develop a rationale for adopting such group facilitation rules.

Task Complexity

Decision quality has been related to the frequency of interaction and task complexity such that increases in task complexity require increases in interaction in order to improve decision quality (Hirokawa & Gouran, 1989). The Consensus and Tool Rules provide opportunities to structure task interaction. The Consensus Rule promotes interaction directly by soliciting members' input and agreement on all decisions whereas the Tool Rule helps a group to address the task and relational dimensions of communication posed by the group's task; relational climate (e.g., friendly, cohesive, defensive, etc.), and the members' characteristics (e.g., apathetic, domineering, etc.). That is, selecting a procedure to facilitate discussion is more than a tool for managing a task; it must also be chosen in view of the group's communication climate and the level of interaction needed from its members. In effect, groups can select techniques to facilitate discussion of complex tasks that spreads participation among the members and increase interaction.

Broome and Keever (1989) identified three design laws for problem-solving meetings that bear directly on task complexity. The first is the *Law of Requisite Variety*, which posits that complex problems are multidimensional in nature, requiring the identification of all relevant aspects of the problem. Overall, the rules of the Interaction Method are a response to the multidimensional problems of meetings per se and help a group inadvertently to manage complex tasks within meetings. The rules were designed to avoid four key task and relational stumbling blocks in meetings: a lack of focus; ineffective task procedures; lack of participation in decision making; and aggressive behavior. The rules do not provide specific guidelines for conducting meetings or choosing types of tasks (e.g., idea generating). However, the Focus and Tool Rules support and encourage consideration of task identification and methods of treatment that contribute to uncovering the multidimensional nature of complex tasks. Additions to the Focus Rule can increase the group members' capacity to identify dimensions of a task. For example, once a focus is identified, members can determine whether it is a simple or complex task. If complex, the next focus would require identifying the dimensions of the problem or subtasks of a project. Each dimension or subtask could then serve as a focus for action. This suggestion would certainly benefit the CC, which often treated a complex focus as if it were simple. Whether treating the meeting itself or a group task as a complex problem, one needs to understand the dimensions of the problem or task before developing steps for its resolution.

The Law of Requisite Parsimony raises the difficulty of cognitive overload on group members' information processing capacities. It contends that groups must manage the cognitive demands on their participants. Broome and Keever (1989) explain that:

> Facilitation must ensure that the information-processing demands imposed on participants does not exceed short-term memory limits . . . [I]deas should be organized in accordance with some specified relationship by using a series of simple yet systematic steps rather than attempting to comprehend and organize a large number of ideas. (p. 115)

The Interaction Method rules provide a simple and systematic procedure for managing key decisions and tasks. The Focus Rule, with the addendum of determining focus complexity, helps groups fractionate complex tasks into manageable chunks. The Tool Rule, on the other hand, contributes to identifying techniques that separate interrelated cognitive operations associated with the task. For example, choosing Brainstorming to perform an idea-generating task separates the episodes of idea identification, clarification, and evaluation. Additionally, using Group Memory to track task discussion and outcomes reduces the burden on members' short-term memory.

The Law of Requisite Saliency addresses the need for a group to uncover the issues that are of import to its group members. Diversity in the importance of issues or tasks among group members can result in "unfocused dialogue, unjustified decisions, and arbitrary solutions" (Broome & Keever, 1989, p. 115). The Consensus Rule can be used to draw out members' views and issues regarding group decisions, and the Tool Rule provides an additional means for identifying issues of import by requiring members to select techniques that fit the task. Thus, if a group is identifying issues of a project or problem, a technique can be selected that requires members to participate in issue identification. For example, Ideawriting is better at obtaining a variety of ideas from each member than is Brainstorming (VanGundy, 1984). However, group members need to know when issue identification should be the focus and know available techniques that are designed to facilitate participation.

Task Communication Behaviors

Numerous studies have examined the relationship between task communication behaviors and decision quality (see Hirokawa & Gouran, 1989). Several key task behaviors are facilitated directly by the rules of the Interaction Method. Relevant, precise, and goal-directed statements contribute to quality task performance. Hackman and Walton (1986) found that a "clear, engaging direction" is fundamental to task group effectiveness. The Focus Rule requires members to identify the goal of a given task in a precise statement. The focus then provides the basis for guiding and maintaining the relevance of members' contributions.

The performance of task leadership functions and increasing the opportunities for members' participation also contribute to effective task performance. The Interaction Method rules, in general, and the Consensus Rule, in particular, establish the process-facilitation role as the responsibility of all group members. All members have the role of process observer and, ultimately, have responsibility for all process decisions. The Consensus Rule also encourages participation, whereas the Tool Rule can be used to select techniques that require participation from all group members, especially in identifying the variety of issues relevant to members and the task at hand.

Evaluating group members negatively has been shown to create defensive exchanges between members that can interfere with effective task communication (Gibb, 1961). This situation is addressed by the No Attack Rule which restricts members to ideational evaluation and requires intervention when personal criticism is displayed. This rule not only facilitates productive task communication but also reduces destructive relational communication behaviors that may over time undermine a group's morale and cohesion and affect task communication negatively. Thus, groups should not permit personal criticism and should require members to focus evaluative statements on the issue or decision being discussed.

Role of Procedures

Procedures that encourage the analysis of problems contribute to solution quality (Hirokawa & Gouran, 1989). In general, the Interaction Method rules are based on the analysis of fundamental problems associated with group meetings. Even though the rules do not offer specific guidelines for analysis, the Focus Rule does encourage general task analysis, whereas the identification of focuses involving analytic tasks sets up the selection of techniques to perform these tasks through the Tool Rule.

These payoffs, however, are dependent on members' abilities to identify analytic tasks and choose procedures for performing them. This latter point is at the heart of what could be called a "procedural deficit": The more energy members spend on process matters, the less they spend on other necessary task functions. Excessive time and energy devoted to procedural matters detracts from decision quality (Hirokawa, 1980). The rules provide guidelines for the analysis of meeting tasks, but they require additional process knowledge and skills to identify and conduct analytic tasks. Group members would have to be versed in the rules of the Interaction Method and know techniques for conducting task activities to avoid excessive time devoted to process matters.

Adopting Process Facilitation Practices

Regardless of the value of facilitative guidelines, their adoption by group members requires a willingness to accept and an ability to use them. Certainly, all group members will have to learn the basic rules and necessary tools for managing the various types of tasks in order to take on the facilitative role. The willingness to adopt facilitative norms, however, is another matter. Friedman (1989) recommends assessing the cultural context followed by a proactive approach for establishing meeting norms. The first order of business requires an assessment of the cultural context in terms of members' thinking, members' relational and personal agendas, the influence of other groups, and existing norms of problem solving within the particular organization and within the society at large. This assessment is recommended as a front-end analysis prior to a group's adoption of facilitation norms and confrontation of its actual tasks. This practice would be equally useful for assessing an existing work group's reluctance to adopt known facilitative practices. In the particular case of the CC, a contextual assessment by the chair and advisor would be useful in developing adoption strategies.

Friedman (1989) advocates a proactive approach to establishing process facilitation norms. Members need to develop shared task group norms to avoid the discord associated with differing norms. This requires "upstream" direction (the rules of the Interaction Method) from both the facilitator and the members to prepare for what is anticipated "downstream." The upstream direction is developed by identifying the problematic downstream occurrences. This, in fact, was the approach used to develop the rules of the Interaction Method. Groups can develop productive group norms by having members identify concerns and interests associated with their group and their tasks. From this, members can identify common dysfunctional experiences and situations that would interfere with effective task and relational communication and develop norms to prevent their occurrence. The identification of shared concerns can lead to the adoption or development of facilitative norms to manage them. In the present case study, for example, the common perception of the CC's focus problem or its floundering with a complex task could contribute to its members' decision to adopt the Focus Rule or to check for task complexity prior to finalizing a focus. Groups are ineffective if members' behavior is based on different norms, and they are not likely to come to agreement on norms until they experience disorganization and a lack of productivity (Spich & Keleman, 1985). Although the CC cannot be characterized as floundering, it has experienced time pressures and frustration related to ineffective meeting and task management practices. This situation could serve as a breakpoint to look backward with the members to uncover the implicit norms that contribute to the experienced dysfunctions (Friedman, 1989).

CONCLUSION

Research provides evidence to support the efficacy of the rules and roles of the Interaction Method to task and relational functions of group communication, and the analysis of the CC's meeting dysfunctions confirms the value of adopting these rules and roles. The Interaction Method rules can help groups manage task complexity, increase task communication behaviors, and encourage members' participation, thus maximizing the variety of inputs and the ownership of decisions and promoting the effective analysis of the meeting and its tasks.

The recognition of such payoffs alone, however, will not ensure the adoption of a group facilitation method. The adoption process should draw on the needs and interests of the group members and the organization as a basis for identifying and adopting process facilitation norms. When the norms are identified, a group will need to establish a protocol for implementation and provide instruction on its use. Once in use, evaluations should be conducted periodically to determine their efficacy and to identify any problems. End-of-meeting evaluations provide a timely method of evaluation. Operational difficulties or dysfunctional consequences could be identified and addressed, and members could modify existing rules or develop additional practices to support the achievement of member, group, and organizational goals.

Perhaps the most nagging question regarding the Interaction Method and other facilitation practices is the reluctance of groups to use them. Over the past 20 years, this author has experienced little in the way of facilitative rules or techniques as a member of groups in university or corporate settings. This is not to say that group facilitation practices are not being used, but it does suggest that they are not used commonly. As the CC case showed, knowing the Interaction Method and its value alone will not motivate mangers or members to adopt it. Even though Friedman (1989) has provided guidelines for adopting group facilitation practices, he does not address how to get managers or groups to want to develop group communication norms to facilitate meetings and task activities.

There appears to be a large gap between the existing body of facilitation practices and their use (Broome & Keever, 1989; Jensen & Chilberg, 1991). Although the research is inconclusive about the efficacy of facilitation practices to group performance, there is sufficient theoretical knowledge and field-tested applications to warrant a much wider adoption of the Interaction Method. Hirokawa and Gouran (1989) are on target in their argument that the main research agenda should focus on identifying the effects of facilitation practices on performance quality.

Research on the efficacy of the Interaction Method, in particular, is warranted for two reasons. First, it is designed for conducting the overall group meeting regardless of meeting tasks, and thus it can be adopted by a wide variety of groups. Second, the rules and roles are designed to address fundamental problems common to decision-making groups. Research on the efficacy of the rules in managing and preventing common problems experienced during group meetings would further the knowledge of communication norms for meetings as a means to enhance effective group communication. At the same time, the value of such knowledge is questionable if it does not lead to adoption.

The knowledge versus use dilemma raises the adoption process as an additional important research agenda. It is ironic that there is a body of research on factors affecting the adoption of computer-mediated systems for facilitating group decision making, whereas such research is scarce in non-mediated group facilitation. There is a need for research on the sources and conditions of resistance to adopting facilitation methods and techniques in face-to-face group meetings. Until resistance to group facilitation in natural settings is understood, knowledge of group facilitation practices will remain largely in texts and manuals, not in the practices of working groups.

PART II

Facilitation Techniques for Encouraging Constructive Dialogue to Resolve Conflict and Differences in Groups

Conflict is inevitable between those who work and live together. Although many people view conflict negatively, often avoiding it at all costs, this is not the most healthy way to deal with conflict. Handling conflict effectively is especially important in small groups, for research shows that groups that do so improve the quality of their decision-making process (Nemeth, 1986).

Group members, however, sometimes choose to avoid engaging in any conflict, which is one of the symptoms associated with "groupthink," a circumstance in which consensus becomes the highest priority, overriding the motivation to realistically appraise alternative courses of action (Janis, 1972, 1982). The results of such conflict avoidance may well prove disastrous. The Challenger disaster, for example, resulted from the avoidance of conflict during the group discussions about whether to launch it, even in spite of the evidence against doing so (Hirokawa, Gouran, & Martz, 1988; Renz & Greg, 1988). Of course, the opposite problem may occur. Group members may engage in so much conflict that their discussions degenerate and they never reach a collective decision.

If groups are to avoid these two extreme and faulty ways of handling conflict—the total lack of disagreement or endless bickering—they need to deal constructively with conflict. The chapters in this section offer some facilitation techniques for encouraging constructive dialogue to resolve conflict and differences in groups.

In Chapter 3, Murphy examines ways in which organizations may identify concerns and explore solutions to conflicts that arise within culturally diverse workplace environments without damaging collegial relationships. Murphy discusses ways of doing this by combining modified focus group, reflective listening, and graphic facilitation techniques. Her case study examines a situation in which an international professional service firm was concerned about the dearth of women in its upper management and sought during facilitated workshops to create "safe environments" in which men and women could raise salient gender issues in such a way as to maximize mutual understanding and minimize personal blame. The description of this technique and its success serves not only as an historical account but also as a model for exploring sensitive or controversial issues within ongoing groups and organizations and for facilitating constructive organizational change.

In Chapter 4, Pearce shows how the Uroz Foundation integrated the communication theory called "the coordinated management of meaning" with "systemic" family therapy to develop a method of consulting with decision makers in important social conflicts. This method is unusual in that it uses group process itself as a consultation technique: A client is invited to participate in a carefully structured form of group communication that brings "news of difference" and thus facilitates the development of unconventional ways of dealing with social conflicts. The process is described and located within the evolution of systemic consultation as a community and a form of practice.

3

Promoting Dialogue in Culturally Diverse Workplace Environments*

Bren Ortega Murphy
Loyola University Chicago

INTRODUCTION

During the 1950s and 1960s, U.S. corporations such as IBM were known for their homogeneity. Not only did they hire from a relatively narrow band of applicants, but they also developed extensive internal programs to socialize employees into their corporate culture. These programs often extended beyond standardizing business practices to standardizing corporate members' appearance, communication style, and recreational and personal habits. These were the "organizational men" of Whyte's (1956) critique.

By the 1980s, most corporations and organizations, including the Fortune 500 companies, were acknowledging internal diversity and exploring ways to make it beneficial. One reason for this shift was the continuing demographic change in the workforce. A widely disseminated report commissioned by the Department of Labor contended that only 15% of the net new workers between the years of 1985 and 2000 would be young white males (Johnston, 1987). Hence, employers who traditionally relied on this applicant pool for their mainstay hires would be forced to contend with a U.S. workforce that would be populated increasingly by women, ethnic minorities, and older workers. The report

*The author wishes to thank Larry Frey and JoAnn Fricke for their help throughout the writing of this chapter.

concluded that the cumulative impact of this new, culturally diverse workforce would be dramatic.

Although race, ethnicity, gender, age, and socioeconomic class are usually the most discussed sources of organizational diversity, there are others. Most organizations, for example, have structural divisions that are determined by function; the most obvious are labor and management. Issues also develop as a result of perceived differences between such units as production and marketing divisions, creative and technical staffs, or the History and Biology departments. Finally, there may be informal but clear political factions that result from different perspectives on such things as organizational leadership, mission, and methods.

Some organizational analysts argue that diversity is beneficial in that it can stimulate new ideas and multilateral perspectives (e.g., Collins & Guetzkow, 1964; Hall & Williams, 1966; Harrison, 1982; Janis, 1982; Kochman, 1982; and Torrance, 1957). Others simply acknowledge that diversity exists and must be managed effectively in order for organizations to reach their goals (e.g., Johnston, 1987; Solomon, 1989).

Diversity also brings with it problems. Cultural, functional, and political differences within groups or between groups in organizations have resulted in such destructive conflicts as strikes, class-action lawsuits, and severance/takeover struggles. Even when these dramatic situations are avoided, organizations fraught with divisions characterized by distrust and perceptions of unfairness often experience high turnover, low morale, and inefficient performance (Alderfer, 1972; Aldrich, 1979; Duncan, 1972).

The dynamic leading to these outcomes is regrettable but understandable, especially in light of the evidence linking perceived dissimilarity to uncertainty, discomfort, and worse. Berger (1986) contends that in intercultural or intergroup initial interactions, differences are often emphasized and associated with stereotypes. These perceived differences do not always elicit negative reactions, but such early interactions require more energy than usual and this in itself may be viewed as disagreeable. Moreover, if people do not make an effort to value differences, there is an inclination to exaggerate and resent them. Brislin (1986) cites five related but distinguishable negative reactions as a probable consequence of intergroup communication: ethnocentrism, prejudice, in-group/out-group, stereotypes, and discrimination. In Brislin's typology, discrimination threatens an organization most immediately because it entails overt and potentially illegal behavior, but informal socializing (in-group/out-group) and perceptual patterns (stereotyping, prejudice, and even ethnocentrism) can also lead to negative emotions and counterproductive actions.

Citing Allport (1954), Aronson and Osheron (1980), Gudykunst

(1983, 1986), and himself, Brislin (1981, 1986) states that, "Over a large number of years behavioral scientists have asked the question, 'Are there specific guidelines we can provide for the development of intervention programs to reduce prejudice and to improve intergroup communication?'" (p. 81). Brislin observes that there is a good deal of evidence that extended contact between/among groups is necessary but not sufficient to "improve intergroup attitudes and communication," and that attention must be "paid to the conditions under which the contact takes place" (p. 83). He cites four conditions as conducive to the desired change: reduction/elimination of status differences, opportunities for self-disclosure, awareness of superordinate goals (goals shared by all concerned), and support from top management.

This chapter describes one particular group facilitation approach that has been used to promote constructive dialogue and reduce negative perceptions between members of different groups within a large organization. It illustrates how that technique was used within the natural settings of regional corporate offices to address issues arising from gender differences. Before describing this particular approach, however, it is useful to identify some of the obstacles to developing intergroup dialogue as well as elaborate on general guidelines to overcoming those obstacles.

CREATING FORUMS FOR INTERGROUP DIALOGUE

Those interested in "cultivating diversity" in order to reap the aforementioned benefits have used a number of techniques designed to create substantive and constructive dialogue. Such dialogue has as its general goals increased understanding and respect for differences, recognition of common ground and a desire to search for mutually beneficial practices, interactive learning that transcends formal hierarchical structures, and the continuation of the dialogue itself.

Despite the desirability of such goals, there are usually substantial obstacles to achieving constructive dialogue in organizations composed of diverse groups and individuals. In the first place, members of different groups often have seemingly incompatible objectives, making it difficult to achieve superordinate goals. One of the most obvious examples is a labor union's desire to maximize benefits for workers contrasted against management's desire to minimize operating costs. Another example would be a request by African-American students for a separate student union at a time when the university administrators are calling for unity.

As important as actual differences are *perceptions* of incompatible objectives, which often coincide with suspicions of bias and hidden agendas. Workers may believe, for example, that management has only boardroom profits in mind and, therefore, views labor as lower-class fodder, whereas management may view union workers as more loyal to their union than to the good of the company. Both black students and white administrators may see each other as motivated by racism. Such perceptions often go beyond differences in policy preferences to question the very character and good will of "the other side." In this atmosphere of fundamental distrust there usually is no need for the members of an embattled group to specify the hidden agendas of what is considered the opposition. There is simply the certainty on their part that they exist, that they are dangerous, and that every move on the part of "the opposition" is geared toward their adoption.

In addition to differences in real and perceived goals, there are also metacommunicational obstacles to dialogue. Most organizations have communication norms, and, like other types of cultural norms, they tend to be assumed rather than explicit. These norms tend to be the product of those who wield the most power (whether by virtue of formal position, longevity, race, gender, economic leverage, or some other form of power). They are thus seldom negotiated openly by members of an organization. Instead, violators (usually members of whatever groups seem to be challenging those in power) are deemed to be lacking in the desired qualities. For example, some women who complain about relatively subtle forms of sexual harassment have been characterized by male peers as humorless and poor sports. In such cases, little attempt is made to understand the other's point of view because the source's credibility is undermined by differences in what is considered acceptable communication. In other words, the right to speak on an issue is questioned before the argument is understood. Clearly, once members of any given faction find it impossible to consider perspectives other than their own, diversity becomes the basis for self-fulfilling prophecies of struggle and loss.

One means of counteracting this downward spiral is to create forums for promoting mutual understanding and trust. Because tensions between groups seem to arise from communication difficulty as well as from misunderstandings and issue differences, these experiences should offer opportunities not only to learn new information and seek new levels of common concern, but also to develop new ways of relating to one another.

An overriding concern of such forums should be *trust*. Pruitt (1983) defines trust as "the expectation that the other will cooperate if one does so [making] it possible to act on a goal of mutual cooperation" (p. 115). Different definitions exist, but those devised for group and organizational settings have two key elements in common: belief in mutual goals and the willingness to work together toward those goals, and belief that "other parties" understand your party's vital interests and do not seek actively to undermine them (Klauss & Bass, 1982).

There is a good deal of evidence to suggest that trust is both a product of and a necessary condition for effective, constructive communication. We are not concerned here with solving the dilemma of which must come first. Instead, the starting point is Brislin's (1986) premise that intergroup situations are often characterized by states of alienation (e.g., in-group/out-group, prejudice, and discrimination). As described by Brislin, these states of alienation bear strong resemblance to Gibb's (1961) description of defensive climates, which have been correlated with low levels of trust and poor communication (Gibb, 1962, 1964). In such atmospheres, communication among members of different groups is not sufficient to build trust because credibility itself is suspect; speakers are not taken at face value, and thus trust becomes a prerequisite for better communication. Carefully facilitated communication may be a significant means to building that trust, and increased trust, in turn, has a positive impact on "the quality, level, content and directionality of communication" (Klauss & Bass, 1982, pp. 23-24). Increased trust improves the accuracy and creativity of communication and has even been correlated positively with acceptance of diversity.

What, then, can be done to set in motion the constructive dynamics of trust and improved communication? This chapter sets forth guidelines for developing a small group workshop, illustrates them by means of the aforementioned case study, and offers further recommendations based on that series of practical applications.

General Workshop Guidelines

The following are components that should comprise any workshop designed to increase participants' understanding of diverse groups within their organization as well as improve relationships among members of those diverse groups once the workshop has ended.

Opportunities to disclose personal experiences, feelings, and opinions that are relevant to the diversity issues under consideration. The process of appropriate and mutual self-disclosure has long been linked to increased personal attraction as well as to a more open and less defensive climate (Berger, 1979; Berger & Bradac, 1982; Broome, 1983; Gibb, 1964; Jourard, 1971; Pfeiffer & Jones, 1969-1973). As indicated earlier, one source of intergroup tension are feelings of being misunderstood and devalued on the basis of group membership. Thus, the chance to speak about one's identity (or an aspect thereof) and have it understood and appreciated would seem critical to relieving that tension. Ting-Toomey (1986) argues that:

[S]elf-disclosure is the sine qua non of close relationship development, because the communication process itself validates one's most
inner-treasured experience, while simultaneously validating the
empathic role of the significant other. In short, identity validation is
a self-confirming and an other-confirming process. It provides the
underlying motivational force in which intergroup-interpersonal ties
can be developed and blossom. (p. 120)

*Opportunities to dialogue both within relevant groups as well as
between or among them.* For example, African Americans should talk
among themselves, while Anglos do the same; union members should
caucus as should management. Such identity-based discussions are not
meant to polarize factions but rather to provide "a safe harbor" for participants to explore common issues. This is especially important when
there are power differences between groups, as there often are within
hierarchical organizations.

To meet the goals of the workshop, issues considered in identity-based groups must emerge in the larger group discussion. They need
not be identified, however, with the specific individuals who raised
them, nor does all of the intensity that may arise in the smaller groups
need to surface in the larger group. Identity-based groups provide people with some latitude to express half-formed ideas, misattributions, and
deeply felt personal reactions. These smaller groups can then consider
whether these views should be carried forth or modified for the larger
group dialogue.

*Opportunities to identify assumptions each group has about itself and
about the other groups involved.* These assumptions include perceptions of
group members' personal characteristics and motives as well as the consequences of their actions and their general situation. Often this can be
achieved by asking each group to list the advantages/disadvantages of
being in their group vis-a-vis the advantages/disadvantages of being in
another. For example, an advantage/disadvantage list generated by
management might reveal the belief that only people in management
work long overtime hours without compensation. A list generated by
Latino students may reveal their belief that many African-American students are disadvantaged by dysfunctional families.

*Opportunities to present credible information regarding the general
sources and validity of at least some of the assumptions.* For example, the
management group of a firm may believe that most women who quit
work do so to stay at home. Data, however, are certainly available to
counter that belief. Similarly, Anglos may believe that Asian Americans
have a more ingrained work ethic, and reasons for the persistence and

ramifications of such stereotypical attitudes can be explored. Although the forum should not rely heavily on didactic information giving, it is usually necessary to provide sources of more objective information than the participants' opinions. Cook (1984) contends that theoretical knowledge, especially in situations that concern the systematic disadvantages of one group vis-a-vis the other, can provide the "cognitive booster" necessary to extend the lessons learned beyond the workshops into the participants' daily lives.

Opportunities for participants to learn things about each other without feeling preached to or blamed for their lack of knowledge. Participants should be encouraged to believe that they are capable of at least rudimentary understanding as opposed to being targets of such accusations as "you couldn't possibly understand."

On the other hand, individuals' admissions of their own need to change should subtly be encouraged as well. As Harrison (1965) has observed, in order to attain "integrated cognitive growth, a person should at all times have both a 'castle' and a 'battlefield'" (p. 105). By a "castle," Harrison means an arena of mental security; the opportunity to have his/her valued beliefs affirmed. A "battlefield," on the other hand, refers to "a set of experiences in which the individual is confronted with disconcerting and dissonant phenomena" (p. 105). In other words, constructive personal change is facilitated when individuals' belief systems are challenged within supportive atmospheres.

Opportunities for each group to make requests of the other aimed at alleviating the disadvantages discussed previously. These requests should not be insignificant, but they should be feasible, at least in part, as far as the immediate participants are concerned. Although the requests made may well lend themselves to change on a large scale, involving organizational and/or societal reform, it is both frustrating and pointless to ask people to change things over which they have no control.

Moreover, these requests should refer to changes in behavior rather than changes in attitudes. It does little good to ask someone to "Stop assuming . . ." or "Stop feeling . . . ." For one thing, people usually have more control over their behavior than over their beliefs, attitudes, and feelings. For another, discussions of unobservable phenomena are prone to stalemates (i.e., "Stop assuming I'm lazy," is usually countered by, "I'm not assuming any such thing"). Examples of useful requests for behavioral change include nurses asking doctors to exhibit common courtesies, such as saying "Hello" and "Thank you," Canadians asking people from the United States to stop using the term "American" to refer solely to those from the U.S., and the production staff of an organization asking the marketing staff to consult with them more about schedules. Finally, although the bulk of these requests concern behavioral changes, some should refer to constructive patterns already in place; that is, to actions that should continue.

FEMALE AND MALE ISSUES IN THE WORKPLACE: A WORKSHOP ON GENDER

The workshops described in this chapter took place in various North American offices of an international professional service firm concerned about the dearth of women in its upper management. The stated goals of the workshops were to:

1. Increase awareness of all participants regarding gender issues.
2. Begin to identify gender issues relevant to the workplace, especially those that might have an impact on the gender ratio at upper levels of the organization.
3. Promote constructive dialogue throughout the office regarding these issues.
4. Begin to identify what should be done to address the problems arising out of these issues.

Workshop material made it clear that the aims were not to consider only "women's issues," place blame, or serve as the total diversity effort. Thus, although it was clear that the primary impetus for the workshop was the status of women within the firm, the facilitators acknowledged up-front that the discussions would welcome a variety of perspectives and recognize that gender issues can lead to problems for men as well as women. Gender issues were defined as any issues that create problems: (a) more often for one gender than the other; (b) that have a different impact on one gender; or (c) that are more difficult for one gender to overcome. Thus, something could be raised as a gender issue even though the ensuing problems are not necessarily exclusive to one gender.

Each workshop was comprised of 25-30 predominantly white and upper middle class women and men in positions ranging from middle management to upper management. Not surprisingly, given the characteristics of the organization, there were usually many more men than women, especially at upper-management levels. There were always two facilitators, one woman and one man.

Although there were periods within the 1-3/4 day workshop that were devoted to lectures, most of the time, particularly the second day, was devoted to participant discussion, either in same-sex groups or as a whole. For the purposes of this chapter, three key sections of the workshop are discussed, with emphasis placed on sections I and III, both of which focus on group discussion. (See Figure 3.1 for the complete agenda flow.)

Workshop Section I: Perceptions of Advantages & Disadvantages

The purpose of this section was to identify and discuss what participants believed to be gender-specific advantages and disadvantages within the organization. In separate groups, both the men and the women generated four lists on flip-chart paper: the disadvantages of being female in the organization; the advantages of being female; the advantages of being male; and the disadvantages of being male. Participants were told to concentrate on gender status within the organization rather than to compare themselves to women and men in other organizations.

These small group discussions were conducted as traditional brainstorming sessions: participation by all was encouraged, ideas were called out spontaneously, all ideas were listed without evaluation, and consensus was not required (Osborn, 1957). When the lists were presented to the group at large, the spokesperson acknowledged that certain items were more controversial than others although he or she was careful to respect the confidentiality of members of the small group. The items on the lists were thus discussed without reference to the specific persons who originated the idea. If any participant was willing to "take ownership" of an item, it was up to that person to do so.

Once each group generated the four lists, the full group reassembled and discussed them in order. The usual procedure was to have spokespersons for each group post and read aloud the lists referring to disadvantages and advantages of women. After each list was presented, there was an opportunity for people to ask for more explanation (e.g., "What do you mean by 'more emotional'?"; "Are you referring to *all* emotions or primarily crying?"; "What advantage does 'better handwriting' accrue?"). This was not intended to be a time for argument, but was used strictly for clarification. Once people were satisfied that they understood the lists, the gender group being described was given a chance to respond. Hence, after the four lists regarding women were presented and explained, only the women responded. They discussed the validity of the items, the overlap and gaps among the lists, and the relative importance or weight of certain issues. Once they had adequate time to react, the men were then invited to join the discussion. The whole process (posting the advantages and the disadvantages, explaining the issues, targeting each gender's response, and conducting open discussion) was then repeated for the lists referring to men.

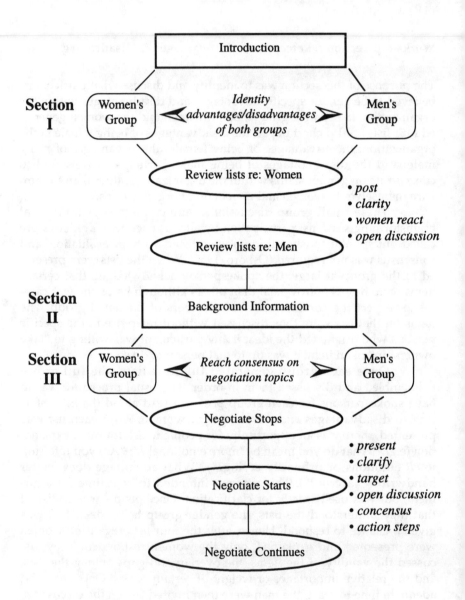

Figure 3.1. Agenda Flow of Gender Awareness Workshop

Participants' reactions to these discussions varied primarily according to different preconceptions regarding the validity and seriousness of the topics raised. Some clung to their preconceptions despite the lack of support for them. Many, however, expressed pleasant surprise at the extent to which each group seemed to understand the other group's issues and concerns. Men were pleased that women (or at least some of them) acknowledged that there are disadvantages to being male, whereas women were impressed that men (or, again, at least some of them) could identify issues critical to women. Occasionally, one group discerned an issue for the other that the other had overlooked. Sometimes this was welcomed as insightful. At other times, however, it was seen as evidence of prejudice. Most participants reported that as a result of the discussion, they had a better understanding of the other gender's situation, a deeper respect for "the other side's" willingness and ability to understand "their side," and more optimism that gender-related problems can be alleviated.

Workshop Section II: Background Information

This part of the workshop was devoted to presenting and discussing scholarship pertaining to gender perceptions and behavior. This information was intended to introduce relevant data and provide a more general context for the specific concerns raised in sections I and III. The theories and data presented were directed toward answering the following questions:

- What accounts for gender differences in perception and behavior?
- Which gender differences in perception and behavior result in significant organizational problems?
- What might make these differences difficult to discuss with one another?
- Why might these problems be difficult to change?

Examples of what was discussed include gender-based patterns of communication, the impact of early socialization, and the largely unspoken, yet significant, constrictions on cross-gender socializing.

Section III: Behavior Negotiations

The most lengthy part of the workshop was the third section, which was organized around participants' visions of the future and specific suggestions as to how the vision might be achieved. Section II usually concluded on the first day, and participants were given a homework assignment and encouraged to "sleep on it." This assignment was two-fold. First, participants were asked to describe a workplace of the future that would be a good place for both women and men to work. They were told not to pay too much attention to feasibility, but to concentrate on their vision—the characteristics, policies, and general attitudes of a place that is able to get its work done while retaining and developing its best people, regardless of gender. Second, participants were asked to think of three behaviors that pertain to the opposite gender: one that members of one group want the other to stop, one they want them to start, and one they want them to continue. These behavioral requests did not need to be applied equally to all members of the target group. For example, a man might ask women to start giving direct feedback regarding offensive remarks. He may know that a few women in the organization do this already, but he would like such behavior to become the norm.

Three guidelines were critical in developing these requests. One was that the requests involve observable behavior. As argued earlier, asking people to stop thinking, feeling, and assuming is generally unproductive on at least two counts. First, they can plausibly deny the charges and second, they remain unaware of whatever signals they are sending.

The second guideline was that requests should include some rationale that makes sense to most participants. For example, a woman could request that men stop laughing or even remain silent when a sexist remark or joke is told by male colleagues because such behavior is seen as giving assent to such attitudes, perpetuating them in the workplace and demoralizing the women who work there.

The third guideline was that the requests be genuine and worth doing. In other words, the "stop" should pertain to actual behavior that is contributing to the disadvantages experienced by one or both groups. "Stop making false sexual harassment charges" is a pointless request if no one has been doing so. A "start" implies that the behavior is not done now or not done nearly enough. Finally, a "continue" should be a genuine pat on the back for a constructive pattern already in place.

When the participants reassembled the next day, they were divided quickly into male and female groups in order to reach consensus about the vision and the three requests they were to present for consideration. In each small group, participants first listed the components of their vision on flip-chart sheets. Because this description usually functions as more of a backdrop than a focal point of discussion, not much time was devoted to it. Members then fashioned their stops, starts, and continues in that order. The most typical process involved listing their homework answers on a flip chart, seeing if any could be combined, and determining which one would yield the most productive discussion. The final version of the stop, start, and continue requests included clear statements of behavioral change or maintenance accompanied by brief rationales, each written on a separate piece of flip-chart paper so that each could be considered individually.

The ensuing discussions were demanding and often proved to be the most profitable for those involved. Because the "stops" often contained the most negative messages and thus required a lot of energy, the large group began with them. Examining "continues" ended the section on a positive note by acknowledging good efforts to date. As a workshop summary, each participant stated one concrete thing he or she would do as a result of the discussions. Thus, the workshop concluded with a hopeful transition back to the "real world" of organizational life.

DISCUSSION

Outcomes

The short-term results of these workshops, as evidenced by formal evaluations and informal discussion, have largely been positive. As mentioned earlier, many participants were surprised and pleased at the degree of perceptual overlap and sympathy concerning certain issues. Moreover, they were impressed with the receptivity of at least some people to new information and ideas. Suspicions regarding "hidden agendas" were also often alleviated. For example, senior management was relieved to hear that few believed the problems were due to conscious discrimination at promotion points.

There was also, overall, a positive reaction to the discussion process itself. Women, in particular, stated that they appreciated the chance to talk with other women, finding kindred spirits rather than feeling isolated. As a female advances up the corporate ladder in traditional, male-dominated firms, it is not unusual for her to find herself the only woman at a given level. It is easy in these situations to believe that all difficulties are caused by her own, personal shortcomings. The small group discussions in these workshops helped many to see that there might be more broad-based factors that are responsible as well. For example, one woman new to senior management ranks and the only woman in her particular division thought she was being ignored at lunch time because her male peers simply did not like her. The interpretation offered by other women (in similar positions but different divisions) was that most men feel uncomfortable initiating even the most innocuous social meeting in such a gender-skewed situation. This interpretation was later supported by the men.

Both men and women reported being significantly more comfortable talking with each other about gender issues as a result of their workshop interaction. Some said that their comfort could even extend to interacting with those who had not attended. Several observed that the most important breakthrough had been acknowledging the legitimacy of the topic itself. Now that gender issues were no longer relegated to bathroom conversations between friends, there was hope that men and women could work together as true colleagues to address the obviously complex situation at hand.

Not all reactions were positive, however. Despite recognition of some perceptual overlap, there was also shock about how much was seemingly not understood. In the cases of certain people and/or certain issues, some of the participants' worst fears were confirmed ("He just doesn't have a clue"). There was some suspicion that double talk and silence had been used to mask resistance to change. There was also a fairly widespread concern that the process would not go any further—that the workshops would function as ends in themselves rather than as the means to reaching more important goals. Although both women and men expressed this worry, they tended to do so from different perspectives. In accordance with Tannen's (1990) findings, male participants tended to find a discussion-focused workshop frustrating, especially when the discussion stopped short of identifying solutions. Female participants, on the other hand, almost always found the dialogue useful and, therefore, tended to believe that the workshop had been a necessary and worthwhile first step. Women, however, did fear that the workshop might function to placate rather than stimulate. Thus, they too saw the need for solutions beyond talk.

On balance, then, the gender workshops appear to have accomplished their short-term goals for most participants. More, of course, needs to take place in order for them to contribute to long-term valuation of diversity.

Limitations of the Workshop

Both the negative and positive reactions of participants point to limitations in this group facilitation technique. The discussions described are lengthy and often difficult to facilitate if they are to prove worthwhile. For "bottom-line," solution-driven people, such an experience is vexing even when it is going well.

Moreover, there are certainly things that can undermine the technique. The value of the dialogue is dependent on its perceived depth and honesty. If people stick to superficial observations, if they say only what they think "should" be said, or if they remain silent, there is a strong tendency for participants to see the time spent as pointless. In the workshops described above, there were several possible constraints on honest disclosures of opinion. For one thing, there were always people who held more powerful positions than others. Sometimes there were even direct reporting relationships, despite efforts to avoid that situation. Moreover, the men always outnumbered and outranked the women in the group. This meant that if a powerful man took a strong position early on and was not challenged, there was a good chance that his view would dominate. Regardless of his position, it was essential that other voices be validated so that the norm could become a true exchange of views rather than an automatic, nonthinking concurrence.

The seniority levels of the participants, particularly those people presenting minority perspectives, also affected the kinds of experiences on which they could draw. Low-ranking women not only were more prone to intimidation than their more senior female colleagues, but they also had less ability to comment on such issues as family responsibilities and "glass ceiling" dynamics. As a rule, they simply had not had the opportunity to encounter either.

A group facilitation technique that draws on an honest exchange of diverse ideas is thus necessarily dependent on the composition of a group and the ability and willingness of its members to articulate different points of view. However, the extent to which this honest exchange happens raises the problems that usually attend any discussion involving controversy.

Participants sometimes have difficulty tolerating or even understanding very different viewpoints. Sherif, Sherif, and Nebergall (1965) suggest that there is a tendency to exaggerate conceptual differences in many situations of disagreement or perspective diversity. Moreover, because these workshops dealt with gender, they often raised issues that concerned very personal beliefs, values, and decisions. At the heart of some discussions were deeply felt differences about such matters as the essential characteristics of masculinity and femininity, what constitutes a healthy family life, and definitions of success. Despite admonitions to the contrary, some people interpreted disagreement or even difference as accusation of blame. For example, some men who had built their careers working long hours away from their families reacted defensively to suggestions that others were not willing to define career commitment in terms of hours.

Because diversity within organizations often involves issues of identity, emotions can run high when the bases for various identities are examined. Furthermore, the discussion of issues related to such identity factors as race, class, and gender invite volatile questions about discrimination and power. Although some emotion may be necessary to guarantee discussants' investment in the dialogue, too much undermines the mutual understanding sought.

In sum, one limitation of the group facilitation technique described in this chapter is the difficulty in constructing the discussion, both in terms of getting the best group composition and developing constructive dialogue. Another limitation, alluded to earlier, is that the process may not be sufficient to yield comprehensive solutions to the problems raised. If there is no follow-up, participants eventually may believe that the process was worthless or even harmful.

Recommendations

The facilitators' experience of these workshops as well as participants' formal and informal evaluations yield several recommendations for the conduct and application of the group facilitation processes described. First, it should be clear that skillful and credible facilitation is required. Although facilitators are, by definition, outside parties with no direct vested interest, they must also demonstrate an understanding and sometimes even a "feel" for the specific issues being discussed. In all cases, it is advisable to have at least two people in this role. In certain cases, these people should be drawn from the diverse populations in question. For example, a female and a male should facilitate gender diversity workshops, whereas both an African American and an Anglo should handle "black/white" discussions. Such balancing should be more than cosmetic; it should provide a range of perspectives and establish credible bases for empathy. This is not to say that a female facilitator champions some official female view. It means that she can understand fundamental female experiences well enough to elicit articulate explanations from participants. Moreover, the facilitators should model constructive dialogue. Thus, if the facilitators mirror the participants in terms of salient characteristics and model constructive dialogue, they serve as "living proof" that such diversity does not necessitate antipathy.

A second recommendation is to hold the sessions over at least a two-day period, even if those two days are not full. The overnight period provides time for reflection and helps the conversation about the behavioral requests.

Third, top management or their organizational equivalent should support strongly the ends and means of these meetings. When participants believe that the workshops are "just P.R.," they are much less willing to engage in the process. Employees often have a strong sense of what "really counts" in their job. If their ability to contribute to this process or its long-term goals seems irrelevant to advancement, many employees will not make any commitment to the workshops or their goals.

Finally, there is some disagreement over whether or not such sessions should be mandatory. On the one hand, there is abundant evidence that at least the perception of free will is important to building trust and promoting attitude change. On the other hand, requiring participation can indicate organizational commitment as well as the possibility that an organization-wide mandate for change can be developed. Requiring participation also gives the workshop organizers some control over the participant configuration of any given session.

CONCLUSION

The introduction to this chapter mentioned several types of groups that are making today's organizations more culturally diverse and thus might benefit from the kind of workshop described herein. Corporations, manufacturing plants, hospitals, educational institutions, and correctional facilities increasingly have expressed the need to identify and address issues arising from diversity. In most cases, this diversity stems from differences in gender, race, and/or ethnicity. The group facilitation technique described could work well in almost any organizational situation made difficult because of ignorance, misunderstanding, or distrust of cultural differences. In such environments, the suspicion of "hidden agendas" clouds almost every policy discussion, and groups who see themselves in competition for uncertain resources routinely measure their gain by the other group's loss. Such a situation could occur within a university between the "old guard" and "young turks," between "the jocks" and "the brains" at a high school, between the part-timers and full-timers at a factory, or between the professional and volunteer staff in a hospital.

Although virtually every small group communication text warns against the negative effects of hidden agendas, there are seldom any suggestions for how to counter them. As with many other communication phenomena, moreover, it is the *perception* of hidden agendas or the accusation that they exist that is sufficient to cause trouble, regardless of their actual existence. It is virtually impossible for a group to allay these fears with simple denials.

The group facilitation technique described in this chapter proved to be one way of establishing common ground and trust, two interpersonal processes that function as gender antidotes to the ills of hidden agendas. The discussions engendered provide opportunities both to learn and be understood and to benefit as well as give. When people believe that their perspective is known and valued, they are more willing to acknowledge and accept others' perspectives. In sum, they are more open to the organizational richness diversity can bring.

4

Bringing News of Difference: Participation in Systemic Social Constructionist Communication

W. Barnett Pearce
Loyola University of Chicago

In July 1991, I was invited to be a participant-observer in an international group called the Uroz Foundation. "Uroz" is a Norse rune; it denotes termination and new beginnings. It refers to discontinuous changes such as the agricultural cycle of death and rebirth. The original symbol for Uroz was the wild ox (aurochs), whose originally threatening strength was domesticated and used by the Norse civilization.

The seven participants in the Uroz Foundation were brought together by three factors. First, we were all interested in the processes of peacemaking. Like many others, we noted that the quality of life for millions of people is affected directly by the success of politicians and business managers in dealing with conflicts. The conflicts we had in mind included the restructuring of the relationship between the North Atlantic Treaty Organization (NATO) and the Warsaw Pact nations (What should be the Swedish position on potential membership in the European Community for eastern European states?); the evolution of the political system in South Africa (Should the African National Party confront or cooperate with Chief Buthelezi and the Inkatha Freedom Party?); the relationship between the U.S. and Iraq (Should the U.S. attempt to depose President Saddam Hussein?); and the role of the government in achieving social justice in Colombia (Should the government seek a peace agreement with the narcotrafficers or oppose them militarily?).

These were real situations in which one or more of us had a particular interest. We envisioned ourselves in the role of consultants or trainers. Specifically, we posed the question, "If we were called in to help the primary decision makers in the major conflicts in the world today, what could we do that would help?" The role we envisioned was not unrealistic; other than myself, all the members of the group had advised or consulted with people who were major decision makers in world affairs, and who were likely to do so again.

The second factor that brought us together was our shared concern about what it meant to "help" decision makers in conflicts like these. The rune "Uroz" struck us as an appropriate symbol because we wanted to explore ways of transforming these conflicts into more prosocial forms of communal activities, not simply change the distribution of power or the "spoils of war" so that our clients' pile was larger than those of other participants. We recognized the power of social systems to reproduce themselves, converting the best-intended efforts to end conflicts into energy that only intensifies them. The venerable symbol of death and rebirth focused our attention on those ways in which the patterns of conflict themselves—not just the placement of groups within those patterns— might be changed. We wanted to explore the ways and means of producing, literally, unconventional interventions in important social conflicts.

A common conceptual orientation was the third factor that brought us together. Taking a "social constructionist" stance informed by the American Pragmatists, the social ecological concepts of Gregory Bateson, and the analytical method of Ludwig Wittgenstein, we looked at these conflicts as made, and in a continuous process of being remade, in interlocked networks of conversations. The patterns of these conversations reproduce conflicts; by changing the structure of those conversations, we believed, we could transform the conflicts.

During a week of intensive work, we devised a 7-step process of consulting with decision makers in large-scale conflicts (see Figure 4.1). Among the many styles of consultation, this one is distinctive for two reasons. First, in most consultations, an individual consults with a group of clients. Instead, we devised a process in which a group of consultants works with a single client. Second, in many consultations, the consultant acts as an "expert" either on the problem confronting the client or on the "process" of decision making. Our group explicitly eschewed both expert roles. The *content* of our consultation consisted of the opportunity for the client to join with us in a conversation structured by systemic, social constructionist communication theory. That is, we offered participation in a particular form of group process as the consultation itself.

1. Initial description
2. Commissioning
3. Hypothesizing
4. Action decision
5. Interview
6. Reflection
7. Client's response

**Figure 4.1. Steps in the Process of Inviting a Client to Participate in a
Systemic Social Constructionist Conversation**

This form of consulting is "labor-intensive" in that it uses many consultants. It is used appropriately in situations in which the client is a person whose decisions will have far-reaching, important impacts on him- or herself and others and who needs to think beyond the normal range of options. We envision clients as deeply enmeshed within the logic of the conflicts in which they must act and thus unable to discover unconventional alternatives without help. However, conventional acts, prefigured by the logic of the situation, are almost always homeostatic; that is, no matter how sincerely *intended* to intervene in or reduce the level of a conflict, they often have the effect of perpetuating and intensifying the conflict. If the recurring problems of war, famine, and ecological deterioration are to be solved, community and world "leaders" must find creative ways of acting that transform the contexts in which those acts take place (Branham & Pearce, 1985; Freeman, Littlejohn, & Pearce, 1992).

We set ourself to find a way of enabling clients to imagine lines of action other than those prefigured in the existing discourse. We thought of our process as a group facilitation of creativity that works by bringing "news of difference."

THE COMMUNITY IN WHICH THIS PROCESS DEVELOPED

We fully expected to develop something novel, but we did not start *ex nihilo*. Our work occurred at a particular moment in the reciprocal development of theory and of a form of practice in an international community. The best way of understanding what we did is to locate it within the still-unfolding history of this community.

The community within which we work is best known as, but described imperfectly by the term, "systemic therapy." As this story shows, the community includes more than therapists and it includes more than just "systemic" concepts.

However named, the nature of this community is best understood by focusing on the medium on which it relies. Ong (1982) argued that communities that use oral speech for their most significant social functions develop different "forms of consciousness" than those that use print. "Primary oral" communities have different notions of the form and function of argument, of the nature of memory, and preferences for rhetorical forms than "primary print" communities.

Although the members of the "systemic therapy" community write and read, the community is structured around oral speech as supplemented by videotape (Pearce, McAdam, & Villar, 1992). In fact, the intellectual legitimacy of this group is often challenged by more print-oriented academic or managerial communities because it rests on an evolving set of common practices known to all its members rather than on a set of canonical texts. If asked to explain itself, this group naturally invites the skeptic to watch it in action rather than referring to a set of books or journals that inscribe its beliefs or data. If challenged to prove that its methods are effective, the natural response within the community is to invite the skeptic to participate, not to refer to a compendium of "outcome" measures or "effects" studies.

Because it combines the extrasomatic memories of videotape and print within a collective conscious that has the "agonistic" structure of an oral community (Ong, 1982), the practices of this community evolve rapidly. Any attempt to inscribe the practices of this community is bound to be obsolete before the journal article or book is published. My attempt to account for the development of this consultation procedure is similarly vulnerable to being made quickly obsolete by continuing innovation. There is no official count of the number of times this consultation process has been used, but I am quite confident that it has *never* been practiced the same way twice or exactly as we developed it in July 1991.

In the *Nicomachean Ethics*, Aristotle differentiated between *theoria* and *praxis*. The "systemic therapy" community has little interest in *theoria* as Aristotle described it: knowledge of things that are eternal. Rather, the members of this group are committed to *praxis*: knowing how to act within situations in which things can be other than what they are. The form of knowledge appropriate for *praxis* is *phronesis*: the practical wisdom that allows a virtuoso artist or master craftsman to make good judgments in particular situations (Cronen, in press; Shotter, 1993). The best practitioners of systemic, social constructionist forms of communication thus often act inconsistently, responding to the particularities of different situations, including their own positions within those situations.

THE EVOLUTION OF SYSTEMIC, SOCIAL CONSTRUCTIONIST PRACTICES

Bateson's (1972, 1979) "ecological epistemology" defines the meaning of a "thing" by its location within a network of relationships, the totality of which comprise a system. Human beings as a species are located within a *physical ecology*, and the failure to take these relationships between ourselves and the environment into account as we act is, according to Bateson, both foolish and dangerous. In the same way, individual human beings or specific social situations are located within a *social ecology* and should be understood by tracing the various relationships that comprise them.

Bateson's presentation of these "systemic" ideas had an enormous effect on both clinical psychologists and communication theorists. The original members of the "Palo Alto" group worked with Bateson at the Mental Research Institute. The first book-length description of the practices based on these ideas, *The Pragmatics of Human Communication* (Watzlawick, Beavin, & Jackson, 1967), was one of the most influential books of the 1960s in the discipline of communication, and the notion of "strategic therapy" became one of the major schools in clinical practice.

The "strategic" approach to therapy presumed that the relationship between therapist and client was one of combat. Therapists were cautioned to guard against the patient's attempts to co-opt him or her into the patient's world. Furthermore, power was assumed to be the primary dimension of patients' social worlds. The therapist had to develop interventions that would overpower or evade the resistance of the patient. (Bateson himself subsequently disavowed the strategic and belligerent nature of this therapy and moved on to different fields of inquiry.)

The Centro Milanese Di Terapia Della Famiglia (in Milan, Italy) was influenced by the Palo Alto group and invited Watzlawick to conduct a seminar for them (see Cecchin, 1992; and Cecchin, Lane, & Ray, 1992). Like the Palo Alto School, the Milan School accepted the metaphor of combat between therapists and clients. However, even during this early period (the 1970s), the Milan School displayed its creativity.

One innovation was the use of group processes among the therapists as a means of working with the clients. They insisted that the whole family come to the therapy sessions, where they were met by a team of two therapists, one male and one female, who were supported by an "observing team" who monitored the process through a one-way mirror or on closed-circuit television. The mixed-gender therapeutic team was intended to take advantage of the client's propensity to make cross-gender "coalitions" with therapists. The observing team had a telephone connection to the therapeutic team and monitored the session to prevent the therapists from becoming co-opted into the family's world view or succumbing to the temptation to think about the family's problem in a "linear" or nonsystemic manner. If the therapist got into trouble, the observing team would call on the telephone to intervene. Regular consultations between the therapeutic and observing teams were built into the plan for the session, in part to reinforce the therapists' identity as "outside" the family.

The Milan group became uneasy with the antagonistic metaphor they inherited from the Palo Alto group and did their own study of Bateson's writings. Impressed by his notion of ecological epistemology, they deliberately divested themselves of the "combat" metaphor, substituting for it a more systemic story in which they dealt with families whose natural evolution had become "stuck," causing pain. The therapist's role was understood to be that of helping the family to get past the "stuck point" so that its systemic evolution could continue in a direction unknown and unknowable to either therapist or family. In addition, they developed a distinctive "systemic therapy" approach, which they characterized as featuring "circularity," "hypothesizing," and "neutrality" (Selvini Palazoli, Boscolo, Cecchin, & Prata, 1980).

Circular questioning is the most widely adopted of these innovations (Boscolo, Cecchin, Hoffman, & Penn, 1987; Cronen, 1990; Penn, 1982). It consists of a technology of asking questions with four distinctive features.

First, circular questioning focuses on "differences" within the social system. Bateson believed that we only perceive differences and that those differences comprise information. The problems that lead us to therapy often come from a "false epistemology" that makes us overlook some of the information in our social ecology. By asking questions that focus on differences, clients can be brought "news of difference" in their situations. This "news of difference" permits clients to gain new insights on their position within the social ecology, thus reframing the original problem and permitting them to envision unconventional lines of action that can transform their social worlds.

Circular questions involve comparisons between more or less, before and after, first and last, and so on. For example, "If Mother were no longer depressed, who would have to change their behavior the most, Father or Brother?" "Before Mother was depressed, who was the most emotional person in the family, Father, Brother, or Sister?" "To whom does Mother show her depression most often, Father, Brother, or Sister?"

Second, circular questions move systematically among the various perspectives in the family, giving particular attention to those perspectives to which the family does not customarily attend. For example, the children are asked to comment on the relationships between the parents in front of the parents, allowing the parents to hear how their relationship appears from a "third person" perspective. The children might be asked, "To whom does your Father think your Mother shows her depression most often, to him, to you, or to your Brother?"

Third, circular questions often pose alternatives to the "punctuation" of relationships within the system. For example, if the family perceives Mother's depression as "caused" by Brother leaving home for college, then the therapists will ask questions based on a hypothesis that Mother's depression serves a function; that it is purposive. For example, "If Mother were no longer depressed, would Brother come home more or less often? So, Mother needs to be depressed to keep Brother from really leaving the family?"

Punctuations are never "right" or "wrong"; they are made by those who perceive them. The purpose of proposing different punctuations in circular questioning is not to prove that the therapist is "correct" or knowledgeable, but to offer the client an alternative way of looking at the pattern of relations within his or her social ecology. If done well, circular questions offer a glittering variety of perhaps mutually exclusive alternative punctuations that serve as a buffet table from which the client can sample many different ways of understanding his or her own situation.

Finally, circular questioning focuses on how the events and objects of the social world are made. Viewed positively, this consists of foregrounding what people actually do and the relations between those doings and others. Viewed negatively, this consists of determinedly avoiding: (a) intrapsychic interpretations (i.e., "how" questions take the place of "why" questions); (b) using the verb "to be"(i.e., the therapist asks how Mother *shows* depression, not *why* she is depressed); and (c) giving negative evaluations. The Milan School is famous for giving "positive connotations" of troubled families; for example, the family might be complimented for being a strong, loving family, one in which the members love each other so much that Mother has learned how to show depression as a way of maintaining a connection with Brother who has gone away to college.

Hypothesizing stands in contrast to other therapeutic schools whose practices include making a "diagnosis" of the problem. Systemic family therapists believe that the therapist often "makes" the problem for the client and even more often coaches the client in how to have the problem. In contrast, the Milan School engages in an "orgy" of hypothesizing in which none of the hypotheses are thought to be "true" or "false"; the orgy itself is designed to produce a wild variety of alternate, contradictory descriptions. One systemic therapist said that his reason for adopting this form of work was so that he could be "promiscuous" with hypotheses.

The orgy of hypothesizing is not without its rules, of course. The "better" hypotheses are those that connect as many bits of information about the system as possible; that suggest systemic, interdependent relationships rather than linear, causal ones; and that do not "blame" anyone or anything. Systemic family therapists use hypotheses to "positively connote" the symptom and/or the system rather than to criticize it, believing that this frees the system to continue its own evolution, whereas criticism "freezes" it in its current painful condition. For example, in the formal "interventions" that characterize this stage in their development, Milan-style therapists might positively connote the "presenting problem" and paradoxically urge the "designated patient" to continue to do/experience it until such time that someone else might pick up the burden. For example, a daughter's anorexia nervosa would be positively connoted as self-sacrificial "work" that she was doing in order to keep the family together, and her willingness to do this work was a sign of the strength of the family's ties to each other, but her obvious physical deterioration indicated that she needed to allow someone else in the family to take over the responsibility for keeping them together.

Neutrality has always been a troublesome concept and has evolved over time. In its first, "Palo Alto" phase, neutrality was thought of as remaining outside the client's system. This form of neutrality was achieved by "going meta"; that is, by taking a position in which one escaped enmeshment in the system by talking about it. In the second, "Batesonian" phase, neutrality was thought of as forming a coalition equally with everyone in the system.

As the Milan method continued to develop, its primary conceptual metaphors shifted from: (a) energy to information; (b) entities to social constructions; and (c) a focus on family to a reflexive focus on the therapist (Cecchin, 1992). In the early 1980s, the Milan school appropriated some ideas from the theory of the Coordinated Management of Meaning, or CMM (Cronen, Johnson, & Lannamann, 1982; Pearce & Cronen, 1980). The crucial concept appropriated was that of the unity of meaning and action. Pearce and Cronen (1980) argued that there can be no meaning without action and no action without meaning. The Milan School interpreted this to mean that they could produce change in behavior by helping the family construct new meanings about themselves and their actions. In the early days of combat with families, they regularly had employed formal, sophisticated, "counter-paradoxical" interventions and behavioral prescriptions (Selvini Palazoli, Boscolo, Cecchin, & Prata, 1976); as they changed to an emphasis on information, these were used less frequently, and they dispensed with "combat" metaphors in describing the relationship between themselves and their clients. They realized that participation in an interview in which circular questions were used was itself a therapeutic intervention.

With the continued movement toward information, the Milan School borrowed from CMM the concept of multiple, simultaneous contexts for action, or what CMM refers to as *hierarchies of meanings*. These hierarchies describe the relationships among, for example, the self-concept of each person in the family, the interpersonal relationships among them, the "family myths" that they tell to characterize their family, and the "episodes" in which they participate. These multiple contextual frames provide one way of talking about the social ecology of families.

The concept cited most frequently from CMM was the "strange loop." As shown in Figure 4.2, a "stable hierarchical relationship" describes, in this example, the "episode" as the context for the "relationship" and the "relationship" as contexted by the "episode." That is, the "contextual force" that moves from the episode to the relationship is stronger than the "implicative force" that moves from the relationship to the episode. If the meaning of the relationship and episode conflict, the episode prevails. However, some levels of contexts are "looped" in that the strength of the contextual and implicative forces are equal. Properly speaking, neither is the context of the other. In real life, however, in which one thing follows another, each is, for a period of time, first the context for and then contexted by the other as they loop around each other.

In a "charmed loop," the meanings of the two levels of context do not conflict; each reinforces the other. In a "strange loop," each level of context is mutually exclusive with the other. If a strange loop is frozen in time, it is a paradox; if it is fluid, flowing with a conversation, it oscillates back and forth first with one level as the context and then the other.

Strange loops are hard to describe in the straight lines of text. Figure 4.3 shows a strange loop of the frequently cited alcoholic's para-

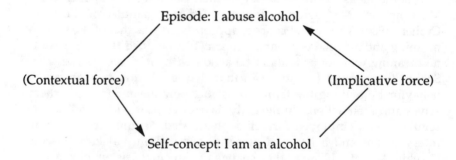

Note: In a stable hierarchical relationship, "contextual force" is stronger than "implicative force."

Figure 4.2. A Stable Hierarchical Relationship

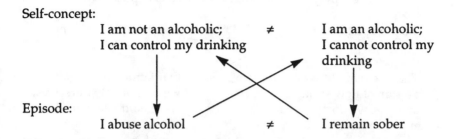

Self-concept:
      I am not an alcoholic;   ≠   I am an alcoholic;
      I can control my drinking   I cannot control my
                                  drinking

Episode:
      I abuse alcohol   ≠   I remain sober

Note: In a strange loop, the relative strengths of contextual and implicative forces are equal or change as a result of the actions that people take. At one time, the self-concept is the context for the episode; at another, the episode is the context for the self-concept. This reversal of what is the context and what is contexted makes this a loop; it is a strange loop because each reversal shifts to a different content. In this example, the person alternates between periods of abstinence and abuse and those in which he or she thinks of him- or herself as an alcoholic or not an alcoholic.

Figure 4.3. A "Strange Loop" of Alcoholism

dox. Start at any point of the diagram and follow the arrows. One punctuation shows the self-concept as saying, "I can control my drinking." This leads (following the arrow) to episodes in which the person drinks. Because she or he is an alcoholic, these episodes ultimately include states of drunkenness. At some point, the implicative force from these episodes exceeds the contextual force from the self-concept, producing not only a change in which is the context for which, but of the content of the self-concept. A series of drunken experiences leads the person to the "other" aspect of his or her self-concept; "I cannot control my drinking." With this as the context, episodes of "refusing drinks" follow. At some point, she or he may conclude, "Since I have been sober so long, I can control my drinking," and the pattern of the strange loop starts all over again.

    Because both the Palo Alto and Milan Schools had an affinity for paradoxes, the Milan School picked up on the concept of the "strange loop" with little difficulty. They used the concept to explain why families would get "stuck" in a particularly painful pattern of interaction, and they used the ratios of contextual to implicative force to explain how talk in a therapy session could bring about a behavioral change later (see Figure 4.4).

    In the late 1980s, the Milan school was influenced by the "second-order cybernetics" of Maturana (1991), specifically his notion that organisms are "structurally closed" and hence there can be no "instructive interaction." Many therapists incorporated the "radical constructivist" perspective that meanings are "in" the organism and determined by the structure of an individual's nervous system. This perspective allowed them to hold clients responsible for their own meanings,

The family's understanding of what is happening:

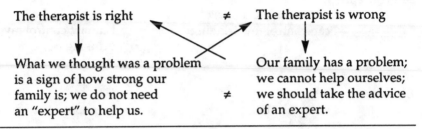

The therapist positively connotes the family's symptoms, saying that, in his or her expert opinion, these symptoms signify that the family is strong. For example, daughter's refusal to eat is not a disease but a means of keeping the family together.

Note: The therapists positively connote the painful symptom by describing it as purposeful rather than as caused and as serving an important function within the ecology of the family rather than as causing a problem. This creates a confusion about whether the therapist is an expert who can help and whether the family can act to solve its problems. (Adapted from Cronen, Pearce, & Tomm, 1985.)

Figure 4.4. A Therapeutic Strange Loop

regardless of what the therapists—or anyone else—told them. Therapy became a process of "perturbing" the clients. Some adopted the adage "Give it a bump and watch it jump" to characterize their effects on the social systems with which they worked.

This "radical constructivist" principle fit in with two discoveries that the Milan School had made: The hypotheses developed by therapists were shaped fully as much by the interaction among the therapeutic team as they were by the interaction between the therapists and the family; and their clients often "improved" whether or not they "accepted" any of the hypotheses offered by the therapists. As a result, these therapists focused more on their own role as a participant in an "observing system" that includes them and the family and less on trying to describe or intervene in the family as an "observed system." That is, they clarified their perspective as *within* the client's system rather than being *outside* it. Among other things, this development continued the evolution of the way "neutrality" is understood. Currently, the Milan School defines the *neutral* therapist as one who remains "curious" about the family (Cecchin, 1987) or adopts an "irreverent" role (Cecchin, Lane, & Ray, 1992).

For present purposes, the history of the development of systemic practices shifts from Milan to London. In the early 1980s, the Kensington Consultation Centre (KCC) was formed as a "second generation Milan school." Within the larger community of systemic workers, it is distinguished by the extent to which it uses social constructionism rather than radical constructivism as its conceptual base (see Leppington, 1991) and by the extent to which it has incorporated concepts from CMM. Although the Milan School adopted the ideas of multiple levels of meanings, the inseparability of meaning and action, the "implicative force" that can change the contexts in which it occurs, and the possibility of "strange loops," the KCC foregrounded these ideas and also adopted some of the CMM apparatus for describing them. For example, they use the CMM "hierarchy" of levels of meaning as a way of structuring circular questions, the technology of "reflexive questioning" (developed by Tomm, 1985) based on CMM's notion of implicative force, and the structure of the "strange loop" as an intervention.

The KCC began as a school for therapists and has continued this function, now offering a Masters degree. However, they were increasingly oppressed by the model of therapist as "expert" and of the "medical model" in which the therapist prescribes a solution for a problem diagnosed on the basis of symptoms. Even though they carefully avoided using this model, they found that their "patients" employed it when talking to them as "therapists." In order to redefine the conversations, they began referring to themselves as "consultants" with "clients" (rather than "therapists" with "patients") and thinking of a wide array of potential clients, not just families (Cecchin & Stratton, 1991). By the end of the decade, the KCC was joined by a sister organization called the Institute for Systemic Management (ISM) and began offering systemic consultations to a wide variety of organizations.

DEVELOPING A NEW WAY OF WORKING
WITH CLIENTS IN CONFLICT

In 1991, under the auspices of the KCC and the ISM, the Uroz Foundation was established to explore the utility of this systemic, social constructionist way of working in large-scale conflicts. The seven members met in a secluded site in England for a week. Our method was to review a wide array of specific practices, concepts, experiences, and research, all with the question in mind, "If we were called in to consult with the 'prime movers' in the major conflicts in the world today, what could we do that would help?"

All members are part of the "systemic" community in that they are familiar with the ways in which systemic therapists/consultants work. For most of our members, such conversations are their daily form of life; for me, it is a special research topic that I have studied for over a decade.

A typical day began with a lecture by one of the members on a topic (e.g., Wittgenstein's analysis of language or Dewey's analysis of activities) that the others thought might provide some useful concepts. These lectures were followed by sharp questioning that probed the utility of the information for our ability to do something about large-scale conflicts from the role of consultants. These ideas were tested in simulated consultations in which these new concepts were incorporated deliberately into the "standard" systemic practices. The day ended with an intensive critique of our way of working and the utility of the ideas that had been tested.

Through this process, we developed the 7-step procedure shown in Figure 4.1. The first two steps—initial description and commissioning—involved the team talking among themselves and with the client. During the second two steps—hypothesizing and action decision—the team members talked among themselves in front of the client but without including the client. This is a variation of the technique of "reflective teams" in which clients are allowed to listen to the therapeutic team discuss them (Andersen, 1991, 1992). The fifth step—interview—involves the team as an interlocutor with the client. The team members talk among themselves again in the sixth step—reflection. The form of conversation in the seventh step—client's response—is completely up to the client.

Initial Description

We assume that the world is a big, buzzing, booming confusion in which any number of different "facts" can be picked out and any number of stories constructed. The relationship between stories and facts is sufficiently slippery that equally valid stories about a single set of facts may be incommensurate with each other.

In this phase of the discussion, we attempt to articulate all available "facts" about the conflict. We make no attempt to organize them into coherent stories; however, as each "fact" is presented, we note how it is situated: Who picks this fact out of the buzzing confusion? From whose perspective are these facts described? Who "tells" or "shows" these facts to whom? When?

Commissioning

This phase of the process may be seen as a very crass attempt to determine who is going to pay the group for their services as consultants. This concern serves as a means of finding out some important information about the client and the conflict, however.

Specifically, we want to know to whom we are speaking. Is the

client a rogue or acting on behalf of the leadership of one of the conflict-
ed parties? Does the client have the power to make and enforce decisions or is the client located somewhere within a matrix of decision makers? If the latter, at what place within the system will our consultation
occur? Assuming that whatever we do will be brought into a
social/political context of which we are largely ignorant, how will our
contribution be used and by whom?

A second question we pose requires the client to describe the
process by which the decision was made to consult with us. Who was
involved in the conversation in which this decision was made? Who else
had to be consulted? Whose approval was required? We listen to these
answers with this additional question in mind: If these people were
involved in the decision, why are they not here for the consultation?
Should they be?

Hypothesizing

At this point, we tell the client that we must consult with each other. By
subtle rearranging of chairs and body positions, the client has become an
eavesdropper, outside the group but listening to it. We address each
other, referring to the client in the third person or by name, but not
addressing him or her directly.

We engage in a process of extemporaneous storytelling. The
content of the story is the conflict described in the first step and the role
of the client as described in the second step. This storytelling is an art
form that we find is hard to describe and not easily taught. With that
caveat, I summarize it as telling particular *kinds* of stories, using the
information we have just heard as the "raw materials."

First, these stories have a particular internal structure.
Specifically, they connect as many of the "facts" as possible. All stories
are incomplete, but the "better" stories are those that incorporate the
most facts. There is also little place in these stories for simple, one-step
linear relationships among the "facts." To say that "x caused y" to happen is considered poor taste. Instead, these stories seek to reverse the patterns of cause and effect that are offered by those involved in the conflict.

For example, the U. S. trade deficit might be described as something that was "intended" rather than "caused." A military coup might be
described as a graceful way for an incompetent President to relieve himself
of the responsibilities of office, so we might say that the President "needed"
to be deposed by a coup, or that the coup "helped" him enjoy his retirement
villa. Sworn enemies might be described as working together closely to
enhance each other's position as the leader of their respective constituen-
cies. The flow of refugees across a national border might be described as an

opportunity for cultural enrichment rather than as an economic problem.

In the same way, there is little room in these stories for simple relationships between two facts. Such relationships are embedded within larger patterns of connections in which there is reciprocal causality or coevolution. Whenever anyone gets excited about the relationship between a set of facts, the next storyteller seeks to embed that relationship within a matrix that extends beyond it. For example, then-President Bush's conspicuous adversarial relationship to the Congress can be seen in the context of his appeal to the voters; his appeal to the voters can be seen in the context of his desire to maintain the "Most Favored Nation" status of his friends in the People's Republic of China; his feelings for China can be seen in the context of his attempt to maintain an Asian economic competitor to Japan; and so on.

These stories move systematically among the perspectives of the parties engaged in the conflict. That is, we move imaginatively from one perspective to another, describing the way the story is told from each. By comparing and contrasting these stories, we bring "news" of the "differences" to the client.

Second, these stories have a particular relationship to other stories. Specifically, they "connect" with or "make distinctions" between other stories; they do not "agree" or "disagree." They include "positive connotations" of the other people in the group. Even if we have to be quite "creative" in thinking about a way of positively connoting what was said, we must not criticize other stories. For example, "That's a useful way of describing the relationship among the Inkatha Freedom Party, the de Klerk government, and the African National Congress, because it contrasts so nicely with what I was hearing from the ANC's own perspective."

The "positive connotation rule" is based on the observation that the chief obstacle to creativity is defensiveness and that if someone is criticized, they will "marry" their hypothesis. The purpose for having this rule is not just to get the group thinking creatively, but to provide the client with an experience or model of a supportive, creative, nondefensive conversation.

Third, these stories have a particular relationship to the client. The client is put in the position of the "third person" listening to stories about a conflict in which she or he is a participant. This is accomplished both by telling the stories from the client's own perspective but in the third person ("She feels that the Congress is incapable of keeping secrets, so . . .") and by telling the stories from the perspective of the other participants in the conflict ("The Iraqi Ambassador thinks that the Joint Committee on Intelligence feels that the White House has a double standard about 'leaks' of information—the Administration's selective releases are matters of policy but the Congress's leaks are irresponsible").

The "rights and duties" of the first person are quite different from those of the third person. Persons in conflict are used to telling their stories from the first-person perspective; being exposed in a non-threatening manner to second- and third-person perspectives on their own stories opens up new ways of thinking.

Action Decision

Continuing to talk among ourselves, we expand our hypothesizing to include ourselves, specifically our relation to the client and to the conflict. The ostensible purpose of this discussion is to decide whether we should continue or whether we want to withdraw as consultants. The process itself, however, serves the more important function of clarifying our voice. Specifically, we construct for ourselves a perspective independent of any of the participants in the conflict, legitimating our making judgments that do not align with any of theirs.

This discussion is important for several reasons. First, we might well decide to withdraw because of ethical or tactical reasons. Perhaps the client is not situated at a sufficiently influential position to make decisions, or perhaps the client wishes to use our intervention for purposes that we find unconscionable. Second, this discussion is the one in which we create a "neutral" voice, at least in the sense of not being identical to the voice of any of the participants.

Interview

In this phase, we turn to the client and engage in a sustained interview using circular and reflexive questions. The purpose of this interview is to help the client locate his or her own perspective within the social system in which the conflict occurs. The client should be led to differentiate his or her own perspective from that of others while at the same time becoming better able to understand how the conflict looks from the perspective of the other. The questioning leads the client to take into account the differences among these stories and thus generates "news of difference."

Reflection

After the interview, the team again talks among itself in front of the client. The talk is free-flowing and not structured formally, but generally follows these three steps. First, we comment on those things that were said in the interview that "stick out" of the discourse for some reason. The phrase of choice for our team is "I was struck by . . .," as in the statement, "I was struck by how [client] described the ANC as 'a subversive organization.'"

Second, we comment on possible connections and distinctions among parts of the story or the stories as told from various perspectives. Our statements often use the phrase "I wonder if . . .," as in, "I wonder if there have been some secret meetings between the Botha government and the Zulu leadership?"

Third, we speculate about the lines of action that might be generated by various decisions or events. We find ourselves saying "I wonder what would happen if . . .," as in, "I wonder what would happen if [client] were to reverse her position on inspections, declaring that the criterion should be 'any place, any time'?"

Client's Response

At this point, the team turns to the client and asks if she or he wants to tell us or ask us anything else. We find that clients often do not say anything in this seventh step other than to affirm that they have developed new ideas about how to deal with the problem and that they have considerable confidence in implementing those ideas; somehow they do not feel it is good or necessary to tell the consulting team what are these ideas. We choose to interpret this response as the client's "ownership" of the ideas they have generated.

APPLICATION

The Uroz Foundation had several visions of how this process might be applied, ranging from formal incorporation of the group as a consultant-for-hire to an informal use of these procedures by the members of the group in whatever situation they found themselves. In the intervening 18 months, the less formal model has prevailed; the members of the group have had numerous opportunities to consult with "major players" in large-scale conflicts and have drawn upon this procedure as a resource rather than announcing it as a structure. For several reasons, I cannot report these applications of the process. To give a sense of how it works, I recount some portions of one of the simulations in which we were trying to incorporate some of Wittgenstein's notions of language-games and grammar in systemic forms of consultation. I am deliberately vague in identifying people and places in my description of the case.

One of the members of the group was approached by a member of a Presidential Commission in a third world nation charged with developing a national policy about abused women. In the *initial descrip-*

tion, the client described the commissioners as outraged by the statistics on violence against women. They were engaged in working out the details for a national system of shelters for abused women. Our client reported a disturbing incident in which she asked, "What do we propose to do for the men who are abusers?" The group's reply was intimidating as well as disappointing: "Nothing! Why should we do anything for *them*?" She felt as if she had been treated contemptuously for suggesting that shelters provide only temporary solutions for the symptoms of abuse and that when women are ultimately discharged from them to return home, they will likely be abused again. She hoped to learn how she could introduce this systemic idea into a group whose thinking about a problem is linear.

Because this was a simulation, the member of our group who had been approached played the role of the client. After the initial description of the situation, we interviewed the client using standard "journalistic" types of questions, such as: How many shelters are there now? How long do women stay in them? What services are provided when the women leave? What are the statistics on women who return to the shelters because they have been abused again? Are there any programs in place for men who abuse women? Is spouse or child abuse illegal? How are the laws enforced?

As we shifted to the *commissioning* phase, the questions became more personal and pointed. They included: Who appointed the commission? How many people are on the commission? What are its powers? To whom will it report? What is your position on the commission? Are you alone, or are there others who think as you do? How did you decide to contact us? What do you expect us to do for you? Whom did you tell that you were going to ask us for a consultation? If we agree to work with you, whom will you have to tell? Who will authorize the check that pays our fee?

To signal the transition into *hypothesizing*, we rearranged our chairs to form a circle that included the consulting team and defined the client as an observer. The team's hypothesizing followed the usual systemic form of extending each idea by moving systematically among perspectives and by including more relationships within the system. As usual, some of the hypotheses were playful and outrageous.

One line of hypothesizing assumed that the commission was controlled by militant feminists and that the shelters were designed to separate abused women and abusing men permanently. These abused, separated women would become a constituency for a political campaign based on the feminist agenda. That is, the "shelters" were really recruitment centers for a nascent political movement, and their "success" was defined in terms of the number of women recruited, not a reduction in the amount of abuse that occurs. In the context of these hypotheses, we reinterpreted the statistics of repeatedly abused women and the incidence of marital separation and divorce as indications of the "success" of this plan.

Another line of hypothesizing assumed that the commission was deeply enmeshed in a feminist language game that sincerely wanted to help women but also included a retributive concept of justice; as a result, "men" inhabited a grammatical place in which "punishment" rather than "therapy" was the only appropriate treatment.

Yet another line of hypothesizing assumed that this country was trying to impress its neighbors with its commitment to social justice and hence needed to develop a showcase program of caring for a politically correct problem. In the context of this hypothesis, solving the problem of the abuse of women was really beside the point; what was needed was an expensive program of government shelters for abused women that could be shown to other countries.

A very serious playfulness characterized this orgy of hypothesizing. Similar to improvisational theater, the members of the group spoke quickly, each picking up what the previous person had said and extending it. Each extension sought to bring yet another relationship into the hypothesis, or to show how this hypothesis suggested a redefinition of the meaning of some element that the client presented in the initial description. As the discussion moved from one hypothesis to another, the meanings of all of the major elements in the client's description of the situation were changed, usually several times.

It should be noted that none of these hypotheses were presented as "true"; the movement among many hypotheses itself allowed the client to separate herself from the "obvious" interpretations and to consider alternatives playfully. This process also works to identify what elements of information are missing from the client's initial description. The development of each hypothesis suggests the question, "What more would you need to know to decide whether this hypothesis is a useful way of framing the issue?" This is a surprisingly useful heuristic because different hypotheses direct the client to very different forms of information.

When our hypothesizing was no longer interesting—that is, when it no longer incorporated additional features of the situation or reversed the meaning of particular elements in it—we shifted to a discussion of our *action decision*. We asked ourselves whether we should accept the role of consultant to this client. In this discussion, we continued our hypothesizing, but this time focused on the client's relationship to the group and our relationship with the client. The primary function of this discussion is to clarify these relationships.

For example, we explored several hypotheses about why this client had been appointed to the commission. Several hypotheses focused on the client's differences with the other commissioners. Since she was a systemic thinker, we suggested, her appointment reflects the commission's commitment to explore alternative ways of thinking; they *want* and *expect* her to address them in ways that they would never have thought of without her; to sound "foolish" is her role. On the other hand, we developed a hypothesis that she was appointed by mistake or as a token and that her "foolish" talk is an embarrassment and obstacle to the commission.

We explored several roles that we might play, ranging from writing a speech that she would deliver to the commission or at a press conference denouncing the commission to various expressions of our own helplessness, claiming that her expertise is absolutely necessary to decide how she should act.

The "helpless therapist" is a standard part of the repertoire of systemic consultants. When the client believes that she or he has a problem that requires an outside expert to solve, a therapeutic strange loop is set up when that outside expert—the therapist—says, "As an expert, I tell you that only you can solve your problem." If the client accepts the consultant as an expert, this advice should be heeded, but if the advice is heeded, then the client should not accept the consultant as an expert (see Cronen & Pearce, 1985).

In the "Shelters" case, we accepted the commission as a consultant to our client and began a process in which we alternated asking the client circular questions and engaging in additional hypothesizing.

To explore the hypothesis that the shelters were part of a feminist plot to split the country down gender lines, we asked questions about our client's perceptions of other members of the commission. Specifically, we asked with whom they talked about the project, how their lives would be different if there were a militant feminist movement in the country, and whose favorable opinion they most desired.

To explore the hypothesis that the shelters were tokens of political correctness to show other countries, we asked about our client's perceptions of who in the government other than the commission members was talking about the shelters, whether they "showed" the shelter program to other groups within the country or to leaders of other countries, whether this program was receiving more or less financial support than other programs designed to improve the lot of women, and whether these shelters were being placed in conspicuous places (e.g., where the news media could find them) or in the places where the needs were the greatest.

When these questions were no longer interesting—that is, the client seemed to be making no more "discoveries" and the answers were no longer incorporating new event/objects or relationships into the description of the system—we oriented ourselves so that the team was talking in front of the client. In this *reflection* phase, we deliberately avoided evaluating various hypotheses or bringing the discussion to a point of closure. Instead, recognizing that we are participants in the conversation that occurred and that we, as much as the client, co-constructed what happened, we focused on things that stood out as unexpected or unexplained. These "stand-out" features are likely to be those which are *not* simply reproductions of our own participation; by calling attention to them, we are able to guide the client's attention to the points at which several stories about the situation give different meanings to particular features.

Finally, we asked the client if she had anything she wanted to tell us. This is more an invitation for the conversation to continue than a request for feedback. In this instance, the client said, "No. I think that I know exactly what I want to do." We never did know what that decision was, but—in this form of consultation—we do not need to know. Our job is to facilitate the client's creativity, not to evaluate the decision he or she makes.

CONCLUSION

In his development of what has come to be known as the "scientific method," Francis Bacon said that our imaginations need "chains, not wings." Such oracular pronouncements should be subjected to the tests of time and place. We believe that one of the problems besetting those who must make important decisions in large-scale conflicts is that their imaginative wings are clipped too short by their deep enmeshment in a particular, often linear story of what is happening. As a result, they do not envision a sufficiently wide array of alternatives, do not think systemically about the consequences of their actions, and do not have the requisite conviction to act in unconventional ways.

The process developed by the Uroz Foundation uses a particular form of group process as a means to inculcate the client's creativity and confidence. Based explicitly on a systemic, social constructionist theory of communication and located within a rapidly changing community united by participation in particular forms of practice, the consulting group creates a conversation in which the client is invited to participate. This conversation is intended to differ from the client's usual way of relating to others and to the situation and functions to bring "news of difference" to the client.

Although this group facilitation procedure has been used as a resource for members of the Uroz Foundation, there have been few formal applications of the process. There are two reasons for the scarcity of such attempts: In the spirit of "hypothesizing" described in this paper, note that these are not mutually exclusive.

First, the process does not lend itself well to packaging and marketing. To invite a client into a strategically constructed conversation with the promise that this conversation will facilitate creativity and thus transform the social systems in which the client works sounds as if tarot cards are the next step. Advertising the expertise of the consultant fits better into the dominant discourses; the "soft forces" of participation in a playful conversation in which the consultants often talk about their inability to make decisions are, at the very least, harder to "sell" as a commodity. As a result, the members of the group employ this process without conspicuous fanfare when they find the opportunity to consult with others, or ask for a willing suspension of distrust from the client. For example, the members of the Institute for Systemic Management explain to clients that they "work systemically," and they obtain a "contract" that allows them to act in unusual ways as consultants without giving anticipatory explanations of what they are doing.

The second hypothesis focuses on the power of the process. By the time Step four—Action decision—is reached, in which the group asks itself whether to take on the role of consultants, some potential clients have decided already that they have realized the benefit of the consultation and terminate the relationship.

Those of us in the systemic, social constructionist perspective are delighted by such ambiguities as clients who say, at the end of Step four, that they have had enough. Does this mean that they have not been helped by the process and despair of finding anything of use? Or does it mean that the first four steps of the process are sufficiently powerful that they have already been brought "news of difference" and have decided what to do? From a marketing standpoint, both alternatives are disappointing; from the perspective from which we began this project, we choose to believe the latter.

The unconventional criterion of "success" presupposed in the second hypothesis is the clearest possible clue to both the future use and limitations of this group facilitation process. The staged sequence of events listed in Figure 4.1 do not constitute the heart of this process; rather, whatever effect occurs results from the client's participation in a conversation having distinctive features. The ability to call into being such conversations—and to enable an unpracticed client to join in—requires considerable proficiency in unusual conversational forms. This proficiency cannot be attained simply by reading about it; it is learned best by participation. The Uroz Foundation's modest innovations are likely to be incorporated within the larger "systemic" community but to be of little use to those who are not experienced in the use of circular questions, hypothesizing, and reflexive teams and who are unwilling or unable to let their performance of these techniques be dominated by curiosity and irreverence.

PART III
Feedback Techniques for Empowering Groups

Feedback is undoubtedly one of the most popular words in the English language, and it has come to mean virtually any response a listener gives to a speaker. In Chapter 5, Keltner takes exception to such a ubiquitous definition, arguing that when someone asks for "feedback" nowadays, we hardly know for what he or she is asking. Does he or she want an evaluation, a replication, an addition, a new idea, or just some kind of response to acknowledge the sender? Keltner suggests that facilitators and group members should focus on a limited conception of feedback called *message feedback*, the process of sending back the message received so that the sender can check to see whether the intended message was received and make whatever modifications are needed. Based on his work as a communication consultant, Keltner shows how this technique is useful in a number of group situations, including task groups in general, arbitration hearings in which disputing parties select a neutral third party to make a binding decision, and mediation situations in which a mediator helps parties in a dispute work out the solution themselves.

In Chapter 6, Keyton shows how ongoing organizational groups that experience interactional problems can turn to self-analytic feedback techniques to identify those problems and to develop more effective interaction patterns. These techniques can empower the group to become its own facilitator and thus be responsible for the continued effective development of the group. Her chapter introduces *SYMLOG* as a self-analytical feedback technique and describes its use in a 6-month field intervention into the interaction dynamics of a medical resident group. The facilitator chose Bales and Cohen's SYMLOG to capture perceptions about group interaction at the individual and group level to provide feedback concerning the group's communication effectiveness. Feedback sessions were designed to help the group better manage its interaction with attending physicians and nursing staffs. Individual

SYMLOG field diagrams focused group members' attention on their perceptions of the group. The facilitator found, however, that the group average field diagram was less useful than expected, as the group diagram significantly collapsed individual differences and hid some of the significant positions and negative relationships in the group. The chapter concludes with some recommendations for using SYMLOG an an intervention technique.

5

Message Feedback in Work Groups

John W. (Sam) Keltner
Consulting Associates

> Something's wrong here. The missing link in the evolution of person-to-person communication has been discovered, studied at universities like a wonder drug, and employed by a striking number of psychotherapists and other mental health professionals. Yet over 98 percent of the population doesn't even know the missing link exists. This unknown talk tool is used unwittingly on rare occasions, and people probably feel good when they do it, but they don't realize what they've done or how to do it again. If they did, they'd have in their communication repertoire the most effective talk tool that exists for demonstrating understanding and reducing misunderstanding. (Goodman & Esterly, 1988, p. 38)

This chapter examines a communication process that can facilitate interactions within a task group as members attempt to pursue a common goal. The efficiency and effectiveness of a task group, it is argued, depends primarily on the quality of the internal processes that characterize its attempts to accomplish its goal(s). One of the most important communication processes that can be facilitated directly is *feedback*.

The first part of this chapter clarifies the importance of communication processes within task groups, the concepts of messages, meanings, and feedback, and the character of *message feedback* as a group facilitation technique. The second part examines the message feedback technique in three types of groups: task groups in general, task groups involved in struggle management through mediation, and task groups involved in struggle management through arbitration.

CONCEPTS AND CONTEXTS

The Centrality of Communication Processes in Small Groups

Basic to our understanding of groups is an assumption that they involve processes that affect both the individual members and the group as an entity. Alderfer (1972) defined human groups as:

> [A] collection of individuals (1) who have significantly independent relations with each other, (2) who perceive themselves as a group, reliably distinguishing members from non members, (3) whose group identity is recognized by non members, (4) who as group members acting alone or in concert, have significantly interdependent relations with other groups, and (5) whose roles in the group are therefore a junction of expectations from themselves, from other group members and from non group members. (p. 204)

This definition implies that a group (two or more people) is defined by interaction among group members or by interpersonal behavior. Although effects may emerge out of the interaction of individuals gathered together that could not be accomplished by any single individual alone, the basic interaction within a small group is interpersonal in nature.

We have over the years given many small groups popular names, such as couples or dyads, discussion groups, work groups, task groups, quality circles, total quality groups, process groups, encounter groups, growth groups, teams, staffs, and so on. No matter what we call them, all groups are characterized by similar internal *processes*. Of course, one of the internal processes that suffuses much of what a group does is *communication*. One-to-one (interpersonal), group-to-one, and one-to-group communication all characterize group interaction.

Hirokawa (1990) argues that the importance of communication on group performance varies according to three characteristics of a group's task: task structure (goal clarity, path clarity, goal-path mechanics, and goal-path obstacles); information requirements; and evaluation demand. Although communication is fundamental for solving all types of group tasks, he contends that communication is less important when the task is simple and more critical as the task becomes more complex, because task performance now requires more information exchange, collaboration, and input from the members of the group.

Although the type of task is an important variable, many times it is desirable to study and facilitate group processes exclusive of the nature of the task. Observers who focus on process often have little or no concern with the nature of the purposes and goals except to identify their presence or absence. Process observers thus focus on the emotional nature of the processes that characterize group interaction. As process engineers, observers are not concerned with the passengers as such, but only with the machinery that serves them. Nor are they concerned with the destination, only the means to get there.

Note, for example, the following two quite common group situations:

> The union representative and the company employee relations director, along with their bargaining teams, seemed to be moving along toward a settlement of the terms of a new contract for the next two years. There remained the difficult issue(s) surrounding the layoff of workers because of slower business and falling profits for the company. The following dialogue took place between the union and employer representatives with the bargaining teams present:
>
> Company: Our financial condition is deteriorating fast and we are facing some serious cutbacks in the immediate future. Can we count on you to assist us in dealing with this situation?
>
> Union: We've always been willing to work with you in dealing with problems like this. We realize that times are difficult for this company and our members are concerned that the company may fold.
>
> Company: We're not at that point, I hope, but we are in trouble financially because of the declining market for our product. Our raw materials are higher and the orders for the products are very low for this time of year.
>
> Union: Yeah, we know. We realize that our people will probably have to tighten their belts, so we're ready to help you work out a plan to deal with the problem.
>
> Company: That's great! We really appreciate your attitude. Now that you're willing to help us, we plan to lay off 20 people by reverse seniority. We'll need your help in determining who these people will be.
>
> Union: Wait a minute, we didn't say we would go for a layoff. We will not agree to a layoff under any conditions.
>
> Company: That's what you did say and we believed you. Now you're denying what you said. I must remind you that we have the right to lay off workers for economic reasons and we simply can't continue to operate and carry these people in the workforce. We're not asking for your approval, we're just asking for your help as you offered it.

Union: You didn't listen very well. We are not going to stand still for a layoff.

Clearly, the information the union was trying to get across was not received by the company, or if it was, it was rejected out-of-hand without acknowledging the union.

> The personnel director was meeting with two vice-presidents concerning the development of a strategy for presenting a proposal to the Board of Directors. One vice-president suggested that the personnel director, "Put together a statement of what we want to achieve." The other vice-president nodded. The personnel director did not understand what actually was desired but did not reply and made a note on his pad. A few days later the three met again and the personnel director handed the two vice-presidents copies of a statement that listed some goals the personnel director had for his office. The two vice-presidents looked at each other in some shock, and one finally said, "This is not what we want." The other one, in a reflective way, said, "You know, if I had been asked to do what we asked you to do I'm not sure I would have known what to do."

In this example, the information the officers were seeking was not clear and neither was their request. The task itself was not defined well nor discussed. Instead of checking the matter at the beginning, several days were lost on a false start, and considerable time was wasted.

In these group situations, and many like them, the process of *message feedback*, or "reflection," as Goodman and Esterly (1988) called it, could have helped the situation. Let's take a look at that process in the context of people trying to send messages to each other through spoken communication.

Effective communication demands a system in which people can correct misreceptions and responses that run contrary to what they think they are transmitting in their messages. People need to find ways to correct their transmissions so that the essential message they are trying to transmit is perceived accurately by the receiver(s). They also need to find ways to determine when a transmission must be altered because the actual responses of the receiver are not consistent with the intended response the sender sought.

A sender has at least two prime sources from which he or she can determine whether a message was received accurately. One is to request that the message be returned to the sender as it was received so that he or she can check on its perceived accuracy. Another is to observe the receiver's resulting behavior to see whether it coincides with the intent of the sender's message.

Messages and Meanings

Let's begin with the assumption that messages and meanings are different things. Meanings are inside of us, are not transmittable as such, and in fact are our perceptions of, our interpretations of, and our responses to the many worlds around us. Meanings emerge from our interpretation of the decoded messages that each of us receive through our various senses of reception.

Messages are composed of signs, symbols, and signals referring to or representing meanings and are coded into organized forms as words and sentences, nonverbal behaviors, pictorial representations, and so forth. Messages also contain information concerning what is going on inside of us. When the message you are sending to me stimulates me to feel, recognize, or experience what you are experiencing, there is a merging of meaning, or what Howe (1963) calls a "meeting of meaning."

I recognize, however, that your perception of the world will never coincide precisely with my perception of the world. The closest I will ever come to seeing the world as you see it is when I become empathic and while in that state discover what some of your world is like.

Messages are what actually is transmitted from one person to another. The intention of the sender is what he or she wants the receiver to know, understand, or do, but the receiver does not perceive the intent, content, or form of a message in the same way as the sender. There are several reasons for this difference. One reason is that the experience base of the receiver is not such that the particular message stimulates a meaning comparable to that held by the sender. Another reason is that the message itself may not be coded in a way that actually performs what the sender intended. For example, there may be errors in the message, the message may not be explicit enough (an inadequate amount of information), or the code used simply is not familiar to the receiver (as when you encounter a person speaking a language you do not understand).

Because we have different sets of experiences with which to react to messages, the likelihood that we will respond in exactly the same way to any given set of messages is quite remote. It is possible, however, to check our messages with each other so that the *information transmitted* can be made more consistent with the *information received*.

Feedback

Richards (1951) stated that, "The problem is how to find out what we have done, take account of it, and proceed in the light of what we have done . . . There is no escaping that . . . what we say next will be in part controlled by *feedback* from what we have said up to that point" (pp. 52, 54; emphasis added).

The general concept of *feedback* may be understood in terms of the input and output of a system. Clement and Frandsen (1976) stated that feedback is "a process wherein a system's own output controls its subsequent input" (p. 11). This view is consistent with a system devised by Weiner (1954) in which the control of the system would be based on its actual performance rather than on its expected performance. That is, a person is controlled on the basis of what he or she does rather than what we may expect him or her to do.

Related closely to this way of looking at the matter is the function of purpose. Littlejohn (1983) pointed out that, "Purposeful behavior is directed toward an object or aim . . . All purposeful behavior requires feedback" (p. 33). Feedback thus allows us to determine whether our behavior has accomplished the purpose for which it was designed and to modify it if it appears to be missing the target.

If we think of persons and the processes involved in their communication with each other as a system, then feedback is a process whereby the behavior of the target of the output (the receiver[s] of a message) is used by the initiator of the output (the sender) to control what output or other behavior will follow.

Feedback, therefore, is related to the idea of a servomechanism whereby a machine is controlled by the consequences of its own behavior. As Annett (1969) explains:

> The ingredients of such a device are a source of power, a transducer, which is activated by the power source, a sensing device which measures the output or activity of the machine and a feedback loop which translates the output measure into a signal which can control the input. (p. 16)

These concepts have, of course, been associated closely with human communication processes for a long time. Watzlawick, Beavin, and Jackson (1967), for example, wrote that:

> [I]nterpersonal systems—stranger groups, marital couples, families, psychotherapeutic, or even international relationships, etc.—may be viewed as feedback loops, since the behavior of each person affects and is affected by the behavior of each other person. Input into such a system may be amplified into change or may be counteracted to maintain stability. (p. 31)

Leavitt and Mueller (1951), in one of the earliest studies on feedback, explain how a machine is controlled by the consequences of its own behavior:

The servomechanism needs a sensory system that is capable of transmitting cues about the errors of its own motor system. The human being learning some motor skill apparently utilizes the same process. But when the human being (A) seeks to transmit information to another human being (B), A's own sensory system is hardly an adequate source of information unless B takes some action which will help A to keep informed of A's own progress. If A were trying to hit B with a brick, A's eyes combined with an inactive B would probably be adequate to permit A to hit his target after several trials. But if A seeks to hit B with information he will probably be more successful if B helps to provide some cues which A's own sensory system cannot pick up directly. In other words, where communication between A and B is the goal, feedback, in the form of verbal or expressive language, should make for greater effectiveness. (pp. 401-402)

Leavitt and Mueller set out to test the effect of feedback on students' ability to replicate in graphic form a series of geometric patterns communicated orally by an instructor. Four feedback conditions were used: *zero feedback*, in which the instructor sat behind a screen and could not receive either visual or verbal feedback; *visual audience feedback*, in which the instructor and students could see each other but no speaking by the students was allowed; *yes-no feedback*, in which the students were allowed to answer only yes or no to the instructor's questions; and *free feedback*, in which students could talk freely with the instructor. Differences among these feedback conditions were then measured in terms of accuracy, confidence level, and time.

The findings showed that feedback in general increased the accuracy with which information was transmitted and also increased both the sender's and receiver's confidence in what they accomplished. Of the four feedback conditions, visual audience observation had the least effect on the outcomes whereas free feedback had the greatest effect. This finding suggests that free expression by receivers is the best way to achieve the purpose of a communication. But what are the communication forms in which free expression emerges? These differences were not explored explicitly, but the assumption underlying the effects found was that free feedback essentially was seeking clarification of the message. Hence, the concept of feedback is tied inextricably to the ability to clarify messages.

The basic concept of feedback, however, has devolved into one with many referents, some of which appear to be contradictory (see Cusella, 1980). It is an extremely popular term in professional areas such as counseling and therapy, interpersonal communication training, and management training, and currently is tossed around almost indiscriminately in communication theory and practice with little real understanding of the referent for which it should be used.

A typical example of the extensive confusion that has developed about the feedback process is given in a recent study by McLeod, Liker, and Lobel (1992) that equated feedback with reports to a group on its "equality of participation, group orientedness, and task versus socio-emotional balance" (p. 27). They identified "process feedback" as the experimenter presenting to the groups at the conclusion of their task, "the results of the observers' ratings of group process, and a set of norms against which to compare their results" (p. 22). Their review of the literature found that such process interventions (which they called feedback) had no measurable effect on task performance while increasing group cohesiveness and member satisfaction.

It is not surprising that feedback, as they defined it, had no effect on task performance. Such a broad and ambiguous use of the term cannot lead to substantive results because what they describe as feedback simply does not fit the basic concept and because they did not examine the communication process for which feedback is designed. What they actually observed was more of an instructional intervention.

Although we assume that there is some feedback whenever interpersonal communication takes place, there is a problem in the typical use of the term. For example, when someone asks for "feedback" nowadays we hardly know for what he or she is asking. Does he or she want an evaluation? A replication? An addition? A new idea? A reaction? All of the above? Or just some kind of a response to acknowledge the sender? Unless the context is such that the kind of response desired is already understood, it actually is hard to tell what is really meant by this use of the term.

Close scrutiny indicates that perceptions of feedback fall onto a continuum. At one end of the spectrum are references to any kind of *response* offered by a receiver. I have heard people say such things as, "I would like some feedback on your perception of my talk," "Give me some feedback on my job performance," or "Would you like some feedback on your management style?" What these people actually are asking for is some kind of *evaluation* or *judgment* about their performance.

This view sees any response by a receiver as "feedback" to the sender. In a technical sense, this would be useful if it were understood that the purpose was the control, modification, or refinement of the original message and its intent. However, this is not always the case. The general use of the term has become so ubiquitous that it now covers all kinds of responses, including responses that are not intended as feedback information for the sender.

Although almost any observable response can be viewed as containing information that affects the subsequent behavior of a sender, it can also be so far removed from the sender's intent and nature of the original message that *the sender never knows whether the original message actually was received*. Under this condition, the sender does not know to what messages the receiver was responding , and the consequent change or adjustment of the message becomes almost a matter of chance.

For example, a process consultant was meeting with the conference planning team of a local service agency. During the meeting she outlined several procedures that would need to take place during the conference. The group members listened quietly but said nothing about her suggestions and showed little nonverbal evidence of understanding, acceptance, or rejection. After the meeting she moved on to another task in another place and did not meet again with this group nor did she attend the conference they were planning. She never knew whether her message and the information in it had been received accurately, much less whether it was accepted.

By generalizing the referent of the term "feedback" at this end of the continuum we have vitiated its usefulness. If our intent is to get some evaluative information concerning the effects of a speech, we can say just as easily, "How good was my speech?" or "Did you like it?," instead of "Give me some feedback on my speech." Indeed, the resulting information would probably be a great deal more precise and useful.

At the other end of the continuum is a limited and precise use of the term feedback whereby the message itself and the information it contains is replicated and returned to the sender so that alterations in the information in the original message can be made by the originator. This type of feedback has been called "reflection" (Goodman & Esterly, 1988), and the analogy to a mirroring effect is used to describe the process (Cushman & Cahn, 1985). I prefer to call this process "message feedback." I have more to say about this type of feedback later.

The various interpretations of the concept of feedback may appear at first confusing. One of the most confusing is the mixing of feedback with response. Taylor, Meyer, Rosegrant, and Samples (1989) say that:

> If you think of response and feedback as the same thing, you can run into trouble . . . Properly used, feedback can be a way to check on the accuracy or effectiveness of a message sending. Improperly used, feedback can lead to ineffective or scrambled communication. (p. 9)

They suggest that all feedback may be viewed as a response but not all responses are feedback. Feedback is a particular form of response that is different from other forms.

Feedback works best when the goals of an interaction are understood by the originator of the information and can be used as the criterion to determine whether the information returned is meeting those goals.

When a budget planning team is attempting to balance income and expenditures, the goal of the group allows for more effective feedback than if there were no clarification of the purpose of the session. In Leavitt and Mueller's (1951) study, for example, the goal of replicating the geometrical design was understood by both the sender and receivers from the outset. The presence of these goals helped to channel the kind of feedback the receivers provided; in other words, their feedback was related primarily to the goal they all sought, the replication of the design.

Furthermore , there is always some confusion about who is the sender and who is the receiver, for people perform both functions simultaneously in conversation. As people interact, they are both giving off verbal and nonverbal signals all the time. Clement and Frandsen (1976) explain it this way:

> In one-to-one communication, while conversant A observes conversant B for information signals that indicate B's degree of understanding, agreement or interest, B is also accumulating information about A's effectiveness, A's knowledge or A's interest in B. For both A and B to gather such information both must provide informative signals regarding their effectiveness in their respective roles. Thus, each conversant both observes and provides signals that, in the fullest sense, fulfill feedback functions. (p. 25)

The question of who is providing feedback to whom thus becomes difficult to answer. It can only be addressed in terms of specific messages within specific times and conditions. That is, what statement is feedback to what other statement may be difficult to identify in the rapid flow of conversation. That does not mean, however, that the process is not taking place.

Although there are a number of varying interpretations and derivations of the concept of feedback, some significant factors seem persistent:

- General feedback does not only occur when people think about it and provide it consciously—it goes on all the time. When we control it consciously, we probably can increase the quality of the communication process.
- We adjust our future statements on the basis of what we perceive as being the results of past statements. Future development and performance of messages are dependent on the perceived past effect of a message on a receiver(s).
- Both interactants are sending and receiving data simultaneously so that subsequent messages are being modified according to the degree to which past messages have satisfied the goals of the

interactants. The process is nonlinear; it is circular and helical.
- When a segment sample or a copy of a message is returned to a person, he or she then has an opportunity to alter the message if it does not meet his or her perceived intent.
- Feedback is a method of testing whether a message (input) sent meets the purpose for which it was formulated.
- Feedback provides a way in which what is happening can be brought into closer congruence with what we want to happen.

Message Feedback

In the message feedback process the information contained in the original message is returned to the originator through a paraphrase, a more or less exact copy, or other form of mirroring that allows the originator to know that the initial message and its information content was received. If the originator gets back a garbled account of the original message, then attenuation or alteration in that message is called for to allow the receiver to know what message actually was intended.

A very common, simplistic illustration of this is the "line-loss" demonstration in which a single specific message is given to two lines of people, similar to two "chain" networks (see Shaw, 1981). One chain is instructed to pass the message down the line with no "feedback," whereas the other chain passes the message down the line but with the added instruction that the message may not pass from one person to another until the originator of the message is satisfied that the receiver has the original message.

By the time the message reaches the end of line one, it consistently is garbled (distorted), much of the original data are missing (deleted), information of little relevance to the original data may be included (addition), and, in general, what was said at the beginning and what came out at the end is significantly different. On the other hand, the line that is instructed to use message feedback typically ends up with a message that is highly similar to the original with little distortion, deletion, or addition (hence, no significant difference from beginning to end).

There seems to be several forms in which message feedback appears. If I give you directions to my home, my goal is to get you there. When you arrive at the front door without further assistance, I have evidence that my message was received accurately. This is a form of feedback I call *behavior feedback*.

Reflective feedback (mirroring) is also a form of message feedback that occurs when one person reflects back to another the exact message with words and phrases intact so that the sender can see whether the message was received as intended. If the receiver rephrases the message into his or her own words but does not add basic information to the message, the sender can also determine whether some of his or her goal of sending that message was achieved (Keltner, 1992).

If we think of interaction between people as an information system and the amount of information in that system as being generated by the participants in that system, then when I originate and send a message to you, I am adding new information into our system. When you reflect back what I said by giving me a replication or "copy" of my message, there is a limited amount of *new* information introduced into the system. Mirroring my message tells me that you have received the new information or "copied" my message accurately. However, when you respond to what I sent you by giving me your feeling, judgment, or other analyses about what I said, you are *adding* considerably more new information into the system. You are, in fact, initiating a *new* message and new information into the system that did not exist in the original message. Depending on the nature of your response, there may hardly be any evidence that you received or are responding to the actual message I sent.

The significant character of message feedback, therefore, is that it does not add substantially new information into a system. It simply provides the sender with evidence that the receiver has, indeed, received the message sent and no more.

Realistically, it is very difficult to provide pure message feedback. Nonverbal behavior alone attenuates the feedback and adds information into a system. For example, Joe told Harry that he should open the discharge valve before turning on the power. Harry replied, "You said to open the discharge valve *before* turning on the power?" (The italics indicate a rising vocal inflection and visible nonverbal behaviors showing disbelief.) In fact, what Harry provided was message feedback but it included, through his nonverbal behavior, *additional* information about his reaction to the message.

In short, message feedback provides more of an opportunity for correcting and attenuating messages than any other form of feedback. It allows the source of a message to modify it in order to get the desired information to the receiver(s). It is, in fact, a basic and fundamental form of the feedback system. Its simplest form is a replication or reflection of the message received, whereas a more complex form is paraphrase. Another form is subsequent receiver behavior in response to a message. (This form can be quite confusing as behavior can be produced by many other factors than just a message sent.) As we see below, using the replication and paraphrase forms of message feedback in small group interaction is a practical way to keep communication channels open and to reduce the amount of loss in information that can occur from sender to receiver.

APPLICATIONS OF MESSAGE FEEDBACK

The following applications illustrate instances of how message feedback has been used to facilitate several types of task groups in natural settings and some of the techniques for promoting its use.

Message Feedback and the Task Group

The use of message feedback in any task group is an important process, and in the hands of well-trained professional facilitators it is a very valuable tool. It is also a valuable facilitation technique when group members learn to use the process themselves.

Using message feedback throughout task group deliberations is important. In many instances, the very nature of a group's task is not clear and considerable deliberation must take place in order to reach agreement and focus on the job at hand. For example, the following discussion, which took place in an organization of officers of state and local governments illustrates how confused members can be about their task:

Member 1: As I understand it, we're to decide on what health and welfare proposals to make to the legislature.

Member 2: That's crazy. Everybody knows that we have no power in the legislature. Why are we spending our time on this?

Member 3: You don't understand. Somebody has to start the process and we're it. Let's get on the ball. If we don't make an effort, who will?

Member 2: It's a waste of time. We don't know how to deal with that bunch of crazy politicians. And further, I don't trust them.

Member 1: Nobody is asking us to deal with the politicians. We're just given the responsibility of working out proposals.

Member 3: First we should find out what our members want. I propose that we send out a questionnaire. We could list several . . .

Member 2 (Interrupting 3): That's not a good way. It's better to get out and talk with our membership face-to-face. But I don't think we have time for that. Anyway, what's the use of formulating proposals if we don't know how to sell 'em?

Member 1: That's not the point. What we decide here will be taken up by our association lobbyists to the legislature. They are the ones who will do the selling.

Member 2: Why didn't you say so?

Member 1: I thought I just did.

Observe the contrast if the same group were to operate like this:

Member 1: As I understand it, we're to decide on what proposals on health and welfare to take to the legislature.

Member 2: Did you say that we're going to make the decisions and this group will take these to the legislature?

Member 1: Not exactly, we're to make the decision about what our lobbyists take to the legislature.

Member 3: Oh, you mean we won't take the proposal forward ourselves but our lobbyist will?

Member 1: Yep.

Member 2: Okay, how do we begin to formulate our position?

Notice that the message feedback in the second example had a different effect on the group members than the effect from the first dialogue when there was no message feedback. The message feedback clarified the task more quickly and reduced the incursion of elements that distracted progress toward the task. In the first example, the group very nearly got blindsided by a proposal to conduct a questionnaire before it knew just what was the nature of the task. The first group could be distracted more easily because the goal or task was not clear at the outset.

The second example is typical of work groups that use the message feedback process. Although in some instances it may appear that message feedback slows down the process, it does in fact help to screen out unrelated information and in the long run expedites group decision making.

There are several phases in group decision making in which message feedback can play a very important role. Certainly in the process of reaching a shared perception of the goal or task it can be used to clarify different points of view and thus help group members to find a focus. Even when members' perceptions are different, message feedback helps members confront those differences openly so that they can be resolved.

When different opinions and proposals emerge, it is useful to provide message feedback so that there are no misunderstandings. Message feedback can be performed by a process observer, by the chair, by informal leaders, or by any group member sensitive to the communication problem and skilled in the message feedback process.

In groups in which there is no reasonable message feedback, people often agree on a solution but each person may have a different idea of what was agreed to. For example, an elementary school faculty task force team was given the responsibility to provide suggestions for preventing violence on the playground. The group came up with the proposal that the dispute be "mediated" by the faculty. When the members were asked privately what the "mediators" would do, the results were appalling. One third described the role accurately, half of them perceived "mediators" as decision makers or arbitrators, and the rest perceived the role as a "police" function.

The use of the message feedback process will not in and of itself remove differences once they are clarified. Negotiation, collaboration, and so forth, are necessary for dealing constructively with differences. Message feedback, however, allows those differences to be recognized. Too often people think they are at odds when in fact actual differences do not exist, and message feedback helps to clarify these situations.

In short, message feedback in task groups provides a facilitation technique that members can use to clarify task concerns and enhance effective decision making. At many stages in the deliberations of a group it is useful to use the process. Of course, when there is a high degree of understanding and a mutual meeting of the minds, using the process is unnecessary.

Group members' willingness to use message feedback is a very important requirement. Note the problem below:

> Two members of a faculty group were having a heated discussion about what should be included in a certain course. Each had, at some length, stated their position. Sherry, however, felt that Cliff had neither perceived nor understood her position. In order to check, she asked Cliff to "Tell me what you think I have said." Cliff glared at Sherry with a flushed face and refused to answer. A tense silence ensued. Cliff finally said, "Are you implying that I haven't listened to you?" Sherry answered, "I really don't know, you've given me no evidence that you heard a word I said."

It is quite possible that had Cliff been willing to check with Sherry about what she was saying, many common agreements would have emerged. As an onlooker, I was quite aware that the two of them were not really far apart in their positions but each felt that the other was opposed strongly. Thus, when Cliff refused to provide some message feedback, there was no way for the matter to be resolved under those conditions.

The type of words used is also important in message feedback. Words and phrases that are synonyms and reflect the same content are often useful. It's very important that the essential message be reflected, as in the following example:

A team of section managers was given the responsibility to prepare a budget for the larger division of the company. Early in the meeting one of the managers stated strongly that his section had to have enough money to buy important new equipment. Another manager answered, "You're saying that new equipment is a high priority on your list?" The answer was, "You got it!"

Although the term "high priority" was not stated in the original message, it expressed the intent of the original statement.

One of the most valuable outcomes of well-placed and designed message feedback is that it gives persons receiving it a chance to examine the effects of their statements and behavior. This is a valuable outcome in any group, as illustrated in the following case:

The director of a small consulting agency called her consultants together to review bidding procedures for consulting contracts. One of the consultants consistently had been underbidding contracts and then running up extra time on the contract that would not be reimbursed by the client and thus lost the agency money. The director outlined the problem and stated that in the future all bids were to cover actual projected costs and time consumption, plus a contingency deposit to cover variations that could arise between the bid and the delivery that would be returned to the client if no additional costs were encountered.

The consultant who had been underbidding seemed to sulk and gave no response. Finally, after the other consultants answered questions about the procedure, the director asked the erring consultant if she had any comments. The reply was, "I don't like to charge our clients for work not done."

The director pointed out that there would be no such charge in the proposal and that the contingency fee would only be charged when actual contingencies existed. The consultant continued to sulk. Finally, the director asked the consultant directly to feed back what the procedure was to be. The consultant said simply, "I know what you're doing, you're trying to get more money by charging a hidden fee. I don't agree with it and I won't do it." The director then said, "You're telling me that you don't agree with our plan and refuse to follow the directive?" The consultant replied, "No, I'm not refusing to follow a directive, I just don't agree with it."

It was clear that when the consultant heard her message returned to her through message feedback she thought better of her refusal to follow the procedure and changed her response. The feedback gave her an opportunity to look at the message she had sent and to realize that she was on the brink of being insubordinate, which could put her job in jeopardy.

Message feedback is quite effective as a group facilitation technique when used as an intervention by a facilitator. The nature of the facilitator's role in the group, however, affects the use of this technique. If the facilitator is a nonmember serving as a process observer, using message feedback as an intervention runs the risk of drawing the facilitator into the content of the discussion which can then create a power problem (in relation to the group's decision-making capability) because of the added power that the facilitator now has. However, used carefully by a facilitator, the technique can be very effective.

The following excerpt is from a task-force group that was formed to help plan a community dispute resolution service. The group had run into difficulties in its deliberations and, at the suggestion of one of the members, had invited a process specialist to sit with them and to facilitate their interaction:

Chair: We need to make a decision about who is going to direct the program. What do we have before us?

Member 1: The Normal Mediation Service, whom I am representing on this task force, has offered to take over the community dispute resolution program and administer it for this task force.

Member 2: How much will it cost?

Member 1: That depends.

Member 2: On what?

Member 1: On how much you have to offer.

Chair: The state dispute commission is willing to make a . . .

Member 2 (Interrupting): We don't have anything to offer. We're starting from zero. We need to get help from the county and the city at least.

Member 3: I'm wary of that NMS bunch. They go off half-baked on a lot of issues . . . and their staff is all volunteer with only minimum training, and they're always trying to get more money from the United Way and other grant groups. I understand this year they went for a 30% increase from United Way . . . [and] the director takes half of what they get from donated funds for her salary . . .

Member 1 (Interrupting): That's not accurate. The director is an MSW and is specially trained in mediating family disputes, and they are a nonprofit group.

Facilitator (To the Chair): I thought I heard you say a minute ago that the state dispute commission was willing to make a contribution.

Chair: Yes, the last I heard from the state director was that they were peeling off a percentage of the filing fees in court cases in each county for this purpose.

Member 1: How much will that amount to?

Chair: We do not know.

This intervention by the facilitator did several things: She focused the group's attention on what the Chair said; gave the Chair an opportunity to acknowledge or correct what was said; made it possible for the Chair to elaborate or continue what he had started to say before he was interrupted; and evaded an emerging struggle between two of the members. At the same time, the facilitator was on delicate ground because by affecting these events she was dangerously close to controlling the content of the discussion and those who were taking part.

There might have been a message feedback intervention at the point at which Member 3 expressed some negative feelings about the NMS. A statement such as, "I hear you saying that you have concerns about NMS and your project," might have resulted in some less negative dialogue. Even such an intervention at that point, however, would have controlled in part the direction in which the discussion was going. It might have focused the group's attention on the negative perceptions, and the funding matter could have been lost. Process facilitators, therefore, must be very careful about controlling a group they are supposed to be facilitating. Of course, the same is true for any facilitator who has more power than is usually assumed by a group member.

Another way that facilitators can assist a group in which some struggle is emerging is to suggest that the adversaries take time to provide message feedback to each other. This is quite similar to what a mediator might do with parties in a dispute.

If the facilitator is a member of the group with the particular role assignment of facilitating the process as well as participating in the content of the discussion, using the two basic forms of message feedback—paraphrase and direct reflection—can be effective. By seeing the value of such feedback, others in the group will begin to use these techniques. However, if the facilitator-member uses these techniques and they detract the group from its central task, the other members may avoid their use and resist the efforts of the facilitator-member.

Underlying all message feedback techniques is the absolute necessity that users be good listeners. If feedback attempts show that a user really has not been listening, a negative response sets in. This is different from "pseudo-feedback" in which the message may be altered purposely in order to check the sender's surety as to what information is to be transferred.

In conclusion, there are many opportunities for using message feedback as a facilitation technique in task groups, but the technique must be used carefully by intervenors, facilitators, and others who attempt to aid a group. For simple tasks the opportunities and values of message feedback are minimal, but for complex tasks the opportunities and values are high. Of course, in the final analysis, it is best used by the members themselves as they interact.

Message Feedback in the Arbitration Process

The arbitration process involves a special type of group that exists when disputing parties select a neutral third party, an arbitrator, to hear their respective arguments and to make a decision that they have agreed to accept prior to entering the process. Message feedback is a useful tool for an arbitrator in several ways: It allows an arbitrator to check and confirm the information provided; assures the parties that what they say is being heard; demonstrates neutrality toward both parties; and provides opportunities for the parties to modify their arguments and testimony after they have heard it fed back to them.

When an arbitrator meets with adversaries in a dispute, the parties usually are polarized and view each other with varying degrees of distrust, alienation, and suspicion. The positions of the parties have become somewhat rigid, and each side usually is into a win-lose perception of the situation (see Keltner, 1994). The tendency for each side is to miss the statements of the other side, misinterpret them, or be unable to provide reasonably accurate reflection or message feedback to each other. Under these conditions, the arbitrator introduces message feedback through performance rather than edict; that is, he or she uses it frequently him- or herself. Some interesting results are apparent when this happens.

The parties usually begin an arbitration by summarizing what they intend to prove. An arbitrator using the message feedback process reflects back that summary by stating as accurately as possible what he or she has heard. In one case, after hearing a company present its opening statement concerning its reasons for terminating an employee, the arbitrator said, "Your position is that termination was for just cause, for repeated absences, for ignoring the manager's instructions, and for not notifying the manager when you were going to be late or absent. Have I missed anything?"

Several kinds of responses to an arbitrator's message feedback emerge typically. The most common response is for an advocate to acknowledge the accuracy of the feedback by a nod of his or her head or by saying something like, "Yes, that's where we are." An advocate may, however, feel that the arbitrator has missed something in the presentation and will repeat the perceived missing information. Another common response is for the advocate to ask if the arbitrator needs more information at this point.

When I, as an arbitrator, provide message feedback to one side in this manner I try to provide the same kind of feedback to the other side. This is an important part of the neutrality function of an arbitrator.

Once the opening statements have been completed, each party takes its turn presenting witnesses along with documentary evidence. The testimony of the witnesses provides a significant opportunity for message feedback to be used constructively. The arbitrator may intervene at an appropriate moment and provide message feedback to the witness, such as, "Did I get this right? You said . . .," or "I heard you say . . . ." The witness usually will confirm the feedback or adjust the message. When hearing the information come back, a witness often realizes that what was said is not what was intended and will make corrections. This is when the use of paraphrase by an arbitrator can be quite effective.

From time to time, I have used "pseudo-feedback" to check the message by altering the original message deliberately as I reflect it back so that the information is truly not the same as in the original message. When the originator of the message corrects my pseudo-message, I gain further confidence about the intent and nature of the original message. I have discovered, however, that this technique should not be used too often because the parties either sense that I am playing games with them or begin to believe that I am a lousy listener. I once used pseudo-feedback twice with a single witness within a half hour of testimony. After the second time, the witness looked at me with disdain and said, "Mr. Arbitrator, do you have your hearing aid turned down?"

In spite of its value, the use of message feedback by an arbitrator during the presentation of testimony by witnesses is a delicate matter. The feedback is an intervention by the arbitrator and he or she must be very careful not to affect the strategy of the presentation. It must not be too frequent, but it may be used to check important testimony.

One desirable outcome of an arbitrator using message feedback is that the parties will begin to use it with each other. This is quite common in the cross-questioning of witnesses by opponents. In some cases, the parties may become so adept at it that the arbitrator need not intervene, a highly desirable state of affairs, albeit an infrequent one. I remember the pleasant shock I experienced when after a company manager said, "We have a long standing rule that employees must not fight with each other or do physical injury to each other. Joe, with intent to hurt, hit Sam with the handle of a sweep broom and raised a big lump on his head," the union attorney replied, "Counselor, you have just claimed that the Grievant purposely hit the foreman with a broom handle and that is against the rules. Is that right?"

Most arbitration hearings are recorded in some fashion, either by a tape recorder or by a court reporter, so what is said becomes a matter of record, although it is not a public record. However, that does not alter the necessity to provide message feedback because it serves to clarify the dialogue and facilitate the dynamic nature of the exchanges as they are taking place.

Of course, in those instances in which an arbitrator gets the message or testimony and feels reasonably sure that he or she understood what the witness said, the need for message feedback is reduced. When testimony is confusing, erratic, and contradictory, however, it is important for the arbitrator to check with the witness as to what was said. This clarifies the testimony for the arbitrator and allows the witness to clarify the evidence presented.

Keep in mind that it is the responsibility of an arbitrator to get the facts so that a decision can be based on full information regarding the situation. There is some concern by professional adversaries that when an arbitrator takes a very active role in seeking the facts the strategy of the presentation may be disturbed. This is a continuing issue among arbitrators and professional adversaries and harks back to the essential purpose of the arbitrator as a decision maker (see Keltner, 1994; Sacks & Kurlantzick, 1988).

The following passage is taken from an arbitration hearing where message feedback was used with some success. The Grievant was appealing a termination by his employer and is testifying under direct interrogation by his union attorney:

Union Attorney: In your judgment, why were you fired from your job?

Grievant: Well, it's really hard to say. I had this argument with the floor manager about how we were supposed to close down the deli section. He insisted that I should wrap all the uncovered foods from the display cases and put them in the cooler before I did anything else and that it should not take me more than 30 minutes. I told him that if we did it right it would take more time than that, at least an hour.

Union Attorney: Obviously you disagreed. Is there more to it?

Grievant: Well, yes. Our argument kind of set him against me and he kept criticizing me about the way I closed down each night. Finally, he told me that he was going to clock me and if it took more than 30 minutes he would dock my pay. That made me mad and I told him that if he could do it right in 30 minutes he could have the job.

Arbitrator: You told him that if he could do it in the 30-minute time that you would quit?

Grievant: No, that he could have the job. I didn't mean I'd quit. And really I was just mad and makin' talk at him. He was really bullying me.

Attorney: Was that why you were terminated?

Grievant: I think so.

Arbitrator: You were terminated because you got mad at your supervisor and wouldn't close the deli in the time he wanted?

Grievant: That's not what he told me when he handed me the notice. It said that I was late to work without notice too many times. I was late for work several times, but I always let him know I'd be late for work before I was supposed to be there.

Attorney: How much time before you were due to appear would you give the manager when you were going to be late?

Grievant: It differed, but it was always before my shift started. Usually it was more than ten minutes or so.

Arbitrator: Let me see if I've got this right. You testify that you were fired because the manager and you didn't agree on how to close down the deli and that you were tardy too many times. Is that what you're saying?

Grievant: Well, the notice of termination mentioned only the tardinesses.

The use of message feedback by the arbitrator gave the arbitrator more accurate information and allowed the Grievant to adjust the information that was given to meet his goals. Notice that the arbitrator did not use the same words as the witness in the feedback and, at one point, changed the witness' words "he could have the job" to "quit." This led immediately to a clarification by the witness of what he meant by this phrase.

This type of message feedback, if used carefully, can boost an arbitrator's perceived credibility by the parties in a dispute. It also provides better information for an arbitrator, who must make a decision based on the information gathered at the hearing.

If, however, message feedback is used inappropriately, in an untimely manner, or reflects bias on the part of an arbitrator (such as lengthy interrogations in the manner of a prosecuting criminal lawyer), it can harm the process as well as alienate the arbitrator from either or both parties to the dispute.

When message feedback is used by the adversaries themselves, the presentation of the witnesses appears more clear than without it, the process is more objective, and the cross-questioning phase of each testimony proceeds with greater precision. Notice the following passage in which the attorney for the employer was interrogating a witness in the cross-questioning phase:

> Attorney: You said that you always let your manager know when you were going to be late. Is that right?
>
> Grievant: Yep.
>
> Attorney: On June 9th, were you late for work?
>
> Grievant: Let's see, that was a Monday. Yes, I was late that day.
>
> Attorney: Did you call your manager to let him know you were late?
>
> Grievant: I think so.
>
> Attorney: How late were you?
>
> Grievant: Not more than ten minutes.
>
> Attorney: You were late ten minutes or less?
>
> Grievant: Well, it could have been a few minutes more but not many.
>
> Attorney: The time clock record (exhibit 3) shows that you were late 30 minutes on June 9. That's more than ten minutes.
>
> Grievant: I guess I didn't check my watch.
>
> Attorney: Now, let's look at your notifying your manager. You said that you called the manager to let him know you were late on that day. When did you call him?
>
> Grievant: I really don't remember whether I called in or not.

As this example shows, when a witness is confused or malingering, message feedback can be a powerful tool in pointing out the confusion and identifying the contradictions.

Message feedback in an arbitration hearing is a valuable tool for an arbitrator and for the parties to a dispute. My experience over the years with the process has been that it helps me as an arbitrator get a clearer perception of the issues and factors involved in a dispute, which leads me to make a more effective decision.

Message Feedback and Mediation

The mediation process is quite different from arbitration (see Keltner, 1987, 1994). In this special form of group process, a mediator is selected by the parties in a dispute to help them work out the solution themselves. Mediators usually are called in when the parties feel unable to resolve their differences themselves and yet do not want to relinquish their right to make the decisions resolving the difference. The mediator does not make the decisions and serves primarily to facilitate the communication between the parties as they work out their own resolution.

Brand (1992), in advising lawyers about the use of process-centered mediation, identifies message feedback as active listening. Brand states: "The mediator repeatedly restates, in his or her own words, what the disputant has said. Each time the disputant is asked to confirm the accuracy of the re-statement. Discrepancies are explored as an aid to identifying the interests of the disputants" (p. 10).

Whereas the feedback process appears to focus on the arbitrator in an arbitration process, it focuses on the participants or adversaries in a mediation process. That is, a mediator uses message feedback to encourage the parties to use the process themselves. The request for message feedback thus occurs more frequently in mediation than in arbitration. The intake or orientation session typically should include some discussion of the message feedback process and how it can be used. A mediator may suggest at this stage that when the parties feel they are not being listened to, they may request the other party to provide message feedback. This opens the door for more careful examination of what each is saying to the other.

When the parties to a dispute reach the stage at which they seek intervention by a mediator, they undoubtedly are having considerable difficulty communicating with and listening to each other. In addition, the emotional concomitants of their dispute often affect them so much that they block out efforts to understand each other. Using message feedback performs a valuable function under these conditions. For example, the following dialogue took place in a session with a divorcing couple who were very angry at each other:

> Woman: You are not a good person to be with this child. Your drinking and your constant criticism of me upsets her. You are so damned concerned with your own girlfriends and nobody knows what else that you really can't take care of her . . .
>
> Man (Interrupting): I'm tired of you playing the martyr and acting like you're being mistreated at every turn. You make people think that you're a downtrodden woman. That

women's lib bunch you hang around with have poisoned
you. You can't even take care of your own child.

It is clear that they were not listening to each other because each
was interested in attacking the other. Either they had heard these
charges many times before or were putting them on to influence the
mediator; in either case, they were not dealing with each other. The
mediator asked each one to repeat what the other had said and neither
could do it. At that point, he reflected back what each had said and
asked if they thought they were communicating with each other. There
was an angry silence.

Two types of sessions occur during the mediation process. The
first type, the *joint meeting*, brings both parties face-to-face with each
other and with the mediator. The second type, the *caucus*, separates the
parties and allows the mediator to meet with each side alone.

In the joint meeting, mediators who use message feedback set a
standard of performance for both parties. Even more important is the
use of message feedback by the parties. When the parties clearly are
unable to listen to each other, the mediator needs to suggest that they
use message feedback to set them on track.

For example, in the child custody case in which the divorcing
parents were exhibiting strong feelings, one person said to the other,
"You have given me no reason to change my mind about the support
payment." The other responded, "I want you to stay away from alcohol
when our daughter is with you." It appeared that each was on a different track and that they were bypassing each other. The mediator could
have assumed that they purposely were avoiding the issue that the other
was raising or that they simply were not able to hear what each other
said. Assuming the latter to be true, the mediator intervened by saying,
"Let's try something here. I want you both to tell the other what you
think was just said." Neither could do this.

The mediator then suggested that they try to provide message
feedback to each other in order to clarify what was happening. After
several stumbling efforts, they used the process more frequently and the
issues became clarified. In this instance, the mediator kept demonstrating the process by paraphrasing their statements until they began to do
this themselves.

In the caucuses with each party, a mediator must provide frequent
message feedback to the persons involved. In this way, messages are tested, tried again, and the positions of each party can become more clear.

Many times in mediation the parties are in need of catharsis
because the stress and anger emerging from the dispute has blocked
their ability to deal with the actual issues. In such instances, message

feedback is less useful than when the parties are working on problems more soberly. Mediators should provide opportunities in both joint sessions and in caucuses for parties to release their anger without interference. Once the pressure has been released, they are more able to get down to business. During the catharsis, mediators may intervene with such statements as, "Sounds like you're really angry" or "I hear your anger." These statements are not message feedback in a technical sense but represent a more general type that allows the initiator to reflect on the nature of the messages being sent. Such statements also assure the party that the mediator understands his or her feelings and may even be able to empathize with them. (This level of intervention, however, is often dangerous unless it is couched in terms that do not suggest to the other side that the mediator is biased for or against him or her.)

Part of the problem in encouraging the parties to use message feedback occurs when the process seems to slow down the interaction and they become frustrated with each other. However, some ground rules can be established for mitigating against these potential problems. An example is the agreement that when one party feels that he or she is not being heard or listened to that he or she asks for message feedback from the other party. This agreement leads participants to be more open to each other and, after several attempts, their listening behavior appears to improve.

Throughout the mediation in the child custody case, the parties exhibited varying responses to efforts to use message feedback. When it seemed to interfere with or slow down their deliberations they avoided it, but when they each began to recognize the cues that indicated the other was not getting the message, they would try the process again (somewhat self-consciously). When it became apparent that they were again reverting to their old behaviors, the mediator suggested they needed some message feedback. This resulted in renewed efforts to provide message feedback.

One of the difficulties in introducing message feedback with persons who have known and been with each other over a long period of time is that they assume they understand what each other is saying. Quite often each believes that he or she knows what the other is thinking and feeling and behaves on his or her biased perceptions of the other. Although this may be the case in some instances, it generally is not the case by the time the parties come to the mediation.

Another resistance to message feedback occurs when a person is uncomfortable with hearing his or her own ideas returned. I have found this particularly critical in those instances in which parties are in a dominant power position over others and fear that others are attempting to gain power by using message feedback.

In mediation involving larger groups, such as labor-management disputes or environmental disputes, the parties usually are represented by professional advocates and the dynamics of the interaction are somewhat different from the one-to-one situation. In those instances, the advocates speak on behalf of their constituents and the immediate constituents are present. The messages being exchanged across the table are often sent mainly for the satisfaction of the constituency and not aimed necessarily at the counterpart across the table. They are designed to convince the constituency that the representative truly is speaking on its behalf, is strong, will not be swayed by the opponents, and can be depended on to get the best possible solution for them. During that type of interchange (often called "putting on a show"), message feedback is not very useful. It is when the parties get down to working out proposals and alternatives that the message feedback process becomes helpful.

When larger groups are involved, the message feedback process is particularly useful in the caucuses. As the constituent group and the spokesperson struggle with the issues, the members are involved in deliberations with each other and frequently need to clarify messages. The mediator can then introduce and encourage the use of message feedback through demonstration.

Message feedback is also very useful when the mediator carries proposals and counter-proposals from one group to another. The mediator can use message feedback to check whether a proposal is as the group wants it. Note the following dialogue which took place in a caucus with a union during a series of negotiations in mediation:

Mediator: What you're asking me to propose to the company is that all wages be increased by 3% retroactively. Have I got that right?

Team Member 1: We also said we wanted another holiday beginning next fiscal year.

Mediator: Okay, so we add the additional holiday to the 3% wage increase?

Team Member 2: Don't forget we want it next year.

Mediator: Which, the raise or the holiday?

Team Member 2: The holiday. We want the raise retroactively.

Mediator: You're asking for a wage increase of 3% retroactively plus an additional holiday beginning next fiscal year?

Team Members: That's it.

The mediator in this exchange fed back the information persistently until the group members were satisfied that he had it right. Under such conditions, it is very important that the mediator have the message clearly in mind before approaching the other party. When the mediator reports the demands to the other side in separate caucus, it is often useful to request message feedback from the group as a way of determining whether the proposal was received as intended. After all, one of the basic requirements for mediators is the ability to listen well.

In short, the mediation process provides an excellent opportunity for a mediator and the parties to use message feedback to facilitate reaching agreements. The amount of effort required by a mediator to get the parties to accept and use message feedback as part of their communication processes varies with the sophistication of the parties, the stage of the struggle, and conditions surrounding the mediation itself.

CONCLUSION

Message feedback has a number of advantages. It allows persons originating messages to check on the effects of their messages, to adjust and modify those messages when they do not fit the goals the messages were designed to satisfy, to change the message when it does not seem to come across to the listener, and so forth. Message feedback also provides receivers with opportunities to test their perception of what the message contained, to get clarification when the message seems unclear or incorrect, to acknowledge to the sender that the message has been received, and so forth.

There are, however, times when message feedback may not be appropriate. They include situations in which the parties have developed a working relationship over time in which they exchange messages accurately, the parties do not know how to use the process, the parties perceive the process as an attack on their ability, and when messages are of sufficient simplicity that they usually are not misperceived.

The message feedback process is best performed by persons who are basically good listeners. The process not only stimulates listening but serves notice to senders that someone is taking care to hear what they are saying. In the process of group decision making, the technique is most effective when all group members use it. That level of sophistication, however, is rare. The facilitator of a group, therefore, must be an effective user, regardless of whether he or she focuses on process facilitation, content facilitation, or both. In those groups in which effective facilitation takes place, the message feedback technique becomes accepted and used by the members.

Facilitators who seek to improve the communication of a group need to use the process regularly. Some facilitators use it almost exclusively for content matters, as it is more difficult to apply to process matters. For example, it is hardly possible to create significant message feedback about the quality of leadership being exhibited by a member nor is it functional to use message feedback in facilitative interventions dealing with the development of goals in group decision making and problem solving. In these situations, it can be used to reflect back those messages that deal with goals, and so on, which allows senders to check on whether their statements are as they want them to be. In this way, the facilitative intervention is useful to the group.

A basic factor in message feedback is that it deals with specific messages emanating from an individual to another person or to a group. To generalize a message from the accumulated behaviors of a group or from a collection of messages from an individual thus may not be subject to very effective message feedback. There simply may be too much to cover effectively.

The main forms of message feedback are paraphrase, reflection, questions about the content received, and actual behaviors consistent with the message request. The difference between response and message feedback must also be kept clear. Finally, message feedback is not a tool that can be used indiscriminately or without care and concern for the conditions of a group and its members. A facilitator who intervenes too frequently with such feedback will soon be ignored, whereas the facilitator who never uses it will soon find him- or herself functioning ineffectively.

Message feedback may take time but the correction and clarification that it provides more than compensates for the loss that would occur had such a process not been used. It is a viable and valuable process and facilitation technique that can be used effectively in almost any interpersonal or group situation.

6

Using SYMLOG as a Self-Analytical Group Facilitation Technique

Joann Keyton
The University of Memphis

An ongoing organizational group that develops processual problems has three options. First, the group can ignore the interactional difficulties that inhibit its goal attainment. Second, the group can turn to outside facilitative help to "fix" the group's problems. Finally, the group, with the help of an outside facilitator, can practice principles of self-analysis and empower itself to identify its interactional problems and enact procedures for continued group improvement. The third alternative is particularly useful when a work group is intact for a long period of time and does not have the authority to alter group membership.

The techniques of self-analytical groups have largely been developed in the social psychology discipline. One of these techniques, called the System for the Multiple Level Observation of Groups (SYMLOG) (Bales & Cohen, 1979), describes and analyzes group interaction by capturing perceptions of group interaction at both the individual and group levels. The goals of this chapter are to: (a) introduce and explain SYMLOG as a self-analytical group facilitation technique; (b) demonstrate its efficacy through a case description of an intervention that used SYMLOG[1]; and (c) provide recommendations for using SYMLOG as an intervention tool.

---

[1]This case study is based on the author's M.A. thesis (1985), directed by Victor D. Wall, Jr.

SYMLOG

SYMLOG was developed by Bales and Cohen (1979) as a theory and method for studying naturally occurring groups. It is a conceptualization, representation, and measurement of interaction built on personality variables that are exhibited in interpersonal interaction and group dynamics. The method allows a group to reflect on its interaction in order to better understand individual interactional differences and group interaction fields.

The works *Interaction Process Analysis* (Bales, 1950) and *Personality and Interpersonal Behavior* (Bales, 1970) provide the theoretical basis on which SYMLOG is built. Bales (1985) developed SYMLOG as a field theory of interpersonal behavior, seeing group members' interpersonal behavior as constituting "an interactive gestalt in which the parts flow together and influence each other systematically in such a way that some inclusive relatively simple pattern often emerges" (p. 1). As such, the theory assumes that the tendency to separate good from bad can be used to identify the unification or polarization of the group (Bales & Cohen, 1979). When group members are unified, they are clustered together in the *reference circle* (characterized typically as friendly and task-oriented). When a group is polarized, some of the members are perceived opposite the reference circle in the *circle of opposition* (characterized typically as unfriendly and task-oriented, or unfriendly and emotionally expressive). The circles identify those group members with similar interactional patterns. Contrasting the two circles helps to identify which group member or members would be most effective in bringing all group members into the reference circle in order to develop greater cohesiveness within the group. This comprehensive view of individual perceptual-evaluative fields and the inclusive social interaction field is one example of the advantages of field theory.

The SYMLOG Rating Method

The theoretical foundation of SYMLOG is based on the existence of three orthogonal dimensions of interaction: (a) dominance-submissiveness; (b) friendliness-unfriendliness; and (c) instrumentally controlled-emotionally expressive. The SYMLOG rating method is used in interventions in which a group ultimately will become responsible for monitoring its own progress. It is user-friendly and can be administered with minimal instruction (see Keyton & Wall, 1989, on the use of SYMLOG in organizational groups). Adjective phrases represent each dimension and dimensional combination, resulting in 26 items for the rating scale (see

Table 6.1). Group members rate retrospectively their own and other group members' behaviors based on a specific group interactional situation. SYMLOG encourages the comparison between individual and group perceptive fields because of the unique ability of this method to provide both by using the same three dimensions. This establishes a consistent framework for evaluating individual and collective interactional behavior within a group.

The ratings result in a *field diagram*, an image of a group as it

Table 6.1. SYMLOG Adjective Rating Phrases

U	Active, dominant, talks a lot	N	Unfriendly, negativistic
UP	Extroverted, outgoing, positive	NB	Irritable, cynical, won't cooperate
UPF	Purposeful, democratic task leader	B	Shows feelings and emotions
UF	Assertive, business-like manager	PB	Affectionate, likeable, fun to be with
UNF	Authoritarian, controlling, disapproving	DP	Looks up to others, appreciative, trustful
UN	Domineering, tough-minded, powerful	DPF	Gentle, willing to accept responsibility
UNB	Provocative, egocentric, shows off	DF	Obedient, works submissively
UB	Jokes around, expressive, dramatic	DNF	Self-punishing, works too hard
UPB	Entertaining, sociable, smiling, warm	DN	Depressed, sad, resentful, rejecting
P	Friendly, equalitarian	DNB	Alienated, quits, withdraws
PF	Works cooperatively with others	DB	Afraid to try, doubts own ability
F	Analytical, task-oriented, problem-solving	DPB	Quietly happy just to be with others
NF	Legalistic, has to be right	D	Passive, introverted, says little

Note: 0 = seldom/never; 1 = sometimes; 2 = always/often. Table reprinted from *SYMLOG: A System for the Multiple Level Observation of Groups* by Robert F. Bales and Stephen P. Cohen with the assistance of Stephen A. Williamson. © 1979 by the Free Press.

appears to its members—not an idealistic, prescriptive model of how the group should be. The three dimensions visually form a cube that is a "representation of a total theoretical space in which all possible types of behavior in groups can be represented" (Bales, 1988, p. 13) (see Figure 6.1). Although somewhat confusing to the uninitiated, SYMLOG dimensions are referred to by the mnemonic language of the measurement and by the conceptualization notation of U-D (dominance-submissiveness), P-N (friendliness-unfriendliness), and F-B (instrumentally controlled-emotionally expressive). The adjective phrases that represent the three

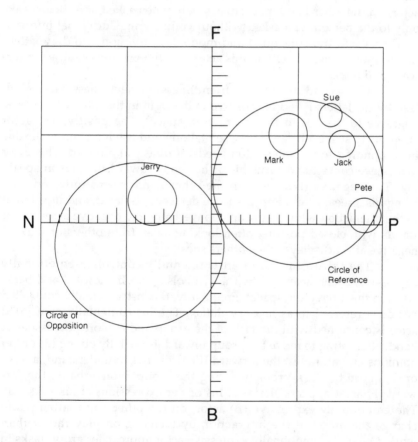

Note: Figure reprinted from *SYMLOG: A System for the Multiple Level Observation of Groups* by Robert F. Bales and Stephen P. Cohen with the assistance of Stephen A. Williamson. © 1979 by The Free Press. Adapted with the permission of the publisher.

Figure 6.1. Group Average Field Diagram of Initial Perceptions

dimensions were developed by Bales to correlate minimally with one another in order to enhance the independent nature of the dimensions. Additional support for the reliability and dimensional structure is provided by Polley, Hare, and Stone (1988).

The first dimension, dominance-submissiveness, is characterized by the U and D symbols (upward and downward in the interaction space). The dominant (U) actor takes the initiative in speaking, speaks loudly, holds the floor, and addresses the entire group rather than speaking specifically to individuals. Nonverbally, the dominant actor moves strongly and rapidly and can be rigid or stiff. The submissive (D) actor, on the other hand, participates only when asked and then speaks only to the person who asked without volunteering additional information. This actor remains quiet and motionless, trying not to draw attention to him- or herself. Often, this actor's body posture is contracted forward and inward.

The second dimension, friendliness-unfriendliness, is symbolized by the letters P and N (positive to the right in the interaction space; negative to the left in the interaction space). The positive (P) actor attempts to strike a balance between talking and listening and is flexible in responding to the interaction needs of others in a group. This actor makes eye contact and turns his or her body toward the person speaking. The negative (N) actor, on the other hand, seems unfriendly by being disagreeable and appears to be detached, isolated, and indifferent to the interaction within a group. Nonverbally, the negative actor sits or stands with closed posture, often looking away from others or making negative affect displays when others speak.

The third dimension, instrumentally controlled-emotionally expressive, is characterized by the symbols F and B (forward and backward in the interaction space). Frequently, the instrumentally controlled vector is referred to as *task orientation*. The instrumentally controlled actor is concerned with the task of the group and explores the issues at hand, attempting to move the group toward its goal. By giving his or her opinions and attitudes, the forward (F) actor tries to understand, assess, or diagnose the task problem facing the group. Nonverbally, the forward (F) actor appears alert, but his or her expressions are impersonal. The emotionally expressive (B) actor, on the other hand, attempts to change the mood of the interaction by focusing on play rather than work. Often, the emotionally expressive actor approaches group tasks in a creative and expressive manner rather than through reason and logic. Nonverbally, the emotionally expressive actor appears to be preoccupied with personal thoughts or feelings, but in an animated manner so that other group members are reminded vividly that activities other than the current task could be the focus of the group.

The rating process produces a numeric value that represents an actor's location on each dimension. Using the ratings as plotting points, each group member is placed on the field diagram to illustrate patterns of the recalled group interaction. Visually, the P-N dimension is displayed on the horizontal axis, and the F-B dimension is displayed on the vertical axis. The point at which these dimensions intersect provides the placement for a circle whose size represents the actors' U-D rating. Using the field diagram, actors can compare themselves in the three-dimensional interaction space and follow their movement in space over time.

SYMLOG dimensions and the rating methodology have been validated by many group researchers (e.g., Benjamin, 1974; Borgatta & Cottrell, 1955; Borgatta, Cottrell, & Meyer, 1956; Breiger & Ennis, 1979; Carter, 1954; Cattell, Saunders, & Stice, 1953; Forgas, 1978; Isenberg & Ennis, 1981; Leary, 1957; Solomon, 1981; Varghese, 1982; Wiggins, 1979; Wish, D'Andrade, & Goodnow, 1980; and Wish, Deutsch, & Kaplan, 1976). Findings from these studies show that the three SYMLOG dimensions are valid representations of actors' perceptions of interaction behavior. Assessments of SYMLOG have concluded that it captures the complexities of interpersonal relations among individuals as well as the emergent group structure that develops as roles, norms, coalitions, and subgroupings (Ichiyama & Reddy, 1987).

The Link between Communication Research and SYMLOG

Poole and Hirokawa (1986) point out that Bales's work is one of a handful that paid direct attention to interaction within a group context. For this reason, SYMLOG is extremely useful to communication researchers and practitioners. As Kelly and Duran (1992) note:

> SYMLOG was not created specifically as a theory of small group communication . . . we believe the system has much to offer teachers and scholars of communication . . . most appealing to communication specialists is the emphasis on group interaction and the developing relationships among group members. (p. 39)

For all of its strengths in describing interaction behavior, however, SYMLOG has received minimal attention in the communication literature. Of the few published studies, Wall and Galanes (1986) found that the P-N SYMLOG dimension correlated with group member satisfaction and perceived style of conflict management. As expected, they found that P-N was related negatively to the amount of conflict a group experienced. Wall and Galanes concluded that large dimensional dispersion within a group inhibits the quality of decisional outcomes. Cegala, Wall, and Rippey (1987) found that the U and P vectors of SYMLOG were related to those group members classified as highly involved on Cegala's interaction involvement scale and that SYMLOG essentially performed theoretically as expected. In studies specific to group decision making and communication, Kelly and Begnal (1984) found that SYMLOG was capable of tracing the interactional processes that give rise to group decisions, whereas Waagen (1984) used SYMLOG to discriminate between interaction that characterized group consensus and that which characterized group cohesion. Later, Keyton and Springston (1990) discovered that SYMLOG ratings did predict group cohesion as measured traditionally if the group was interacting in the friendly and instrumentally controlled (PF) quadrant of the field diagram.

SYMLOG as an Intervention Tool

As an intervention device, Schantz (1986) used SYMLOG in a work group in which a suspected drug addict was inhibiting the group's productivity, whereas Boethius (1987) used SYMLOG with administrative teams to diagnose group unification and polarization. Bales (1988) argues that using SYMLOG theory and methods "can produce remarkable increases in both direct knowledge and new insights. Leaders and members alike begin to see strategic ways to help the group move towards improved relationships and better performance" (p. 24). Returning diagrams to group members or displaying the group average diagram at a group meeting stimulates curiosity about individual members' behavior and interaction within the group. As an intervention, participants find the field diagrams easy to understand and easy to extrapolate to their group experience (Keyton & Wall, 1989).

Kressel (1987) noted that one of the advantages of SYMLOG is its compact and operational definition of target behaviors. Instead of removing the description of interaction behaviors from actors to observers, SYMLOG uses group members' ratings to reveal the overall pattern of behaviors. Wilson, Goodall, and Waagen (1986) argue that, "A participant observer has a definite advantage in knowing what group members are really saying while not disturbing the ordinary group interaction" (p. 222). SYMLOG has been recommended over other self-report measures composed of highly abstract traits (e.g., dominance) far removed from observable behavioral acts because it asks actors to rate 26 vectors of interpersonal behavior "that reflect a more concrete level of behavior" (Schneider, Schneider-Duker, & Becker-Beck, 1989, p. 478).

The SYMLOG Consulting Group (1986) believes that the rating and feedback processes improve the effectiveness of a group's teamwork. Specifically, group members can achieve the following objectives:

1. Will be able to discover and correct some misperceptions.
2. May recognize the reasons for some behavior not realized earlier.
3. Will very likely find some things that can be improved quite easily.
4. Will come to like one another more than less as they express their dissatisfactions and get to understand better the reasons for behavior they do not like about one another.
5. Will be able to express their appreciation and satisfaction for the things they like about their group and reinforce the effective teamwork operating in their group.
6. Will be able to formulate clearer conceptions as to how they want to behave and expect each other to behave.
7. Will be able to make some important decisions.
8. Will have their attention to the way the group operates raised to new levels.

THE INTERNAL MEDICINE RESIDENT GROUP

This intervention was developed for a group of internal medicine physicians in residency training at a 300-bed, urban osteopathic teaching hospital. The residency program is three years in length and has a long history at this hospital. The group was comprised of one third-year resident, five second-year residents, and two first-year residents who ranged in age from their mid-20s to mid-30s. These physicians had successfully completed their medical school education, interned in a general medicine program for a year, and passed their physician licensure exams.

Being a medical resident requires interacting in relational oxymorons. Although empowered to take responsibility and make life-altering decisions, a resident works within an environment in which the patient is responsible financially to the attending physician for services rendered by the resident and in which the nursing staff frequently is more familiar with the patient's case than is the resident. The power structure and reporting relationships of resident-attending and resident-nurse relationships give residents the difficult task of balancing relational needs, maintaining professional composure, and developing medical competence. It's no wonder, then, that stress and strain find their way into the interaction among residents and between that group and the attending physicians and the nursing staff.

This is a case description of an intervention into such dynamics. An internal medicine resident group asked for help in managing how they interacted with one another and with the attending and nursing staffs. The primary objective of the intervention was to improve the residents' internal group identity by identifying individual and group interactional problems. The secondary intervention objective was to strengthen the relationships between the resident group and the nursing staffs.

Sue[2] is the only senior resident of the group and the only female resident in recent history. She was elected unanimously by the rest of the group to represent them as chief resident. In this role she sets rotation and on-call schedules. She is the facilitator of the group and the primary contact person when problems occur. Historically, hospital administrators have left management of the group to the chief resident. Jack, Pete, and Mark are second-year residents who were with this program last year as first-year residents. Joe and Tim are second-year residents who transferred into the program at the beginning of the resident year. The first-year residents, Kevin and Bob, both interned at this hospital and are familiar with the other residents and the task demands of residents in this hospital. Once they were accepted into the residency program (four months prior to beginning the residency program), they began to interact with the resident group socially and professionally.

The group's primary task is to learn the subspecialties of internal medicine. To that end, the group provides medical services for the hospital by satisfying the role of primary physician for night, weekend, and holiday on-call coverage for the intensive care and the critical care units (ICU/CCU). First-year residents do the most call, whereas third-year residents do the least. However, each resident does the same amount of weekend call. Each resident is also assigned to a different physician for a month-long period. Although assigned to different physicians, these attending physicians may be in the same subspecialty, and the residents see one another on a regular basis in the hospital. As a group, the residents do not have any other group tasks except to provide education for themselves. Because patient care must be continuous, and several residents may provide health care for any one patient, the sharing of information must be coordinated at every shift or rotation change. The group also meets every morning for reports on the status of patients. To satisfy the educational requirements, the group meets once a week at night after normal duty in a journal club to discuss the latest medical literature. Scheduling and other problems are discussed at monthly meetings. Here, residents discuss problems with attending physicians, police their own behavior (assigning penalties for being late or missing ICU/CCU coverage), and examine new educational programs.

The Hospital Environment

In the past, this resident program had 10 members, and schedules and

---

[2]Names of the residents have been changed.

physician coverage were created for this level of staffing. Even though the hospital administrators and the attending physician staff knew that only eight residents would participate in next year's residency program, nothing had been communicated to the residents to reflect different performance expectations. Compounding the reduction in residency slots, the hospital required that this resident group also cover the ICU of its satellite suburban hospital. This reduction in staff increased interaction tension. Because there are fewer residents to provide coverage, the second- and third-year residents are on-call more hours this year, thus removing a perk of seniority.

The resident group is an example of a human service team—a group in which performance "ultimately depends on the degree to which clients are better off for having experienced members' ministrations" (Hackman, 1990, p. xix). As evidenced in studies of other human service teams (i.e., Perkins, Shaw, & Sutton, 1990), this group displayed three endemic tensions of such groups: (a) a struggle for control; (b) conflict over efficient versus quality service; and (c) the act of balancing client needs and team member needs. These tensions exist due to the group's permeable boundaries with the nursing and attending physician groups within the larger organizational environment (see Putnam & Stohl, 1990). Interaction with these other organizational groups causes the resident group to continuously cycle its members into other temporary, but often repeating, subgroups of residents, nurses, and attendings to make medical decisions and provide medical care.

The Interaction Environment

The interaction environment of the hospital requires residents to make effective life-saving decisions. Two primary factors affecting resident interaction are decision-making style and inequity; both illustrate the group's interdependence with their organizational context.

Decision-making style.

The decision-making process used by residents, critical to patient care, is the primary factor on which they evaluate one another. Janis and Mann (1977) describe the decision-making process as a psychological analysis of conflict, choice, and commitment. Residents make decisions within the stressful hospital environment in the presence of their peer group, the nursing staff who carry out their orders, and attendings who evaluate their decisions. Residents frequently seek the advice and recommendations of other residents; less frequently and directly, they seek the advice of the nursing staff. Once a resident makes a decision, the decision is conveyed to the nursing staff and to other residents assisting in procedures. Residents are also required to communicate and justify patient-care decisions to attending physicians. According to Janis and Mann (1977), the psychological stress experienced by residents within this type of setting imposes limitations on the rationality of decisions.

From a functional aspect, the residents exist in the hospital to make decisions in place of attending physicians. Given the congested layout of ICU/CCU and the crisis nature of decisions to be made, patient-care decisions were not made in isolation. The decisions of these group members frequently received a wider audience as the hospital was a teaching one, and other residents, interns, and medical students were present to watch and learn.

A review of the medical decision-making literature indicates that effective medical decisions are based on the assumption that they are made rationally, logically, and are void of emotion (Bergman & Pantell, 1984; Politser, 1981; and Pozen, Lerner, D'Agostino, Belanger, & Buckley, 1982). Quick, Moorhead, Quick, Gerloff, Mattox, and Mullins (1983) identify consensual decision making as the most effective style in medical situations. Typically, when the situation is complex or ambiguous, the decision process becomes progressively more group-oriented as other medical personnel provide input to develop sound clinical judgment. A sound clinical decision is operationalized as the efforts of a physician to achieve the most favorable outcome possible in light of available information and resources. In SYMLOG parlance, residents making effective medical decisions would be perceived as being dominant, positive, and emotionally controlled (UPF).

Inequity.

Inequity is an issue for residents in two ways. First, residents on night and weekend call have to make up for other residents who have not completed customarily prescribed medical procedures during the day shift. This problem increases the work load and the perception of inequity for the resident on-call whose primary responsibility is to deal with medical emergencies. Second, residents also evaluate inequity as to who is doing procedures correctly with a minimal amount of supervision from attending physicians. Residents fear that those who seek excessive procedural assistance from their attending physician will cause other residents to lose privileges.

THE INITIAL INTERVENTION

The initial intervention was designed to introduce the SYMLOG feedback process to the resident group. The first ratings were completed in

May, three months prior to the new resident year.

Expectations of the Feedback and Intervention Process

The intervention and interaction feedback process were intended to provide information about the functioning of the resident group. The only other feedback residents received were individual evaluations from attending physicians. Although it would have been ideal for attendings to rate the residents, they declined to participate in the study. Their decision not to participate is in line with their autonomous management style.

This initial rating period provided a baseline for identifying group interactional patterns that the resident group wanted to change. This first rating period was important, not only for sanctioning the continuation of the intervention, but for the residents as well. The current chief resident was not well liked. Sue had already been elected as chief resident and she, as well as the other residents, voiced publicly their intentions to develop into a more harmonious group. The first ratings occurred after the majority of the residents had been to an educational meeting. Residents rated themselves first and then the other members of the group. The objective of the first rating was to "test" this feedback procedure with the residents and to introduce group development and feedback about group development as useful tools for creating a cohesive group.

As expected for this type of group, all members saw themselves as being emotionally controlled and task-oriented (F). The instrumentally controlled (F) vector taps into purposeful leader action, assertive management, authoritarian and controlling interaction, insistency, and willingness to accept responsibility (see Figure 6.1). For this group, the highest F score was 11.4; the lowest was 0.4. The nature of the job requires this instrumentally controlled interaction even if a resident's personal interaction style is more emotionally expressive. An emotionally expressive style simply would not be viewed as appropriate physician behavior by attending physicians or as effective in the crisis setting of the ICU/CCU.

Sue was seen as the most forward member (11.4). Although her official term as chief resident did not start until August, Sue had been working for some time on schedules and proposals for changes for the coming resident year. The other most forward members were Mark and Jack (7.8 and 8.0, respectively) who, at this point, were both first-year residents. Mark was perceived by the group as the medical expert, and his command of the literature was so complete that others used him as their reference source. Besides being task-oriented, Mark was considered the most dominant member with the exception of the current chief resident. His knowledge base provided him the opportunity to speak for the group and to hold the floor in group interaction. Jack also served as a reference for the group because in addition to the DO degree, he had earned a PhD in physiology. Although respected, he was not as talkative or purposefully active as Mark.

The most striking feature of the first rating was that Jerry, the current chief resident, was perceived in the negative or unfriendly side of the field diagram and thus polarized opposite the rest of the group. Jerry's leadership style contributed to these ratings. The other residents described Jerry as biased, domineering, abusive, and pushy. As a result, Jerry was perceived negatively (6.3N), whereas the other group members were perceived positively (an 11.0P average). The group clearly perceived Jerry to be at odds with the group, primarily because he administered decisions from an authoritarian position without consulting the other residents or including them in the decision-making process. The other residents commented that what Jerry accomplished was acceptable in content, but the manner he used to get there was not acceptable.

Sue recognized the potential negativity that comes with the role of chief resident. This prompted her proactive approach in working on schedules in conjunction with the other residents. Additionally, Sue announced that decision procedures would change to include more group decision making. She did not want to end up in the interaction position (UNF) Jerry had developed for himself. Part of Sue's self-designed strategy as the only female in the group and as the chief resident following Jerry was to be less dominant and to be perceived as one of the group, not apart from the group. She believed her leadership potential would be maximized by being a less aggressive leader than Jerry.

The Individual Field Diagrams

The individual field diagrams for each resident, except Pete, were similar to the group average field diagram. For example, although the other residents saw Jerry as polarized against the group, Pete perceived the entire group to be clustered in the positive side of the space. Overall, there were minimal variations in perceptions, but the same general interactional patterns existed.

Reaction to the Initial Intervention

The facilitator met with the residents at a monthly business meeting to present the results of the first SYMLOG ratings. The individual residents' field diagram and the group average field diagram were delivered back to each resident with notes from the facilitator about group strengths and weaknesses. She prompted their responses and suggested that the group would receive valuable feedback from continuing the intervention. Sue, the chief resident, monitored reactions to and subsequent comments about the initial ratings. Generally, the process was seen positively because it provided confirmation that Jerry was a negative force in the group. In her role as chief resident, Sue requested that the facilitator provide the intervention and feedback in August once the work group was operating officially. The group as a whole agreed to continue; however, only three of the residents (Sue, Mark, and Pete) appeared eager. The new residents (Kevin and Bob) agreed to participate, but more out of peer pressure from the more senior residents than from their own interest. Joe and Tim joined the group after this session and agreed to participate at Sue's request. Jack was the lone group member who did not want to continue with the project; he even tried to redirect this conversation. Jack indicated that although the feedback was informative, medicine was the real issue of the group's meeting and should take precedence over any other topic or task.

THE INTERVENTION

Introducing SYMLOG

At the next meeting, the facilitator introduced SYMLOG as a theory of interaction behavior and explained the three dimensions to the residents. The facilitator explained how it would be possible for the group to use SYMLOG to describe its interaction and analyze individual interactional patterns and those of the group to help each individual and the group reach their interaction potential. Group members were told that the objective of such a process was to judge their own interaction effectiveness and to learn to emphasize effective behaviors and to refrain from ineffective behaviors.

Residents were cautioned that SYMLOG was not a personality analysis. Rather, any analysis of why they behaved the way they did would be left to them, and this was part of the group's learning. Although the dimensions of SYMLOG are relevant to psychoanalytic concepts, the focus is not on why someone interacts in a dominant fashion, for example, but what dominant interaction exists and what happens in the group as a result of that dominant interaction.

The residents were encouraged to recognize that all interaction represented by the three dimensions were naturally occurring behaviors. To offset the notion frequently held that all group members should be rated similarly, several illustrations were given. Although the stereotype for an effective group frequently assumes that all group members should strive to be rated as slightly dominant, friendly, and instrumentally controlled (UPF), a group in which members interact too similarly could become immobile. A group with members who are too friendly, for example, could fall into a pattern of "groupthink." A group without members who interact in an emotionally expressive manner may be missing out on the ability to be innovative or creative in solving problems. Or, a group with too many dominant members may find themselves in constant battle. Thus, each group must find its own effective interactional patterns which are, in turn, dependent on the group members themselves, the group task, and the environment in which the group operates. Whereas some interactional patterns are more effective than others—and that is what SYMLOG can help groups discover—contemporary group effectiveness models (Hackman, 1990) do not prescribe that all groups need to interact in one way. Groups should be looking for the fit of the interaction to the situation and the objectives of the group.

The Feedback Process

Residents filled out the SYMLOG adjective rating form four times at about 5-week intervals. Several ratings are desirable because SYMLOG is most useful as an intervention tool after participants have become accustomed to the rating and feedback processes. Trust in the rating methodology and feedback procedures encourages participants to rate themselves and each other truthfully and honestly.

The first ratings were made in August as the resident group began operation officially under the new chief resident; the last rating was completed prior to the Thanksgiving holiday. Each time, residents received a copy of their own individual field diagram, a copy of the group average diagram, and a written analysis of both diagrams. The analyses included the researcher's interpretation of the diagrams, identifications of relationships with potential for conflict, and similarities and dissimilarities in perceived interactional patterns. Residents were not required and, to the knowledge of the facilitator, did not share their individual field diagrams with one another. Each time field diagrams were distributed back to the residents, the facilitator extended an invitation to meet with individuals to discuss the diagrams, and on several occasions, residents asked for these sessions. The facilitator also met with the resident group to discuss the group diagrams.

Because of the problems between the ICU/CCU nursing staff and last year's resident group, Sue asked the shift supervisors of nursing at both hospitals to participate in rating the residents on the adjective rating form after each resident had rotated through the ICU/CCU monthly rotation (November). The issue of which group controlled the ICU/CCU had surfaced during the last year. Residents believed that they should control the interaction and procedures of these units because, as a result of their scheduled coverage, they made most of the patient-care decisions. Attendings, however, believed that they should control the units because these were their patients, and the nursing staff believed that they should control the units because they were the group assigned permanently to patient care. The ratings made by the nursing staff were introduced in the last feedback session.

Results of the Feedback Sessions

The feedback sessions revolved around the displayed group average field diagram; these are the basis for the descriptions below. Examples of individual field diagrams and how they differed are explained for Rating Periods 2, 3, and 4.

Rating Period 1.

At this rating period, the resident group was operating as a new social and professional entity; Joe and Tim had yet to join the group, however. This first rating of Kevin identified him as extremely submissive (6.0D). From the group average field diagram, some group members changed slightly from the initial rating. Sue became more instrumentally controlled (13.9F) as she assumed official duties for the group but remained positive in the eyes of the other residents. Perceptions of Mark became less positive (4.0P). Pete's and Jack's positions essentially were unchanged. The group was unified, interacting in the UPF quadrant of the interactive space, which the SYMLOG Consulting Group has identified as the effective teamwork quadrant.

Rating Period 2.

At this rating period, the entire resident group was now intact. As a group, all members were unified within the effective teamwork quadrant. Sue's position was the most positive (16.0P) of the group, whereas Pete was seen as more instrumentally controlled (3.6F) than in the first rating period. Jack was less positive (9.0P) and more instrumentally controlled (8.4F) than in Period 1. Although still submissive (4.7D), Joe was positive (11.9P) and moderately instrumentally controlled (7.5F). Tim was submissive (3.0D), moderately friendly (6.9P) and slightly instrumentally controlled (4.4F).

As examples of individual differences in field diagrams, Pete perceived the group members as more unified in the friendly vector of the space and not as task-oriented in comparison to other residents' perceptions. More striking was Mark's perceptions of the group's interaction. His images of group members stretch across the entire friendly-unfriendly dimension (from 16P to 11N) and throughout the task-oriented vector (0.0 to 17.0F). He rated Sue as most intense (17F) and rated Kevin and Tim neutral (0.0F) on the task-oriented vector.

Rating Period 3.

Perceptions at the group level showed that the group members were relatively unchanged in relationship to one another. All members were still unified within the effective teamwork quadrant, but the group as a whole, however, was less instrumentally controlled (see Figure 6.2).

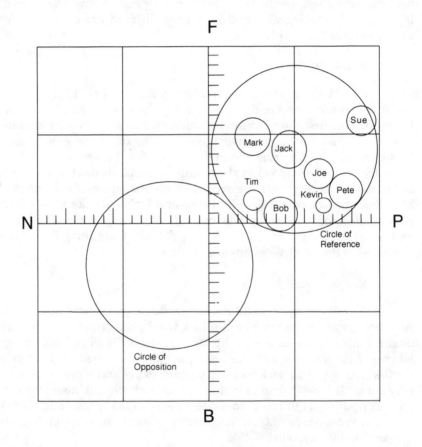

Note: Figure reprinted from *SYMLOG: A System for the Multiple Level Observation of Groups* by Robert F. Bales and Stephen P. Cohen with the assistance of Stephen A. Williamson. © 1979 by The Free Press. Adapted with the permission of the publisher.

Figure 6.2. Group Average Field Diagram at Intervention Time 3

Using Pete and Mark as examples of individual differences, both group members perceived the group's interaction as scattered widely. This time Pete perceived group members as being polarized along the friendly-unfriendly dimension (16P to 9N), whereas some group members were perceived in the emotionally expressive vector (see Figure 6.3). Mark's perceptions also stretch the width of the friendly-unfriendly dimension, with some group members seen as being emotionally expressive (see Figure 6.4). Although they perceived the same general group interactional pattern, each perceived Sue and Bob occupying critically different interaction positions which reflected their individual relationships with those residents.

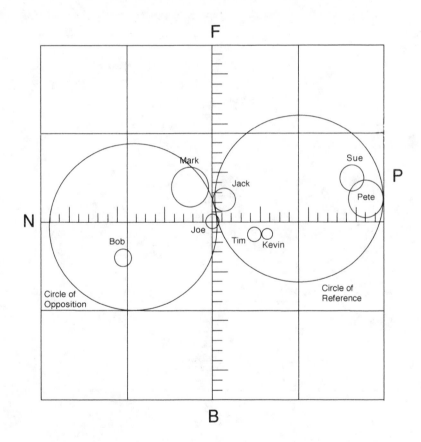

Note: Figure reprinted from SYMLOG: A System for the Multiple Level Observation of Groups by Robert F. Bales and Stephen P. Cohen with the assistance of Stephen A. Williamson. © 1979 by The Free Press. Adapted with the permission of the publisher.

Figure 6.3. Pete's Individual Field Diagram at Intervention Time 3

Rating Period 4.

This rating period was where the performance problems of one resident began to surface. Although the other group members clustered together, Tim was perceived as separate from the group because he was the least intense on the friendly (2.9P) and the instrumentally controlled vectors (0.2F). Tim's position was now in the circle of opposition. Viewing Tim's polarized position helped the group understand that ineffective interaction with one group member could disrupt their entire communication network with one another and their interactions with other medical groups.

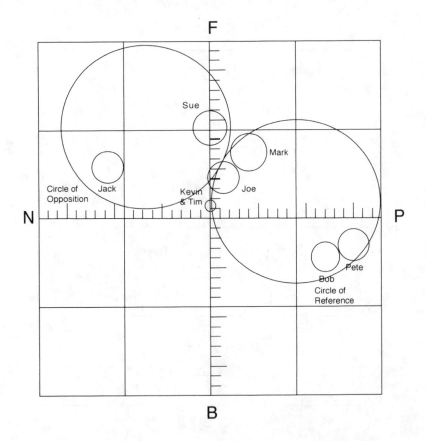

Note: Figure reprinted from *SYMLOG: A System for the Multiple Level Observation of Groups* by Robert F. Bales and Stephen P. Cohen with the assistance of Stephen A. Williamson. © 1979 by The Free Press. Adapted with the permission of the publisher.

Figure 6.4. Mark's Individual Field Diagram at Intervention Time 3

Ironically, Tim perceived his own interaction quite differently than did the other residents. Tim perceived himself to be dominant, friendly, and task-oriented (UPF). Bob, however, perceived Tim's interaction as submissive, negative, and very emotionally expressive (DNB). Tim clustered perceptions of himself and other residents in the PF quadrant, whereas Bob's perception made use of all four quadrant vectors.

Interaction with the Nursing Staffs

One of the objectives of the intervention was to repair interaction with the nursing staffs. Residents spend most of their on-call duty in the ICU/CCU. Besides providing evening and weekend coverage for these units, each resident rotates through the ICU/CCU for at least three months each resident year. Decisions made here typically are crisis-oriented (as in the event of a cardiac arrest). Due largely to the types of decisions made in this environment and the autonomy the hospital and attending physicians gave to the resident group, residents saw the ICU/CCU as their responsibility.

Approximately 75% of the nursing staff agreed to participate in the study. Thirteen nurses from CCU and 11 from the adjoining ICU represented the nursing staff at the main teaching hospital, and 8 nurses from the ICU at the satellite hospital also participated. All shifts were represented; no attempt was made to control for proportional representation because many nurses alternated between shift assignments. To determine their perceptions of the residents, the ICU/CCU units at each of the hospitals rated the resident group. Nurses rated the residents based on their most recent interaction with them; the ratings occurred just prior to the residents' final rating of themselves.

Ratings of critical care nursing staff.

Although overall this group of nurses perceived the resident group as positive and instrumentally controlled, there were some exceptions. Tim was perceived as unfriendly (3.4N), whereas Bob and Pete were not seen as instrumentally controlled (0.1F and 0.2B, respectively). Otherwise, the other residents were perceived as instrumentally controlled (2.4F to 9.0F). Sue was the most friendly (16.1P), and Mark was the least friendly (3.4P). This nursing staff perceived the group unified in the PF (friendly, task-oriented) quadrant, except for Tim, who was positioned in the circle of opposition (DNF).

Ratings of intensive care nursing staff.

This group of nurses perceived the resident group similarly to the critical care unit with two exceptions. In this unit, Bob was perceived the least favorably (2.9P), whereas Tim was perceived more favorably (4.0P) than in the other unit. Otherwise, the resident group was unified in the PF quadrant, and the dynamics among the other residents were basically the same.

Ratings of intensive care suburban staff.

There were several exceptions to be noted in the ratings of this nursing group. Tim was seen as submissive (1.3D), unfriendly (0.5N), and emotionally expressive (0.6B), and in the circle of opposition, polarized from the the rest of the residents. This group of nurses perceived Pete as the least friendly (11.2P). These differences may be due to the differences in the working environment. In this unit, residents were isolated from other residents and frequently on their own in making medical decisions. Thus, different interactional patterns are likely to surface.

The Final Feedback Meeting

The final feedback was delivered to the residents at one of their monthly evening meetings. Sue gave residents less than 24 hours notice for the meeting and did not inform them that it was also a feedback session. (Facilitator's note: I did not feel that these deceptive techniques were called for. It had been my experience that the group was responding well to the diagrams and was curious about them to the point that they were engaging in self-analysis of the group. However, Sue insisted that the meeting be handled in this fashion.)

The meeting began with Sue's agenda of business issues. The residents appeared surprised that some of these issues were worthy as topics of discussion. A second problem was that Tim did not attend the meeting. He had not checked out of the hospital but had failed to answer pages. Other residents perceived him as having little excuse for not attending. Finally, he appeared as the business portion was concluding. Unfortunately for the group, his performance was one of the topics of discussion.

An attending physician had complained about Tim's decision making and asked the resident group to establish policy so that the problem would not reoccur. The group knew who the offender was and spoke of the problem as being an individual's problem, but did not identify Tim specifically. His offense caused the others to feel deceived because policy changes were being considered. Once Tim appeared at the meeting, however, no one mentioned these changes. At the conclusion of the business meeting, another resident asked Sue to summarize all the important issues so that Tim would know what happened. When she got to the policy change, she glossed over the problem as a group problem with a long history. She summarized the policy change with little direct focus on Tim. The other residents appeared nervous as Sue approached this part of the meeting and withdrew nonverbally from the interaction.

The meeting was then turned over to the facilitator for the last set of residents' SYMLOG ratings of one another and the nursing staffs' SYMLOG ratings. Large field diagrams from the three nursing units were displayed. The residents became quiet as they made two types of comparisons: (a) comparing their individual locations from each nursing unit, and (b) comparing how the nursing staff rated them in comparison to the other residents.

Reactions to nursing ratings.

The high internal reliability coefficients (.89 to .97) from the nursing staffs' ratings indicated that the residents' interaction was perceived similarly. Overall, the nursing staff perceived residents as being slightly dominant, positive, and only slightly instrumentally controlled. The low F scores surprised the residents as they expected these ratings to be much higher because they perceived themselves as managing the ICU/CCUs. The facilitator pointed out that the nurses may not share this perception because the residents rotated through the units sharing responsibility for patient care among them, whereas the nurses provided more continuous care over time. Prior to distributing the nurses' ratings, the residents expected to be rated less positively by the nurses because they admitted they became overly task-oriented, negative, and emotionally explosive in the crises that developed in the ICU/CCUs. Although the residents did not receive formal, direct evaluation from the nursing staff, nursing staff input about the residents did find its way to the attending physician staff. More importantly, negative interaction among residents and nurses resulted in a negative performance cycle in which nurses became more resistant to carrying out residents' orders.

The resident group was, therefore, relieved that the nurses perceived them so positively, and they attributed this to the fact that they were trying to get along with the nursing staff by treating their patient care opinions as valid options and by recognizing that their familiarity with patients was crucial to obtaining information in making medical decisions. From the nurses' ratings of the residents, it appeared that the control issue was more salient to the residents than to the nurses. The residents felt that they were being trained to walk into the ICU/CCU and take control from the nurses. Their identification with the control issue may be compensation for their inadequacies of not knowing patients as well as the nurses did.

The group talked about the differences between this resident group and last year's resident group with the nursing staff. At this point, the facilitator pulled out of the conversation and let the residents take over the analysis and discussion of interacting with the nursing staff. The discussion moved eventually from comparing last year's to this year's resident group to examining the residents' behavior with the present nursing staff. Encouraged by the facilitator, the residents were able to determine what they were doing to develop and maintain positive interaction with the nurses. This discussion thus represented a significant step in group empowerment.

Reactions to self-ratings.

This conversation chained into the residents' feelings about their own SYMLOG ratings. Tim broke the ice by stating that the diagrams let him know what others thought of him. He felt that knowing others' honest reactions to him would help him to be more open in the future. Kevin, typically seen as very submissive, said, "There I am, that little circle again!" His remark evoked laughter from the group and he grinned, appearing to realize that this remark was not submissive.

The facilitator summarized the progress of the group's discussion. Suggestions developed by the residents to manage effective interaction included: encouraging social interaction; expressing concern for other residents as people rather than physicians; expressing dissatisfaction with others' behavior when annoyances occurred rather than suppressing the annoyance; and expressing appreciation for favors other residents did for one another.

Accomplishments of the Intervention

The primary objective of the intervention was to improve internal group identity by diagnosing interactional problems; the intervention was somewhat successful in this regard. Through the feedback process, residents finally were using the diagrams as a basis for improving their interactional patterns. Although it took a substantial length of time (four months) for residents to become involved actively and willing to use the feedback to recognize ineffective interactional patterns, the facilitator believes that this particular group could not have moved through the process more quickly. The group members were not accustomed to generating or receiving feedback about their interaction and had taken the intervention on in addition to their other group and individual tasks. It took this period of time for the group to become comfortable with the process and to recognize that identifying interactional problems was more beneficial than ignoring them.

The secondary objective was to strengthen residents' relationships with the nursing staff. Although hesitant initially to have the nursing staffs rate them, feedback from the nurses indicated that the relationships among nurses and residents were not as strained as the residents believed. This feedback provided a useful benchmark for the residents and encouraged them to seek interaction actively with the nursing staffs.

RECOMMENDATIONS FOR USING
SYMLOG IN INTERVENTIONS

Before introducing a specific feedback technique, a facilitator should consider several issues. First, the facilitator must consider whether the design of the intervention is relevant to the needs of the client group. In other words, whose agenda will be met by the intervention process? A group will reject feedback if it does not meet its needs. Facilitators also need to gauge how much information individuals and a group can handle. If a group interacts in a context void of regular feedback or one in which feedback is always negative, then the feedback process must be introduced slowly. If learning is to occur, the facilitator must make sure that resources for ongoing coaching and other group resources are available to or within the group.

Before using SYMLOG as an intervention device, the theory and its methodology must be introduced to group members. Doing so decreases levels of anxiety as participants recognize that they are measuring their own behavior rather than having it assessed by someone outside their interactive context. As such, participants need to understand that individual perceptions will be different and need to understand why differences exist. The facilitator must help the participants understand that each member's view of the group's interaction is valid. Those familiar with SYMLOG and its feedback process as an intervention tool recognize that SYMLOG is strongest when the facilitator simply guides the description process and encourages group members to provide their own evaluation.

The facilitator should discuss the advantages and disadvantages of anonymity, but allow participants to decide the level of anonymity with which they are comfortable. As group members become more comfortable with the SYMLOG feedback process, it is likely that they will drop most anonymous procedures. When the tension of anonymity is relieved, group members are more able and willing to integrate their self-generated feedback into their individual and group learning. This tension must be resolved by group members if they are to use self-analytical techniques effectively after the facilitator has left the group.

Facilitators also need to plan the scheduling of rating and feedback sessions. Ratings should be completed immediately after important group meetings. Feedback sessions should not be too close together; otherwise, change will not be recognized in the field diagrams. Bales and Cohen (1979) recommend that ratings be made several times about a month apart so that changes can be traced.

Impact of the Group Average Field Diagram as a Feedback Tool

SYMLOG methodology was developed initially to provide feedback to self-analytical groups. Recommendations for facilitating feedback are from that perspective, but can be adapted to other settings. Bales and Cohen (1979) believe that the group average field diagram is the most useful summary of ratings information for feedback to a group:

> It can hardly fail to make salient some of the most important things about the group and the constellation of relationships in it. The facts revealed are likely to compel attention, and often a large degree of consensus as to their truth, since they represent, after all, the average of the perceptions of all the members. (p. 308)

Although the field diagram may point out information that individuals do not welcome, it acts as a beacon for bringing issues that are otherwise not discussed to the surface. The group average field diagram also provides a benchmark for individuals as they examine their own field diagram.

When field diagrams are part of a group's feedback process, new insights and inferences are likely to develop. In introducing the diagrams, the facilitator should help group members understand that the diagrams do not represent "some absolute hidden truth" (Bales & Cohen, 1979, p. 308), but are the group members' perceptions of their own interaction and that "inferences made from the data are only heuristic hypotheses" (p. 308) which must be validated as useful points of reference. If the facilitator can introduce feedback in this type of tentative and inquiring spirit, group members are more likely to participate in a process of discovery about themselves and their group.

Facilitators should recognize that there are many appropriate methods for providing feedback to groups. Selection of the feedback strategy should be based on the objective to be accomplished and the willingness and ability of group members to participate in the feedback and intervention process. Facilitators need to use tact and sensitivity in introducing field diagram locations, particularly if group members fall in the unfriendly vector (and sometimes in the emotionally expressive vector). Facilitators should also encourage group members to take over the description and analysis of the interaction. This can be accomplished by asking group members how they react to the ratings, what they think the ratings mean, if the ratings are a good reflection of the group's interaction process, and how the group should proceed. The more group members share in and own the analysis of their group's interaction, the more likely the feedback process will develop into learning that affects group member behavior.

The group average field diagram has both advantages and disadvantages in providing feedback to group members. As an advantage, individual positions are hidden from the group, thereby minimizing personal attacks. Hiding individual perceptions of interaction behavior, however, prevents group members from receiving honest and constructive feedback about others' perceptions of them. In rating periods in which individual perceptions differ substantially, the group average field diagram loses its potency by averaging extreme locations from both poles of the same dimension. This disadvantage is particularly important to the interpretation of the P-N (friendly-unfriendly) dimension, which tends to be the location of personal and group conflicts. If the entire group engages in the conflict, variation in perceptions is minimized and identification of the conflict via the diagram is less problematic. However, if dyadic or subgroup conflicts develop in the group, these tensions can be hidden by the group average locations. Using the group average field diagram can diminish the impact of an intervention if the objective is to repair strained interaction relationships or to develop positive relationship links.

Individuals should have access to their individual field diagrams, and the decision to share them with others belongs to them. The facilitator in this case encouraged residents to discuss their individual perceptual differences by talking about (not showing) how their individual diagram differed from the group diagram. To initiate these discussions, the facilitator highlighted the importance of individual differences and discussed her own diagram of the group's interaction and how it differed from the average group diagram. If these differences do not surface to the group level of interaction, they can continue to be a source of irritation and possibly disrupt group cohesiveness and effective group interactional patterns.

CONCLUSION

This case study illustrates the complexities of introducing a feedback system into an organizational group context in which feedback about group interaction does not occur normally. The further removed a group is from a culture of organizational learning, the longer it will take for group members to accept and use feedback techniques. The time it takes to establish such techniques, however, can be worthwhile if the group adopts the feedback technique and learns to facilitate its own learning. The more a group owns its intervention, the more likely the learning will take hold.

As a feedback technique, SYMLOG is grounded in a theory and methodology that provides descriptive and diagnostic help for groups with interactional problems. Its primary advantages are that the feedback instrument is accepted easily by organizational groups and the process can be taught to groups so that they can continue group development with minimal guidance from the facilitator. After all, the primary objective of self-analytical techniques is for the facilitator to remove him- or herself from describing and diagnosing group interaction and for the group to take over these responsibilities.

This case study demonstrates that group members are able to develop the skills of group facilitation over a period of time. Group members incorporated what they learned from the feedback sessions into their behavior and into the interpretation of their behavior, thus undoing problematic behavior and leading them to more effective levels of group interaction.

PART IV

The Focus Group Technique: Generating Information About Respondents for Communication Campaigns

The techniques discussed so far have focused on how facilitators help groups interact better for the purpose of accomplishing group members' goals. Sometimes, however, group interaction is facilitated in order to accomplish researchers' goals. In applied communication research, for example, researchers often are interested in obtaining information from a particular group that they can use in designing persuasive messages aimed at members of that, or other, groups.

One popular method for obtaining relevant and revealing information about the beliefs, experiences, and needs of specific populations is the *focus group method*. In a focus group, a small number of people are interviewed by a facilitator in a relatively unstructured discussion about a specific topic. The interaction generated in focus groups stimulates the sharing of relevant ideas, encourages self-disclosure, and helps facilitate group problem solving. Such information can then be applied to address important problems these populations face. The chapters in this section explain the procedures and dynamics of focus groups and show how they generate information that can prove useful in designing persuasive messages for communication campaigns.

In Chapter 7, Kreps describes the benefits of using focus groups in health communication inquiry and identifies important guidelines for conducting effective focus group discussions. Strategies are examined for selecting individuals to participate in focus groups, facilitating group interaction, preserving group interaction, and evaluating focus group data. These strategies are exemplified in the presentation of two applied communication field studies that employed focus groups to generate data for directing health promotion efforts. In the first study, focus

175

groups were used to gather information about public perceptions and attitudes toward an urban substance abuse center for the purpose of identifying strategies for increasing public acceptance, support, and utilization of the program. In the second study, focus groups were used to refine the development and implementation of media messages (posters) for preventing the spread of sexually transmitted diseases within a university community. Kreps concludes by pointing out how focus group discussions enhance organizational reflexivity, enabling program administrators to see the strengths and weaknesses in their systems.

In Chapter 8, Bormann, Bormann, and Harty report the results of a study designed to use fantasy theme analysis with focus group interviews to discover the rhetorical visions of a group of teenage tobacco users regarding smoking and chewing. Their chapter begins with an explanation of symbolic convergence theory (SCT) and then explains a special kind of focus group interview technique based on this theory that is designed to examine the shared stories or dramatizations and to discover the clustering of attitudes, opinions, images, and feelings into coherent rhetorical visions of experience. Six SCT-based focus group interviews were conducted with teenagers who smoked or chewed tobacco. The psychographic analysis from these focus group interviews revealed three coherent visions of the way teenagers interpret their recreation and health practices with an emphasis on the role that tobacco played in their lives. The investigators used these findings to make recommendations to the Center for Nonsmoking and Health of the Minnesota Department of Health in their media efforts to promote a tobacco-free lifestyle. The chapter includes the information that was provided to those planning the campaign regarding communication strategies and messages that would be likely to appeal to the target audience, what messages they would reject, and what communication media would be effective for reaching them. The chapter concludes by explaining how symbolic convergence theory offers information unlike other focus group techniques and how it can be employed effectively.

In Chapter 9, Cragan and Shields extend the discussion of SCT-based focus groups by explaining a five-step procedure for conducting them and describing three case studies that demonstrate different approaches to solving client-centered, applied communication problems. A newspaper case explicates a typical use of SCT-based focus group interviews in the testing of the acceptability of a consumer product. A simulated jury case using randomly selected members of the target population illustrates the use of SCT-based focus groups to develop a plaintiff attorney's persuasive opening and closing statements. Finally, a police academy study shows the use of SCT-based focus groups in doing a quantitative assessment of a training program.

7

Using Focus Group Discussions to Promote Organizational Reflexivity: Two Applied Communication Field Studies

Gary L. Kreps
Northern Illinois University

Interviewing is a powerful information-gathering tool in modern society. It is used in a wide variety of contexts by practitioners and researchers alike to explore people's experiences, needs, beliefs, values, attitudes, intentions, and behaviors. Indeed, Brenner (1981) estimates that 90% of all social scientific investigations use interview data.

One important variation on the interview technique is the *focus group discussion*. In a focus group, a group leader (facilitator) poses questions about topics of research interest to group members (respondents) and encourages them to discuss the questions and elaborate on their answers. Focus group discussions help stimulate the disclosure of information by encouraging a chaining-out of shared perceptions (fantasy themes) (see the next two chapters by Bormann, Bormann, & Hasty and by Cragan & Shields; as well as Shields, 1981). The technique produces a wealth of information because outspoken respondents often encourage the more timid respondents to share information. By observing group members' verbal and nonverbal behaviors, the group facilitator can encourage maximum participation, information sharing, and creativity, thus obtaining more relevant information in less time from one focus group discussion than would be possible by conducting personal interviews with each member of the group.

The focus group technique is a popular applied research method because it reveals relevant and important information about respondents' personal experiences and interpretations of reality. It also enables researchers to learn quickly and inexpensively about the needs, values, beliefs, expectations, and behaviors of *specific* populations (Herndon, 1993). Focus group discussions are thus often used in advertising and marketing research to interpret consumers' ideas, attitudes, and behaviors because the data generated can be used to understand how audiences have responded in the past and to predict their future responses to specific messages, products, services, or programs. Such data are crucial in developing products, designing messages to promote these products, evaluating the products and messages, and for directing program interventions. Finally, focus group interviews are of particular interest to communication researchers because they provide examples of *metacommunication*, statements that report, describe, interpret, and evaluate communication acts and processes (Briggs, 1986).

This chapter first describes the general benefits of using focus group discussions in communication inquiry and identifies important guidelines for conducting effective focus group discussions. Strategies are examined for selecting individuals to participate in focus group discussions, facilitating group interaction, and preserving and evaluating the data. These strategies are then illustrated in two recent applied health communication field studies that employed focus group discussions to generate important evaluative information. The first study used focus group discussions to evaluate the performance of an urban residential adolescent substance abuse rehabilitation center for relevant publics and to provide data for refining and improving the ability of the center to meet the needs of community members who seek rehabilitation services. The second study used focus group discussions to refine the development and implementation of health promotion media messages for preventing the spread of sexually transmitted diseases within a university community. In both of these studies, the data generated from the focus group discussions were used to evaluate and refine communication efforts for the purpose of promoting public health.

THE FOCUS GROUP RESEARCH STRATEGY

Composition of a Focus Group

Selecting participants is a critically important aspect of focus group research. Careful sampling strategies should be used to select respondents who are representative of populations to which the researchers would like to generalize the findings. This is especially important because nonrepresentative samples have limited utility in explaining responses beyond those individuals who constitute the research sample. To enhance the generalizability of focus group research, random sampling techniques should be used whenever possible to select respondents. If nonrandom samples must be used, researchers should at least strive to select respondents who are as representative as possible of the larger audience the researcher wishes to understand, and caution should be taken in generalizing from these samples (see Frey, Botan, Friedman, & Kreps, 1991).

Respondents should be selected who share key characteristics of relevance to the research topic (such as exposure to similar social, educational, or occupational activities or environments) to ensure a common base of knowledge and insights about the topics to be covered in the discussion. Selection of a narrow sampling frame and the use of stratified sampling strategies (by sampling respondents from lists of the members of specific groups, organizations, or occupations) thus help guarantee that group members will share salient demographic characteristics and experiences. Researchers should also strive, whenever possible, to select participants who are not personal acquaintances to serve in the same focus group so that participants' interpersonal relationships do not unduly constrain group interaction (Krueger, 1988).

The size of the focus group can range from as few as 3 to as many as 12 respondents, with 5 to 8 respondents being the typical group size. The group should be small enough to give all participants opportunities to interact, yet large enough to generate a range of ideas and perspectives (Herndon, 1993; Staley, 1990). To ensure a sufficient number of respondents, it is a good idea to recruit a few more individuals than needed for each focus group, because it is not uncommon for one or more to fail to show up. It is better to a have a few more group members than needed than to have too few respondents.

Small cash payments (usually from $10 to $100) or gifts (such as coupons for products, tickets for movies or performances, etc.) are sometimes offered to recruit participants and increase attendance. Such incentives are most appropriate when the focus groups clearly are being conducted for commercial purposes (selling products), but not necessary when the purposes are for public benefit (as in studies that are designed to address popular social causes, such as improving public health, promoting environmental conservation, or enhancing elementary education), or when the participants have a personal stake in the issues being discussed (as in studies that are designed to solve problems experienced directly by the focus group respondents, such as rectifying problematic working conditions for employees or living conditions for public housing residents).

Preparing for a Focus Group Discussion

The setting for a focus group discussion should be located conveniently for the respondents in order to increase attendance. Focus group discussions work best when held in small, comfortable private meeting rooms where the group will not be interrupted and where participants can see and hear one another easily. It is often useful to have participants sit around a table (as they can in a typical conference room). It is also helpful to provide all focus group participants with easy-to-read name tags so that everyone can be addressed by name. Before beginning a focus group discussion, all respondents should sign an informed consent form that indicates their willingness to participate in the discussion.

Time is also an important issue in preparing a focus group interview. The amount of time needed to conduct focus group discussions can vary from as little as 20 minutes to as much as 2 hours, with most groups lasting about 1 hour. It is important to provide enough time to give all participants the opportunity to speak their mind, provide all relevant information, and allow group interaction to develop and proceed uninterrupted, but it is also important to keep the discussion brief enough to preserve participants' attention, involvement, and energy.

Conducting a Focus Group Discussion

In conducting a focus group discussion, a facilitator leads a relatively open, yet directed, conversation among a small group of respondents about a specific topic (Lydecker, 1986). The directed group conversations are used to stimulate introspection and group deliberation about relevant topics. The facilitator should begin the group discussion by providing a general overview statement that explains the purposes of the research, describes the way the discussion will proceed, expresses gratitude to the participants for sharing their valuable time and expertise, encourages all participants to speak their mind, and ensures that all information provided in the discussion will be kept strictly confidential.

The facilitator introduces the conversational topics by posing specific questions to group members from the *interview schedule*, sometimes called the *discussion guide*, which lists the questions in the order they are to be discussed. The questions should be sequenced such that they direct group conversation logically from one related issue to another, which helps make the discussion flow smoothly, and at the same time provides full coverage of all issues of concern in the study. It is often useful to provide each participant with a copy of the interview schedule, with the schedule serving as the agenda for the meeting, in order to orient participants to the issues to be covered in the discussion and to enhance their understanding of each primary question (Greenbaum, 1988).

Open-ended questions are also better discussion starters in focus group discussions than closed questions. The *funnel format* is a typical questioning sequence used in focus group discussions, in which the facilitator moves from asking general introductory questions to asking more specific and complex questions over the course of the discussion (Frey et al., 1991). For example, initial primary questions could ask about basic issues related to the discussion topic, progress to more in-depth analytic questions as group members become oriented more fully to the topic, and conclude with questions that ask for summary evaluations and recommendations.

Focus group discussions are often *moderately scheduled*; that is, there are specific primary questions listed on interview schedules for facilitators to ask of group members, but facilitators are also encouraged to follow up with additional probing of respondents. The open-ended and moderately scheduled nature of focus group discussions thus place great responsibility on the facilitator to pose *secondary questions* as needed to probe for additional information, stimulate group interaction, encourage the involvement of all group members, keep the discussion moving and on target, summarize issues covered, and help the group reach conclusions, without influencing or biasing members' responses unduly.

The facilitator should try to avoid having one vocal person dominate the conversation so as to exclude participation by others. It is particularly important to draw out silent group members by gently asking these individuals their opinions on issues raised and providing feedback that legitimizes their viewpoints. The facilitator should encourage interaction by accepting and validating all responses and avoid disagreeing openly with group members or engaging in debate with any participants (Krueger, 1988). The best facilitators thus engage in minimal discussion themselves, and encourage maximum interaction among respondents.

The facilitator must also be sensitive and responsive to the wide range of verbal and nonverbal messages sent by group participants to keep track of group process and to know when and how to encourage optimal interaction (Staley, 1990). For the method to be effective, focus group leaders should be well trained in communication and interviewing techniques that enable them to facilitate group interaction competently.

Preserving and Analyzing Focus Group Data

Focus group discussions generate a great deal of rich information, yet preserving this wealth of data is a challenge. It is extremely difficult to lead a focus group discussion and take notes of group members' responses at the same time, especially because it is imperative for facilitators to give their full and undivided attention to keeping track of and directing group interaction. It is possible to have an assistant take notes during the group discussion, but an additional person can distract the attention of group members and hinder full participation. To preserve data from focus groups, it is useful to *record* group interaction, using the least obtrusive technologies available (such as using a small audio-cassette recorder). Unobtrusive recording technologies enable facilitators to keep track of group interaction without minimizing their own or their respondents' involvement.

Although videotape technology preserves more information than audiotaping, audiotaping is more useful for focus group discussions. Audiotape recorders are relatively small and unobtrusive compared to the larger and more complex videotape recording equipment, and, if placed in a central location, audio equipment can record unobtrusively the vocal messages of all respondents. Videotape recording is more complex because multiple cameras must be placed in different positions to capture the nonverbal behavior of all members of the group, often necessitating the use of camera operators to move the camera positions in response to group members' movements. Furthermore, the fact that videotaping preserves more nonverbal data than audiotaping poses a series of coding problems for focus group researchers, complicating analysis of the data beyond the benefits provided by the additional nonverbal data preserved.

As mentioned earlier, informed consent must be received from participants both to participate in the focus group discussion and to have their comments recorded. The purpose of recording the discussion should be described to potential participants both verbally and in writing (on the informed consent form), making it clear that the recordings are to be used only for preserving information for the purposes of that research project and that the confidentiality of all respondents will be strictly maintained.

The recordings made should capture clearly the comments of all participants from the beginning of the discussion to the end. Small recorders with built-in nondirectional microphones are unobtrusive and are usually sensitive enough to preserve all of the group members' comments. Recording tapes should be used that will last the entire length of the group discussion, without having to be replaced or reset during the discussion. To increase the accuracy of the data, the tape recordings should be transcribed carefully to identify in writing each individual member's comments.

Content analytic procedures generally are used to analyze the data generated by focus group discussions. Content analysis of the transcripts is used to identify primary content categories within the responses. For example, a focus group discussion might contain different categories of suggestions or problems identified by respondents. The analyst must take care that the content categories established are mutually exclusive, equivalent, and exhaustive, with all comments made during the discussion fitting into one of the categories (Frey et al., 1991). Once all the comments are coded into categories, the number of comments made in each content category can be tallied to determine which categories are represented most often within the discussion. If desired, statistical analyses can then be conducted to test for differences between categories or relationships among categories, both within each focus group discussion and/or between different focus group discussions. Analysis of these data should reveal which issues and ideas are most important to the respondents, enabling the researcher to reach conclusions about the topic examined in the focus group discussions.

In summary, the focus group interview is a very useful and increasingly popular social scientific tool for gathering in-depth data about the experiences, ideas, and expectations of specific populations. The often spirited interaction among members of a focus group encourages member identification, participation, the sharing of relevant information, and the generation of new ideas and recommendations. With careful planning in selecting respondents, setting up the group session, and competent group facilitation, the focus group interview can be used effectively to evaluate as well as to develop intervention strategies to improve and enhance messages, products, services, and programs. Two exemplar studies that have employed focus group interviews effectively for the purposes of evaluation and intervention are described in the following sections of this chapter.

USING FOCUS GROUPS FOR HEALTH PROMOTION: TWO FIELD STUDIES

Study 1: The Substance Abuse Rehabilitation Center Research Program

An applied field study was conducted to gather information about public perceptions and attitudes toward an urban Residential Adolescent Substance Abuse Rehabilitation Center (the acronym RASARC is used in place of the real name of this rehabilitation center to preserve confidentiality). The research was designed to help RASARC meet community members' needs for rehabilitation services at a time when reports of adolescent substance abuse within the surrounding geographic area indicated that this problem was at an extremely high level. A primary goal of RASARC was to provide needed treatment to as many of the adolescent substance abusers who were not being served as adequately as they possibly could. The data gathered in this study were needed to help RASARC examine the reasons why these adolescents were not receiving treatment, as well as to identify strategies for increasing public acceptance, support, and utilization of their health promotion programs.

Sample

It was determined through analysis of archival records that the parents of adolescent substance abusers were the primary decision makers for enrolling clients for treatment in residential care facilities like RASARC. Therefore, parents of adolescents were identified as the population to be studied in this research effort. Three different relevant groups of parents were selected for participation in this research program: (a) parents with children who had already *completed* treatment at RASARC; (b) parents with children who were *currently* in treatment at RASARC; and (c) representative parents with children who were within the *potential* age range and geographic region served by RASARC. Focus group participants were selected randomly from these three lists (sampling frames) to ensure that the groups were representative of the larger populations of parents within the community served by RASARC. Names from each of the three sample-frame lists were randomized systematically to create three potential sample lists, and participants were recruited over the telephone. From these lists, nine parents were recruited for each focus group.

Letters were sent out from RASARC to all of the parents on the original three sample-frame lists prior to recruitment to explain the research project, identify the researcher, inform them that they might receive a recruitment call from the researcher, and encourage their participation in this research program. After the recruitment calls were made, follow-up letters were sent to all parents who agreed to attend to confirm the day, time, and place of their focus group, as well as to encourage their actual attendance at the focus group. Additionally, the researcher called each of the parents recruited for the focus groups two days prior to their group meeting to remind them of the session.

Method

Focus group discussions were held with each of the three groups of parents to identify their key experiences, ideas, and concerns about the specific programs and services at RASARC, as well as to explore the more general problem of adolescent substance abuse and their sources of relevant health information about substance abuse treatment and support. The focus groups were scheduled and conducted on the same day in the same place with 90 minutes set aside for each group discussion. Each of the three focus group discussions lasted approximately one hour in length. To increase participation, the sessions for Group A (completed) and Group B (current) were scheduled at times when these parents were likely to already be coming to RASARC. The focus group meetings were held in the conference room in the main administration building at RASARC. The actual size of the focus groups ranged from four to seven members, with four members (2 men, 2 women) in Group A (completed), six members (4 men, 2 women) in Group B (current), and seven members (3 men, 4 women) in Group C (potential), including the facilitator.

A general discussion guide (interview schedule) was developed to direct the focus group discussions, and minor alterations were made to adapt it to the different experiential sets of the members of the three different groups. For example, Group A (completed) was asked about their experiences with aftercare, Group B (current) was asked about their expectations for aftercare, and Group C (potential) was asked about their knowledge about the goals of aftercare (see Figures 7.1, 7.2, and 7.3).

Results

Each group discussion was audiotaped to preserve group members' comments for later analysis. The audiotapes were then transcribed and content analyzed by the researcher into the following 13 primary content themes, which provided the basis for the recommendations:

1. *Motivation to Seek Treatment:* The most intriguing finding in this content category was that almost all of the responses to this query by members of all three groups involved confrontation themes (family crises and conflicts). In future promotions it may be wise to use the theme of family confrontation as a motivating factor in urging parents to seek treatment at RASARC. Several of the comments in this category potentially can serve as storylines for future advertisements, pamphlets, and public relations media.

It is also interesting to note how resistant the majority of parents in the potential group (C) were to seeking treatment for their children, especially in contrast to the other two groups. The theme expressed most commonly by parents in group C was that they would not seek treatment for their children at RASARC, or at any other treatment facility, unless it was their very last alternative. This response suggests avoidance and denial, which is not really surprising. Because this group is the least familiar with RASARC and its services and is least invested in treatment (their children have probably not been diagnosed as substance

1. What motivated you to seek treatment?
2. What motivated you to seek treatment at RASARC?
3. How did you find out about RASARC? (Doctor's referral? Media ads? School referral? Legal referral? Support group?)
4. What are your general feelings and impressions about RASARC?
5. What are the barriers that prevent parents from seeking treatment for their children?
6. What information sources do parents need to recognize the need for treatment?
7. How can RASARC help parents recognize the need for treatment?
8. What information sources are there about available treatment services?
9. What prior experiences do you have with social services and treatment services?
10. What kinds of family support services could be offered?
11. What are your experiences with and expectations for aftercare services?
12. What are realistic expectations for treatment services and the outcomes of treatment?
13. What problems are there with current treatment services, including those offered by RASARC?
14. How can RASARC improve its treatment and aftercare services?

**Figure 7.1. Discussion Guide for Group A
(Completed Treatment Group)**

abusers), they do not want to imagine their offspring needing treatment, lest those thoughts become self-fulfilling prophesies. In future advertising it may be important to confront parents with their tendency to avoid and deny their children's problems.

2. *General Referral Sources:* The courts were the source of general referral mentioned most frequently, which indicates that court officials must be made aware of RASARC and the benefits of its services. The most up-to-date promotional materials should thus be sent to lawyers and court officials. The second general referral source mentioned most frequently was television advertising, which reinforces the importance of RASARC using television advertising to reach potential clients.

3. *RASARC Referral Sources:* Radio and television advertising, as well as personal recommendations from parents who have used RASARC services, were the referral sources mentioned most frequently. Media advertising was most important for the potential audience, which indi-

1. What motivated you to seek treatment?
2. What motivated you to seek treatment at RASARC?
3. How did you find out about RASARC? (Doctor's referral? Media ads? School referral? Legal referral? Support group?)
4. What are your general feelings and impressions about RASARC?
5. What are the barriers that prevent parents from seeking treatment for their children?
6. What information sources do parents need to recognize the need for treatment?
7. How can RASARC help parents recognize the need for treatment?
8. What information sources are there about available treatment services?
9. What prior experiences do you have with social services and treatment services?
10. What kinds of family support services could be offered?
11. What are your expectations for aftercare services?
12. What are realistic expectations for treatment services and the outcomes of treatment?
13. What problems are there with current treatment services, including those offered by RASARC?
14. How can RASARC improve its treatment and aftercare services?

**Figure 7.2. Discussion Guide for Group B
(Current Treatment Group)**

cates that it is a good channel for reaching new customers (as mentioned in the discussion of the previous content category). Word-of-mouth referral from other parents was most important for the parents who had already been through the program and is a relatively inexpensive and highly trusted advertising channel. It may be wise to keep in contact with parents who have been through the program, provide them with materials, and keep them involved with RASARC in advisory capacities. The majority of other referral sources are from area professionals (such as lawyers, judges, psychologists, and police) who should be kept up-to-date about RASARC and given current promotional materials.

    4. Positive Impressions of and Experiences With RASARC: This was by far the largest and most impassioned of the 13 content categories. The data clearly indicate that RASARC is thought of highly and appreciated by all three groups of parents. Several of the comments can be used as testimonials or advertising copy for future promotional media. To be cautious, how-

1. What are your general feelings and impressions about RASARC?
2. How did you find out about RASARC? (Doctor's referral? Media ads? School referral? Legal referral? Support group?)
3. What circumstances would motivate you to seek treatment for your child?
4. What might motivate you to seek treatment at RASARC?
5. What are the barriers that prevent parents from seeking treatment for their children?
6. What information sources do parents need to recognize the need for treatment?
7. How can RASARC help parents recognize the need for treatment?
8. What information sources are there about available treatment services?
9. What prior experiences do you have with social services and treatment services?
10. What kind of family support services could be offered?
11. What are realistic expectations for treatment services and the outcome of treatment?
12. What are realistic expectations for aftercare?
13. Do you know of any problems with current treatment services, including those offered by RASARC?
14. How can RASARC improve its treatment and aftercare services?

**Figure 7.3. Discussion Guide for Group C
(Potential Treatment Group)**

ever, it should be noted that a selection bias may explain this finding. That is, the parents who were most supportive of RASARC were likely to be the ones who agreed to participate in this research program, whereas the parents who were disenchanted with RASARC were likely to be unwilling to participate. (During the recruitment of participants, however, parents who mentioned being upset or unhappy with RASARC were strongly encouraged to attend the meeting to express their feelings and to help improve the system.) Regardless of this potential selection bias, the data generated in the focus group interview appear to be sincere and moving.

5. *Negative Impressions of and Experiences With RASARC:* There is a clear and troubling consistent pattern of negative first impressions and public images of RASARC that are held by all three groups of parents. These negative stereotypes identify RASARC as a place for delinquent children, orphans, runaway boys, bad boys, and rough kids. Furthermore,

there is a penal-system, punishment image of the services provided at RASARC that discourages parents from sending their children there for treatment. This image must be changed if RASARC is to be promoted effectively. Perhaps promotional materials that explain the historical developments and transformations at RASARC can emphasize the long history of the institution and its name recognition by coupling this information with knowledge of the new services and philosophy of RASARC.

6. *Barriers That Prevent Parents From Seeking Treatment for Their Children:* The most significant barrier to seeking treatment voiced by members of all three groups, and mentioned twice as often as any other response, was denial. (This supports the implication drawn from the responses of the potential group to what might motivate them to seek treatment at RASARC discussed in content category 1.) The denial theme has to be a central part of promotional messages to reach parents who do not want to think about substance abuse and their children. The second barrier mentioned most frequently was by the potential group (C) who stated that they needed to know the warning signals to determine whether their child was engaging in normal adolescent behavior or whether there really was a substance abuse problem. Providing parents with promotional materials that identify warning signs can be very powerful. In fact, immediately after the focus group meeting with the potential group (C), the parents asked for handouts identifying the warning signs and even took some home for their friends and neighbors. Parents who want to handle the situation themselves have to recognize the severity and complexity of the problems their children may face. Guilt and parental problems with drugs and alcohol are additional barriers mentioned frequently that should be addressed in marketing themes and advertising messages. Cost issues are also of concern to parents, and information about insurance coverage might encourage parents to seek treatment when needed.

7. *Information Sources To Recognize the Need for Treatment:* School programs and parent networks are the information sources parents most want to use to help them identify their children's need for treatment. Parents want the schools and their peers to provide them with timely and honest feedback about their children's deviant behavioral patterns to help identify instances of substance abuse. Perhaps in promotional materials RASARC can present a community orientation to this problem, encouraging parents and neighbors to work together and help fight substance abuse by sharing relevant information. Parents should also be encouraged to initiate communication with representatives from the schools on a regular basis to find out if their children are behaving peculiarly or if teachers, administrators, and counselors suspect substance abuse.

8. *Suggestions for RASARC to Help Parents Recognize the Need for Treatment:* Parents responded to this question with many suggestions for

RASARC to engage in increased information dissemination efforts. The suggestion mentioned most frequently for getting relevant information to parents was increased use of television and radio ads. (This finding is consistent with the data in content category 3, in which parents stated that television and radio advertisements were important sources of information in referring them to RASARC.) The respondents suggested using advertising scenarios that depict family breakdowns to attract the attention of parents. Furthermore, group members encouraged using public affairs, news, and other television and radio programs to present information about RASARC and its services. The second suggestion mentioned most often was for RASARC to work closely with educational institutions in offering lectures, courses, and other programs for parents and children to inform and motivate them to recognize and deal with the problem of substance abuse. Another interesting suggestion was to disseminate widely promotional and informational literature (leaflets) about substance abuse and RASARC for parents to pick up at schools, department stores, grocery stores, businesses, medical facilities, police departments, and shopping centers.

9. *Experiences With Other Social Services and Treatment Services:* Many respondents had experience with several other treatment services in the area. The organization mentioned most frequently was Family Anonymous, which was seen as a very good family resource. Affiliating with and working closely with Family Anonymous may be mutually beneficial to both organizations. In contrast, local hospitals were mentioned often, but were generally disliked for their high levels of bureaucracy and their medical orientation, although parents did like one hospital's radio advertisements and half-day school program for children. Parents in the current group (B) were also very interested in proposed aftercare support groups (core groups) at the local high schools, and perhaps RASARC can help schools in the area get these groups started.

10. *Suggestions for Family Support Services:* Interestingly, this category received the fewest responses, including no responses from the parents in the potential group (C), even after probing. Perhaps these parents were so removed from facing substance abuse problems that they did not envision a need for any family support services. There was, however, interest expressed by parents in the completed (A) and current (B) groups to reinstate the sibling program (in which counseling is provided to brothers and sisters of the children receiving treatment) at RASARC. There was also strong agreement among the parents in the completed group (A) about the need for aftercare services for parents and families.

11. *Experiences With and Expectations for Aftercare Services:* Parents generally supported the need for and the importance of aftercare services, especially parents in the completed group (A), who are probably

participating and want to be more involved in aftercare. Parents in the completed group (A) want RASARC to inform them about the attendance of their children at aftercare meetings, educate them about aftercare services, offer special aftercare sessions for parents and children, and start a parents' alumni group for peer support and future projects. Another suggestion for aftercare services was to provide children with healthy social and occupational opportunities, such as identifying safe (drug- and alcohol-free) places to go, establishing a youth center or halfway house, and helping children find jobs.

   12. *Realistic Expectations for Treatment and Outcome of Treatment:* There is a dramatic difference between parents experienced with RASARC (groups A and B) and the parents in the potential group (C) with respect to expectations for treatment. Parents in groups A and B were realistic about not expecting miracle cures at RASARC, recognizing that it is their children's responsibility to stay straight and learn coping skills. These parents even expected some relapse from their children. In contrast, several parents in the potential group were unrealistic in their expectation that treatment would cure their children so they would never desire drugs or alcohol again. These results indicate a strong need for educating parents about the nature of addiction and the realistic outcomes of treatment. On the other hand, several parents recognized the psychosocial elements of effective treatment, mentioning the role of support systems, ego-strength, withstanding pressure, and self-esteem in recovery.

   13. *Suggestions for RASARC to Improve its Services:* This content category provides a good summary of the implications drawn from earlier questions, as many of the suggestions offered have previously been discussed. There is a wealth of ideas offered here that, with some refinement, can be of great benefit to RASARC. For example, information and social support programs are high on parents' list of suggestions. Several parents in the completed (A) and current (B) groups suggested that RASARC do a better job at the Wednesday night meetings of educating parents about the potential for relapse, the signs of relapse, and how to handle it. Parents from all three groups suggested improving the alumni group so that children can keep in contact with each other to provide an on-going support system after treatment. Several parents encouraged efforts to enhance community awareness of RASARC services through radio and television coverage and advertising, as well as offering a drug or alcohol abuse hotline. Information dissemination can also be enhanced by a videotape that describes RASARC, its treatment philosophies, and its programs (i.e., showing the facilities and the kinds of activities kids go through) for parents to view while waiting during the initial evaluation and during the first Wednesday night meeting. (Such a program may be able to get some free television air-time on public

affairs programs.) They also suggested that when parents first bring their children in for treatment they should be given books and other reading material about substance abuse, treatment strategies, and family strategies to help children.

Parents in the completed group (A) desired follow-up telephone calls from RASARC after treatment is over to identify any problems and provide needed information or support. They suggested setting up a system in which successful alumni of the program can work as peer counselors for current children going through the program. Parents are interested in RASARC helping to get their children back into school and making sure that they stay there. They want to be informed about whether their children are attending aftercare meetings. Parents also suggested that RASARC can provide parents with information about Family Anonymous, provide more privacy in the basement for families meeting with their children, and take a more preventive approach with advertising, educational services, and pamphlets. Parents also would like RASARC to help keep costs down by encouraging insurance companies to offer more coverage for aftercare services and by providing low-cost options for aftercare services.

Study Summary

This study illustrates how focus group research can provide a wealth of information about public perceptions and attitudes toward an organization such as RASARC, identifying parents' concerns about adolescent substance abuse treatment and generating specific suggestions for increasing public acceptance and support for RASARC. The focus group interviews indicated that the public's support for RASARC appears to be high, although the public's image of RASARC is sometimes tainted by false stereotypes. Parents generally are concerned about adolescent substance abuse and indicated a clear need for more information about risks, symptoms, and services. The data indicated that RASARC can attract business and community support by developing and implementing information dissemination promotional programs to meet the information needs identified by parents in this study. Many of the recommendations from this study were implemented at RASARC, which has helped the organization to provide the public with relevant health information, enhanced the public image of the rehabilitation center, and attracted greater public support for its programs and services. RASARC was also able to increase client enrollment significantly over the six months following the completion of this study, enabling the rehabilitation center to provide health care services to a larger segment of the adolescent population who were in dire need of such care.

Study 2: Pretesting Posters to Help Students Resist Sexually Transmitted Diseases

The staff of the Department of Health Enhancement at Northern Illinois University's Student Health Services Program were concerned about the increasing number of cases of sexually transmitted diseases (STDs) reported at the Campus Health Care Center. A decision was made to develop an on-campus health promotion campaign to encourage students to engage in "safe sex" practices in order to prevent the spread of STDs. Several prevention communication strategies were introduced, including advertisements and articles in the campus newspaper, lectures in classes and for campus groups, pamphlets distributed around campus, condom vending machines in campus buildings, and posters encouraging safe-sex practices displayed prominently in residence halls.

Four different poster designs with different health promotion messages were developed. Each of the four posters used a provocative line from a popular song as a title, were done in bright colors, and included photographs of students in playful and romantic poses to attract student attention. Each poster also listed seven safer sex tips as primary health education messages. This study was designed to generate data that could be used to refine these posters as effective health promotion messages. To determine the potential response of students to these posters, focus group interviews were conducted to evaluate the effectiveness of the four posters to promote safe-sex practices on campus and prevent the spread of STDs.

Sample

Because the vast majority of students who seek treatment for STDs at the Campus Health Care Center are undergraduate students, undergraduate university students were identified as the primary audience for the health promotion media evaluated in this study. It was also anticipated, based on past experiences with health promotion media, that there might be differences in responses to the posters by students who resided on-campus or off-campus, as well as by students who were freshmen/sophomores or juniors/seniors. Because most freshmen/sophomores live on-campus and most juniors/seniors live off-campus, two different groups of undergraduate students were selected for participation in this study: (a) freshmen and sophomores who resided on-campus in the university residence halls and (b) juniors and seniors who resided off-campus.

Focus group participants were selected randomly from lists of all students in these two groups provided by the University Office of

Registration and Records (sampling frames) to ensure that the groups were representative of the larger populations of undergraduate students at the university. Names from each of the two sample-frame lists were randomized systematically to create two potential sample lists, and participants were recruited over the telephone. Respondents were offered $10.00 to participate in the focus group discussions. Ten students were recruited for each of the two focus groups.

Follow-up letters were sent to the students who agreed to attend to confirm the day, time, and place of their focus group, as well as to encourage their actual attendance. The letters explained the purpose of the study, thanked them for agreeing to participate, reminded them that they would receive $10 for participating in the study, let them know that the discussions would be tape-recorded, and promised that their participation would be kept confidential. Additionally, telephone calls were made to each of the students two days prior to their focus group meeting to remind them of the session and to answer any questions they had.

Method

Focus group discussions were held with each of these two groups of undergraduate students to identify their reactions and evaluations of the health promotion posters. The focus group interviews were scheduled and conducted on the same day in the same place with 90 minutes set aside for each group discussion. The two focus group discussions each lasted approximately 45 minutes in duration. The focus group discussions were held in a conference room at the University Student Health Center. The actual number of focus group participants in the study were nine members of the Freshmen/Sophomores Group (4 men, 5 women) and seven members of the Juniors/Seniors Group (3 men, 4 women), including the facilitator. A general discussion guide (interview schedule) was developed to direct the focus group discussions. The questions were designed to provide a complete evaluation of each of the four posters, including a ranking and rating, as well as to suggest specific refinements for improving each poster (see Figure 7.4)

Results

Each focus group discussion was audiotaped to preserve group members' comments for later analysis. The audiotapes were transcribed and content analyzed by the researcher into evaluative comments and recommendations offered by each group about the four posters. Additionally, evaluative ratings and rankings made by each group were calculated numerically for each poster.

Ask the following questions for each of the four posters:

1. What characteristics of this poster attract your attention? Why? What, if anything, do you dislike about this poster?
2. Do you find this poster to be interesting? Would you stop and read this poster if you passed by it in a building on campus? Why?
3 How comfortable are you with this poster? Do you find anything about this poster to be offensive? Why?
4. Would you describe this poster as being easy or hard to understand? How informative is this poster? What are the main ideas this poster is trying to get across? What does this poster make you think about?
5. Is there anything in this poster that you find hard to believe? What? Why?
6. Did you learn anything from this poster? If so, what? Do you think this poster might influence your attitudes or behaviors? In what ways? Why?
7. Do the artwork and the written messages on this poster complement each other or does one detract from the other? Explain.
8. What elements of this poster would you change to make it more effective in influencing student attitudes and behaviors?
9. Please rate each of these four posters on a typical academic scale of A through F, and rank-order these four posters from 1 to 4, with 1 being most effective and 4 being least effective.

Figure 7.4. Discussion Guide for Pretesting Posters to Help Students Resist STDs

Poster 1, titled "All You Need Is Love," was green and black with one large and three small photographs of a male and female student in friendly and romantic poses. The seven safer sex tips were placed in the top third of the poster. This poster received a rating of C- and a ranking of 4 from the Freshmen/Sophomores group and a rating of C and a ranking of 3 from the Juniors/Seniors group. Both groups agreed that the print was too small on the poster and that the use of the message about "love" was unclear and connected poorly to the STD issue. The Juniors/Seniors group recommended adding a question mark after the word "love" to provoke thought, whereas the Freshmen/Sophomores group suggested changing the message used in the poster to: "If you love someone, you will protect them from STDs."

Poster 2 was titled "I Want Your Sex," with the first three words listed in medium size print at the top of the poster and the word "sex" listed in large letters below the first three. It was green with black lettering and had five photographs in the center of the poster. Three of the photographs were of different couples and two were of individual students.

The seven safer sex tips were listed across the bottom of the poster. This poster received a rating of A- and A from the Freshmen/Sophomores and Juniors/Seniors groups, respectively, and both groups ranked it as 1. The Freshmen/Sophomores group commented that the poster was very interesting, they liked it a lot, and they particularly liked the use of the word "sex" in big letters on the poster. The Juniors/Seniors group commented that they liked the big print too, the poster was easy to read, it attracted the attention of the viewer, and it was very realistic. The Freshmen/Sophomores group recommended providing statistical information about the incidence of STDs on the poster, while the Juniors/Seniors group recommended making the poster more colorful by using different colored bullets before each of the written messages at the bottom of the poster.

Poster 3, titled "What's Love Got To Do With It?," was blue and black, with black lettering. One large photograph of a couple was placed in the upper left-hand corner of the poster, with six smaller photographs placed within a triangle in the center of the poster. The seven safer sex tips were listed beneath the title and to the right of the triangle with the photographs. This poster received a rating of B- from the Freshmen/Sophomores group and a ranking of 2, whereas the Juniors/Seniors group gave it a rating of C and a ranking of 4. The Freshmen/Sophomores group commented that although they liked the layout and angles in the poster, the print was too small, the word "love" in the title was distracting and contradicted the primary message of the poster, the female model used in the poster was unattractive, and the couple's interaction depicted in the poster was too tame. The Juniors/Seniors group commented that the models used in this poster were atypical and ineffective, the poster looked off-center, and there was too much information in one place. The Freshmen/Sophomores group suggested that the poster should highlight the word "sex" rather than the word "love," use a different (more attractive) female model, and depict the couple in a "wilder" position. The Juniors/Seniors group also suggested that the couple be depicted in a more "sexy" position, moving the photograph over to create more balance, and combining the photographs with the messages, rather than listing them separately.

Poster 4 was titled "Bad Case Of Loving You," which was placed in the upper left-hand corner of the poster. The poster was blue and white, with black lettering. Four small photographs of couples were interspersed with the seven safer sex tips. This poster received a rating of C and a ranking of 3 from the Freshmen/Sophomores group and a rating of B- and a ranking of 2 from the Juniors/Seniors group. Both groups commented that there was a contradiction between the title and the photograph of a happy couple used in the poster. The Freshmen/Sophomores group commented that the poster had too much white space and that the layout was too green. The Juniors/Seniors group commented that the green color in the poster attracted attention, but that the poster looked too cluttered. Both groups suggested that the couple in the photo should look more worried. The Freshmen/Sophomores group also suggested that more space be used in the poster, that different couples be used in the photograph (such as both a white couple and a black couple), and the messages on the poster be rearranged so that they stand out more (perhaps by putting a message on each side of the photographs used). The Juniors/Seniors group suggested that bullets be used before each message, moving the photographs over to the left to make the messages easier to read, and enlarging the words on the poster to make them easier to read.

In their overall evaluation of the posters, the Freshmen/ Sophomores group commented that they did not like poster 4 and suggested that posters 2 and 3 should be combined into one poster. The Juniors/Seniors group concluded that they definitely liked the use of the word "sex" in Poster 2.

Study Summary

These focus groups provided excellent evaluative data about the health promotion posters by identifying their potential limitations, as well as specific ideas for improvement. Both focus groups identified Poster 2 unequivocally as the best health promotion poster. Efforts were taken immediately to refine this poster by adopting the specific strategies for improvement suggested by the focus groups, and copies were then posted in strategic, high-traffic areas of buildings on campus. The other three posters were also refined over time in accordance with suggestions made by the focus groups and were displayed in campus buildings. The posters were also displayed at meetings of the American College Health Association, where they received a great deal of attention from student health center personnel. Upon request, the poster design formats were made available to other college health professionals to use in designing their own health promotion media, and the poster designs have been used in educational institutions throughout the country.

FOCUS GROUP DISCUSSIONS
AND ORGANIZATIONAL REFLEXIVITY

A focus group discussion is a powerful group facilitation technique and research tool that can be used to generate valuable evaluative data about the effectiveness of various messages, products, services, and programs by encouraging representatives of relevant audiences to share their experiences and beliefs concerning these messages, products, services, and programs. Program administrators depend on feedback from individuals who have insights into their programs, such as the people their programs serve and the people who work in their organizations. Relevant populations such as these have the ability to assess critically the quality of programs and to help improve them. Focus group discussions can also be used to generate relevant feedback from key populations to identify strategies for program intervention and refinement. Feedback from such populations can thus enhance *organizational reflexivity*, enabling program administrators to see the strengths and weaknesses in their systems from the perspective of key internal and external audiences (Kreps, 1989, 1990).

In this chapter, two health communication field studies were described to illustrate the ways focus group discussions were used to enhance health promotion efforts. The first study described the use of focus group discussions to assess the health promotion efforts of an urban adolescent substance abuse rehabilitation center, whereas the second study reported the way focus group discussions were used to evaluate health promotion media developed by a university health care program to prevent the spread of STDs on-campus. In both of these studies, representative consumers were recruited to participate, and the focus group discussions elicited evaluative information from them about health promotion programs and communication efforts. The interactive nature of the focus group discussions encouraged the respondents to analyze the programs and messages critically and to identify specific directions for improving these health promotion efforts. The data gathered via these discussions increased organizational reflexivity in the two programs, enabling system representatives to refine and improve their health promotion strategies.

The studies presented in this chapter illustrate the value of focus group interviews for evaluating messages, products, services, and programs by providing researchers with a relatively quick and inexpensive way to gather in-depth information, evaluations, and recommendations from relevant populations. There are, however, limitations to focus group interviews. One important limitation concerns the generalizability of the data gathered, for even when participants are selected randomly, the small size of the actual focus group represents a problem. To overcome this limitation it is useful to triangulate focus group interviews by using other larger sample research strategies, such as surveys, to make sure the data generated by the focus group interviews are representative of the larger population to which the researcher wishes to generalize. Focus group interviews can also be used to complement other data-gathering techniques. For example, in multiphase research efforts, in which each data-gathering phase builds on previous ones, focus group interviews can be used to further investigate and evaluate data gathered in an earlier phase and/or to identify topics to investigate in later research phases (see Kreps, 1989).

In the final analysis, although focus group interviews are not necessarily the best method to use in every applied research context, they are a powerful group facilitation technique that can be used to stimulate group discussion. They are, indeed, an important tool for many applied communication researchers.

8

Using Symbolic Convergence Theory and Focus Group Interviews to Develop Communication Designed to Stop Teenage Use of Tobacco

Ernest G. Bormann
University of Minnesota
Ellen Bormann
Curtis-Bormann Associates
Kathleen C. Harty
Minnesota Department of Health

This chapter presents an overview of symbolic convergence communication theory and explains how applied communication researchers can apply it in order to study, understand, and communicate effectively with various target audiences. The chapter then demonstrates the techniques in terms of using focus groups to gather information for the study of teenage tobacco users in the state of Minnesota. The Center for Nonsmoking and Health of the Minnesota Department of Health developed an initiative aimed at discouraging tobacco usage among teenagers. The initiative was to result in televised public service messages aimed at teenage tobacco users in Minnesota to be aired during the broadcast of the state high school hockey tournament. This chapter reports how researchers utilized symbolic convergence theory in order to conduct an in-depth psychometric study of the audience of teenage tobacco users in Minnesota for the purpose of developing a communication program for the Center for Nonsmoking and Health. The results from the study were then used to develop televised messages to encourage teenagers to quit smoking or chewing tobacco.

OVERVIEW OF SYMBOLIC CONVERGENCE THEORY

The *symbolic convergence theory of communication* (SCT) is a general theory within the broad framework that accounts for human communication in relation to *homo narrans* (Bormann, 1985). The theory explains the appearance of a group consciousness, with its implied shared emotions, motives, and meanings, not so much in terms of individual daydreams and scripts but rather in terms of socially shared narrations or fantasies.

Symbolic convergence communication theory explains how groups of people come to share a common social reality. The basic communicative dynamic of the theory is the sharing of dramatizations that bring about a convergence of appropriate feelings among participants. The process of sharing interpretations was uncovered in the course of studying the effects on groups of dramatizing messages that contain a pun or other word play, double entendre, figure of speech, analogy, anecdote, allegory, fable, or narrative (Bales, 1970; Bormann, 1985, 1990). Investigators noted that some dramatizing messages fell on deaf ears but others picked up the tempo of the conversation; people grew excited, interrupted one another, laughed, showed emotion, and forgot their self-consciousness. The psychological process of being caught up in imaginative language is illustrated by such examples as people being engrossed in a novel, attending raptly to a play, film, or television show, enjoying a folktale or anecdote, or identifying with a supernatural persona in a sacred myth. The people who shared the fantasy did so with the appropriate responses. The result of people sharing dramatizing messages is a *group fantasy*.

Fantasy is a technical term in symbolic convergence theory and does not mean what it does in one of its common usages; that is, something imaginary, not grounded in reality. The technical meaning of fantasy is the creative and imaginative shared interpretation of events that fulfills a psychological or rhetorical need for a group of people. Symbolic convergence theory distinguishes between the ongoing unfolding of experience and the messages that discuss events in other than the here-and-now. If several members of a teenage gang or clique begin to have a fist fight, the situation might be dramatic. Yet, because the action is unfolding in the presence of the observers, it would not qualify as a group fantasy for them. If, however, some of those present recount structured narratives of the same event after it has taken place, their stories would count as dramatizations that could lead to shared fantasies.

When members of a target audience share a fantasy they experience jointly the same emotions, develop common heroes and villains, celebrate certain actions as laudable, and interpret some aspect of their common experience in the same way. They have thus come to symbolic convergence about that facet of their common experiences.

The power of symbolic convergence theory stems from the human tendency to try to understand events in terms of people with certain personality traits and motivations, making decisions, taking actions, and causing things to happen. We can understand the idea of a person making plans in order to achieve goals and succeeding or failing to do so because our personal fantasies and daydreams often interpret our own behavior in that way.

Fantasy themes, in contrast with the way we experience the here-and-now, are organized and artistic. Because fantasy themes are always slanted, ordered, and interpretative, they provide a rhetorical means for people to account for and explain an experience or an event in different ways. The way several or more people come to some meeting of the minds and emotions is by participating in dramatizations in which an explanation of the events is acted out by the personae in the drama.

When we share a fantasy we make sense out of what prior to that time may well have been a confusing state of affairs and we do so in *common with the others who share the fantasy with us*. We have created a group consciousness and have come to share some symbolic common ground. When a group of people share a fantasy theme they share a consciousness with similar meanings and emotions that can be set off by a commonly agreed cryptic *symbolic cue*. The inside-joke phenomenon is an example of such a trigger; only those who share the fantasy theme that the inside joke refers to will respond in an appropriate fashion. The symbolic cue need not be only an inside joke, however. The allusion to a fantasy shared previously may arouse tears or evoke anger, hatred, love, or affection as well as laughter and humor. Among the best evidence available to a scholar that fantasies have been shared is the presence of such inside cues.

The symbolic inside-cue phenomenon makes possible the development of *fantasy types*. When a number of similar scenarios or outlines of the plot of the fantasies, including particulars of the scenes, characters, and situations, have been shared by members of a group or larger community they form a fantasy type. A fantasy type is a stock scenario repeated again and again by the same characters or by similar characters. Rhetoricians, for example, often use the fantasy type as a rhetorical device in their discourse. Rather than dramatizing a fantasy theme with specific characters in a specific setting, they instead present the general plot line. Rhetoricians also use an archetypal fantasy as a way to fit the breaking news and the unfolding of experience comfortably into a community's social reality.

When people come to share a group of fantasy themes and types, they may integrate them into a coherent *rhetorical vision* of some aspect of their social reality. A rhetorical vision is a unified putting-together of the various scripts that gives the participants a broader view of things. Rhetorical visions are often integrated by sharing a dramatizing message that contains a master analogy, such as "Cold War" or "Christian Science." The master analogy pulls the various elements together into a more or less elegant and meaningful whole.

A rhetorical vision usually is indexed by a key word, a slogan, or a label. Such indexing is a special case of the symbolic inside-cue phenomenon, but in this instance the cryptic allusion is not just to details of fantasy themes and types but to a total coherent view of an aspect of the participants' social reality. Recent examples of terms functioning as inside cues for rhetorical visions include Cold War, Yuppies, New Populism, and Political Correctness.

The following report was prepared from the analysis of data provided by the use of focus group interviews that employed symbolic convergence theory to conduct a fantasy theme analysis of the rhetorical visions of various segments of the audience.

SYMBOLIC CONVERGENCE THEORY-BASED FOCUS GROUPS

Kreps provided a thorough and useful description of the focus group research strategy in the previous chapter. We recommend that the reader unfamiliar with the focus group as a group facilitation technique read that section of Kreps's chapter in conjunction with this chapter.

Kreps illustrates the importance of understanding group communication principles when using the focus group method to gather data. The characteristics of a one-time meeting (Bormann & Bormann, 1992) are important as are group cohesiveness, role emergence, leadership, and norming behavior. Pressures for group conformity and communication related to deviance are also relevant. Kreps provides an excellent discussion of how to select individuals to participate in focus groups, how to facilitate group interaction, how to preserve group interaction, and how to evaluate focus group data.

Shields (1981) describes a special kind of focus group interview technique informed by symbolic convergence theory that is used to discover how attitudes, opinions, images, and feelings cluster into coherent rhetorical visions of experience. The *symbolic convergence theory-based focus group* technique enables investigators to see the interplay of fantasy sharing and rejection and to discover the various rhetorical visions shared by the members of a focus group. A careful discourse analysis of the transcripts enables the investigator to segment the audience on the basis of psychographic (rhetorical visions) rather than demographic (e.g., age, income, religion, ethnic background, etc.) dimensions.

Other focus group and market research techniques often collect and report summaries of answers to specific questions that are of interest to a client. Still other focus groups are used to provide records for content analysis that can result in quantitative analysis. Traditional focus group studies often emphasize the importance of demographic information by discussing the results in terms of age groups, social class, ethnic, religious, or political backgrounds. In contrast, the SCT-based focus group technique examines the shared stories, or dramatizations, that occur during a focus group while questions are being answered. The rhetorical visions that emerge reveal a coherent picture of how the respondents view the world, both in general and in relation to the specific topic under discussion.

Investigators who wish to study a community's shared consciousness and communication by using focus groups can seek several kinds of evidence in order to infer and derive the shared fantasies and rhetorical visions. The evidence consists of: (a) members redramatizing and chaining during a focus group; (b) the recurrence of the same drama being shared from group to group; (c) respondents' use of inside cues; and (d) respondents' use of fantasy types.

One of the virtues of SCT-based focus groups is the opportunity they provide to study written or electronic records of the interviews. A trained interpreter can find the sharing process in the verbal and nonverbal communication chains discernible in videotapes or audiotapes.

To illustrate the way investigators can interpret fantasy chains we use examples from our study of teenage tobacco usage. Our first example shows a fantasy chain indicative of the sharing process. Note particularly how many different members of the focus group chime in with full understanding of the drama that is unfolding. No one member tells the entire story but by adding to and embroidering a number of participants shape the drama jointly. This sort of chain is usually one that has been shared prior to the group coming to a meeting. The group members are not creating a new meaning but rather retelling a familiar part of their culture. To indicate the chaining nature of the communication process our format is to indicate the questions with the sign "?=" and the turn taking with a dash "—."

?= Do you like doing things that are on the edge a little bit?
—(In unison) Yeah.

?= A little bit of danger?

—Yeah.

—Yeah.

—Bridge jumping in the summer.

—Bridge jumping.

?= Tell me about bridge jumping, what's it like?

—Go down to the lake . . .

—Go down to Lake of the Isles and you stand about 30 feet above the water and just launch your body. (Some laughter) It's the best.

—And hope it's a 20-feeter.

?= At Lake of the Isles?

—Yup.

?= But you aren't supposed to go swimming in Lake of the Isles—

—Yup.

—That's right.

—Yeah, that's when the cops come.

—That's living on the edge.

—And canoes go underneath the bridge.

—. . . splash 'em.

—Scare 'em.

The recurrence of similar dramatizing material in different focus groups also provides evidence of symbolic convergence. There is always the possibility that a group will share a novel fantasy and begin to build a unique culture. The recurrence of shared fantasies from group to group is evidence that the material is not new but part of the group members' established rhetorical vision.

Additional evidence of an established rhetorical vision is furnished by cryptic allusions to symbolic common ground. When participants share a dramatization, they have come to symbolic convergence in terms of common meanings and emotions that can be set off by an agreed cryptic symbolic cue. For example, in one focus group the members responded verbally and nonverbally to the cryptic phrase "beer goggles" in a way that indicated it was for them an inside cue. Only those who share the dramatization to which the inside cue refers will respond in an appropriate fashion. When the questioner probed for explanation, the group explained the symbolic cue in detail as follows:

—See, if you're drunk at a school dance you're yourself. More aggressive. You can pick up a chick. (Laughs)

—Yeah.

—You got your goggles on and you're ready.

—Maybe get in a fight or two.

. . .

—The (name) situation is where you've been drinking too much and you get into what is known as the "beer goggles" and you don't have a good-looking girl but you end up fooling around with her.

(Laughter)

—You put your beer goggles on, the girls get skinnier, they're looking good though.

(Laughter)

—They get blonde hair.

. . .

—There you go. Like we'll be sitting in the commons around our little benches and stuff that we've got and we'll rate the girls going by by how many beers we'd have to take to, you know . . .

(Laughter)

—Sometimes it comes out to a keg or two.

(Laughter)

Members of a group or larger community may share abstract dramatizations that refer to specific scripts detailing similar plot lines, scenes, characters, and situations. These stock scenarios are further evidence that people have shared a series of specific dramatizations to which these more abstract stories refer. The general story that reflects all of these specific stories would be a *fantasy type*. Generally, when the story relates to personae such as fathers, friends, or cops, it is a fantasy type. An example from the transcripts about chewing tobacco illustrates the use of fantasy types as follows, ". . . but if you're going to try and get people to stop, the pressure that you might want to put on is to say that it's not cool and you're not going to pick up chicks, they're not going to get in your car because you have a chew because they say, 'Aw, that's gross.'" Notice that this is a story about generalized personae (*people* and *chicks*) rather than about specific individuals. The use of fantasy types or allusions to types in their messages is further evidence that dramatizations are shared.

People who come to share a cluster of fantasy themes and types typically integrate them into a coherent *rhetorical vision* of some aspect of their social reality. Using SCT as an explanatory account thus forces the investigator to search for the boundaries of rhetorical communities.

The focus group is particularly useful for determining boundaries between rhetorical visions because if several individuals from one rhetorical community are in a focus group with several individuals from another, the first cluster may share a fantasy, whereas the second cluster does not. Those who do not share may be either apathetic or clearly against that interpretation. The following transcripts represent boundary-defining dramatizations. One group responded to questions about athletics as follows:

> —Well, there's a lot of games that I really like but usually everyone just plays to beat up on each other.
> (Some laughter)
> ?= You like the . . .
> —The physical part.
> ?= It's physical, it's violent?
> —Yeah.
> (Some laughter)
> —You're sick.
> ?= Do you like athletic events in general?
> —(In unison) Yeah.
> . . .
> ?= You're a bunch of jocks, is that right?
> —(In unison) Yeah.

Another group of respondents, however, were negative about athletics. Here is an excerpt from their transcript when they were asked if they like athletics:

> —No.
> —Naw.
> . . .
> —Cause all the jocks think they're big stuff and they ain't nothin'.

When investigators find one group of respondents sharing the fantasy but another group rejecting it, these differences allow them to draw boundaries that divide the various rhetorical visions.

Using SCT as an explanatory account enables communication scholars to search for the boundaries of rhetorical communities and reveal the complex and complicated symbolic terrain of the typical audi-

ence for constructing persuasive messages relating to such matters as
quitting the use of tobacco or other addictive substances. Such an analysis is a strong antidote to interpretations that select out of such complexity a cluster of ideas and suggest that this cluster represents the essence
of a general audience's psychometrics.

The SCT-based focus group method leads investigators to analyze
the very same series of complex events, such as chewing or smoking tobacco, from the perspective of the rhetorical visions of the various communities in the target group. To illustrate, members of one group celebrated the
fun and adventure of recreation based on the daring and dangers involved
in wild parties, racing automobiles, drinking, and using tobacco, whereas
members of another group saw tobacco usage as a response to boredom
and an attempt at rebelling against parental and school authority.

METHOD

Participants

We gathered the data for this study from six focus group interviews
involving 63 participants. A sample of 63 participants for in-depth interviewing provides a good basis for conducting a symbolic convergence
analysis. The participants were young men and women enrolled in
junior or senior high schools. There were 22 male tobacco chewers interviewed; 8 of them were junior high school students from portions of the
state other than the metropolitan area, whereas the others were senior
high school students from the metropolitan area. Eighteen of the other
participants were male smokers; 12 were junior high school students
from the metropolitan area and 6 were senior high school students from
other parts of the state. The remaining 23 participants were female
smokers attending senior high schools; 6 were from the metropolitan
area and the remainder from other areas. Every effort was made to get a
substantial sample of respondents from the population of teenagers in
the state of Minnesota who use tobacco.

Procedures

Five interviewers, three women and two men, conducted the focus
groups. The interviewers had studied small group communication and
were trained in using symbolic convergence theory and fantasy theme
analysis. The interviewers were trained to conduct SCT-based focus
groups and used a common outline to conduct the interviews. (For an

excellent discussion of the administration and conduct of SCT-based focus groups, see the next chapter by Cragan and Shields.) Male interviewers conducted the three focus group composed of all male subjects, female interviewers conducted the two groups that were composed of female subjects, and a male/female team of interviewers conducted the equally balanced mixed-gender group.

The focus groups began with open-ended questions and then focused on the main purposes of the interview as the discussion proceeded. The investigators prepared a brief discussion outline of the main questions to focus on and used this outline as a guide rather than as a straightjacket. In all instances, they succeeded in bringing the conversations around to the main questions. Often the groups took tangents and this free-wheeling was likely to take place early in the interview. As the meetings continued and group members began to dramatize more and more and the fantasy sharing picked up, the interviewers began to focus the discussions more sharply. This method allowed the audience members themselves to explain their social reality relating to the issue, rather than relying on preconceived notions of what should be important to the audience.

Evidence that this method was effective is provided by the fact that by the sixth meeting the interviews were becoming repetitive of the first five interviews. Reaching the point of diminishing returns for new shared fantasies is evidence that the universe of discourse under study has largely been surveyed.

The interviews lasted for about 50-60 minutes each. All participants agreed to have the interviews audiotaped and videotaped. The audiotapes were transcribed and when there was difficulty in deciphering them they were checked against the videotapes. The transcriptions plus the repeated analyses of the videotapes formed the basis for the detailed analysis. The videotapes proved to be particularly helpful in studying important nonverbal interactions that indicated the sharing or rejecting of dramatizations.

Symbolic convergence theory when combined with knowledge about group dynamics offers information unlike traditional focus group techniques. Often investigators using the traditional approach only report direct answers to direct questions. An example of how the two approaches differ can be found in the answers given to the question, "Why did you start using tobacco?," posed during these interviews. The male chewers in one segment of the respondents responded definitely, "It wasn't peer pressure." The stories that they shared, however, revealed that peer pressure was indeed a strong motivational factor. To report only a summary of their responses would have missed this factor. The female tobacco users in another rhetorical community responded to the question by answering that "peer pressure" was the main reason they started using tobacco. However, the stories they shared most revolved around family members and relatives who used or introduced them to tobacco. Again, a strict summary of their responses would have given a faulty picture of what was most important regarding the factors contributing to their use of tobacco.

RESULTS

Our analysis of the focus group discourse revealed three coherent visions among the various groups of tobacco users in regard to the meaning of tobacco use in their lives. We have voluminous data supporting our discovery of three rhetorical visions, and we reported much of it to the Minnesota Center for Nonsmoking and Health. In the discussion of the visions here we include only representative segments from the tapes to support and illustrate our descriptions of the rhetorical visions. These excerpts are edited to eliminate redundancies and restatements but contain the essential meaning.

Vision One: The Adventuresome Jock in Control of His World

The central fantasy of rhetorical Vision One is the teenage male as a special breed of macho, adventuresome jock, living on the edge, savoring the rush of adrenaline as he stretches the limits of societal codes and rules to live dangerously. There is little excitement and not much fun in this rhetorical world without danger. Active and passive recreation, revolving around automobiles, sex, danger, sports, excitement and violence, gain much of their fun from danger and rebellion against authority.

Recreation involves such things as drinking parties with lots of women and beer where unexpected and violent things may happen. Getting drunk, driving fast, having sex, and physically fighting represent a good time. Recreation for members of this rhetorical vision involves watching and participating in athletics, particularly those characterized by violence, such as football, hockey, and rough broomball games (they reject basketball and other less violent sports). They enjoy movies and TV shows that stress sex and violence. However it is accomplished, the main ingredient is risk and flirting with danger.

Automobiles are fun in and of themselves as they can provide thrills because of the danger in speeding, reckless driving, and driving while drunk. The following fantasizing communication documents the presence of this element of the rhetorical vision:

?= What about automobiles? Do you like automobiles?

—(In unison) Yeah.

—Driving fast.

—Four-wheel driving, fast cars, and fast women. (Laughs)

—. . . four-wheel down there.

—Muddin', muddin'.

?= What do you do when you get in the car?

—Abuse it. (Laughs)

—Music.

—Turn on the music loud.

—Crank the tuners as loud as they can go . . .

—Put in a chew, and you're off.

—Put in a big chew.

Teenagers in the first rhetorical vision see drinking alcohol and chewing tobacco as integral parts of the scene when they are having a good time. Because they view themselves as athletes (jocks), they generally reject smoking and smokers because they see smoking as having a negative influence on athletic performance, whereas chewing does not. Smoking is also less macho than chewing and more likely the province of females. They also see smoking as more dangerous to their health and more unpleasant for others.

Vision One teenagers see their high schools as filled with cliques of students. Cliques include students who take academic subjects and study hard ("They stay home all weekend to do their homework . . . They don't drink . . . They don't party."); those who dress and wear their hair in the style of the larger cultural group known as punks; trendies who wear nice clothes, have money to spend, and do not smoke; dirtballs who smoke tobacco; druggies or headbangers who listen to loud music and are "stoned out of their heads"; and so forth.

—No, like, okay, our school is like really "cliquey," you know, and if you go to a party with a different clique, the party will end up separating, you know. One clique will go over here, the other clique will be over there.

. . .

—You guys are rednecks. Every single one of you is a redneck.

The participants in the first rhetorical vision are also part of a clique. They are rednecks, jocks who drive four wheelers or pickups and dress southwestern style with cowboy boots, and chewing tobacco is an important part of their self-identity. Although they testify that they did not start using tobacco because of "peer pressure," they also report that it was natural to begin when hanging out with group members, most of whom were chewing. Group norms are thus an important reason for their use of tobacco. They recognize that many others in their school environment as well as in the larger society find their chewing repulsive or "gross," but they are defiant about their use of tobacco and see it as an important way of rebelling against societal restraints and repressions, and in this defiance and rebellion they gain strong support from the bonds within their high school clique.

Teenagers who participate in the first rhetorical vision indicate their rebellion in a number of ways. One of the strongest villains in their symbolic world is the "cop." They are hassled by the police who often pull them over when they are driving to check if they have been drinking. Cops have it in for them and give them undue attention.

—The cops, when you're our age, like maybe you're driving down the highway, you know . . . and whenever you pass a cop you have to turn down your radio . . .
—They look for you.
—Yeah, they're looking for you, and every teenager's bad.

Another set of rules are part of the high school environment. They develop ways to chew in class without detection because discovery will result in punishment. They have difficulty finding approved places to chew. The smoking lounge is blue with smoke and, as indicated, members of the first vision have some animosity toward smokers in any case.

Interestingly enough, participants in the first vision are not particularly worried about parental response to their chewing. Their families may not approve, but their rebellion against parental authority is apparently over, and they are now bucking the society of the school and the larger community.

Concomitant with their love of danger is the recognition that there is a downside to their lifestyle. Aside from such mundane considerations as the cost of tobacco, the members of this vision realize that they might not be able to attract the woman of their dreams because of their macho, daring, and rebellious ideals.

?= Do you guys have problems with girls because you chew?
—Yeah.
—Yeah. When your girlfriend comes over to your house, they

always check your lip before they kiss you, and they take it out of your teeth.

—Yeah.

—His girlfriend chews anything.

(Some laughter)

—My girlfriend wouldn't kiss me for a whole day if she saw me with it in. She'd say, "Well, you're going to have to wait until tomorrow."

—"Brush your teeth."

As we mentioned previously, a prominent inside cue in one focus group that was shared widely was that of "beer goggles." A participant who began a party or school dance with a clear-eyed appreciation of sexy and attractive women might have failed in his attempt to attract such a person, and as he continued drinking he found a female whom he would not look at twice while sober becoming more and more attractive. In general, attractive women often found tobacco chewing repulsive and were turned off by the practice, and, hence, the substitution of less desirable women required "beer goggles."

Participants in the first rhetorical vision also recognized that their lifestyle posed hazards to their health and well-being. Driving while drunk is dangerous, so they often had a designated driver who stayed sober and "did not have any fun" but could console himself with a chew while the others lived it up.

Although they perceived smoking as more dangerous to their health than chewing, they were informed fully about the dangers of cancer and other ailments of the mouth that stemmed from chewing tobacco.

?= You mentioned your health. Is it bad for your health to chew?

—Yeah.

—Oh, yeah.

?= What's the problem?

—The bottom half of your face can fall off.

(Some laughter)

—Or your tongue, or the back of your mouth, or your face can get mangled and you die.

—A little lip-rot sometimes.

—Esophagus cancer.

—Everybody knows . . .

—Yeah, we all know it's bad for you.

—We can live with . . . (Hard to hear)

—It's a risk, a fun risk.

—It's another risk.

—You think, "Oh, it won't happen to me."

—The thing is, you believe it but they try and scare you. I mean they take out, I mean if they told you the actual numbers of this . . .

—Yeah, right.

—. . . it's so minimal. They make it sound like it's going to happen to you automatically if you chew, which is a big scam. I mean, chances are maybe your dentist will say, you know, you're going to have to have your lip scraped in order to check it out. I mean, the thing that happens, I mean, they act like it's just going to, bam! It's just going to happen like that . . .

—One (dip?) and your jaw's going to fall off.

(Some laughter)

—. . . and chances of that happening are so minimal.

—Oh, yeah.

—They're trying to scare ya.

—The thing is, if your lip hurts you don't put a chew in for a while. You let it heal up.

In general, the hero in rhetorical Vision One is a persona who is in charge of his own life. He takes risks and enjoys living in the fast lane, but when troubles come he is willing to take responsibility for them. In his vision, things do not so much happen to him as he chooses to make them happen. Participants in Vision One are young, vigorous, and healthy, and feel that dangerous health problems are likely to come upon one gradually. If in a dozen years or so they find themselves suffering symptoms from their chewing then they will quit. Withdrawal symptoms would be difficult but they would manage.

If a suitable reward for quitting were presented to them, members of Vision One felt that, as with most things in their lives, they could control their chewing habit, and quit.

?= But if someone offered you a new car you'd take the withdrawal and quit?

—Yeah.

—Oh yeah.

—Yup.

—You could sit in the car and twitch all you want.

—Guys get over withdrawal, that's no big . . . (Hard to hear).

Participants in rhetorical Vision One tend to live in the present much more than they recall the past. Very few of their shared fantasies related to older family members or acquaintances or to events of even the recent past. They did, however, have some sense of the future and a feeling that their high school days might be a unique time and that their dedication to chewing might be tied closely to their present lifestyle and reference groups. Perhaps chewing is a passing fad they will drop when they move on to other activities.

—There's another guy, a guy I work with, who's twenty-five, you know, he chewed for seven years and he's out of college and all that and he just said, "Screw it, why should I do it, you know? It's over now and I can quit, and, you know—"

—It's only fun when you're in school.

—Right, right.

Vision Two: Bored and Drifting Middle School Males

The core of rhetorical Vision Two is the young male as a bored and drifting immature but maturing man-child living in a world of things and appetites that are largely beyond his control. Participants in Vision Two are not talkers and do not elaborate on events. Instead, they react, often in literal ways, to what life presents them. Active and passive recreation gains much of its fun from the satisfaction of basic appetites. Like the members of Vision One, their recreational world revolves around automobiles, sex, danger, excitement, and violence. Unlike participants in Vision One, however, members of the second group do not talk about and elaborate imaginatively on their interests. Instead, they tend to have trouble putting their recreation into any but the most basic and monosyllabic terms.

The participants of Vision Two are not athletes and, indeed, are anti-jock. They view jocks as undeservedly popular high schoolers who often gain their place on the team and in the school because they have money and their parents spend it on them to assure their standing. Jocks would not dare to come to a party dominated by participants in Vision Two because they might get "beat up." Members of Vision Two, much more than members of Vision One, are likely to seek rather quiet recreation, such as hunting, fishing, or camping in the outdoors.

Like the participants in Vision One, part of the excitement in life for members of Vision Two comes from the danger of rebelling against authority, including the rules and regulations of their school. They enjoy an element of risk and danger, and they too are particularly fond of violent movies.

One of the important aids to recreation is the automobile. Like the members of rhetorical Vision One, they see cars as fun in and of themselves and as an avenue to sexual popularity, as well as providing thrills because of the dangers of speeding and riding on slippery roads. However, those in the second vision also see the automobile as fun to work on and tune up.

These teenagers are also part of a culture filled with cliques and groups. They believe their status and standing in the school community are related closely to membership in these subgroups. Indeed, in the two focus groups of 8th- and 9th-grade males, in each instance the eighth graders sat on one side of the table and the ninth graders sat on the other.

Like the members of rhetorical Vision One, members of Vision Two also see "cops" as villainous personae trying to hassle them.

—They drive around on (street name), just looking for kids.

—Yeah, they sit in front of the liquor store just waiting for you to come up drunk.

—Yeah.

—They're supposed to be on the highways to assist you, and not to trap you like that.

—Yeah.

—Yeah, I don't know, any time you go by Country Kitchen there are always four cops there, sitting.

—Just staring out the windows.

—Yeah.

Unlike members of rhetorical Vision One, however, those in Vision Two are more preoccupied with their families and are sometimes in conflict with parents about their lifestyle and, particularly, their tobacco usage.

—Now my mom's quit smoking and now she's really, she's giving me all these lectures and stuff, like, "You know every time you have a cigarette you're going to die six minutes earlier," and stuff like that.

—Oh, my mom, she just says, "It's going to kill you someday," I say, "Yeah." "So you should quit!" (Hard to hear, perhaps "Yeah I'm quitting.") She just gives me hell.

(Laughter)

?= Are there people you admire who chew?

—My grandpa. He started chewing since he was younger than us and he's still living.

(Some laughter)

—Yeah, with no teeth!

Despite the enjoyment of parties, beer, tobacco, automobiles, and the outdoors, the overwhelming character of Vision Two is that of a drifting persona in a boring world. The aimless nature of the present, as well as their preoccupation with the present, are indicated by the following attempts by the interviewer to get the participants to dramatize about their work plans and their view of the future.

?= . . . Let's talk a little bit about work. How do you view work? Is it a necessary evil to make some money or do you enjoy working?

—Need the money.

—Depends on what you do.

?= What do you think you'd like to do if you had a chance to get a job?

—Mechanics.

?= Work on large, small engines, cars?

—Cars.

?= Any other thoughts on that? People who said you didn't have a job, do you want a job?

—Of course.

?= What would you like to do if you got a job.

—I don't know of anything right off.

—Something besides dish washing.

. . .

?= Say ten years from now, what would you like to do?

—Nothing. Be retired.

(Laughter)

?= Anybody want to add to this notion of getting a job where you could work on motors or cars? Or anything else that you see around here that you'd say, "Well, I'd kind of like to do that?"

(Long pause)

The central persona in the second rhetorical vision participates in a world that views the drawbacks to tobacco usage as more mundane and less important than those in Vision One. Members of Vision Two have a much greater concern for the expense involved in using tobacco than do the teenagers in Vision One. Vision One participants were preoccupied strongly with women and their response to tobacco use, whereas those in Vision Two are interested only mildly in these matters.

?= . . . What do girls think of chewing?

—They don't really like it . . .

—I don't know. I think they just blow it off. I don't think they really care that much.

—If they want to be part of (hard to hear) they can learn to chew, right?

(Laughter)

—My old girlfriend chewed.

. . .

?= Can you think of a time when a girl hasn't liked it when you were chewing?

—No.

—Well, maybe . . . gross.

—Well, I was at her house and I put a chew in and I tried to give her a kiss and she—

(General laughter). . .

—She said, "No, no!" (in a high voice). . .

Whereas participants in Vision One are well informed about the dangers of chewing and have well-thought-through and elaborate arguments to deal with health issues, those in Vision Two have some of the basic information but in much simpler form, and they are much less concerned about the dangers.

?= What is your response to those other messages, where somebody says it's going to be hard on your health, all those messages?

—Gets on your nerves after a while.

—Most of them don't smoke and they don't even know what

they're talking about.

—Kind of sick of hearing about it.

?= Is it bad for you?

—The bottom lip. Well, that's just what people tell us, we don't really, we haven't seen anything bad happen, other than what's appeared on movies.

?= Was that scary?

—No, 'cause look at all the other people that have been chewing for so long that are still going.

—How long have people been chewing? How many hundreds of years, and now in the last ten years why is it so bad?

—Yeah.

—Yeah.

. . .

?= Do you see a reason to quit chewing?

—No.

—Nope.

In general, the participants in rhetorical Vision Two are 8th-or 9th-grade males who either smoked or chewed tobacco, although some did both. The smokers felt little antagonism toward the chewers and vice versa. They were, for the most part, from outstate Minnesota or from the outer suburbs. In their rhetorical vision, events are often controlling and the participants are often at loose ends. They need a job but either cannot find one or those that are available to them are menial and uninteresting. They are bored and not sure what to do about it. They live in a world that is confined largely to an immediate present that is literal and basic. They seem to deal with it better at the level of action than at the level of language. Unlike members of the first vision, who had little sense of the past but did have some feeling for their future, participants in the second rhetorical vision have little thought for what is likely to happen to them in the next 5 or 10 years. Any danger to their health that is not immediate is not interpreted as a threat.

They live in a rhetorical vision in which they are largely reactive. They are not active participants in sports or other school activities. At a loss for anything better to do, they might go home and "crash" or go "play pool." Other people or fates are responsible largely for what happens to the participants in rhetorical Vision Two. When the police arrest a person for being drunk, it is the fault of the police for lying in wait for the teenager rather than being out on the highway helping people. If someone gets cancer from using tobacco it is because his time is up and it was his fate to get sick.

Vision Three: Family-oriented Teenagers Testing Limits and Searching for Ties

Although all of the members of rhetorical Vision Three are teenage, female smokers, we conducted one focus group with an even number of males and females and include some comments from the males when appreciable numbers of females shared the dramatizations. In using material from the mixed-gender group, we indicate whether the speaker is male or female.

Participants in the third rhetorical vision live in a world that differs most dramatically from those in Visions One and Two in the way the extended family dominates the scene. Whereas the immediate family was almost nonexistent in the communication of members of rhetorical Vision One, it provides the symbolic ground for many of those in the third rhetorical vision. The dramas of participants in the third rhetorical vision are populated first by their immediate family (their fathers, mothers, sisters, and brothers), but they also tell stories of their cousins (often involved in their starting to smoke), uncles and aunts, and grandfathers and grandmothers.

On the question of parental authority, participants in Vision Three are divided. Many important stories come from the central story line that has a young female smoker gaining some excitement from testing the intrafamily limits. They dare to break the family rules and often get harassed, grounded, "bawled out," and punished in other ways when discovered.

Others in Vision Three portray the family as having been too permissive in allowing smoking. There is a tone of wistfulness to these dramas that suggest that the participants might have desired stronger rules to test themselves against.

Participants in Vision Three often refer to health problems and smoking practices of members of their extended family, including even grandparents and cousins as well as parents and siblings:

> (F)—My mom's dad, and her stepdad, all her relatives have all died from lung cancer from smoking . . .
>
> (F)—Okay, I thought of that, and . . . But then again, in my family, 'cause my great-grandfather smoked from the time he was nine years old until he was, like, I think he died when he was like ninety-six. He smoked a pack and a half to two packs a day every single day from the time he was nine and when he died he did not have one bit of cancer in him.

Although they are ambivalent about their family experience, in that for some it is a source of comfort and support, whereas for others it is a source of pressure and frustration, it is nonetheless the major feature of their rhetorical vision. The importance of family is indicated by a substantial sharing of the "crush and flush" fantasy type in which an elementary school student first learns about the dangers of smoking and then goes home to crush and flush a parent's cigarettes. Ironically, when the same students reach junior high school, they find themselves bored and experiment with smoking out of curiosity and in a search for "something to do." They thus end up as teenage smokers.

Second only to family members in rhetorical Vision Three is the persona of the "boyfriend." Although the presence of the females may have inhibited the males in some regards, it is also possible that by participating in a mixed-gender focus group the men found themselves expressing a more balanced approach to male-female relationships or at least another dimension to it than did the members of the all-male groups. Even though participants in rhetorical Vision Three share dramas about male-female relationships and "cruising" and "chasing boys," they do not share fantasies about "one-night stands," "scoring," or "getting laid," as do participants in Visions One and Two. They have an implied sense of commitment in that if they were in a serious relationship with a male who wanted them to quit smoking they might well do so.

Participants in the third rhetorical vision, like those in the other two, live in a high school culture filled with cliques of students. They specifically do not view themselves as losers or drifters. They are busy with school activities, such as plays, and with school work. They recognize that many others in their school environment find their smoking repulsive or not "cool." Their portrayal of such groups is that the members' antismoking attitude is too bad and "their problem." They have a "live and let live" approach to smoking. As one participant said, "It doesn't matter, though, I mean. If they don't like me because I smoke that's their problem. I've got other people, you know, that are my friends."

Members of rhetorical Vision Three live in a recreational world that revolves around automobiles, parties, drinking, smoking, and doing things with "best" friends. They portray themselves as active and knowledgeable, adventuresome, and interested in fun, excitement, members of the opposite sex, and the future:

?= So, how do you think of yourselves? Do you think of yourself as an athlete, or—

(F)—Stoner. Just kidding. (Laughter) Just kidding. I don't do that.

(F)—Original.

(F)—Yeah.

. . .

(F)—You're not stuck-up or anything but then you're not real down low.

(F)—You're not in a clique.

(F)—I'm not in a clique.

(F)—Just regular.

(F)—Yeah.

(F)—You're not trendy, you're not with the cheerleaders, the headbangers.

(M)—It used to be cool to smoke, or whatever, back in the fifties and sixties. (Laughter) I don't know, I guess, that's what they tell me anyway. But nowadays it ain't cool to smoke. But, it's not just wastes that smoke and losers that smoke, you know, leather jackets, long hair and pierced ears that smoke . . . It's, you know, a lot of people smoke.

Participants in the third rhetorical vision are active and seldom bored. Their rhetorical vision portrays recreation as revolving around automobiles. Automobiles are fun in and of themselves but they also are fun to cruise around in and for the purpose of seeing and meeting people. Cars are a means to sexual popularity in that female teenagers who have cars will often give males rides, and visa versa. Automobiles provide additional thrills because of the danger in speeding and reckless driving. Music is also an important part of the recreational scene for these teenagers. In addition, they like a greater variety of movies than the horror or action films preferred by respondents in Visions One and Two. Athletic events are also important to members of Vision Three, both as participants and spectators. They also recognize that their lifestyle poses hazards to their health and well being. They may deny that the dangers are imminent or suggest that when they are under less pressure to do well in school, plan their future, or deal with personal problems, they will be able to quit. Sometimes they portray an ideal situation in which nonsmokers would simply leave them alone and cease "bugging" them to quit. As one respondent said, "After all, it is my body."

In general, the participants in rhetorical Vision Three have a broader view of time than those in Visions One and Two. Perhaps their kinship orientation provides them with a sense of the past, at least of their family's past. Even though they have this sense of the past, they are very much living in the present, and the present is often one in which they are pressured and harried by family conditions or their school environments. They also have a strong sense of the future and some of their daily, current pressures come from contemplating this future.

Some share fantasies about the pressures of the immediate future as they contemplate leaving high school and going into the world. Others dramatize the "who wants to live forever scenario," and still others share the drama that if health problems appear in the future a person can always quit smoking and their lungs will return to normal.

(F)—Smoking is good when you're under pressure.

(F)—Yeah.

. . .

(F)—I think, well everybody's going to die sooner or later. I really don't want to get old in the first place.

(F)—Yeah.

(Laughter)

(F)—It bothers me, growing old. It scares me.

. . .

(M)—If you get lung cancer you're going to die. I don't know what the percentage of smokers, how many smokers do actually get cancer, and how many smokers don't. I've heard that you can smoke a pack a day for ten years and if you quit smoking for one year your lungs will be completely white again. I've heard that too.

(F)—If you quit smoking your lungs will turn back to normal unless you've smoked for so many years that the cilia in your lungs have dropped off.

Still, they portray themselves as capable of responsible action. The world may be difficult and filled with pressures, but they can make choices and control their fate somewhat.

RECOMMENDATIONS FOR CONSTRUCTING PERSUASIVE MESSAGES

Analysis of the rhetorical visions of the respondents allowed the investigators to make a series of recommendations about the persuasive communication campaign planned by the Center for Nonsmoking and Health. The researchers presented these findings to the planners who created dramatized scenarios for public service announcements on televised broadcasts of the state hockey tournament. This section explains the implications and recommendations for each rhetorical vision.

Recommendations for Vision One

The participants in Vision One are probably reached best through the electronic media, although the print media should not be ruled out entirely. They are very much interested in sports, both in terms of participation and watching on television. They prefer action and violence in their sports. They do not care for basketball, but like football and hockey and are likely to watch professional games in these sports, as well as state high school tournaments. They also like loud, modern music and listen to radio stations, particularly when driving around. Members of rhetorical Vision One also commented about magazine and newspaper stories they had read and were generally well informed about the basic health hazards of tobacco usage.

With regard to the content of the persuasive messages, there are certain themes that could catch the interest of those who share Vision One, whereas others would most likely not do so. For example, they are unlikely to be influenced by significant others. Of all the interviewees, the participants in this vision are least preoccupied with or influenced by immediate family members. They are also unlikely to change their chewing habits because of the influence of a girlfriend.

They also see the police as villainous personae who hassle them. Secondarily, the school authorities who punish them for infringement of the school rules are viewed negatively, although their attitude toward coaches who would kick them off a team for using tobacco is ambivalent.

Members of this rhetorical vision are very much involved in thinking about automobiles and women. Messages that include interesting automobiles and good-looking women, therefore, will catch the favorable attention of this audience. Hijinks, practical jokes, escapades like bridge jumping, and bathroom humor are additional action lines that appeal to these teenagers.

There is also an apparent and important contradiction in the first rhetorical vision that can be used in developing persuasive messages for this audience. Two major preoccupations of these teenagers are at odds: the central place that chewing holds in their clique or group versus their preoccupation with sexual relationships with attractive women. Males who share this vision made it clear that many attractive women are turned off by their chewing and thus their sexual success is handicapped by their tobacco habit. In this instance, they may feel a frustration with how chewing interferes with their desire to be smooth and successful with women, and this can be used as a persuasive theme in changing their behavior.

They also are probably feeling the contradiction between their interest in sports and health and their use of tobacco. Some are clearly trying to alleviate this strain by diminishing the importance of the health hazard, whereas others are suggesting a change sometime in the future. Consequently, when asked for suggestions on how to appeal to this audience, a vocal minority suggested the use of high fear arousal appeals to health:

—If you're trying to stop a future generation from chewing well, then, have them look at some mangled faces.

—Right, and then, it helps if like in the paper or in a *Time* article or something you'll see this kid that was, ah, Joe Football Player, All-Star all this, and he was a really heavy chewer and then he started getting cancer and then, you know, he had to get all this surgery on his face and everything, you know. He was Joe Stud until he got all this, until his face got mangled up.

The usefulness of high fear arousal appeals in changing attitudes and behaviors has been investigated extensively, and the early studies indicated that medium fear arousals were more effective than low or high fear appeals (Janis & Fleshbach, 1953; Leventhal, 1967). These studies have been reevaluated, however, in light of their methodology and changing circumstances. Smith (1982) noted that the facilitating effects of appealing to fear may be short-lived. There is some evidence that initial exposure to high fear appeals may have longer effects than moderate appeals. Fear arousal messages need to include or be accompanied by further messages that provide a workable remedy, clear steps on how to implement that remedy, and images that suggest that the remedy is effective. In this instance, some use of appeals to health and perhaps some high fear arousals might be indicated at the beginning of a campaign to catch the interest of the audience and make the contradiction in their rhetorical vision clear and unavoidable. Care should be taken, however, not to overdramatize the dangers or to oversimplify the threat because members of rhetorical Vision One are suspicious of instant dangers and quick fixes. Then, too, since they do not feel that chewing has been the subject of much attention in persuasive campaigns to this point, some strong messages pointing out the contradiction between athletic performance and health, on the one hand, and chewing tobacco, on the other, might be a possibility. Respondents in Vision One, however, noted the way good athletes often chew tobacco when their games are televised, so such messages would have to be drafted in light of this factor.

Appealing to health concerns is supported further by the fact that although members of rhetorical Vision One share dramas about excitement and risk, they also are concerned about safety as represented by stories about the dangers of driving while drunk and having a designated driver to assure against such risks. They also shared stories about plans to take steps to change or stop chewing when a dentist or a doctor discovers they have a health problem. These latter fantasies indicate a realistic understanding of the future. Their sense of future, coupled with their "locus of control" in being able to take charge of their lives, poses some promising openings for persuasion aimed at this particular audience.

Recommendations for Vision Two

The participants in rhetorical Vision Two are more difficult to reach through the mass media than those in Vision One. Vision Two members report that they do not watch much television. They are also not interested very much in music and, therefore, probably do not listen to the radio a great deal. They are not language-oriented and probably do not read very much. Perhaps television would be the best medium for reaching this segment of the audience if personal contacts are unavailable.

Participants in the second rhetorical vision are more concerned with the reactions of their families than those in the first rhetorical vision, but they are just as unlikely as the first group to be influenced by family members who might urge them to quit using tobacco.

The teenage males in rhetorical Vision One were all chewers and with the young male chewers in rhetorical Vision Two they comprise the sample of young male chewers in the focus groups. Both audience segments were involved with automobiles and women. What was said about the power of the images of the automobile and of attractive teenage females for the first group holds true for this audience as well. The younger group is probably more shy and in even earlier stages of learning how to relate to females, but they are already showing evidence of the emergence of dramatizations of male-female relationships that are very similar to those in rhetorical Vision One. Some of this is undoubtedly braggadocio in this audience, but the same attitudes are implied strongly by the shared dramatizations.

The participants in rhetorical Vision Two, however, are not very open to persuasive messages that imply that attractive women will not go out with teenage males who use tobacco. In the first place, women are not as important for the younger audience as they are for senior high school males. In the second place, they are not yet convinced that using tobacco really makes a male less attractive to women.

Strong, direct fear appeals to their health are also less useful with audience members in rhetorical Vision Two than they might be with those in Vision One. Although their argumentative defenses are less sophisticated than those in Vision One, the younger group is so immersed in the present that any future health threat seems largely irrelevant.

Members of rhetorical Vision Two seem to be creatures of whim, and many report that they have tried to quit, although their efforts seem halfhearted. They began using tobacco casually and on the spur of the moment. They also may have decided to quit in the same manner only to just as casually start up again. The casual aimlessness of these teenagers makes it difficult to achieve lasting nonsmoking behavior on their part.

The one problem that members of rhetorical Vision Two dramatize as a real difficulty is the growing expense of supporting their tobacco habit. Messages that appeal to the high cost of using tobacco might possibly appeal to this segment of the audience. Still, given their drifting, reactive stance, they might start up again with a shift in their financial fortunes or a change of friends or group membership. Indeed, some of these teenagers shared the drama of learning about the dangers of tobacco as elementary school children and trying to "crush or flush" their parents' cigarettes, only to start smoking themselves at a later time. All in all, the members of this rhetorical vision pose some of the greatest difficulties in constructing effective persuasive messages of all the interviewees in the focus groups.

Recommendations for Vision Three

The participants in rhetorical Vision Three are probably reached more easily through all media of communication than those in the other visions. They are interested in sports and watch television, and they also like music and listen to the radio. They did not comment much about reading habits, but they told more stories and longer stories than members of the other rhetorical visions. They even commented about anti-smoking slogans, such as "Kiss a nonsmoker, taste the difference" and "Ashtray mouth."

Members of the third rhetorical vision provide, perhaps, the most options of all the interviewees for persuasion aimed at changing their smoking habits. Like members of the other visions, the participants in Vision Three are interested in automobiles and persons of the opposite sex. They like to party, drink beer, go to the movies, and listen to music. All of these activities represent powerful images to be considered in constructing persuasive messages.

Members of this rhetorical vision also often feel pressured and harried, and they dramatize smoking as a coping mechanism that enables them to deal with the problems of their life. They also worry about the withdrawal symptoms if or when they quit, the effect of their stopping on their friends and the groups with which they are associated, as well as their tendency to substitute eating or drinking for smoking and the resultant gain in weight. These barriers to stopping need to be dealt with in a persuasive campaign, although the negative suggestion inherent in such messages should also be considered. Some of these teenagers also noted the expense of smoking as a reason to quit, and this positive message needs to be stressed.

The greatest motivation present in this audience segment for stopping smoking is to be found in their web of interpersonal relationships, and the most powerful, significant persona is that of the boyfriend. This teenager would probably quit smoking if she loved her boyfriend and he urged her to stop.

> (F)—I was going with someone who didn't like it so I quit. And then I started smoking again after I broke up with him.
>
> . . .
>
> (F)—Well, (boyfriend's name) hates it when I smoke too.
>
> (F)—Yeah, but he hates it because he doesn't like the taste.
>
> ?= What does he not like about it?
>
> (F)—I don't know. He just doesn't like the smell of it, and . . .
>
> (F)—He doesn't like it, 'cause I'll give him a kiss and then . . .
>
> (F)—Ooooh, pooh, I'm tasting after-taste.
>
> (Slight laughter)

One interviewee dramatized a future child and portrayed the persona of the child as a reason to quit.

> (F)—I know when I go to have a kid I'm not going to smoke while I'm pregnant.
>
> . . .
>
> (F)—'Cause I don't want to endanger the life of my kid, and I know that can become a hazard when you're pregnant.
>
> (F)—But can you quit smoking?
>
> (F)—Yeah.
>
> (F)—For an important cause.
>
> (F)—Yeah.

Another set of powerful personae who can influence members of this rhetorical vision to quit or to try to quit are their parents:

> (F)—Yeah, to make your parents happy.
>
> . . .

(F)—I don't know. My mom found out about it. I think that's
why.

(F)—She can't smoke because of her dad. (About a member of
the focus group who has decided to stop.)

Some members of rhetorical Vision Three were also open to appeals to
the health dangers of smoking:

(F)—My mom's dad, and her stepdad, all her relatives have all
died from lung cancer from smoking, so . . . It's kind of, just
thinking about that. It makes you think, "Well, I'm going to die
too," you know. (From an interviewee who had decided to quit.)

(F)—I began to smoke really heavy and one night, my heart, I
had trouble sleeping, it would go "b-b-b-b-b-b" and then it
would stop for a couple seconds and then "b-b-b-b-b-b" again
(slight laugh) and it really scared me, so I really thought
about quitting and I cut down a lot and since then I smoke
occasionally, but I don't smoke real heavy.

The participants in the third rhetorical vision thus seem more open
to messages about giving up tobacco than do those of the other two rhetorical visions. They have tried to cut back or quit more often. They also have a
strong orientation to the future and, particularly, to human relationships as
represented by their families, their boyfriends, and their future progeny.

CONCLUSIONS

Symbolic convergence theory is a general theory of communication that
is useful both for basic research (Bormann, 1989; Bormann, 1990) and
applied research. A growing number of communication scholars and
practitioners are using symbolic convergence theory to segment markets
for products or to analyze audiences for health, political, and public service messages (e.g., Cragan & Shields, 1992; this volume).

Investigators who employ symbolic convergence theory need to
use research methods that allow them to find the fantasy themes, inside
cues, and fantasy types that provide data about the rhetorical visions of
the various communities of people in a given audience. Some investigators analyze written messages, some use individual interviews, and
some use focus group interviews. These methods yield information that
researchers can analyze further through Q-sort techniques (e.g., Cragan
& Shields, 1981), content analysis, or the statistical discovery of factor
types that represent rhetorical visions.

Because symbolic convergence theory is a social theory, the use of focus group interviews to find shared fantasies is often indicated. When investigators use individual interviews there is always a possibility that the dramas they collect will be idiosyncratic. Indeed, one of the things that facilitators conducting focus group meetings must guard against is being overly distracted by the contributions of one talkative member whose comments represent only that respondent's opinions in the group. The dynamics of a symbolic convergence focus group, however, often encourage members to reveal the nature of their rhetorical visions. Group members have difficulty malingering or faking their responses to previously shared or rejected dramatizations. The excitement of the past fantasy chains tends to pull members into supporting them when they are redramatized.

SCT-based focus groups are not, however, always the best method for gaining information about an audience for the purposes of creating and evaluating messages. This method is considerably more sophisticated and complicated than other forms of focus groups. Not only do the interviewers need to know about group dynamics, but they also need to be well versed in the technical concepts of symbolic convergence theory and must stimulate respondents to dramatize during an interview.

Another important limitation of the focus group technique in general applies to this particular type of focus group and is illustrated by our study. The use of systematically selected participants does not allow any statistically significant estimate of how participants in these visions may be distributed throughout the total population of young female and male users (chewers and smokers) of tobacco in the state of Minnesota. Such information would require a survey of a large, representative sample. However, Bormann, Kroll, Watters, and McFarland (1984) have developed a technique in their voter studies that allows the results of focus group studies such as this one to be used as the basis for conducting a large sample survey that could provide evidence as to how these visions are distributed throughout the state of Minnesota.

Kreps's chapter on using focus group discussions in field studies illustrated the strengths of a typical investigation in the analysis of four posters designed to encourage "safe sex." The facilitator focused the group on each poster and gathered information about such things as attention, interest, comfort, understanding, and believability. Much of the early focus group work in marketing followed this technique of providing group members with a product, having them use the product, and then having the focus group discuss the things the respondents liked or disliked about it.

For some specific campaigns, such as the poster development study explained in the last chapter, the focus group that is organized tightly around specific questions related to already formulated messages is often best. The Center for Nonsmoking and Health, however, hoped to use the results of the focus group studies not only to evaluate the three programs under development, but to provide an understanding of the audience of teenage tobacco users and to guide future campaigns as well.

Approximately the last 20 minutes of each focus group interview in this case study of teenage tobacco use was devoted to market testing three anti-tobacco commercials that were in the planning stages for the Minnesota Department of Health. The commercials were later aired during the Minnesota State High School Hockey Tournament. The interviewers based their questions about the commercials around four main areas of: (a) Were the messages memorable?; (b) Were the commercials believable?; (c) What did the messages communicate?; and (d) How might the messages be improved for this market? We were thus able to compare the usefulness of the symbolic convergence analysis in the larger portion of the interviews with the specific testing of the commercials at the end of the meetings. This comparison then led to changes in the commercials.

An example of the way that symbolic convergence theory aided in improving the announcements is provided by the "Cooper's Station Script." The script was set in a gas station, and the relevant portion of the first script was as follows:

Charlene and Rhonda walk to the pumps with cans of diet pop. Rhonda is smoking.

Rhonda: Hi, Coop, stayin' outta trouble?

Bobby: Hi, Rhonda. Hi, Charlene.

Coop: (Gesturing to the pumps) Rhonda, get rid of that smoke around the pumps.

Rhonda: (Disgusted) Oh, Coop.

A new, gold Camero careens into the station. Dwayne honks his horn.

Coop: Nice wheels.

Dwayne: I'd like some service here.

Bobby: Neat car. What's it got in it?

Dwayne gets out of his car. Spits. Bobby runs his hand over its fender.

Coop: Neat car like this, all you need is some place to go.

Dwayne: Hey, girls, let's go for a ride!

Rhonda and Charlene get in his car and they speed off.

The main conclusion from the specific questions asked about the commercial indicated that it was confusing for the teenagers to follow.

They were generally attracted to Coop as a character, whereas Dwayne made less of an impression on them. The women, however, became a focal point for the chewers, even though they appeared only briefly.

Our analysis of the reactions of the members of rhetorical Vision One resulted in a revision of the commercial that was tied closely to the tension in their vision. Here is the relevant portion of the revised script that was broadcast:

> Charlene and Rhonda walk to the pumps with cans of diet pop.
>
> Rhonda: Stayin' outta trouble, Coop?
>
> Bobby: Hi, Rhonda. Hi, Charlene.
>
> A new, gold Camero careens into the station. Dwayne honks his horn.
>
> Charlene: Nice car.
>
> Dwayne gets out of his car. Spits. Bobby runs his hand over its fender.
>
> Dwayne: (Holds two dollars in his fingers) Two bucks, Coop.
>
> Bobby: It's awesome. What's it got in it.
>
> Coop gives the car a good looking over. Frank comes out of the garage to look. His dog comes with him.
>
> Coop: Nice car, too bad you've got no place to go.
>
> Dwayne: (Glares at Coop and spits, drooling a bit) Girls, hop in, let's go for a ride.
>
> Rhonda and Charlene: Gross—no way!

In conclusion, symbolic convergence theory in conjunction with the focus group technique is a powerful method for analyzing audiences. As our study of teenage tobacco users in Minnesota demonstrates, SCT-based focus groups can reveal the major rhetorical visions that comprise a target audience. These rhetorical visions provide communication scholars and practitioners with a richly textured analysis of the heroes and villains, the celebrated scenarios, the motives, and the emotions of the audience members. Such a careful audience analysis provides the basis for any successful persuasive campaign, including one designed to stop tobacco usage by teenagers.

9

Using SCT-Based Focus Group Interviews To Do Applied Communication Research

John F. Cragan
Illinois State University
Donald C. Shields
University of Missouri—St. Louis

Conducting applied communication research using SCT-based focus groups requires three knowledge bases. First, one needs knowledge of and experience in moderating focus groups. Second, one needs a working knowledge of symbolic convergence theory (see Bormann, 1983, 1985, this volume; Cragan & Shields, 1992). Finally, one needs an understanding of the product, service, or organization being studied. The two preceding chapters by Kreps and by Bormann, Bormann, and Harty showed how to conduct focus group research in general, and how to find and analyze the fantasy themes that occur in focus group discussions.

In this chapter, we build on this groundwork to explain the specific steps one needs to follow when conducting applied communication research using SCT-based focus groups. We then present three different case studies that demonstrate the use of SCT-based focus group interviews to solve client-based problems. A newspaper case study explicates a typical use of SCT-based focus group interviews to assess consumers' reactions to suggested improvements in a product. A jury case study that involved refining a plaintiff attorney's opening and closing statements illustrates a new approach to using SCT-based focus group interviews to develop persuasive messages. The third case study demonstrates the use of SCT-based focus group interviews to generate a qualitative data base to develop quantitative research instruments, such as surveys and Q-sorts (see Cragan & Shields, 1981, 1992), to assess the law enforcement training provided to recent police academy graduates.

SCT-BASED FOCUS GROUPS

Since the early 1950s, focus group interviews have served as a standard qualitative method for conducting market research (Cragan & Wright, 1991; Greenbaum, 1988). Operating from the premise that the interpretation of data becomes more insightful when analyzed through the lens provided by a communication theory, Shields (1981) introduced SCT-based focus groups to the communication discipline. Our experience in moderating more than 200 focus group interviews as part of dozens of applied communication research studies indicates that there are five steps that one should follow to conduct effective theory-based focus group interviews.

Step 1. Selecting Participants

Much of applied communication research occurs because a client organization contracts with a researcher to study a problem unique to that organization. In such cases, the client organization usually specifies the screening questions. We usually recruit participants randomly from such sources as customer lists, professional association directories, voter registration lists, phone directories, shopping mall intercepts, and so forth. Where possible, we use telephone interviews that screen the recruits into a stratified random sample representing demographic characteristics that the client organization has specified. Typical screening questions ask potential participants whether they are a customer or not, use the product or service, and so forth. We would caution that the more restrictive the screening questions, the more expensive the cost of recruiting. For example, gasoline users may be easy to locate, whereas users of a specific drug, such as Halogen, may be difficult to locate. Another viable strategy for recruitment is to go through professional organizations and let a known intermediary recruit the participants who meet the screening criteria.

The amount of money used as an incentive to recruit people to a focus group also varies greatly. Typically, we recruit college students with a $10 incentive, the general public with a $30 to $50 incentive, and professionals such as physicians, attorneys, architects, and veterinarians with a $150 incentive or more. In estimating the cost of hosting a focus group session, one needs to remember that 15 "confirmed" participants may only produce 8 participants for the session; conversely, if all 15 recruited subjects show up, ethically one must pay them all, even though only 10 of them may participate in the discussion. We have found that the ideal size of a focus group is 7 to 12 members.

Step 2. Developing the Focus Group Outline

Kreps called the focus group outline the "interview schedule." He recommended that the moderator give the interview schedule to each participant. With SCT-based focus group interviews, we recommend that only the moderator possess a copy of the focus group outline. In that way, the moderator can maintain a better sense of control, keep the participants from jumping ahead, and provide a sense of novelty to the discussion that ensues.

A great deal of work goes into constructing a good focus group outline that will guide a 60- to 90-minute discussion of a specific topic. First, one meets with the client and determines the objectives of the study. Second, one conducts a document search of previous studies on the product or service, past and existing advertisements and informational material on the product or service, technical material on the product or service, and articles in the popular press. Third, one conducts personal interviews with in-house experts. In a study of a commercial product, for example, one would want to interview the product managers, the researchers who developed the product, and the sales force. In all, a good focus group outline will be the product of half a dozen personal interviews and a review of 100 or more documents. The outline will also go through several revisions honed by client review and approval.

Step 3. Moderating Focus Groups

Scholars from several disciplines generally agree on three expected outcomes of a good focus group interview: generation of new ideas, spontaneous group interaction, and emotionally provocative discussions (Bormann, 1990; Cragan & Wright, 1991; Frey, Botan, Friedman, & Kreps, 1991; Goldman, 1962; Haag, 1988; Kinnear & Taylor, 1983; O'Hair & Kreps, 1990; Shields, 1981; Wells, 1974). Three variables that affect these outcomes are the setting, the moderator, and the focus group outline.

Focus group interviews can occur informally in a room filled with easy chairs and a tape recorder on the coffee table to formally in a room especially equipped with round tables, one-way mirrors, hidden cameras, and overhead microphones. The type of setting depends on the amount of money available. Although the setting is important, the most important variables affecting the outcomes of a focus group interview are the skill of the moderator and the quality of the focus group outline.

We often characterize an SCT-based focus group moderator as a pyromaniac of focus group discussions. The idea is for the moderator to throw out a lit match (a fantasy theme) and see if it catches fire in the group. Sometimes it takes several different matches to light a fire about a given topic. Nonetheless, if the moderator's fantasy theme does not chain-out, a participant will throw out a competing fantasy theme that does. Indeed, it is not unusual for several competing brush fires (fantasy themes) to erupt about a given topic of discussion of the focus group outline.

An SCT-based outline requires the presence of narrative statements that depict characters taking action in a scene. For example, a moderator might use a narrative that goes something like this when studying a newspaper's readership: "Some people say that 'USA Today is like Chinese food. Twenty minutes after you read it, you're hungry for more news.' What's your opinion of this national newspaper?" Our experience indicates that a moderator needs to use both positive and negative, pro and con, or right and wrong scenarios to generate group interaction about a topic.

In an SCT-based focus group run by a skilled moderator, the outline would not even be apparent to the focus group participants, and to the casual observer the discussion would appear to be free-flowing, perhaps even off the cuff. Although it is important for the moderator to cover the outline points that are relevant to the objectives of the study, it is equally important for the moderator not to stomp out forest fires; chaining fantasies in group interaction need to run their course through the group's own volition so that the three outcomes of a good focus group may be achieved. To insure that these outcomes are achieved, a skillful moderator will not interfere with the group's exploration of relevant topics not covered in a preconceived outline. Finally, a moderator who demonstrates an authoritarian style and follows a highly structured, lock-step chronology in asking questions will not be able to generate the type of free-flowing discussion that is crucial for an effective SCT-based focus group discussion.

Step 4. Data Analysis

Cragan and Wright (1991) point out that researchers should look for three touchstones in the data from a focus group study: redundancy, intensity, and creativity. *Redundancy* occurs when a fantasy theme is repeated either within or across group discussions. One discovers redundancy by analyzing the data from several focus groups in which participants discuss the same topic. A set of five focus groups on the same topic will usually exhaust the universe of ideas that exist in the marketplace, but sometimes even three focus groups will be sufficient. For example, the universe of ideas (reactions) in three focus groups on dorm food would readily lose their novelty from the first to the second to the third group. In other words, one would hear the same stories in each of the three groups, and by the third group one would not hear any more new stories.

     Intensity concerns how viscerally focus group participants express their viewpoints. Intensity is often conveyed by excitement, volume, tone, and timbre of the voice, but may also be conveyed through gestures and facial expressions. One of the real advantages of focus group interviews is the ability to observe how intensely the participants hold some fantasies. In quantitative survey research, one usually only assesses the intensity of respondents' reactions from their placement of a mark on a 5-point Likert-type scale. In a focus group, however, the emotions conveyed by tone of voice, pitch, timbre, loudness, animation, and so forth, help flesh out how important a given fantasy theme is to the participants. For example, a focus group study of student responses to a university newspaper once revealed that female students held viscerally to the view that the student newspaper needed to report violent campus crimes, especially rape and rape attempts, within 24 hours of their occurrence.

     The synergistic properties of group discussion will produce *creativity* in idea generation—new ideas that grow out of the group discussion that were not previously in the minds of the participants or the client before the focus group discussion occurred. Focus group participants typically create new ideas that may have significant impact on changing products or services. Such creative ideas often lead the client to conclude that the entire study was justified. For example, in a study we did on Lutalyse, a synthetic prostaglandin used to synchronize breeding in cattle, a number of the focus group discussions among cattle breeders led to the idea of using the product with natural service (bulls doing the breeding) as opposed to Upjohn's original thinking that the drug could only be used in combination with artificial insemination (Bush, 1981). The group manifested creativity through the original fantasy theme: "My hired hand in charge of heat detection is that ol' bull out there."

Step 5. Report Writing and Presenting

We follow a 7-step procedure for writing up and presenting both qualitative and quantitative applied communication research. The seven steps include: Background and Problem, Purpose and Objectives,

Method/Design and Procedure, Data Analysis, Recommendations, Executive Summary, and Oral Presentation.

The typical SCT-based focus group report is about 30 pages in length. The length of the write-up for the background and problem, purpose and objectives, and method/design and procedure sections is usually about seven pages, and data analysis and recommendations take 15 to 18 pages of the report. The executive summary is typically five pages in length.

The background and problem section describes why the study was necessary; that is, what led to the commissioning of the research. The purpose and objectives section contains the one overriding purpose of the research and lists several specific objectives of the study. The method, design, and procedure section stipulates the procedures followed in selecting participants, the time-line for the study, the dates and locations of the focus group discussions, and an explanation of the focus group method, data analysis procedures, and the theory selected for data analysis (in this case, symbolic convergence theory).

Data analysis, the longest section of the report, possesses a distinct organizational pattern that roughly follows the focus group outline and/or the specific objectives of the study. The fantasy themes heard in the groups constitute the data the researcher analyzes and interprets for the client. The data analysis section reports fantasy themes from the focus group discussion(s) that support the researcher's conclusions. Here, the client wants and needs to hear the customers' voices in dramatistic form; as such, the researcher usually presents the key fantasy themes in this section of the qualitative report. The client also needs to know the dominant fantasy themes—those heard most often and most viscerally—as well as lesser themes that may run contrary to the dominant themes. Even though management is not likely to make decisions based solely on the findings from applied research, the consultant's recommendations should flow directly from the findings reported in the data analysis.

Because we live in a world of information overload, executives need a thumbnail sketch (executive summary) of the report that states the objectives of the study, highlights the major findings, and provides specific recommendations. We often include the executive summary as the first section of the written report.

Finally, the oral presentation usually employs a variety of media (e.g., voice, overheads, slides, audio or video snippets, etc.) and does not exceed one hour, with 15 minutes of that time made available for questions. The oral presentation walks the audience through the report. At the end of the presentation, we like to provide six copies of the report to the client.

SCT-BASED FOCUS GROUP INTERVIEWS: THREE CASE STUDIES

In the following pages, we examine three case studies (a newspaper case study, a simulated jury case study, and a police academy case study) to illustrate how SCT-based focus group interviews provide answers to clients' applied communication problems. As we indicated in our introduction, the newspaper case study represents the standard way in which we have done qualitative market research studies for clients. The jury case study uses naturalistic groups, people in a jury pool, to hone the artistic fantasy themes relevant to the attorneys' opening and closing statements in a trial. The police academy case study demonstrates how to use the fantasy themes discovered through focus group interviews in a questionnaire to segment a population according to people's participation in warring rhetorical visions exemplified by the righteous, social, and pragmatic master analogues of SCT (Cragan & Shields, 1992).

The Newspaper Case Study (Cotter & Cragan, 1987)

Most major news dailies regularly conduct market research studies in their on-going efforts to serve their readership and increase circulation and advertising revenues. In 1987, the editorial board of the *St. Louis Post Dispatch* (PD) asked Dan Cotter, Marketing Manager at the paper, and John Cragan, Professor of Communication at Illinois State University, to assist them in redesigning their Sunday supplement, called *PD Magazine*. To meet the study's objectives, the internal staff at the paper met and designed a prototype of a new Sunday supplement; its design varied significantly from the existing supplement. Through focus group interviews, the editors sought to elicit readers' reactions to both the existing magazine and the Sunday magazine prototype. The study's objectives included:

1. Obtain in-depth feedback from PD readers about what they liked and disliked about the existing magazine.
2. Solicit reactions from PD readers about potential additions to the magazine.
3. Collect specific criticisms of the new Sunday magazine prototype from PD readers.

The researchers conducted three focus group interviews with a total of 28 PD readers. The researchers screened participants for "regular readers" who matched the demographics of a 1985 study of PD readers' race, gender, and age. The researchers held the focus group sessions in

St. Louis, MO, in a room that was specially designed and fitted with one-way mirrors and an anteroom for the editors to observe the sessions. Each focus group interview lasted about 90 minutes, and each participant received a $35 stipend.

To understand how an SCT-based focus group proceeds, we include excerpts of the outline the moderator used in the study. The focus group participants first had copies of the old *PD Magazine* in front of them as the moderator walked them through it, and in the second half of the interview the participants had copies of the new prototype as the moderator asked questions about it.

I. General Impressions of *PD Magazine*—Current Uses

    A. General Impression

        About a year ago I conducted three focus group interviews on the newspaper with readers like yourselves. They felt that the *PD Magazine* had been getting thinner and thinner, and there was less in it. For example, one person said there were only two big articles, and the "Question and Answer" section had been dropped. What is your general impression of the *PD Magazine*?

    B. Favorite Part of *PD Magazine*

        Living out-of-state, I tend to read the *Post-Dispatch* infrequently, but I tend to be a regular Sunday reader. What I like in the *PD Magazine* is Elaine Viets's column, and I look forward to reading it. What is your favorite part?

    C. Least Favorite Part of *PD Magazine*

        I talked to a woman yesterday and she said the thing she likes least about the *PD Magazine* is that it does not seem to contain any structure—she does not know what is going to be in it each week. What is your Number One complaint about the *PD Magazine*?

    D. New Additions

        One of my wife's favorite leisure time activities with the newspaper is working out puzzles. She told me before I started this project to suggest that puzzles be added to the *PD Magazine*. What would be your favorite suggestion for something to add to the *PD Magazine*?

II. New Content Added to Sunday Magazine/Repositioning of Old

    A. "Q&A" Feature

        Some readers tell us that they love in-depth knowledge about celebrities. Now that you have looked at this new feature, do you find these personal profiles of local (or national) people a good addition to the magazine?

B. Moving Elaine Viets's Column a Few Pages into the New Maga-
in the "Time Out" Section
The idea would be that Elaine Viets's column, a photo of the
city, a light feature called "Update," and a cartoon would consti
tute the section. How does this change strike your sensibilities?

C. Cover Story
The editors tell me they plan to make the cover story of the
new magazine the best general interest feature story of the
week. Some people have told us they do not want a hard
news story here—they want something more entertaining
and more informative, but not like the stories on the front
page. Do you have any "do or don't do" advice regarding the
cover story? What about local versus national topics? One
reader told us that because this is a St. Louis magazine it
should feature St. Louis stories. What is your preference?

Participants discussed points such as those illustrated above. As
you can see, the moderator threw out fantasy themes like matches to
elicit spontaneous combustion responses. The rest of the outline, some
six pages in length, proceeded in the same manner. The researchers
recorded the three focus group interviews and analyzed the discussions
using SCT as the theory guiding the analysis.

The analysis of focus group data usually entails transcribing the
focus group discussions and then cutting and pasting together similar
fantasy themes within the major headings of the outline as they occurred
across the groups. Kreps, in his chapter, referred to this procedure as
content analysis. Following the advice Bormann, Bormann and Harty
offered in the last chapter, the "content" to be analyzed includes similar
fantasy themes, fantasy types, symbolic cues, and sagas (the basic technical terms of SCT). We usually proceed deductively, beginning with the
conclusion and then providing the "content" descriptions, which
include the important fantasy themes that chained out in the group discussions that support the conclusion. As we indicated above, a complete
analysis of the data for a set of three focus groups takes about 15 pages
in the written report. What follows are excerpts of the first three conclusions presented in the data analysis section of the newspaper case study:

A. General Impressions of Current *PD Magazine*

1. *In general, the readers believed the current PD Magazine lacked structure and identity.* As one participant in Group 3 commented: "Something
needs to be done about the *PD Magazine* because it is the weak-link in
the paper. Most of the time it is just an advertising medium. It doesn't
seem to have any purpose or structure." A participant in Group 2

offered a similar comment: "To me, the *PD Magazine* exhibits an identity crisis. You get some issues that tend to be mostly local and then you get articles that could be appearing in any newspaper or magazine around the country." The following comment by a participant in Group 1 also represented the view that the PD lacked a consistent structure and identity: "Sometimes it's hard news; sometimes it's philosophical. It seems to me that the PD is continually trying to make up its mind as to what it is. It has changed several times over the last several years, so I think it is still looking for what it is."

2. *Elaine Viets clearly is the anchor of the PD Magazine as it presently is constructed.* Participants in all three groups indicated a widespread following and commitment to Elaine Viets's column. Many participants said that her column was the major reason they even opened the *PD Magazine*. For example, a woman in Group 3 said: "Elaine is from the South side, so that makes her column more enjoyable. She writes about the things we know." Another woman in Group 2, who was also from the South side, commented: "I enjoy her column because she always writes about us Southsiders. She writes about what we know in a light and humorous manner." Another participant reflected the strength of her commitment to Viets's column this way: "She is the first thing I read and then I flip through the rest of the pages to see if there is anything else to read."

3. *Apart from Viets's column, participants suggested a local feature story as the next most likely reason why they read PD Magazine.* As one man put it: "PD just doesn't seem to have any bait to get you into the magazine." Another said: "Elaine Viets and a local feature story are the only things that get me into PD at this time." Another group member said, satirically: "PD makes a good fire starter, if you don't like the feature story." One woman in Group 2 captured much of the mood of the participants in all three groups when she said: "I find the PD very uninteresting. I tend not to be interested in its features. I did read about Shanahan [one-time owner of the St. Louis Blues Hockey team] because it was of local interest, but usually I regard it as very dull. I like human interest stories, lightweight material, and local features." Still others argued that all the news on television seems so gruesome and so negative that "it would be good to see the *PD Magazine* provide some positive human interest stories."

As the above excerpts indicate, the moderator's goal in a focus group interview session is to prompt spontaneity, original comment, redundancy, restatement, embellishment, and reconfiguration of important fantasy themes, types, cues, and sagas. Our approach, therefore, is quite at odds with some professional advise about how to run focus groups. Lederman (1990), for example, recommends a non-discussion format in which each member of a focus group responds to each question in turn. Such an approach to moderating focus group discussions, however, will not elicit chaining fantasy themes because the moderator's control of the group's interaction will stomp out the fantasy themes before they have a chance to spread.

In this case study, the management of the newspaper sought to make format and editorial changes in *PD Magazine* based on the results of the qualitative interview data. The written report contained 15 recommendations to the editors of the *St. Louis Post Dispatch*. The following excerpts illustrate these recommendations:

1. The general concept of placing regular features in *PD Magazine* should be adopted; however, the cover stories should be local, or at least have a very strong local tie-in.
2. Leave Elaine Viets's column as the lead column and do not bury her in the "Time-Out" Section.
3. The prototype "Fitness News" section needs to be rethought to include more than just fitness information.
4. Articles in the "At-Large" section should be kept short and supported with photographs.
5. The "Menu" on the inside cover should be kept because it will increase the number of readers who will just read parts of *PD Magazine*.

Communication consultants doing market research through focus group interviews can only make recommendations to management that flow from the findings of the research, and management, of course, is free to accept or reject them. In this case, the *St. Louis Post Dispatch* adopted a number of the recommendations and introduced an improved *PD Magazine*. Follow-up research indicated that newspaper readers liked the new product.

We define *applied communication research* as research that focuses on a client's problem and uses a communication theory to solve it (Cragan & Shields, in press). As we indicated above, the Pulitzer Company, which publishes the *St. Louis Post Dispatch*, was a typical client with a standard problem of needing to improve the quality of its product in customers' eyes. What made this case a communication study is that a communication theory (SCT) drove the research conducted to answer the problem. In other words, SCT allowed the researchers to find communication facts (fantasy themes, fantasy types, symbolic cues, and sagas). The focus group research outline allowed the researchers to use fantasy themes as matches to fire up the discussions. Without this theory, the researchers would not have known the type of communication phenomena for which to search. SCT also enabled the researchers to see the kinds of information that needed to appear in the report. Bormann, Bormann, and Harty's chapter also illustrated the kinds of materials, such as rich chaining fantasies, available for discovery through the lens of SCT.

This case study demonstrates the use of SCT-based focus group interviews to test out the viability of new products and services. As the above case illustrates, the comments obtained in the focus group discussions enabled the client to change and modify its proposed new product in ways that increased substantially its attractiveness to the customer. We would emphasize that product testing provides a major rationale for the use of focus group interviews in business and industry.

The Jury Case Study (Cragan, Dimiceli, Kingsley, Radtke, Steward, & Smith, 1992)

Communication scholars, from the time of the Greeks and Romans, have been interested in the communication processes intrinsic to the judicial system. Recently, however, there has been a resurgence in this interest. For example, Forston (1968) videotaped mock jury deliberations and described the role emergence occurring within these groups. In 1971, the national high school debate question concerned the issue of justice and the jury system (Shields & Cragan, 1971). A number of communication scholars subsequently began employing communication theories to explain how jurors processed arguments in trials. For example, Bennett (1979), Ritter (1985), and Sanbonmatsu (1971) used dramatistic and narrative theory to analyze the arguments made in jury trials. Miller and his associates at Michigan State University (e.g., Miller & Fonts, 1979; Miller, Fonts, Boster, & Sunnafrank, 1983) used information processing theory to guide a four-year study on the legal system sponsored by two National Science Foundation grants to help answer some practical questions about the use of videotaped testimony. From such research interests the professional communication associations added "communication and the law" as a distinct interest group. The *Journal of the American Forensic Association* changed its name recently to *Argumentation and Advocacy*. Finally, Goldswig and Cody (1990) provided an extensive review of research about communication and the law.

Mirza (1992) argues that all good trial lawyers take pains to understand how a jury will react to testimony. He noted that many good trial lawyers "use formal focus groups to test what the average juror's response will be to particular parts of the evidence or testimony" (p. 11). However, there exists little systematic research on how to employ focus groups to study legal argument. SCT-based focus groups thus appear ideal for studying jury deliberation because they enable researchers to identify which fantasies hold jurors' attention and chain out during their group deliberations.

A Chicago trial attorney requested the assistance of Professor Cragan in preparing a personal injury case for trial. Part of this assistance included constructing an opening statement for use by the plaintiff's attorney. As we explain later in the case study, Chicago citizens who reflected the demographics of those comprising the potential jury pool heard the essential arguments of the case, rendered a decision based on those arguments, and then discussed in a focus group interview format their rationale for the decisions they made. The researcher videotaped the jury deliberations and the focus group sessions for subsequent analysis. A graduate student research team then identified the chaining fantasies in each of the three jury deliberations and the focus groups.

We mask the names of the case, the plaintiff and the defense, and the plaintiff's and defense's attorneys because the case, as of this writing, remains in litigation. For this reason, we refer to the case as Jones vs. ABC Oil Company. The facts of the case are as follows. Mr. Jones was a 21-year-old laborer employed by Mr. Block, a retired police officer who makes his living cleaning, repairing, and relining large underground gasoline storage tanks used at every gasoline service station. Mr. Block had cleaned and repaired more than 200 storage tanks for 10 years without an accident. However, on a Monday morning in the mid-1980s, Mr. Block and his laborer, Mr. Jones, returned to finish cleaning a storage tank for an owner-operated gas station flying the flag of the ABC Oil Company. On the Friday before, they had cleaned out the tank and were returning to make repairs on the tank's lids. Mr. Block dropped off Mr. Jones to finish the repairs while Mr. Block went on to a new job. Mr. Jones began to grind on the lid of what he thought was an empty gasoline tank when a spark from the grinder set off an explosion. The explosion blew Mr. Jones some 60 feet away. Mr. Jones received burns on 90% of his body and broke his back. He survived, but is now a quadriplegic.

This case centers on the issue of who is at fault for this accident. Is Mr. Jones at fault because he failed to ventilate the tank properly while he was grinding on the tank lid? Is Mr. Block at fault because he failed to supervise his lone employee? Is the independent filling station operator at fault because he owned the gasohol tank that exploded? Is the manufacturer of the plastic lining of the tank at fault for building a faulty lining? Is ABC Oil Company at fault because it invented and distributed a new fuel (gasohol) and did not warn the owners of independent stations, and their independent cleaning and repair companies, of the volatile nature of gasohol as compared to gasoline? Is the XYZ transporter of gasohol at fault because his transport company knew of the potential dangers but did not inform the independent station owner of them? Mr. Jones regarded ABC Oil Company as responsible for his injuries and sued for $100 million.

A local focus group set-up company recruited 45 participants from registered voters in Chicago for a series of three jury simulation focus groups. The focus group set-up company screened participants to represent a stratified random sample of age, gender, race, occupation, and income reflective of the average demographics of registered voters in Chicago. The mock trial focus groups met on Wednesday evening for three consecutive weeks. At each session, 15 participants conversed socially during dinner provided in the focus group room. Attorneys for the plaintiff observed these interactions through a one-way mirror and simulated *voir dire* by selecting the 12 people they wanted to serve as the mock jury.

The 12 mock jurists then moved to a room designed to simulate a courtroom and took seats in the jury box. They learned that they would serve as a mock jury and would hear the opening statements of a real case delivered by real attorneys. They received a brief description of the facts of the case and learned that they could take notes on the statements they heard. They also learned that at the end of the opening statements they would go to yet a third room and deliberate a judgment. The mock jurors heard a 30-minute opening statement from both the plaintiff's attorney and the surrogate attorney for the defense; then the plaintiff's attorney presented a 10-minute rebuttal. After hearing these statements, the mock jurors received instructions to appoint a foreperson, got a ballot to vote, and were given one hour in which to attempt to reach a decision. After the jury reached a decision (or hung), the communication professor conducted a 30-minute focus group interview to determine what fantasy themes were and were not persuasive, and why.

The mock jury deliberations and focus group interviews generated more than eight hours of qualitative data. Space limitations only allow us to present excerpts from the report submitted to the plaintiff's attorney. In the first mock jury trail, the plaintiff's attorney presented five major fantasy themes in his opening statement. The graduate student research team traced these themes through the mock jury's deliberation and the focus group interview. These themes can be paraphrased as: (a) Mr. Jones is only a 22 year-old single boy; (b) Mr. Block is an expert on tank cleaning and repair; (c) People who re-line gasoline tanks are not Harvard graduates and thus are not capable of understanding the chemical interaction of gasohol and plastic tank liners; (d) Gasohol acts differently than gasoline; and (e) ABC Oil Company never made the independent station owners aware of the dangers of gasohol.

All five of these fantasy themes chained out with the first mock jury, but one of them worked to the disadvantage of the plaintiff and, when it was tied to a major defense fantasy theme, the jury hung and could not reach a verdict. In the first mock trial, the plaintiff's attorney asked the jury to find ABC Oil Company guilty or innocent; this instruction did not allow the mock jury to assess any level of guilt to the other people. Concomitantly, the defense attorney unleashed a negative fantasy theme labeled the "deep pockets" fantasy type. The defense attorney claimed that the only reason the plaintiff was suing ABC Oil Company was because they have money (i.e., deep pockets), yet others also bore some blame. The jury combined the deep pockets fantasy theme with the plaintiff's attorney's fantasy theme that Mr. Block was an honest-to-goodness expert on tank repair and concluded that he should have known better than to leave Mr. Jones, a mere laborer, alone. Thus, the mock jury hung. In the focus group interview, jurors explained that they did not see ABC Oil Company as the only party who could be blamed for the tragedy and thought the plaintiff was too greedy.

Based on the outcome and discussion of this first mock jury simulation and focus group interview, the plaintiff's attorney changed his opening statement. For the second jury simulation, he asked the jury to assign proportionate blame to ABC Oil Company, the gasohol distributor, the independent XYZ station, Mr. Block, and Mr. Jones. He also argued that even though Mr. Block was an experienced gasoline tank cleaner and repairer, he was a neophyte gasohol tank cleaner and repairer because he was unaware of the chemical reaction differences between gasoline contact and gasohol contact with plastic tank liners. Finally, the plaintiff's attorney introduced a new fantasy type that described this gasohol case as similar to a product liability case involving a faulty toy. The plaintiff's attorney explained carefully in detail that if a parent bought a Mattel toy from Sears, brought it home and gave it to his or her child, left the child for a few moments, and the child sustained a serious injury from the toy, then the parent would first blame him-or herself for leaving the child alone, then blame Sears for selling the toy, but ultimately would blame Mattel for manufacturing and distributing a known potentially dangerous toy without providing any warning labels for its use. The plaintiff's attorney then explained that ABC Oil Company knew that gasohol, unlike gasoline, would seep through a plastic lining and be hidden from view. Furthermore, the attorney argued that ABC Oil Company knew of this problem but failed to notify either the independent ABC Oil Company station owner or Mr. Block and did a poor job of informing the distributor who transported gasohol to the independent station. The plaintiff's attorney concluded that these omissions provided justification for blaming most of the cause of the accident on ABC Oil Company.

The second jury found ABC Oil Company primarily liable and ruled in favor of the plaintiff, Mr. Jones. The focus group discussions pinpointed the reason for this ruling. Not surprisingly, the toy product liability fantasy theme was the major fantasy theme that chained out in the simulated jury discussions. In the focus group interview, the mock

jurors indicated that the toy fantasy theme helped them see a clear rationale for why they should judge ABC Oil Company to be the guilty
party. Portraying Mr. Block as a well-meaning but uninformed repair
contractor also led the jury to assign only minor blame to him. However,
this mock jury expressed concerns in both their mock deliberations and
in the subsequent focus group interview that the description of Mr.
Jones's injuries and the impact they would have on his life seemed inadequate. The mock jurors also indicated that it was unclear to them
whether the manufacturer of the tank liner was at fault as well. They
also expressed uncertainty as to the kind of steps ABC Oil Company
should have taken to prevent this tragedy.

In the final jury simulation, the plaintiff's attorney retained the
winning fantasy themes from the second mock trial and tested four new
fantasy themes. The first fantasy theme developed the grievous injuries
that Mr. Jones received, arguing that they were "probably the most
grievous injuries seen in a Cook County courtroom ever." The attorney
described the injuries in detail and used photographs to emphasize their
serious nature. The second fantasy theme dramatized ABC's lack of
proper notification of a dangerous product by saying:

> ABC Oil Company decided not to engage in a safe way of marketing a dan-
> gerous product. ABC had an obligation to provide instructions to make it
> reasonably safe. Can you go to a gas station and buy gas in anything but a
> red can? No you can't. That's the law. You must have a red container. And
> it's also the law for any gasoline delivery. They must have the right con-
> tainer for the right product. If you find, as the evidence will indicate, that
> gasohol is unreasonably unsafe when stored in a plastic container, that
> ABC Oil Company knew it was unreasonably unsafe, and that their failure
> to instruct others that gasohol is unsafe when stored in a plastic tank was
> one of the proximate causes of Mr. Jones' s injuries, then you must con-
> clude with me that ABC Oil Company is at fault.

This fantasy theme proved itself to be the central and winning dramatization in the jurors' minds.

The third new fantasy concerned the "sponge" theme. This
theme dramatized how the chemical structure of gasohol blends with
the chemical structure of plastic, so that the plastic liner sucked up the
gasohol as if it were a sponge and held it within its porous membrane
waiting for a spark to ignite it. The final new fantasy theme argued that
$100 million was not much money when compared to the massive
wealth of ABC Oil Company, and was barely sufficient to provide medical care to Mr. Jones across the next 50 years of his life expectancy.

The third simulated jury found for the plaintiff and awarded the
entire $100 million. In the focus group, they wanted to know when the

trial would take place and they looked forward to seeing ABC Oil found guilty for their obvious negligence. Unfortunately, we cannot report to you what the real jury did because ABC Oil Company continues to delay this case, perhaps in the cynical hope that Mr. Jones may well die of his injuries, thus reducing the amount of damages. The actual trial could still be years away. However, the arguments/themes developed from these mock juries and focus groups will be used when the trail comes to court.

Most trial attorneys today recognize that their professional obligation to their clients includes the need to develop, practice, and then refine oral arguments based on systematic feedback. This case study illustrates the use of SCT-based focus groups, in combination with mock jurors deliberating the facts of the case, to develop and refine fantasy themes that are likely to chain out and prove decisive when an actual trial takes place. The testing of persuasive messages through focus group interviews, of course, is not restricted to the legal system. Advertising agencies use consumer focus groups routinely to test potential advertising themes in print, radio, and television commercials. Just like the attorney adapted and changed his oral arguments based on the findings of each focus group, so too do advertising agencies change and refine the themes in their commercials. SCT-based focus groups can thus be used to develop and test a wide variety of persuasive messages.

The Police Academy Case Study (McCafferty, 1988; McCafferty & Vasquez, 1992)

Researchers often use the data from SCT-based focus groups to construct questionnaires that allow them to sort people out by their participation in different rhetorical visions. Our experience tells us that people in groups, organizations, and collectivities participate in rhetorical visions that compete with one another. Cragan and Shields (1981, 1992) explain these warring differences based on three master analogues: righteous, social, and pragmatic.

A rhetorical vision based on a *righteous master analogue* emphasizes the correct way of doing things with its concerns about right and wrong, proper and improper, superior and inferior, moral and immoral, and just and unjust. A rhetorical vision with a *social master analogue* reflects primary human relationships as it keys on friendship, trust, caring, comradeship, compatibility, family ties, brotherhood, sisterhood, and humaneness. A rhetorical vision with a *pragmatic master analogue* stresses expediency, utility, efficiency, parsimony, simplicity, practicality, cost effectiveness, and minimal emotional involvement. Segmenting customers and employees by their identification with these three master analogues proved valuable in our work in marketing, advertising, and strategic planing in organizations (Cragan & Shields, 1981, 1992). Such a segmentation allows a client to tailor messages and products to specific targeted audiences (market segments).

Let's assume that someone wants to buy a "quick-change" oil and lube franchise like Jiffy-Lube. The three master analogues of SCT tell us that there are three potential customer types who participate in different rhetorical visions regarding automobile oil changes. There is the righteous vision, which in all likelihood portrays an automobile owner who changes his or her own oil because he or she wants to make sure it's done right. This person probably has a shelf in the garage for storing the special tools and equipment necessary to do the job. He or she may also buy Pennzoil by the case because it's the best. There is also a social rhetorical vision that portrays the automobile owner as getting his or her oil changed at the friendly, neighborhood gas station because he or she has known the owner for years and trusts that person to change the oil. Finally, there is a pragmatic rhetorical vision that portrays the automobile owner as viewing oil as a generic product and an oil change as a minor inconvenience that needs to be taken care of as quickly and cheaply as possible. Efficiency (speed) and cost (cheap price) are what matters in this latter drama, not quality of the oil or friendliness of the service.

Given this knowledge of the marketplace, our potential franchise purchaser might want to do a quantitative market survey to determine the size of the pragmatic market segment and the best location for the Jiffy-Lube station. Finally, the segmentation study would help in designing advertising messages that would emphasize the franchise's speedy service and low-cost products.

Not only are the master analogues important to the segmentation of customer markets, but these analogues can serve as guides to the development of training programs in organizations. For example, if a researcher conducted an SCT-based market segmentation study of the student body of a university, he or she might find that 20% of the students participated in a righteous academic drama, meaning they wanted rigorous, challenging courses taught by top-flight university professors. On the other hand, 40% of the students might participate in a social academic drama, meaning they wanted empathic, caring, friendly professors who took the time to advise them about all matter of academic and social problems. Finally, another 40% of the students might participate in a pragmatic academic drama, meaning they wanted a degree as cheaply, quickly, and easily as they could get it and, therefore, wanted a professor who was clear, precise, and easy. For such a pragmatic group, this professor ideally would only teach what related to the student's ability to get a degree and get a job upon graduation.

If a survey of the faculty, however, revealed that 80% of the faculty participated in a righteous vision of academics (theory-building, researching, and publishing), 10% participated in a social vision of student-centered learning, and 10% taught their courses and went home, then the university might want to initiate a training program to make righteous professors appear more social so that student needs would be met more closely.

Michael McCafferty, an attorney and police officer working in the legal division of the Chicago Police Training Academy, wrote a master's thesis at Illinois State University in which he identified the rhetorical visions in which police officers participate. After conducting three focus group interviews with Chicago police officers to collect the universe of fantasy themes regarding their personae, he found three rhetorical visions: the righteous vision of *The Enforcer*, in which the officer's primary objective is to arrest criminals; a social vision of *The Social Worker*, in which the officer's primary objective is to solve human problems; and a pragmatic vision of *The Survivalist*, in which the officer's primary objective is to put in 20 safe years on the job and retire.

As an instructor in the academy, McCafferty became interested in the degree to which new cadet school graduates participated in these respective visions. This question was important to both McCafferty and other police academy instructors because they recognized society's need for officers to participate in all three dramas, but worried that an insufficient number of recruits participated in the enforcer drama. To segment the graduates of the police academy, McCafferty solicited the assistance of Gabriel Vasquez, a recent Illinois State University graduate student and a PhD candidate in the Department of Communication at Purdue University.

This police academy case study shows the chronology of events needed to use SCT-based focus groups to initiate large sample quantitative studies. Several sources explicate how to construct and analyze statistically the data from market segmentation and organizational training studies that depict participation in righteous, social, and pragmatic visions (see Cragan & Shields 1981, 1992; Kapoor, Cragan, & Groves, 1992; McCafferty, 1988). Space limitations prevent us from explaining these procedures.

McCafferty's MA thesis contained 45 fantasy themes about police officers that he built into a structured Q-deck; that is, a deck structured specifically to include statements reflecting the three rhetorical visions of police officers (Enforcer, Social Worker, Pragmatist) across 15 issues pertinent to the training of recruits. McCafferty (1988) asked a sample of 60 Chicago police officers to sort the 45 statements on a rank-order continuum from most-like to least-like their view of a police officer's persona. McCafferty factor analyzed the data and found three significant factors reflective of the righteous, social, and pragmatic analogues depicted in the visions portrayed by officers participating in his focus group discussions. He then used the average z-scores for police officers comprising each rhetorical vision to determine the most salient, neutral, and least salient fantasy themes.

McCafferty and Vasquez (1992) selected the five most salient fantasy themes reflective of each rhetorical vision. They built these 15 statements (5 statements by 3 visions) into a questionnaire that asked respondents to react to each fantasy theme depiction on a 9-point Likert-type scale ranging from "least like," through "neutral," to "most like" their view of each issue's importance to a police officer. One hundred and twenty-five recent graduates of the Chicago Police Academy completed the fantasy theme questionnaire along with a 30-item, 4-point job satisfaction scale ranging from "very satisfied" to "very dissatisfied."

In analyzing the data from the survey of recent police academy graduates, McCafferty and Vasquez used fantasy theme marker variables to identify vision participation. A recent academy graduate whose high mean score occurred on the five righteous, or on the five social, or on the five pragmatic statements was identified, respectively, as a righteous, social, or pragmatic police officer. Table 9.1 displays the 15 salient fantasy themes by vision type, the average persona type, and the mean scores of the participants in each vision. In turn, the data reflect the warring nature of each diametrically opposed vision statement. If an officer participates in the Enforcer drama, then he or she tends to reject the fantasy themes from the social and pragmatic visions. Similarly, an officer who participates in the Social Worker vision tends to reject the fantasy themes in the Enforcer and Survivalist visions.

Fifty-four percent of the recent police academy graduates participated in a pragmatic rhetorical vision, 25% in a social rhetorical vision, and 21% in a righteous rhetorical vision. To McCafferty and Vasquez's surprise, they found that more than half of the freshly graduated police officers participated in a Survivalist vision in which the Number One fantasy theme depicted the role of the police academy as "teaching police academy trainees to be safe."

Follow-up SCT-based focus groups helped explain this finding. As one officer put it: "The Rodney King case, the Wilson case, and the Los Angeles riots show what a dangerous job it is for a cop. The Wilson brothers were cop killers who were arrested and put away. But then, 10 years later, the arresting officers were suspended without pay because they didn't follow procedures in making the collar." Another officer pointed out: "Half of the police recruits come from police families, so they know the score before ever going to the academy." In other words, survival is the first order of business. Both of these fantasy themes

Table 9.1. Mean Scores of Police Academy Graduates' Fantasy Themes by Master Analogue

Master Analogue Type:	Enforcer (21%)	Social Worker (25%)	Survivalist (54%)	Total Population (100%)
Righteous Fantasy Themes:				
"Our primary objective is to arrest criminals."	5.6	4.2	4.2	4.5
"The only way to learn the job is by working the streets."	5.1	2.7	4.1	3.9
"The way to quell a riot is by using a maximum show of force."	6.2	4.0	4.6	4.8
"The main purpose of a field report is to assign in jailing the offender."	7.1	6.4	6.3	6.5
"Police need to be aggressive in controlling the street curb-to-curb."	6.8	4.8	5.7	5.7
Social Fantasy Themes:				
"A good officer can put on a social worker's suit to solve problems."	4.5	5.7	4.6	4.9
"The best reason to fill out a case report is to keep the citizen happy."	2.0	2.6	2.2	2.3
"In a riot it's important to communicate with community leaders."	4.7	6.6	4.6	5.1
"The Academy should sensitize recruits to deal with cultural diversity."	5.4	7.8	6.8	6.7
"Being aggressive is over rated; communication is the key."	5.1	7.9	6.0	6.3

Table 9.1. Mean Scores of Police Academy Graduates' Fantasy Themes by Master Analogue (cont.)

Pragmatic Fantasy Theme:

"In a riot I need to act cautiously and avoid lawsuits."	3.4	3.2	5.1	4.3
"Being aggressive does not add anything to your paycheck."	4.9	5.2	6.9	6.1
"My goal is to safely put in 20 years and retire."	4.2	4.3	5.7	5.1
"The best reason to fill out a case report is to cover yourself."	5.4	4.1	6.0	5.4
"The main purpose of police training is to teach recruits how to stay alive."	6.4	7.1	7.4	7.1

because they came from the follow-up, SCT-based, focus groups, help to explain the intensity with which the majority of cadet graduates were adhering to the pragmatist vision. They also provide insight into the participants' rationale for holding the pragmatist vision.

The data contained in Table 1 show the war among the righteous, social, and pragmatic rhetorical visions. The righteous fantasy theme—"Our primary objective is to arrest criminals"—is accepted by the Enforcers ($M = 5.6$), yet rejected by the Social Workers ($M = 4.2$) and the Survivalists ($M = 4.2$). The social fantasy theme—"A good officer can put on a social worker's suit to solve problems"—is accepted by the Social Worker graduates ($M = 5.7$), but rejected by the Righteous Enforcers ($M = 4.5$) and the pragmatic Survivalists ($M = 4.6$). Finally, the pragmatic fantasy theme—"My goal is to put in 20 years safely and retire"—is accepted by the Survivalists ($M = 5.7$), but rejected by the Righteous Enforcers ($M = 4.2$) and the Social Workers ($M = 4.3$).

The 15 fantasy themes taken in the three righteous, social, and pragmatic clusters demonstrate that 21% of the recent academy graduates are into a righteous street scene in which they are pursuing and arresting criminals aggressively (Enforcers), 25% believe that communication with civilians is the primary way to get the job done (Social Workers), and 54% believe that they must work cautiously and safely so that they can be around to collect their pension in 20 years (Survivalists).

Although all the police officers indicated satisfaction with their job, Enforcers appeared as the least satisfied segment. They expressed concern about the opportunity for promotion, acceptance of their ideas, the ability to transfer, and their relationship with the police union. The focus groups also revealed that police officers adhering to the Enforcer vision knew that their view represented the minority view in the department. Furthermore, they indicated that they received few rewards for their righteous police work. As one officer put it, "I feel like an outsider within my own police family."

This case study demonstrates the use of SCT-based focus group interviews to derive salient, warring fantasy themes that flow from the three master analogues (righteous, social, and pragmatic). The study also illustrates how a researcher may use the data derived from such group interviews to build a quantitative instrument to segment organizational personnel to assess the effectiveness of training programs. The case indicated that only 21% of academy graduates participated in the law and order Enforcer Vision. The researchers thus recommended that the client revisit the training program to raise the consciousness of cadets regarding the bread and butter issues of investigation and arrests.

This case study is typical of the design of applied communication research that falls within the heading of market segmentation studies. Here, vision participation serves as the breaker variable to segment markets, thereby enabling the client to design advertising and sales stories compatible with the vision reflected by each targeted segment. In this way, a company or client is able to position a product or service within the most profitable segment or segments (Cragan & Shields, 1992).

CONCLUSION

Focus groups have been used as an information-gathering tool for 50 years in market research and are part of the communal tool-kit of the social sciences. However, focus groups conducted by a psychologist or sociologist would bring psychological or sociological theories, respectively, to bear on the construction of the focus group outline and the interpretation of information gathered from the group discussions. In these case studies, the communication researchers used a communication theory to construct the focus group outlines, conduct the interviews, interpret the data, develop subsequent large sample survey instruments in one case, and guide recommendations.

What made these studies communication studies is that they used a communication theory, symbolic convergence theory (SCT). Our point here is that even if we have not persuaded researchers and practitioners to use SCT when conducting focus group interviews, we certainly hope that we have established the advantages of theory-based focus group interviews; that is, some communication theory must drive the collection and interpretation of data and inform the recommendations offered for the solution of the client's applied communication problems. We have argued elsewhere (Cragan & Shields, 1981, in press) that there is nothing more practical than a good theory. In fact, we do not think one can conduct theory-free applied focus group research; so, don't leave campus without one.

In this chapter, we sought to demonstrate that SCT is a good communication theory. For us, the advantage of using SCT as the communication theory to develop a product for a newspaper (Case 1), prepare successful messages for an attorney (Case 2), and segment the graduates of a police academy (Case 3) is that the attributes of a product, the themes in a persuasive message, and the content of a training program are all explained coherently by the use of the same general communication theory. The general theory lends consistency to the collection and interpretation of data and drives the recommendations for new product attributes, messages, and training programs. Of course, other good communication theories may be used.

The two preceding chapters and this chapter amply demonstrate the virtual universal application of focus group interviews as a qualitative procedure for conducting applied communication research about client-centered problems. Each chapter provided variation in the designs and procedures used to conduct focus group research. Each chapter also provided various gradations in the interview outline and the interview schedule, and even moderator involvement. We believe it may well be impossible to determine vicariously which approach and which communication theory is best for you. Just as one never really knows a statistical procedure without using it in a real study, we submit that one will never really understand focus groups without moderating a few. To borrow from Nike's commercial, "Just do it."

PART V

Facilitation Techniques for Building Teams

The ultimate challenge for task groups is their ability to work together effectively as a team. The advantages of group work over individual work, after all, are only realized when group members coordinate their lines of action in an interconnected effort to achieve a mutually defined goal that results in a high-quality decision.

The recognition of the importance of teams and teamwork has started to radically transform many U.S. businesses. Not only are groups used extensively in organizations to accomplish what used to be done by individuals working alone, but many function as self-managing teams that are responsible for all aspects of their efforts, including personnel decisions, budget allocations, and even self-assessment. Decisions are thus no longer made solely from the top and then communicated to those in the middle and at the bottom of the hierarchy.

Implementing self-managing teams into an organization—especially organizations in which traditional, top-down bureaucracy has reigned—and getting them to work well is not always an easy task. The chapters in this section examine ways to facilitate high-quality team efforts.

In Chapter 10, Felkins reviews three group facilitation techniques that can help organizational members to contribute to change and development: action research, organizational simulations, and employee involvement. Action research cycles provide a process through which groups can define issues and concerns related to change, collect data, and conduct feedback sessions for collaborative analysis, interpretation, and action planning. Organizational simulations allow managers and team members to practice change in a microworld in which they create and manage their own organization over a period of time, making decisions, taking action, and seeing the consequences in a simulated social and economic context. Employee involvement in quality teams, self-directed groups, and clusters provide opportunities for

257

organizational members to join together around specific tasks and take responsibility for managing change. Each of these techniques is examined in a case study of teams working in an organization. This chapter concludes by exploring some developmental challenges related to group facilitation of change, including conflicting roles and relationships, collective information processing, and team renewal.

In Chapter 11, Seibold discusses facilitation techniques employed with a self-regulating team of employees managing a new-design plant. Pertinent literature concerning advanced manufacturing technologies and their relevance for new-design plants is reviewed in the first section, with special attention to the theoretical requirements for facilitation in team-managed organizations. The second section introduces the background, structures, and practices of the case organization. The third section reports the facilitation procedures utilized, with particular emphasis on team building, problem solving, and group process requirements of new-design plants and self-managed teams. Seibold concludes by underscoring the importance of matching the facilitation technique with the needs of the particular group studied, as well as integrating group and organizational research into facilitation practices.

In Chapter 12, Poole, DeSanctis, Kirsch, and Jackson examine the use of a Group Decision Support System (GDSS) that combines communication, computer, and decision technologies to facilitate decision making and related activities of work groups. Most studies of the implementation and use of Group Decision Support Systems (GDSS) have focused on laboratory groups or the use of GDSSs in special meetings with a great deal of planning and facilitation support. This study focuses on the use of GDSSs by ongoing project teams on a day-to-day basis. The theory of adaptive structuration is used as a lens to focus the analysis. Use of the GDSS by four teams over periods of six months to one year was studied. Themes in the analysis include: changes in use patterns over time; adoption and adaptation of GDSS features; meshing GDSS structures with existing group procedures and tasks; how group problems influence GDSS appropriation; general meaning of the GDSS to the teams; and critical junctures of structuration. Differences and similarities across effective and ineffective implementations and their implications for promoting quality team efforts are then discussed.

10

Groups as Facilitators of Organizational Change

Patricia K. Felkins
Loyola University Chicago

The traditional bureaucratic approach to organizational roles, structure, and decision making is being transformed by a fundamental paradigm shift with new ways of thinking about "management," "organization," and "participation." Innovative methods of redesigning work and organizational structures have provided opportunities for groups throughout the system to be more actively involved in creating their collective future. This change is not just a matter of participation or quality improvement; it is a profound transformation of organizational culture based on technology and collaboration within changing structures.

In traditional organizations, power and resources are often concentrated at the upper levels of bureaucratic structures. Employee involvement, self-directed teams, and "clusters" (Mills, 1993) can help to distribute power and decision making to all parts of the system. A team-oriented, "high-involvement" organization (Lawler, 1992) increases knowledge, information, power, and rewards. Rather than simply redistributing authority and decision making within the hierarchy, "empowerment" enables employees and transforms the organizational structure by developing and expanding influence through interaction, cooperation, and teamwork (Vogt & Murrell, 1990). New forms of organizational "architecture" (Nadler, Gerstein, & Shaw, 1992) support these innovative structures based on flexibility, information, and strategic group collaboration. These facilitative group techniques are helping to maximize organizational resources to meet the challenges of complex systems change.

This chapter explores three methods for developing and expanding the resources of groups to understand and influence organizational change: action research, simulations, and employee involvement. Action research methods facilitate data-based change through collaborative inquiry, which involves groups in cooperative data collection and analysis, and in planning, implementing, and monitoring changes based on the data. Organizational simulations provide a learning environment for breaking frame, testing assumptions, and practicing change in both current and future organizational contexts. Employee involvement, from quality teams to self-directed teams and clusters, allows groups to manage change with increasing levels of responsibility and authority.

Through group involvement and cooperation, managers and employees learn to recognize and appreciate different ways of thinking about how they work together within an organizational system. Employees develop new conversations and relationships and recognize new possibilities for development as individuals and as group members within a responsive "learning organization" (Argyris & Schon, 1978; Senge, 1990). Managers can be facilitators, mentors, and partners in this collaborative group process.

A learning organization helps people understand interrelationships and take responsibility for their actions as they help to create the organization in their daily work practices. Most people in organizational systems want to know that their individual and group contributions "fit into a logical whole" and that they can use their intellect, make decisions, and learn through their work experience (Ketchum & Trist, 1992).

Perspectives About Change

Part of team learning and cooperation is a recognition of and respect for different perspectives about change. Competitive challenges and transformations in traditional work practices and relationships are recreating the structure of organizations through integrated teams, collaborative inquiry, and consultative management. Employee involvement and participation reflect a shift from management-as-control to management-as-facilitation (Felkins, Chakiris, & Chakiris, 1993).

Figure 10.1 differentiates four theoretical perspectives about change with respect to their group process focus and their primary result or outcome.

Within many traditional organizations a *rational/behavioral* approach characterizes change as causal and predictable—decisions and actions that can be understood logically and controlled through expert knowledge and precise, objective measurement techniques that help to reduce uncertainty. A management perspective often dominates a ratio-

Perspective	Primary Process Focus	Primary Outcome
Rational/Behavioral	Control	Production
Systems	Interdependence	Transformation
Cultural/Interpretive	Interaction	Coordination
Critical Humanist	Confrontation	Emancipation

Adapted from Felkins, Chakiris, & Chakiris (1993).

Figure 10.1. Perspectives About Change

nal/behavioral approach to change with a focus on performance and production measurements for quality, productivity, leadership, and teamwork. This approach could be expanded to include "continuous improvement," a common goal for many organizational teams. Group training and assessment are essential in this model to support planned, predictable change that leads individuals toward focused, collective action related to production outcomes and organizational objectives.

Networks of interdependent relationships make *systems* change more complex. From this view, realistic change often means transformation, which restructures intergroup relations and total systems into a new and balanced configuration. Mintzberg (1989) describes efficient systems change not as continuous adaptation but as "quantum leaps from one integrated configuration to another" in brief periods of concentrated "strategic revolution" (p. 96).

Changing a system can be costly and disruptive. Often systems change can be implemented most effectively in greenfield sites or start-up facilities, which begin with new configurations and collaborative visions. A systems approach is not prescriptive, but more descriptive. The focus of change is not on individual attributes of the organization, but on a holistic approach that integrates both social and technical components.

A *cultural/interpretive* approach to change focuses on the people within an organizational system by exploring group interactions and ways in which change is constructed and interpreted through cultural practices, human interaction, and collaborative inquiry. Culture as "interpretive structures" (Geertz, 1973) or a "software of the mind" (Hofstede, 1991) provides basic coordination and rules for group interaction. Yet, acting within culture-specific, taken-for-granted cultural controls, group members may not be aware of the "frames" (Goffman, 1974) of roles and scripts and the "recipe knowledge" (Berger & Luckman, 1966) that facilitate their daily interactions and provide competence and predictability in work practices. Some cultural approaches focus on "reframing" organizations from multiple perspectives (Bolman & Deal, 1991; Frost, Moore, Louis, Lundberg, & Martin, 1991).

Giddens (1984) describes "structuration" in the way that "institutionalized routines" create and reproduce the organization, yet also provide in each reconstitution the possibility for change. According to Giddens, the structuration of rules and practices is both the medium and the outcome. The interaction that brings coordination is also an opportunity for change as groups gather information, solve problems, interpret policy, implement procedures, and measure results.

The outcome for cultural or interpretive approaches often is concentrated on more responsive coordination among organizational members based on their shared understandings of mutually accepted or negotiated rules and norms. The organization continually needs "reaccomplishment" (Weick, 1979), and through such activities as data collection, decision making, and negotiation, organizational members continually are creating and coordinating the organization. These activities help group members make sense of the complexity and uncertainty related to change, reinforce or question rules and procedures, and ultimately facilitate or block change.

The *critical humanist* approach is emancipatory in looking at the possibilities for group involvement and empowerment in facilitating organizational change. From this perspective, change most often is experiential, action-oriented, and contested. Greater knowledge and awareness of organizational discourses may lead to increased self-determination and influence for individuals and groups within the organizational system.

However, the emancipation that comes from directly confronting the old ideology and dominant power hierarchy within the organization is elusive. Although employee involvement would seem to imply greater autonomy and freedom, some theorists are skeptical of the democratic potential of participation. In his critical analysis of democracy and "corporate colonization," Deetz (1992) argues that employee participation is just another form of managerial control. Decisions are not "free" and actions are still dominated by "managerialist" concepts and practices as groups work together to increase productivity, quality, and effectiveness. Hierarchical monitoring is simply replaced by team surveillance and internal controls.

Each of these models focuses change efforts in different ways and affects the expectations and applications of group facilitation techniques. Participation reframes and restructures some of the rational/behavioral approaches that concentrated on management control rather than allowing organizational members to be active, involved participants in a dynamic, interdependent system. The systems and cultural models seek to facilitate group involvement by connecting the social and technical aspects of participative change to basic communication processes. The critical humanist perspective critiques the philosophy and practice of group participation and asks provocative questions that can lead to new awareness and learning for organizational leaders and team members in attempting to create more "liberating" organizational structures. The group techniques in this chapter are based on multiple perspectives that integrate both task and social dimensions with emphasis on individual and team development within changing systems.

Change is not just the dramatic sweep of new initiatives or painful cutbacks; it is more often a developmental process of organizational learning, innovative alignments, and reflexive group practices. It is a "shift of mind" (Senge, 1990) to increased awareness and responsibility in a responsive and interdependent system in which change is accepted as a natural and continuous process and an opportunity for learning and group renewal. The following sections examine three facilitation techniques that help groups to participate in change processes to create the innovative, responsive, collaborative organization of the future.

ACTION RESEARCH: GROUPS
FACILITATING DATA-BASED CHANGE

Action research attempts to understand and change a corporate culture by looking at problems and challenges as they are defined by organizational members and encouraging those members to take an active role in collecting and analyzing data and planning for action to solve the problems and meet the challenges they have identified. Action research is a commitment to data-based change through a process of collaborative inquiry that involves groups in gathering and analyzing data, providing feedback to other groups, planning for action, and collecting more data to monitor the results of change. Those who collect the data also are responsible for sharing that data and facilitating collective analysis and planning. This interactive, participative process can increase individual and group learning, build commitment to action, and encourage more responsible and ethical decision making.

There has been an increased interest in action research as part of the "objectively subjective" methodology of "new paradigm" research (Reason & Rowan, 1981), and the critical "emancipatory" (Habermas, 1971) possibilities of collaborative inquiry have been debated vigorously. Elden (1986) proposes democratic action research as empowering worker-managed change. Participatory action research is acknowledged as an applied research strategy with both scientific and practical value (Whyte, 1991).

Applied action research, however, is not a recent phenomenon. Kurt Lewin (1951) is credited with introducing the term "action research." His work provided an understanding of a "psychological field" as it exists for individuals and groups at a given time and a determination of the supporting and resisting "forces" within that interrelated field that affect motivation, learning, change, and conflict. Eric Trist and his associates (1963) developed the concept of sociotechnical systems in the 1950s and established the Tavistock Institute as a center for action research in applied social science.

Ron Lippitt, one of Lewin's colleagues, and Gordon Lippitt, founders of the National Training Laboratory, integrated action research as the core of process consultation (Lippitt & Lippitt, 1986) and organizational renewal (Lippitt, 1982). This team consultation model concentrates on ownership of change and involves the client system in collecting and analyzing data. Chakiris (1992), a leader in the Lippitt consultation group, has integrated these concepts into Action Research Teams (ART) as the essential element in facilitating and influencing organizational change. ART can be the collective foundation for organizational development as members engage in a process of shared discovery and learning and model participative practices for others in the organization.

There are many applications of action research teams, which are often cross-functional and cut across organizational boundaries. This methodology can be used by any group within an organization from temporary groups, such as task forces, project teams, ad hoc groups, steering committees, and design teams, to mature self-directed teams and clusters. For example, a task force might employ action research in a feasibility study to assess readiness for change or in a needs analysis to identify gaps in performance measurements. A steering committee or design team implementing self-directed groups can use action research technology to collect and process information from interviews, plant visits, and questionnaires. The team then shares these data with relevant groups that work together to develop action plans for implementation at a specific site.

Quality control teams also apply the action research model in the Plan-Do-Check-Act Shewhart Cycle (Deming, 1986a) for monitoring and improving production processes. Team members plan for action and after implementation they measure the results and make the appropriate changes as part of a continuing process of quality improvement. Action research cycles also provide development opportunities through increased awareness of group process. For example, in a "pause for learning" (Ketchum & Trist, 1992) after completing a project or an activity, a self-regulating team gathers data, reviews and evaluates its work, and plans for adjustment and future actions. In consultation and group development, "stop-sessions" (Lippitt & Lippitt, 1986) at any time during the project allow team members to assess where they are and how they are working together. In each of these cases, team members are working with applications of data-based change methods in action research cycles.

Application

The process of facilitating change and organizational development through collaborative inquiry in action research is illustrated by the experience of a regional energy company moving from rapid expansion to a more stable, customer-based operating mode (Felkins, Chakiris, & Chakiris, 1993). This directed change process was initiated by senior executives who felt a need to assess overall operations and look at the type of organization they wanted to be in the future.

With the help of a process consultation team, this organization used several action research cycles to assess its current position and plan for the future. The first action research cycle involved a series of management conferences with the General Manager and senior staff members, the Board of Directors, and representatives of their largest customer groups. Biannual conferences were held over a period of three years and coordinated through the combined efforts of an internal/external resource team.

Before the first conference, data were collected from executive interviews and surveys. The conference design followed an action research model: data feedback to participants; interpretation of the data; discussion and validation of relevant issues; and problem-solving work sessions to use the data to plan and propose new action decisions. The issues included strategic planning for change management, team development, quality of work life, concern for the environment and natural resources in the region, relations with customers, leadership style, succession planning, employee participation, and productivity.

The conference provided a forum for exploring the issues and areas of concern and opportunity related to the data collected prior to the conference. Board members and customer representatives had an opportunity to learn more about mutual concerns and visions for the organization's future. They also developed action plans to deal with executive succession and to make decisions about how to move forward as an organization with new leadership.

As a result of this collective learning, the executive group decided to extend the process and collect data from all employees to involve them in the action research process with feedback, decisions, and action planning. The Metrex Human Resource Audit (Chakiris, 1993) was used to collect organizational diagnostic data from all employees about their perceptions of work conditions and relationships as well as the quality of their products and services and areas for improving productivity and efficiency. Feedback sessions were held with all employees to share the general audit results, facilitate employee interpretation and understanding, and give employees the opportunity to prioritize those areas requiring further attention. After the feedback sessions, trained internal facilitators worked with individual units of the organization to initiate an action-planning process to address the organization-wide concerns and areas of improvement identified in the audit.

Suggestions were made for the formation of a more formal action research team as an ad hoc task force with broad constituency representation. Members researched issues and facilitated feedback, decisions, and actions both within and between units. At the executive level, a steering committee of senior staff addressed the issues identified and the action recommendations provided by this inter-unit task force. The overall process of implementing the recommendations and monitoring the effectiveness of this effort was facilitated by an internal Development Coordinator.

By using action research and group facilitation techniques, this organization initiated an ongoing renewal process that addressed both the immediate changes occurring in their operations and the ongoing effect of changes in the industry, the economic environment, and the ecology. Their goal was to be continually responsive to the changing needs of customers, constituents, and employees. The process of action research built a capacity and competency for current and future employee involvement in change management. Some of the processes for ongoing collaborative inquiry and team planning were internalized within the organization and continue to provide a support system for data-based change and continuing renewal.

ORGANIZATIONAL SIMULATIONS:
GROUPS PRACTICING CHANGE

Like action research, "action learning" in simulations can help groups to facilitate organizational change. Managers and other organizational members live and work with mental models based on shared understandings and interpretations of organizational rules and practices. The opportunity to explore the validity of these models and habitual work practices in a simulated real-world context provides valuable information and insight for change management. A typical simulation group includes 15 to 40 people who usually work in teams of 3 to 8 members. Sessions may be conducted in-house or as part of an outside conference or management retreat.

Simulations compress time and space as groups experience a complex organization in a supportive, interactive environment. Managers and team members have an opportunity to "break frame" and get out of the routine of their department or business unit, to create and manage a company, to make their own rules, and to take responsibility for the consequences. This experience also stretches a traditional "time horizon" (Jaques, 1986), which may be limited to months for line employees and a few years for managers. Sitting in the CEO's chair helps to expand these time horizons and, consequently, ways of thinking about the future and making decisions in the present. The simulation allows groups to manage a company for several "years" and see the direct results of their decisions and actions.

Simulations can cover a variety of functional skills in programs ranging from a few hours to several days. Many business simulations focus on analyzing organizational issues and problems, planning action, and making decisions. Teamwork and group process can be assessed as the team works together to meet these challenges. Groups can test their strategy, assumptions, and models for the future. Business simulations often focus on multiple options, alignment, and innovation in a competitive market.

The sophistication of simulations has increased with improvements in computer technology and capability. In business simulations, the computer contains a data base, simulates the market and environmental factors as they affect the organization, and provides accounting functions and financial reports. Each team may have its own computers or the facilitator may work with a master program and give regular reports to each team. The computer allows the group to see the simulated results of its decisions and to compare its results with the competition. During the simulation, teams also may see results in their own "annual report" and receive a brief financial newsletter reviewing the economic forecast, key news events, industry data, and information on competitors. Timely, comprehensive feedback and relevant information are essential to the success of a simulation.

Simulations place groups in a "microworld" where teams can explore, test, and improve their mental models and theories about how organizations work in an interactive learning context. De Geus (1988) notes three major advantages of computer simulations: (a) managers deal with multiple variables over a simulated time period; (b) they see cause-and-effect relationships and trigger points that may be separated in time and place; and (c) they learn what constitutes relevant information. Senge (1990) speculates that microworld simulations may soon become as common as business meetings as a way to focus on creating alternative future realities.

One of the most complex simulations is a computer-aided management program that reproduces the complete operation of a specific type of business, such as manufacturing, financial, or healthcare institutions. Teams begin to understand the interaction among marketing, finance, and operations as they manage the company for a simulated period of three to five years. Participants plan and make decisions related to product development, prices, advertising, hiring, training, research and development, plants and facilities, loans, debts, and credit. They are evaluated at the end of the simulation by their financial position, including final market share, shareholder equity, cumulative sales, and profits. Other simulations deal with the operation of one functional area, such as finance or operations, or focus on a particular competency, such as project management or teamwork.

One effective simulation for organizational development and teamwork, OrgSim (Murrell & Blanchard, 1986), helps leaders and managers to gain insight into their work style, communication, and team relationships. OrgSim is an open simulation in which groups create with maximum freedom their own organization and their own team experience. Although there is a shorter version, OrgSim usually lasts two days with four to six 1-hour sessions on the first day and debriefing and discussion on the second day. The developers of the program recommend that for every hour in the simulation another hour be spent in review and analysis (Murrell & Blanchard, 1986, 1992). OrgSim has been used in many organizations as well as in university classrooms, business schools, and in cross-cultural contexts.

Although there are some general outcomes, each session of OrgSim is different and unique because the people involved create their own organization and rules with a distinct mix of their personalities and experiences. One of the values of this simulation is that it is a fluid model and it is impossible to know or predict exactly what will happen. A variety of different contexts and products can be used. In some cases, the "product" might be solving organizational problems or creating lists of ways to improve quality or productivity. There are many options with this open, creative simulation. It can be used as a "live" case study (Murrell & Blanchard, 1992) with intense learning and involvement tailored to specific challenges and issues within the organization. The following description of one session of OrgSim illustrates the experience of a particular management group.

Application

A major retail organization brought 15 managers from various locations across the country to corporate headquarters for a week of specialized leadership training and assessment. Participants received an OrgSim manual the previous evening. Most of the group did not know each other, and some uncertainty was evident as the participants gathered in the conference room. A group of senior managers were observing, and three outside consultants were serving as facilitators and resources.

The opening statements by the lead facilitator were brief. The participants were asked to form an organization. They began by choosing three people from their group as the Board of Directors, who had the power to hire, fire, reorganize, and reassign. Participants then presented their individual resumés and applied for a job with the Organization. The Board hired a CEO first and then a personnel director. The personnel director then hired the VP Marketing, VP Operations, and VP Finance. The Organization moved slowly in recruiting other employees, and the managers in the "Hiring Hall" were frustrated. They waited for a time and then decided to form a "Rival Organization."

The teams were in different rooms along a long hallway. The Home Office where the Board and the CEO were headquartered was in the first room. Their two production facilities, EZ Operations and HD Operations, were in two separate rooms. The Rival Organization had its operation in one room at the end of the hall. Movement between locations required purchasing taxi or airfare coupons.

The two organizations realized that they needed more market information and financial assistance to begin operations. With one of the facilitators as the Banker, the organizations purchased magazines, scissors, and tape to "produce" neatly cut-and-pasted words. Another facilitator served as the Consumer, buying only certain words and rejecting those that were cut badly or were of lower quality.

As the teams gained some confidence and produced quality products, the facilitators introduced a continuing product development cycle into the simulation—the Consumer would no longer buy the simple product the Organization and the Rival Organization produced. The teams moved quickly to gather data and implement a creative plan to meet the Consumer's needs. Both organizations offered new products in an increasingly competitive market. The Organization began to experience some fragmentation and internal conflict over products and production methods. In the end, the Rival Organization created an innovative product that expanded both quality and capability. As the original Organization endeavored to match its competition, the Consumer kept demanding improvements.

During the breaks between each round of activity, participants completed a brief worksheet describing their level of satisfaction with their team and their goals. The full group met briefly at the end of the last round, but the majority of the debriefing occurred the next day. The facilitators' first task was to recognize any anger or frustration that might have been created during the simulation. Some group members talked about fairness and their lack of control in the initial hiring. Others were upset that the Board and CEO had isolated themselves and not involved anyone else when making decisions.

Each person had his or her own experience of the simulation, and the debriefing allowed them to talk openly. The facilitators concentrated on identifying the learning points and helping the group members to understand the consequences of their roles and how their behavior was influenced by the structure and the norms they had created. Motivation, conflict, power, communication flow, trust, leadership, group norms, planning, staffing, and job design were discussed and processed through the simulation experience.

When the group members were asked if they wanted to work for the organization their team had created, most said they would not. Some characterized the organization that their group had built as "splintered" and "confused" with no vision and a lack of trust and communication among workers and top management. The executive group was blamed for many of these problems. One of the most significant outcomes of this debriefing session was that many participants said that they "learned how to be team members again, and not just managers." For example, one manager returned to his unit and began to share more information and authority to develop the competence of his team.

In this organizational simulation, people discovered that they initially had reproduced the bureaucracy, poor communication, lack of teamwork, executive isolation, unfairness, and mistrust—all the characteristics that they disliked most in their own organization. For many members of this group, there was a real breakthrough in recognizing the consequences of their routine management practices. These managers left with new insights and understanding of their own strengths and developmental needs as well as their responsibility for facilitating teamwork and collaborative inquiry in their daily work.

EMPLOYEE INVOLVEMENT TEAMS: GROUPS MANAGING CHANGE

The goal of collaborative inquiry in action research and team practice in organizational simulations is to develop group competence and knowledge so that people are capable and confident in assuming greater responsibility and authority in creating the future of their organization.

Employee participation was evident in the 1950s with applications such as work redesign and self-management in the Tavistock studies of coal miners in Britain, integrated work teams at Volvo plants in Sweden, and the Mondragon worker cooperatives in Spain. The Mondragon group continues to provide a model for employee ownership and cooperative ideals (Whyte & Whyte, 1988).

The sociotechnical systems approach practiced by the Tavistock group attempted to coordinate the technology and methods of production with the way groups of people work together. Appropriate boundaries defined the team as an autonomous unit but also connected the team to the rest of the organization.

Sharing information and authority within a more flexible structure is not easy for people who have always worked within controlled, bureaucratic systems. For example, both management and team members in those early experiments in "composite working" in the UK coal mining industry assumed initially, or wanted to assume, that their unit would still function in the "ordinary" way that they had always known (Trist, 1989). Some organizations today also believe that they can implement a participative program and still operate with the same bureaucratic structure and procedures. However, employee involvement transforms basic work relationships and helps shift organizational structures related to authority and responsibility.

Employee involvement has stretched the boundaries of ordinary work and group relationships and helped teams to place themselves in more strategic and influential positions within their organizational system. From ad hoc problem-solving teams, quality teams, and employee involvement groups to autonomous units in self-directed teams and clusters, groups are helping to facilitate change within the organizational system.

Some professionals characterize the evolution of participation and employee involvement in four stages: (a) setting the stage for increased involvement; (b) developing parallel structures such as quality teams that focus on one specific problem or issue; (c) creating natural work teams from existing groups without structural change; and (d) redesigning work structure for maximum employee involvement in self-directed teams (Schultz, 1992).

Although there are many employee involvement and quality teams in both manufacturing and service organizations, most self-directed teams, including initial quality teams and employee involvement groups, have been in core manufacturing processes. The impetus for a change to team configurations is related most often to being more competitive by improving productivity and quality, reducing product cycle time, or lowering production costs. This competitive crunch was evident in manufacturing earlier than it was in service industries. In the 1960s and 1970s, some organizations had quality circles and autonomous teams, but during the 1980s, many more corporations were focusing on employee involvement to improve quality and customer service. In the 1990s, organization clusters, high-performance teams, and virtual teams have continued to expand organizational resources and flexibility through group collaboration and technology.

As some organizations are designing new self-directed teams

and clusters and others are dealing with group renewal in conventional quality teams, a number of organizations are still trying to understand what "collaboration" and "empowerment" mean within their organizational culture. For some executives, managers, and employees, these terms sound faddish and hollow; for others, they are a threat and a challenge to a familiar, ordered bureaucratic system. Some management anxiety may be justified. Experts predict that the number of supervisors can be reduced by 50% or more with the use of self-directed teams (Lawler, 1992). There is, however, a clear warning for change facilitation: Self-managed teams will not work if they are only an attempt to cut costs and downsize the organization.

Employee involvement teams require a commitment to a different way of thinking and acting within an organization and the reconstitution of the role of manager, employee, and customer. Teams and business units have greater influence in a business by collectively managing their integrated work processes and dealing directly with suppliers and customers. Many self-directed teams and clusters are more like small business units, profit centers, or mini-enterprises. Drucker (1985) encourages managers to learn more about fostering a sense of entrepreneurship in which organizational members are "searching" for change and embracing change as an opportunity. A participative model of a "collective entrepreneurship" (Reich, 1987) allows the team, rather than just the CEO or senior managers, to be the entrepreneurial hero and to develop ownership and pride in the innovation and quality of its product or service.

The intensive change in a unit with the start-up of self-directed teams can become a "beachhead laboratory for discovery" (Ketchum & Trist, 1992) and a profound learning experience for the teams. Clusters are more loose in their structure than self-directed teams, and jobs are defined broadly in order to respond to rapid market changes and shift decision making close to the point of action (Mills, 1993). Through these participative group processes, organization members develop a different way of thinking about their work and their relationships to each other and to their customers.

The transfer of operational decisions from managers to work teams is a process that may take years as the team moves through distinct and sometimes prolonged stages of development: Start-Up, State of Confusion, Leader-Centered Teams, Tightly-Formed Teams, and Self-Directed Teams (Orsburn, Moran, Musselwhite, & Zender, 1990; see Seibold's experiences with teams in a new-design plant described in the next chapter). In many cases, these teams seem to mirror the classic pattern of group development outlined by Tuchman (1965): Forming, Storming, Norming, and Performing.

In the orientation stage of group development there is enthusiasm for participation combined with some anxiety as the team members begin to gather information and discuss how they can work together most effectively. The attention to work relationships and production methods creates in some cases a moderate Hawthorne effect as plants undergoing redesign show productivity increases, even before the teams are implemented (Ketchum & Trist, 1992). Additional facilitators, trainers, and consultation teams may be used during this phase to provide support for changing structures and roles.

After the initial excitement and the anticipation of influence, group members begin to recognize the reality of their responsibility and the level of commitment required. Managers are often caught between two conflicting paradigms. Job security and success depend suddenly on teams of employees with new and unprecedented authority. This is stressful for everyone involved, but more disturbing is the fact that predictable roles no longer fit the new structures and contexts. One production manager recalled her team telling her to "back up" and let them handle an internal dispute (Schultz, 1992). This is the point at which both managers and team members may have a "trapeze feeling" (Ferguson, 1980) as they let go of one safe context and reach toward another that may be uncertain.

Deming (1986a) urges organizations to "drive out the fear," but this is not an easy task. In the beginning, team members often are afraid to ask too many questions, and managers are afraid they might lose their position. As a manager tries to deal with the loss of control, he or she must be prepared to be a teacher and a mentor to clarify procedures and operations for anxious team members and help integrate and link group activities throughout the organization. At this time, the team needs training and continuing support to develop broad skills, flexibility, and confidence. As the manager lets go of some authority so that the group members can try their skills, teams may lose direction and flounder with no clear leadership role.

This confusion begins to abate as the manager and the team develop better coordination and agreements. They negotiate and clarify their relationship and set clear performance goals. The manager takes on a consultation role and begins to facilitate group learning (Felkins, Chakiris, & Chakiris, 1993). The team appoints a leader or a leader emerges out of the group and helps develop a liaison with the rest of the organization. The manager transfers more responsibility to the group as the team gets better at solving its own problems.

With some success and increasing responsibility and influence, the group becomes highly cohesive, but alignment within the system is not complete. In some ways, self-directed team members within conventional structures are misfits on the margins of the traditional organization. Other units may envy or resent the special position of these self-managed teams. At this point, excessive team orientation can cause the group to focus narrowly on its own interests in competition with other teams. The group might refuse to share information and equipment, cover up internal team problems, or deliberately become isolated from the rest of the organization. Appropriate boundaries and partnerships may be forgotten temporarily as the team tries to establish its own identity as an autonomous self-managed group.

The self-directed teams may mature slowly as they establish a productive partnership within the organizational system. Members become responsive to each other and to internal and external customers and suppliers. They are more confident in their practices as they manage all aspects of their work, from accounting and budget to ordering supplies, meeting production deadlines, maintaining quality control, and assessing their training needs. An area manager or module advisor monitors overall performance and manages the technology and systems that support and link teams throughout the system.

Part of management's commitment to employee involvement is an ethical responsibility to have clear agreements and expectations about the accountability of the teams and the responsibility of the organization to team members. Even with authority, responsibility, and broad-based skills, the team cannot control outside economic factors and market shifts. Committed employees, through team participation, may energize a business with quality improvement, customer service, and cost-effective production, but lose the final battle because of economic factors beyond their control. Employee teams also may assume responsibility for quality and productivity only to find that the system reverts back to old habits and bureaucratic methods when innovative executives and powerful sponsors leave, when production technology becomes obsolete and requires substantial investment and training that the corporation will not support, or when a merger or buyout brings different priorities and ways of working. Successful group involvement requires an investment in people and technology and a long-term organizational commitment to cultural and structural change.

Application

This case study involves a large financial institution that introduced employee involvement not only to improve quality and productivity, but also to increase the motivation and esteem of employees (Aubrey & Felkins, 1988). One of the first steps was to develop a steering committee to maintain top-level support and to plan, implement, and monitor the ongoing process.

The steering committee included the operating general manager, three division managers, three team leaders, three facilitators, quality assurance personnel, and the General Banking Services Operations training coordinator. The group met regularly and was responsible for developing general objectives for quality teams, controlling implementation, determining expense allocation, arranging for training, providing guidelines for measurements of activities, and establishing appropriate rewards.

The initiative began with an overview for the management team. Everyone in the organization then attended an orientation to the new quality program with presentations by senior executives. Each supervisor met with his or her employees after the orientation to discuss the program and how it might affect their department. Employees asked tough questions and expressed their concerns in these informal sessions.

This involvement was entirely voluntary, and a number of supervisors and employees agreed to start pilot programs in their departments. From these volunteers, the pilot groups were chosen based on their departmental morale, past successes, and opportunities for working together to accomplish specific goals related to quality, productivity, and customer service.

The integrated process encouraged individual and group learning and skill development. Facilitators from human resources trained supervisors to be the initial leaders of their quality teams. Group leadership was rotated so that all members practiced various competencies and ways to transfer these competencies to others.

After training certification, the supervisors returned to their departments and trained their teams with assistance from an experienced facilitator. This team training included data collection and analysis as well as specific problem-solving techniques: brainstorming, cause-and-effect analysis, process analysis, project management, flow charting, sampling, survey data collection, work measurement, and project benefits and cost analysis (Aubrey & Felkins, 1988). Team leaders also received specialized training in communication, group dynamics, and leadership.

The groups met for an hour once a week on company time. Over the next 20 weeks, the quality teams moved through basic training and completed their initial projects. One of the first tasks of the groups was to select a nickname. The teams chose such names as the "Wizards of Wisdom" and the "Problem Zappers," indicating their task orientation and increased confidence. The members also determined their overall objectives and developed a code of conduct for their group. This list of rules ranged from "Be prepared" and "Listen to all ideas" to "Have fun." Members could join or leave a team at any time, but they had to explain to their team why they were leaving.

The teams began the problem-solving process by brainstorming about the aspects of their work that could be improved or changed to increase quality, productivity, and service. After choosing a specific focus, such as improving customer response time, they began to apply the techniques they had learned. Some teams developed customer surveys and reviewed the records and charted response time for their department over the past year. They collected data and analyzed it in their group meetings by constructing charts and graphs to identify problem areas and compare information.

The teams found innovative solutions to everyday work problems that they understood better than anyone else in their organization. They prepared a formal presentation with elaborate visual aids to explain their proposal to management. The managers gave immediate feedback and a timely decision on project status. Most proposals were approved. From all the groups, 54 projects were accepted the first year and 119 the second year, with an average acceptance rate of 98% (Aubrey & Felkins, 1988). This high rate is due partly to management screening of inappropriate or redundant projects before they were started.

Although there was support for team development and initiative, these quality teams still worked within a conventional system of authority in which management made the final decision. These employee involvement groups were encouraged to develop cross-team relationships and partnerships, but the focus and control was limited to their own department or unit. They also did not deal with any personnel matters such as salary, hiring and firing, and discipline.

The emphasis in these teams was on developing individuals and groups and the intrinsic rewards associated with team recognition, learning, and esteem. New skills and leadership development were recognized in individual performance appraisals. The coordinators of this process believed strongly that the teams should not receive financial rewards that would distract from the quality focus and create excessive competition and conflict. Because of this policy, groups were recognized as teams in awards ceremonies and in corporate publications. Teams received bank logo items, but the most popular rewards were a half-day off and tickets to major league sporting events, which were reserved for exceptional team performance.

The results of the quality teams were evident in measurable improvements in quality, productivity, service, and work environment. For example, turnaround time was reduced by more than 30% in General Banking Services Operations and defect rates went down by 96%. Specific projects improved turnaround in answering correspondence and faster resolution of differences. The overall savings from the changes and improvements initiated by these teams over the first two years was more than $1 million. Groups also demonstrated increased confidence, improved problem-solving and leadership skills, and greater understanding and knowledge of bank operations.

CHALLENGES FOR GROUP DEVELOPMENT

The benefits of group participation and collaboration are substantial in facilitating organizational change and in developing teamwork, but organizations must invest in technology, training, and support for these groups as they work in often contradictory contexts within organizations that are in the midst of continuous change. Some of the major challenges in group facilitation techniques related to change management concern conflicting roles, access to information, and the need for team renewal.

Change is often a contradictory process for managers, team members, and for the organization as a whole. In attempting to map change processes, McWhinney (1992) suggests that all change produces some conflict, which comes from different ways of constructing reality and defining change. These alternative worldviews can foster conflicting expectations and objectives. Involving groups in facilitating organizational change requires a commitment to a flexible, pluralistic paradigm while recognizing the reality of a unitary bureaucratic model. Dealing with these multiple perspectives can create frustration and conflict.

Part of the challenge comes in understanding and integrating shifting and contradictory roles. In his explanation of the "Janus Effect," Koestler (1967) describes the duality of parts of a system that are at the same time complete in themselves, yet also part of a larger whole. Self-directed teams and clusters can be caught in these conflicting roles because they are included in the organization system and yet autonomous from the system. Managers also play a Janus role in participative organizations because they represent authority in dealing with employees, but they are also expected to empower employees and share authority. Both managers and team members in changing organizations may feel the Janus Effect in their conflicting roles and membership loyalties related to traditional structures. This duality raises many questions: What happens when team values conflict with organizational values? In what ways are managers responsible for autonomous and self-directed groups? How do team members and managers relate in new roles? How can teams and clusters be coordinated within changing organization structures?

The increasing ambiguity related to accountability and responsibility in changing roles and structures creates some stress. Deming (1986a) blames management and the system as causing the majority of organizational problems and preventing people from doing their job. In explaining the principles of organizational transformation, Deming states that it is necessary to "break down the barriers" between different areas of the organization. This encourages teamwork but also raises other questions and challenges related to responsibility, coordination, and control.

In a provocative article, Jaques (1990) suggests that the hierarchy, the essence of bureaucracy, is the "most natural structure" ever devised for managing large organizations because it deals directly with accountability. According to Jaques, none of the group-oriented "panaceas" deal directly with accountability. As he reminds us, companies hire and fire individuals, not groups. Waterman (1990) explains that both "adhocracy" in flexible team structures and "bureaucracy" in a more permanent structural design are necessary to organizations. The challenge is learning to move in and out of these differing structures to adapt to changing needs.

No matter how participation and employee involvement are presented, from ad hoc committees and quality teams to self-directed teams and clusters, the manager is the person who is most often caught between the old way and the new reality. For example, in self-directed teams, the manager is expected to take on different roles—teacher, mentor, and facilitator—while giving up much of his or her traditional authority. To meet this challenge, managers need training in communication, consultation, and group dynamics. Increasingly, managers are becoming consultants and facilitators who work with people and use facilitation rather than control to support and nurture organizational teams, clusters, and alliances (Felkins, Chakiris, & Chakiris, 1993). These new-style managers focus on processes that integrate people and technology and encourage collaborative inquiry to maximize group contributions to the change process.

Access to timely, relevant information is another important challenge for managers and team members in shifting structures and changing organizational relationships. The action research cycle is a valuable group tool for continually collecting and analyzing data related to performance goals and teamwork. Through action research, cross training, and simulations, groups learn about how their organization works and how they help create the organization through their actions, decisions, and work practices. A cultural approach to change is based on coordination through group interaction, information sharing, and team learning.

Team members also require continuing training to enhance their skills and organizational knowledge. They need information on marketing, finance, human resources, and operations in order to make effective decisions. This means more than just production data, control charts, and customer surveys. Groups should have knowledge about how the parts of the organizational system work together, but they also need to understand how they help create the rules, policies, and unwritten norms, and how these social constructions influence them as individuals and as group members.

Knowledge, interaction, and experience begin to break down the barriers between departments and people, but some crucial information barriers remain. Although the technology of the organization is geared toward gathering, processing, analyzing, selecting, and disseminating information (Schrage, 1990), that information is often fragmented by unit or department and not shared as a collective resource for group learning, planning, and implementation. Clusters in a "communication-driven" approach to organization attempt to break down these barriers with the free and open exchange of information and resources to meet customer needs (Mills, 1993).

From a critical perspective, information can oppress or liberate. In the "Era of Technique" in which the machine becomes an "embodied decision procedure" (Barrett, 1978), information can take on its own existence, disconnected from the people who collect it or the people who will be affected by it. The computer-based technology of an "informated" organization (Zuboff, 1988) offers opportunities for learning and development as well as the potential for alienation in decentralized and widely dispersed structures.

Handy (1990) suggests that the majority of people in the organizational system soon may be part-time, temporary, or contract workers, which creates additional challenges and increases the need for effective coordination and operational alliances. Action research and collaborative inquiry can help to reconnect information and people by focusing on the process of collective research and analysis, with data feedback and action planning, implementation, and monitoring by the people who use the information and are affected by it, including managers, employees, suppliers, customers, and communities.

In the "virtual organization" (Davidow & Malone, 1992), individuals and groups with specific competencies coalesce around a task and then separate and reform in a new configuration for another task. Within these shifting and spontaneous alliances, Schrage (1990) stresses the need for a "shared space" for information exchange and team collaboration as part of the architecture of transforming organizations. Computer technology offers some practical options for group facilitation and learning, including unique interactive opportunities in "computer-enhanced" meetings facilitated with a large, shared computer screen accessed from individual terminals. In one application, the Xerox Palo Alto Research Center created Colab software for "interpersonal computing" in the collection, integration, and analysis of individual and group ideas.

Another example is the Software Aided Meeting Management (SAMM) program developed at the University of Minnesota as a group decision support system (GDSS) that includes agenda setting, brainstorming, idea evaluation, and decision tools (see Poole, DeSanctis, Kirsch, & Jackson, this volume). SAMM was designed for and tested with teams at the Internal Revenue Service as part of a large-scale quality improvement program (DeSanctis, Poole, Desharnais, & Lewis, 1991).

People must find innovative and humanistic ways to establish a shared space for generative dialogue to explore organizational possibilities. In many instances, however, organizational members do not take the time to create a space for collective learning as a resource for change and development. The design of "information space" can "illuminate" the organization's current activities and reveal patterns of thinking and decision making to help groups understand, plan, and implement change (Nadler, Gerstein, & Shaw, 1992).

In exploring ideas about developing a common space for group learning, Bohm and Edwards (1991) apply some critical concepts to an understanding of thought as a "collective phenomenon." There is a clear distinction between "discussion," in which group members concentrate on expressing and defending their ideas, and "dialogue," in which participants listen to each other to gain insight and understanding into their shared thinking processes. Thoughts represent common meanings that only can be accessed within the participatory process of dialogue, which makes us aware of our thinking process, our sometimes incoherent thoughts, and the assumptions on which they are based (Bohm & Edwards, 1991).

As executives, managers, and group members better understand their own thinking processes in relationships with others, they are more able to respect multiple voices and deal with the ambiguity of alternative organizational structures as they facilitate collaboration and creatively integrate directed and nondirected change processes.

The greatest challenges for groups facilitating organizational change come from both inside their teams as well as from external forces. Organizational teams must maintain management support and create an internal process for group renewal in order to survive. There are many questions that team members and organizational leaders must confront about the positioning and maintenance of teams within an organization: How do self-managed units and clusters relate to existing facilities and conventional groups? How does the organization support and recognize individuals within team structures? How does the system meet the increased need for information and exchange among groups? How can traditional training programs be shifted into the new paradigm? How can bureaucratic managers move into consultation roles that facilitate teamwork and group development?

Once questions related to external alignment and authority are answered, there are internal challenges to energize teams that have gone stale and lost their excitement for innovation and learning as individuals and as groups. Some characteristic terms related to this extensive organizational change process are "rebirth," "reinvention," and "transformation." Lippitt (1982) suggests the term "renewal" as a continual process of confrontation of the data and the issues, especially in the discrepancy between "where we are" and "where we want to be." Renewal is more than an innovative training program, a successful company-wide quality initiative, or an astounding financial recovery. As a developmental group process, renewal requires critical thinking, collaborative inquiry, team learning, and mutual influence.

Group participation and involvement become routine when teams cease to learn and take their responsibility for granted without recognizing the shared agreements and knowledge on which it is based. As group processes become more routinized and less flexible and collaborative in relation to other parts of the system, members stop looking for creative options and accept the prepackaged solution or the dominant corporate ideology without questioning its viability in a changing environment. When this happens, groups no longer learn from their experiences, and participation and involvement become empty words as teams lose their capacity as agents of change.

Groups within organizations require new role flexibility within a portfolio of skills and assignments, shared spaces for thinking and learning together, and opportunities for team confirmation and renewal. By expanding influence through collaboration and increased knowledge and competencies, groups can help facilitate organizational change. Action research, simulations, and employee involvement can be powerful group facilitation techniques to understand and implement change as groups and organizations move into the future.

11

Developing the "Team" in a Team-Managed Organization: Group Facilitation in a New-Design Plant

David R. Seibold
University of California at Santa Barbara

The great revolution of modern times has been the revolution of equality. The idea that all people should be equal in their condition has undermined the old structures of authority, hierarchy and deference.
(Schlesinger, 1986; cited in Fisher, 1993, p. 10)

Although Schlesinger was discussing post-industrial society human relations in general, his characterization rings true for industrial relations in particular. In today's "second industrial revolution" (Fisher, 1993), the assumptions and structures of traditional workplaces (e.g., control by managers, pyramidal designs, stovepipe operational functions, vertical chain of command relationships, and rigid bureaucratic procedures) are giving way to nontraditional work relationships and practices (e.g., workers' participation in managing, lattice organizations, cross-functional work arrangements, lateral collaborative relationships, and self-directed work teams). Increasingly, hierarchical organizations are being supplanted by "shamrock," "fishnet," and "self-organizing" organizations (see Seibold & Contractor, 1992). The fundamental features of this shift include decreases in traditional forms of supervision and correlative increases in employee involvement. *Working collaborative-*

ly, employees increasingly must gather and synthesize information, interpret and decide jointly how to act on it, and take collective responsibility for implementing, monitoring, and evaluating their actions (Barker, 1992; Versteeg, 1990; Walton, 1985). These changes have important theoretical implications for understanding and practical implications for *facilitating* collaborative group work in organizations.

Variously termed autonomous and semiautonomous work units, self-directed teams, team-directed workforces, worker cells, self-managing workers, high involvement organizations, team-managed plants, and self-regulating work groups (among many other labels), these "teams" have collective responsibility for managing themselves and their work with minimal direct supervision. Self-directed teams share a variety of characteristics: typically they plan and schedule work, order materials and handle budget expenditures, make production/service-related decisions, monitor productivity, and take action on problems—decisions once reserved for management (Fisher, 1993; Versteeg, 1990).

These teams have their roots in the human relations initiatives in the United States between 1930 and 1970, European coal mine and factory studies beginning in the 1950s, and Japanese quality circles following World War II. Beginning with their innovation in U.S. organizations in the 1960s and 1970s (cf. Walton, 1977), what sets these teams apart from their predecessors and counterparts—especially as they are used in U.S. core manufacturing organizations—is their continued and central emphasis on business performance: improved quality, increased productivity, and decreased operating costs. Likert (1967) was among the first scholars to recognize their value in reducing communication distances and pushing down decision making to organizational levels where first-hand information is available:

> Communication is clear and adequately understood. Important issues are recognized and dealt with. The atmosphere is one of no nonsense with emphasis on high productivity, high quality, and low cost. Decisions are reached promptly, tasks are performed rapidly and productively. (pp. 50-51)

Although only 7% of U.S. workers are now organized in such teams, more than 200 major corporations currently rely on them in at least one company location (Fisher, 1993). Furthermore, 83% of organizations using self-directed work teams surveyed in 1990 planned increased use of them by 1995 (Wellins, Byham, & Wilson, 1991).

This chapter discusses facilitation techniques employed during the author's work with a specific type of self-directed team: a self-regulating team of employees managing a new-design manufacturing plant

(Lawler, 1986). Because they referred to themselves as a "team-managed" organization, that term is preserved in the case study. Three tasks are undertaken in the chapter; each is the focus of successive sections. The first section reviews pertinent literature concerning advanced manufacturing technologies in general, and their relevance for new-design plants in particular. In light of the philosophy, structures, and processes endemic to new-design plants, special attention is paid to: (a) the theoretical implications of the requirement for *integrating* (Kanter, 1983; Lawrence & Lorsch, 1967) information, resources, and support across organizational subgroups, and (b) the practical implications of the need for *facilitating* (Friedman, 1989; Hirokawa & Gouran, 1989; Keltner, 1989) team goals, roles, procedures, and relationships. The second section briefly discusses the background, structure, and practices of the team-managed organization itself. Those features that make it a new-design plant are highlighted, implications of those features for self-managed team functioning are identified, and results of a formative evaluation conducted during initial stages of the process consultation are presented. The third section reports the facilitation procedures utilized in response to the evaluation findings, with particular emphasis on team building, problem-solving procedures, and group process requirements of new-design plants (as reviewed in the first section) and self-managing teams (as discussed in the second section).

ADVANCED MANUFACTURING TECHNOLOGY AND NEW-DESIGN PLANTS

The team-managed plant examined in this chapter represents the intersection of two distinct trends in organizations during the last quarter of this century: the incorporation of advanced technologies into core manufacturing operations, and the development of new-design plants. Each of these trends is discussed briefly in order to provide a context for understanding the organization in question and a sensitivity to the requirements for team facilitation in such organizations.

Advanced Manufacturing Technologies

Technologies have evolved during the 1970s and 1980s that are dramatically changing manufacturing. Known collectively as advanced manufacturing technologies (AMTs), they have been defined broadly as "automated production system(s) of people, machines and tools for the planning and control of the production process, including the procurement of raw materials, parts, and components, and the shipment and service of finished products" (Pennings, 1987, p. 198). AMTs include robotics, computer-aided design, engineering, and manufacturing (CAD, CAE, CAM), automated materials handling systems, materials resource planning (MRP) systems, and computer-integrated manufacturing (CIM) systems. AMTs are of great strategic importance in competitive manufacturing, as they can enhance manufacturing effectiveness in terms of cost, quality, flexibility, and lead-time (Dean, Susman, & Porter, 1990). Growing numbers of organizations are adopting AMTs to cope with fragmented mass markets, shorter product life cycles, and consumer demands for customization, because AMTs enable production of specialized products at mass production cost (Zammuto & O'Connor, 1992). AMTs have been integrated into core operations by manufacturing firms worldwide. Malone (1987) estimated that the global market for manufacturing automation would grow to $63.3 billion by the early 1990s.

Technology-based companies, of which AMT firms are the ultimate examples, have the potential to achieve important competitive advantages through the rapid and ongoing development of new product and process technologies (Spencer, 1990). As Elmes and Wilemon (1991) emphasized, these advantages accrue from an organization's ability to communicate freely and effectively across organizational boundaries (Maidique & Hayes, 1984; Souder, 1987), to scan and respond rapidly to data about changing markets, environments, and technologies (Bauer & Hout, 1988), to learn from prior decisions (Meyers & Wilemon, 1989), and to be innovative (Pearson, 1988). Furthermore, as Cushman and King (1993) noted, organizational communication that can operate at "high speed" in environmental scanning is crucial to managing organizations' internal "coalignments," as well as their internal/environmental interfaces. Only in this way can companies achieve the rapid, efficient, innovative, and flexible responses necessary to compete in a turbulent global economy.

There are important *theoretical implications* of these technological and communication-related changes for group/organizational functioning. In particular, if organizational responsiveness, flexibility, innovativeness, and efficiency are dependent on the speed, accuracy, scope, and processing capability of internal and external communication by organizational members, then the *integration* of information, resources, and support across subgroups is vital to the well-being of technology-based manufacturing firms (Elmes & Wilemon, 1991; Kanter, 1979). Lawrence and Lorsch (1967) noted long ago that top-performing organizations are both highly differentiated and highly integrated. Differentiation occurs when members of subunits adopt different cognitive and behavioral orientations in order to cope with environmental complexity, whereas integration occurs when subunits, despite orientation differences, collaborate to achieve "unity of effort."

Most organizations tend toward greater differentiation, or seg-mentalism (Kanter, 1983), primarily as a result of: personal and function-al specialization (Kanter, 1983); difficulties emanating from imbalanced power-dependency relationships (Emerson, 1962); inadequate interde-pendence requirements (McCann & Galbraith, 1981; Thompson, 1967); insufficient coordinating mechanisms (Galbraith, 1973); social catego-rization processes that lead to in-group/out-group identities between subunits (Ashforth & Mael, 1989; Hogg & Abrams, 1988; Tajfel, 1982); inability to moderate levels of intergroup conflict among units compet-ing for resources and often with differing goals (Baburoglu, 1988; Brown, 1983; Pondy, 1967; Pruitt & Rubin, 1986); ineffective methods of managing interdependence, coordination, and confrontation (Walton & McKersie, 1965); and difficulties that differentiated members have in examining their own assumptions about the causes of difficult relations (Kilmann & Thomas, 1978) and difficult problems (Argyris, 1982; Argyris, Putnam, & Smith, 1985). To the extent that these strains toward differentiation result in poor intergroup relations within a technology-based organization, information exchange, awareness of changing envi-ronments, organizational learning, and innovativeness are impeded (Elmes & Wilemon, 1991). Hence, the challenge for AMT companies, in particular, is to counter the tendency toward organizational differentia-tion and to achieve *intergroup integration and group responsiveness*. One organizational design that has enabled achievement of these ends is the "new-design" plant.

New-Design Plants

Patterned after pioneering theory and research with self-regulating work teams in England and Norway (Burns & Stalker, 1968; Herbst, 1962; Rice, 1958; Trist, Higgin, Murray, & Pollock, 1963), as well as high-ly publicized innovative participative management plants created in this country during the 1970s by Procter and Gamble in Ohio and Georgia and by General Foods in Kansas, U.S. corporations designed new plants in the 1980s that continue to be revolutionary in the extent to which they transfer power, information, knowledge, and intrinsic rewards down-ward (Lawler, 1986). These "new-design" plants now exist in many *Fortune* 500 companies, including selected facilities of AT&T, Rockwell, General Motors, Heinz, TRW, Johnson and Johnson, Sherwin-Williams, and Cummins Engine. Indeed, Walton (1985) estimated that 200 new-design plants were in operation by the mid-1980s.

Characteristic of the participative, group-centered practices com-mon to new-design plants are selection of new employees by teams of co-workers, work team participation in the physical layout of the plant, design of jobs by employees, lack of a hierarchy in organizational structure, implementation of egalitarian pay and incentive systems, and the development of management philosophies that emphasize shared participation and shared decision making. As Lawler (1986) summarized:

> Overall, new design plants are clearly different from traditional plants in a number of important ways. Almost no aspect of the organization is left untouched. The reward system, the structure, the physical layout, the personnel management system, and the nature of jobs are all changed in significant ways. Because so many features are altered, in aggregate they amount to a new kind of organization. (p. 178)

New-design plants (and the self-regulating work teams at their core) are direct outgrowths of sociotechnical systems theory (Emery & Trist, 1965), which conceptualizes production systems as composed of both technological and social components. Sociotechnical systems theorists propose that work structures must be designed in ways that are responsive to both the task requirements of a technology and the social needs of workers—structures that are both productive and humanly satisfying in the context of changing external environments. The *group* is the building block of these designs, referred to as "technically required cooperation" (Meissner, 1969). The objective of these designs is to increase team members' capacity to control variance from goal attainment (Cooper & Foster, 1971; Emery, 1967). In turn, the design of self-regulating work groups in new-design plants depends on at least three factors that foster technically required cooperation and control capacity: (a) "task differentiation," the extent to which the group's task is itself autonomous; (b) "boundary control," the extent to which employees can influence transactions with their task environment; (c) and "task control," the extent to which members can regulate their behaviors to convert raw materials into finished products (Cummings, 1978).

A number of positive results obtained from new-design plants have been documented by Lawler (1986): improvements in work methods and procedures due to team problem solving; enhanced recruitment and retention of team members due to increased involvement and pay; high-quality work due to team motivation; fewer supervision requirements because teams are self-managing; improved decision making resulting from increased input; higher levels of skill development and staffing flexibility due to cross-training; and lower levels of grievances because teams resolve issues. These findings are corroborated in Cotter's (1983) review of organizations in seven countries that "transitioned" from traditional work systems to self-directed work teams: 93% reported improved productivity, 86% reported decreased operating costs, 86% reported improved quality, and 70% reported improved employee attitudes.

Still, these advantages depend critically on *facilitating* loose aggregates of individuals into well-integrated and committed problem-solving teams. If new-design plants shift information, power, knowledge, and rewards downward, and if the success of new-design plants depends on empowered first-line employees' ability to utilize these resources collaboratively and to share responsibility for their decisions, then improving members' effectiveness as a team is central to the success of new-design plants. The remainder of this chapter, therefore, describes efforts at team facilitation in one new-design plant. The following section introduces the organization, with particular attention to its features as a new-design plant and problems for its self-regulating workforce that were indicated by results of a formative evaluation undertaken during the organization's early stages. The final section reports team facilitation techniques employed in response to those findings and in light of theoretical/empirical determinants of group effectiveness in general.

TEAM MANAGEMENT AT BFSI

BFSI is a 37-member, team-managed manufacturing plant located in the Midwest. The identity of the organization has been protected at its request and will simply be called BFSI. It is a joint venture of a multinational construction equipment manufacturer and a Midwest-based major manufacturer of filters for such equipment. BFSI's mission is to produce top-quality oil and transmission filters at competitive prices. The impetus for the venture came from the companies' desire to have closer ties between product design and manufacturing design. Joint work began on the plant in 1986. By 1987, BFSI had received delivery of all equipment, much of which had been designed by team members. Members began testing and refining all computer-driven machinery, designing the physical layout of the plant, and bringing the production line into operation by mid-1987. Production did not begin in earnest until early 1988. This chapter focuses on the organization's group processes during 1987-1988.

BFSI as a New-Design Plant

BFSI was designed as an automated factory from the outset, in part for reasons of quality control and in part to achieve the benefits of team management (including a smaller work force). Whereas production functions in traditional organizations are handled by some workers, and functions such as maintaining the equipment and assuring quality control and safety are handled by others, the organizational structure at BFSI cuts across those responsibilities. Multiskilled blue collar workers (technicians), working in "area teams" of 4-5 persons, rotate jobs within and across areas to handle all aspects of the production process. There are also no foremen or supervisors at BFSI. The technicians, with two-year technical degrees and training in electronics and mechanics, are self-directed. They monitor and maintain the production process machinery with specialized support from a small team of certified engineers, who act more as consultants than quality control overseers.

BFSI is designed to foster group participation in planning work, coordinating tasks, and solving problems. Every day, each shift begins with a meeting of everyone working in the plant during that rotation. Meetings of subunits or standing committees may follow or be held throughout the day. Standing committees, such as the Safety Committee, the Good Practices Committee, and the Design Committee exist to address a variety of organization-wide issues. Personnel functions have been absorbed by other groups of employees, including preparation of an employee handbook, development of applicant screening/selection procedures, and monitoring compensation. Team members also administer most aspects of the reward system, including establishing skill-based pay levels, determining raises and bonuses, and monitoring a gainsharing program. All members are cross-trained in every aspect of the production process. Although there is a plant manager and an accountant, they primarily serve liaison roles in interfacing with the parent companies. A strong egalitarian culture exists at BFSI that is reflected in the absence of formal hierarchies (team members rotate as "area leaders") and status markers (e.g., there are no eating areas, restrooms, offices, recreational facilities, parking places, and the like that cannot be used by all members). Training is emphasized: On-the-job and paid off-site technical training is provided for everyone on a regular basis, as is training in interpersonal and group process skills, career planning, and other personal development.

Formative Evaluation of BFSI

Most new-design plants are highly successful by measures of productivity, costs, and work life quality. For example, Procter & Gamble was so successful with new-design plants that: (a) all new plants were mandated to be new-design, resulting in 20 such additions; (b) all traditional plants were to become new-design; and (c) all new-designs were to be closed to researchers and others because Procter & Gamble believed it had a competitive advantage it did not wish to lose (Lawler, 1986). Productivity results at BFSI also were successful, if more modest: nearly on-time startup and at less than projected cost; output equivalent to comparable plants but with 60% less labor; 80% less rework; more frequent inventory turns; less production machinery "down time" than normal; and near-zero turnover in personnel.

Furthermore, the quality of work life at BFSI was high based on results of a self-administered survey of the 37 employees (34 returns = 92% response rate). The questionnaire was developed by the author and his colleagues (Seibold, et al., 1988) as part of a formative evaluation of the organization during its early stages—at the invitation of the Good Practices committee and in answer to the question "How are we doing?" BFSI members felt that there were four major advantages to team management at BFSI. First, there were greater opportunities to elicit input from all members of the organization than in a traditional management organization, thus producing a stronger organization. Second, both human and technical resources could be better utilized in a team-managed organization. Third, members' freedom to express their opinions and ideas increased their morale and satisfaction with the organization. Fourth, members pointed to cross-training as a major strength of BFSI.

These strengths were associated with other advantages of working in a team-managed organization, according to those surveyed and subsequently interviewed. Comparing BFSI to a traditionally managed organization, members felt that they had a greater sense of ownership at BFSI and that there was more worker satisfaction and better decision making, all of which produced a better product. In addition, team members felt that they had greater autonomy at BFSI and that people were highly self-motivated. As one member said, "I had a hard time leaving after twelve hours if something still had to be done." Another commented, "Everyone tried their (sic) hardest." Team management encouraged better communication, a higher level of interaction among its members, and members appreciated being able to talk directly to the plant manager. Other advantages of working for BFSI mentioned by respondents included: allowance for individual differences, such as flexibility in scheduling work hours; the fact that co-workers were more helpful and honest; and the acknowledgement of individual contributions by others in the organization. "In traditional organizations," said one member contrasting his prior employers with work at BFSI, "they (upper management) take credit for ideas."

At the same time, new-design plants are prone to a variety of problems: member expectations can be too high because of the philosophy and selection process; surveillance by other areas of the organization (e.g., management in "parent" companies) can produce pressure and conflict; training costs are high due to the need for cross-training and team training; team meetings take more time and decision processes can be slow; establishing standards can be difficult in the absence of a "history" and meaningful benchmarks; and the timing of new decisions regarding compensation, schedule, and production changes is difficult (Lawler,

1986). Furthermore, members may revert to the practices of traditional workplaces and hierarchical management during times of information overload, environmental uncertainty, decision difficulty, work pressure, and interpersonal conflict (Barker, Melville, & Pacanowsky, 1992).

Similar problems were evident at BFSI. More than 66% of respondents felt that other members cared more about their own areas than the plant as a whole—a serious threat to "team spirit." Nearly 20% felt they did not understand how a team-managed organization should work, and they clung to traditional organizational practices. Approximately 40% felt that interpersonal conflicts had slowed technical progress. More than 85% believed that team-decision processes had slowed work. One of every two respondents perceived imbalances in influence within the plant despite a norm of equality. Although everyone in a new-design plant should feel able to express negative feedback, a sizeable minority (18%) felt inhibited about openly sharing feedback on performance of other members. Ninety-five percent reported that alternate shift teams needed to better communicate and coordinate with each other more effectively. These "problems" became the impetus for the author's facilitation efforts with BFSI, as described in the next section.

FACILITATING A "TEAM" AT BFSI

Team facilitation at BFSI did not entail assisting members in dealing with many problems found in organizations making a "transition" to self-managing teams. Because BFSI had been conceived from the start as a new-design plant, there were no first-line supervisors, middle managers, or union representatives to resist the teams; reductions in existing workforce size were not evident; self-management was not limited to select units of the organization, nor on an "experimental" basis; there were no changes in pre-existing organizational roles or patterns of communication to be facilitated; nor were there the reported dysfunctional correlates to increased "permissiveness" within units suddenly given greater autonomy (for discussion of these problems, see Barker, Melville, & Pacanowsky, 1992; Cordery, Mueller, & Smith, 1991; Cummings, 1978; Lawler, 1986). Hence, some of the facilitation reported here may be less relevant to organizations "in transition" to self-directed workforces. Furthermore, unlike many treatments of facilitation in self-managed teams (Versteeg, 1990), work with BFSI more broadly involved facilitating a team-managed organization, including the timing of start-up decisions about shift work, bonuses, and production schedules; establishing plant-wide standards; interfacing with parent companies; and negotiating the unique role of the plant manager. Of course, the facilitation process did focus on many of the same difficulties observed in self-managing teams in general and evident in the BFSI survey results discussed above: conflict, decision making, efficiency, performance feedback, inter-area relationships, and the like. Finally, the facilitation process also involved attention to theoretical and practical issues concerning effective group functioning in general (Hirokawa & Gouran, 1989). Each of these aspects of the facilitation process is treated next.

Team Process Facilitation

At the broadest level, the facilitation process involved the author's immersion into plant "life" approximately one day per week. This seemed to be sufficient to aid team members to: (a) recognize the ways in which their interactional processes contributed to the aforementioned problems while simultaneously fostering the strengths they acknowledged; (b) work within those same processes (trying simultaneously to improve any that were especially dysfunctional) to identify causes and determine solutions to the problems jointly agreed on; and (c) facilitate team-based learning of the skills and processes employed through the facilitative relationship, so that members could, on their own, utilize them in confronting problems in the future. The facilitation process involved certain aspects of process consulting (Schein, 1988) and team building (Dyer, 1988), and I have characterized it before as "team process consultation" (Seibold, 1986).

Team process consultation emanates from a series of assumptions concerning: (a) people problems and change processes; (b) how an "outsider" can be helpful with both; and (c) conditions under which success is most likely. At BFSI, these "assumptions" were shared and discussed during team meetings with the whole plant over a series of two to three weeks. During all discussions the following matters were explicated as both replicated research findings and principles underpinning the facilitation process. First, concerning people and change, the author discussed research with BFSI members indicating that: (a) people do not resist change so much as they resist perceptions they are being changed; (b) personal commitment is a vastly more powerful motivator than external reward or punishment; (c) focused feedback and coaching can affect more enduring change than criticism; and (d) personal and systemic change are more likely when members feel valued by others in the organization.

Assumptions in the second area, the "outsider's" role, included the following tenets of team facilitation: (a) members beset with difficulties may be motivated to change but not recognize how those matters are part of larger problems, nor what to do about them; (b) through systematic observation, data collection, and discussion, an "outsider" can help members to focus their attention on previously "unseen" difficulties or patterns, but cannot become involved deeply enough to solve problems (nor would this be desirable except in crises); (c) hence, with an outsider's help—over a period of time needed for insight and trust to develop—team members must come to their own understanding of "the problem" and to their own solutions; and (d) because no remedy will be perfect or permanent and because new problems emerge, team members must also learn how to continuously monitor, interpret, analyze, solve, and implement decisions about their own problems.

Third, assumptions about preconditions for success were discussed (with far less treatment of supporting research). Success of team facilitation is most likely when team members: (a) already have some recognition of and insights into problems but are open to alternative perspectives on them; (b) have high commitment to solutions and are willing to become involved in all aspects of the team process consultation; (c) accept responsibility for the outcome(s) of their efforts, whether successful or unsuccessful; and (d) recognize that problems are systemic and require considerable scanning/information gathering by the outsider and themselves (including, in this case, discussions with parent company managers and plant clients). Implicit in all three assumptions concerning team process facilitation were values that the author believes should drive organizational development (OD) facilitations of this sort: promoting a culture of collaboration, engendering ownership of process and outcome, creating openness in communication, increasing personal and group effectiveness and efficiency, and promoting inquiry and continuous learning (for similar positions, see Church & Burke, 1993; Friedlander, 1976; Weisbord, 1982).

For all these reasons, it was necessary and most productive to work with BFSI members as a team. Although some emphasis was placed on enhancing individuals' skills (in the training and coaching discussed below), primary attention was directed to working with members collectively to understand the team processes involved in problem solving, integrating resources, sharing information, and dealing with interpersonal difficulties. To do so required a common conception of "team." What emerged from discussions was their "creed" that BFSI would become a team when members could: (a) share and articulate a common set of goals and a "vision" that unified them in pursuit of those goals; (b) share information and interpretations freely (i.e., "communicate honestly"); (c) work collectively in an effective and efficient manner to solve problems and make decisions; (d) respect and trust each other sufficiently to request and to provide "support"; (e) set high standards for themselves, attain them, and learn from the process how to better achieve their next goals (for which they used the abbreviation "continuous improvement"—itself a part of the Total Quality Improvement program in which they had been involved since the plant's inception); (f) develop procedures for "working smart," by which they meant working efficiently yet with sufficient flexibility to adapt to changes as the plant grew in size and number of products produced; and (g) feel satisfied with their individual contribution to the plant while knowing that others on the team valued that contribution too.

Fisher (1986), a former team leader and internal consultant at Proctor & Gamble's new-design plant in Lima, OH, described five "stages" that such operations experience in the self-directed team "maturity cycle": (a) investigation ("understanding it"); (b) preparation ("accepting it"); (c) implementation ("making it work"); (d) transition ("keeping at it"); and (e) maturation ("keeping it continuously improving"). Like so many phasic models of development that posit a unitary linear sequence of "steps" (see Poole's critique, 1983), Fisher's conception may be somewhat oversimplified. At BFSI, team members seemed to cycle back and forth through investigation/preparation/implementation during their first two years together. At times, it was important for the author to help team members develop common vocabularies, encourage them to keep the "team" abreast of new information, and to continually tie evaluation of how the team "was doing" to BFSI's real business needs. Although these are more representative of the initial phase of self-directed teams (Fisher, 1986), BFSI members simultaneously needed assistance with matters that Fisher would consider aspects of later stages: helping area leaders to "model" appropriate team-centered behaviors; developing patterns of open communication; recognizing how the workplace was evolving and supporting that growth; encouraging personal sacrifice and supportiveness of others; and continually linking team practices to the plant's overarching business objectives.

At the same time that BFSI was developing through certain "team" stages, albeit neither linear nor sequential, the process of team facilitation also was proceeding though certain stages. Normally, team process consultations go through "preparation" and "start-up" phases at the outset (Dyer, 1988; Seibold, 1986). The author's involvement with the formative evaluation and survey discussed above substituted for a more thorough "preparation" period that normally would involve meetings with clients, the parent companies, and team members, as well as considerable archival study of the group's written communication. The series of discussions with BFSI members concerning the survey results and facilitation process assumptions discussed earlier also served as the "start-up" period.

During the next several weeks, facilitation focused on "group problem solving and process analysis." The thrust of the sessions in this phase was to create a "process within a process." The ostensible purpose of each meeting was to focus on processes contributing to whatever problem the group was analyzing. Toward this end, BFSI members were provided with training in a variety of meeting planning, structuring, and problem-solving techniques (see Seibold, 1979; Zander, 1982). In the course of these (videotaped) sessions, the team also came to see ways in which some of these process difficulties (subtle status differences and disproportionate influence, cliques, insufficient testing of ideas, etc.) were manifested simultaneously in their interactions during these meetings. For example, during the problem-solving exercises designed to simulate the complex coordination demands inherent in their work, members began to see their over-reliance on more vocal members' input, the emergence of subgroups in the exercise as the only way to counter these influential individuals, and the withdrawal of other group members while the "fight" was going on. Hirokawa and Gouran (1989) have termed these "relational problems," and Gouran (1982) discussed the ways in which these and other relational problems can impede a group's efforts to satisfy the requirements of decision-making tasks.

Almost at the same time, and especially when environmental pressures affect a team negatively (as did a series of production setbacks at BFSI), team members enter what Dyer (1988) termed a "feedback" phase. At BFSI, members began tentatively or emotionally to share interpretations about each other's behavior and performance, accept (or deny) responsibility, and move toward some resolution of both the specific problems at hand and interpersonal processes contributing to them. The author worked with team members to focus feedback on matters that would aid others' personal and interpersonal effectiveness. Various "skill-building" training sessions were introduced during this phase (e.g., listening, avoiding and handling defensiveness, communicating criticism, and mediating conflict). A variety of traditional OD techniques also were used (Burke, 1982), including role playing, "prescription writing," envelope exchanges, and sessions focused on subareas. As a result of these sessions, techniques, training, and follow-up coaching sessions with individuals (as well as their own continued work), a more cohesive BFSI team emerged.

Now more effective in dealing with each other, team members were able to refocus their attention on plant problems. The author's facilitation activities included assisting with the design of a task-logging system to improve intershift communication, developing strategies for responding to the parent companies' pressures regarding production quotas, designing interarea reporting systems, systematizing "feedback" forms for area team leaders to evaluate their meetings, and facilitating standing committee deliberations concerning safety procedures and skill-based pay raises. Facilitation also involved helping members to codify "ground rules" for discussion sessions that emerged during the team-building sessions. These "ground rules" formalized the team's norms concerning interaction and decision making (e.g., "Everyone participates," "Try for consensus before voting," "Focus on facts before feelings" in problem analyses, "Hold '2nd chance' sessions" before final decisions are reached, "Take risks" in discussions, etc.)

Although the author moved from the Midwest before the normal team facilitation process could run its course at BFSI, team members assumed responsibility for many aspects of the last stage—"termination and follow-up" (Seibold, 1986). For example, some members formulated interpersonal "contracts" with others that might be invoked to adjudicate recurrent and troublesome issues. These "contracts" concerning frequent disagreements included mutually agreeable "terms" specifying what each member would (tactfully "confront") and would not do ("sandbag," "gang up," "hold a grudge") if in conflict in the future. Contracts were voiced before the entire team and "witnessed" by team members. Team members also held a meeting to assess areas in which changes had occurred, identify processes that led to the changes, reflect on what they had learned from the experience, compile a list of problems remaining to be studied (their "agenda"), and institute mechanisms that would ensure team effectiveness (quarterly process review meeting, periodic use of a "process observer" from the team, feedback from the plant manager).

Theory-Based Facilitation Practices

Although space limitations preclude systematic treatment, it may be worthwhile to note in closing this discussion of facilitation techniques at BFSI that theory and research were not used merely to guide the facilitation process but were explicit bases for discussion with BFSI members. The author has always been committed to the interdependence of theory and practice (Seibold, in press). At BFSI, the practice of facilitation included discussion of theoretical concepts which, in turn, facilitated learning (Argyris, 1991; Guzzo, Jette, & Katzell, 1985; Hackman, 1990; Harrison, 1982; Katzell & Guzzo, 1983). For example, team members were interested in what the author termed "non-managerial control" at BFSI. Shortly before this project began, Mills (1983) had written about the "control" that exists in self-managed groups. Although not tied to formal leadership, control derives in part from members' preferences for self-management. More importantly, Mills argued, "normative systems" emerge out of group practices and serve to guide members' behaviors. By extension, they serve as moral justifications for group practices and as standards for judging the appropriateness of one's own and others' actions. From a communication standpoint, these justificatory/regulatory systems emerge from implicit or voiced premises surrounding decision making by a group (see Tompkins & Cheney, 1985). Members found it useful to understand that the same ground rules (see above) "creating" their organization were subtly laying the foundations for "control" of their own and future members' behaviors.

The author also drew liberally on Galbraith's (1973) notion of the "design" of organizations as the result of members' "information processing" activities. Especially in the standing committees, team members could see the benefits for organizational effectiveness and efficiency of such uncertainty reduction strategies as reducing members' need for information processing (e.g., by increasing "slack resources" in areas of inventory or by placing additional shift workers "on call," and by increasing "certainty" viz performance goals, policy manuals, and procedural guidelines for each area of the plant) or by increasing members' capacity for information processing (such as more effective lateral communication structures like those discussed above). Information processing notions were understood readily by technicians familiar with concepts like "sensing" and machine "intelligence" in a computer-automated plant. Other theoretical discussions focused on empowerment (Albrecht, 1987; Pacanowsky, 1987), leadership in self-managing groups (Manz & Sims, 1984), attribution processes (Green & Mitchell, 1979), and dysfunctional decision dynamics (Janis, 1989; Manz & Sims, 1982), as well as functional group processes (Lewin, 1958) and organizational environments and scanning (Daft & Huber, 1987; Daft & Lengel, 1984; for a more recent statement see Seibold & Contractor, 1992).

CONCLUSION

The settings, methods, and variables employed in much group research—even the collectives that have been studied—have both reified and limited the way academics think about "groups" (Seibold & Meyers, 1988). In a similar vein, Putnam and Stohl (1990) urged examination of "bona fide groups," or groups with stable but permeable boundaries and interdependence with immediate intergroup/organizational/environmental contexts:

> We see a dire need to enhance the ecological validity, the vitality, and particularly the creativity of small group research through incorporating models of intergroup systems—variables that reflect tacit and explicit interfaces between groups and their environments, concepts that embody boundary permeability, and new constructs that capture the complexity and exciting quality of the group situations we experience. (p. 261)

Like other discussions of new-design plants (Lawler, 1986), this treatment of team management at BFSI could hardly avoid the boundary permeability and context interdependence aspects of this bona fide group. Parent company pressures, continuous contact with AMT manufacturers who provided machines for the plant, communication with former colleagues from other new-design plants, competitors' effects on the market, interfaces with customers and suppliers, and intershift coordination issues all were part and parcel of team "life" at BFSI. In turn, these matters all were in the weave of members' interactions and the pattern of their decisions.

Just as the "team" at BFSI was never isolated from these intergroup and environmental forces but actually was the manifestation of these forces, facilitation techniques with this bona fide group were more complex than research with laboratory groups would suggest. Even when the problems encountered by team members at BFSI were traditional difficulties in what Hirokawa and Gouran (1989) termed the "substantive," "procedural," and "relational" domains of group decision making, the facilitator's role was considerably expanded beyond the application of knowledge from laboratory studies. As Frey notes in the introduction to this volume, zero-history and concocted groups in laboratory studies typically have no unique interactional problems to solve. Consequently, the facilitation techniques imposed on such groups have limited ecological validity. But, as Frey also notes, facilitation with bona fide groups with unique needs requires the strategic match of facilitator, facilitative techniques, and in situ group. At BFSI, this required the procedures highlighted in the preceding case: building trust and credibility for the facilitator for more than a year viz formative evaluation and immersion into BFSI practices; providing training in problem-solving procedures most consistent with the Total Quality Improvement procedures within which the plant operated; and facilitating team decision making concerning the gainsharing, skill-based pay, bonus, shift, and myriad other matters specific to BFSI.

Finally, facilitation at BFSI entailed application of general principles from group and organizational theory and research. As described throughout this case, issues of organizational integration, information processing, control, scanning, coordination, empowerment, reward systems, physical layout, and personnel systems interpenetrated matters of group relationships, interactions, patterns, problem solving, and decision making. Hence, facilitation at BFSI required a sensitivity to both group and organization perspectives. This would appear to be a necessary consequence of working with bona fide groups, given Putnam and Stohl's (1990) conception of such groups' interdependence with other groups in their environment. Still, communication scholars have too long bifurcated the study of groups and organizations. Consistent with the author's attempts elsewhere (see Berteotti & Seibold, 1994; Lewis & Seibold, 1993), it is hoped this study of team facilitation at BFSI underscores the importance of integrating group and organizational communication research and incorporating both in practice (Seibold, in press).

12

Group Decision Support Systems as Facilitators of Quality Team Efforts *

Marshall Scott Poole
Gerardine DeSanctis
Laurie Kirsch
Michelle Jackson
University of Minnesota

As civilization moves into the post-industrial era, organizations are experiencing an information explosion accompanied by increased complexity and turbulence in their environments. The need for group decision making increases under these conditions because a single person's perspective and expertise is too narrow to address complex, knowledge-intensive deliberations and judgments. In addition, group decisions must be made more quickly and take account of continually changing events. To address these needs, social scientists have been exploring new information technologies which might facilitate effective and efficient group work. Among these are teleconferencing (Johansen, Vallee, & Spengler, 1979), computer conferencing (Kerr & Hiltz, 1984; Sproull & Kiesler, 1991), and group decision support systems (GDSSs), also called electronic meeting systems (DeSanctis & Gallupe, 1987; Dickson, Poole,

*We would like to thank Rebecca Lind for her help with the observations and George DeSharnis and Howard Lewis for their comments and feedback. This research was supported by National Science Foundation grant SES-8715565 to Poole and DeSanctis and by the NCR Corporation. The opinions stated here are solely those of the authors.

& DeSanctis, 1992; Nunamaker, Dennis, Valacich, Vogel, & George, 1991). Topics such as "Computer Supported Cooperative Work," "Collaborative Work," and "Groupware" are enjoying increased attention in popular and scientific literature.

These technologies have great potential for two types of groups that are becoming increasingly common in today's dynamic organizations—self-managed teams and quality teams. To add flexibility and responsiveness to their structures, many organizations are moving toward self-managed teams as the locus of work and responsibility. Operational units are subdivided into workgroups with the authority and flexibility both to set goals and to accomplish work toward them. The teams are fairly autonomous but with strong reporting responsibilities that communicate the outputs and productivity of the team to management (see Felkins, this volume; Furino, 1988; Pasmore, 1988). In addition, quality programs often emphasize a team-based approach to improving communication flow and work quality. These programs vary in their particulars, but most emphasize common principles of management-employee cooperation, participative decision making, and systematic problem solving. To bring about quality improvement, managers and employees meet in small groups to identify problems and chart out methods for setting goals, solving problems, and monitoring work processes and outputs (Deming, 1986b; Wood, Hull, & Azumi, 1983).

This case study focuses on the impacts of one important group technology, the group decision support system (GDSS), on quality teams. A GDSS combines communication, computer, and decision technologies to facilitate decision making and related activities of work groups (DeSanctis & Gallupe, 1987; Jessup & Valacich, 1992). In a GDSS, communication technologies such as electronic messaging, teleconferencing, and large public screens visible to all members provide additional channels for communication. Along with these come other technological features such as multi-user operating systems, fourth generation languages, and graphics facilities. These communication and computer technologies are knit together by decision support technologies such as agenda setting, decision modeling methods (such as decision trees or risk analysis), structured group methods (such as Nominal Group Technique or Integrative Structural Modeling), and rules for directing group discussion (such as parliamentary procedure). GDSSs have been designed to handle face-to-face or distributed meetings and to support both synchronous and asynchronous (nonsimultaneous) work by group members. The potential of GDSSs is in their ability to enhance individual and group information-handling capacity, to provide additional media for interpersonal communication, and to provide procedural structures for group work.

The technology of advanced computing—hardware and software—tends to monopolize our attention, so there is a temptation to attribute the impacts of GDSSs to the system itself. However, Poole and DeSanctis (1990) have characterized GDSSs as social technologies because the group's interaction processes are just as important to their operation as the software and hardware. The features designed into a GDSS do not determine automatically how groups interact; they must be worked into the discussion to have an impact. To understand how GDSSs work, then, we need to focus on communication and decision-making processes.

Research on GDSSs has been increasing in recent years, but there are still relatively few studies. Most studies of GDSSs fall into two categories: laboratory experiments with student subjects and field investigations of the use of GDSSs in special, one-time meetings with a great deal of planning and facilitation support. This case examines the adoption and use of a GDSS in the day-to-day work of four teams over periods of six months to a year. The study is unique in that it focuses not on encounters with novel technology in the laboratory or in a specially planned session, but on teams trying to incorporate the GDSS into their normal operating procedures on a long-term basis. Therefore, it is more likely to highlight the prospects and problems inherent in widespread applications of this technology in "everyday" groups.

A number of different theoretical perspectives could be used to study how GDSSs and other advanced computer and communication technologies influence and are influenced by group communication processes. Recent books edited by Fulk and Steinfield (1990) and Jessup and Valacich (1992) have explored frameworks as diverse as temporal interaction process theory, structural symbolic interactionism, critical mass theory, social information processing theory, and the theory of adaptive structuration.

Although they have much in common, each of these theories focuses on different social processes and variables. In this study, adaptive structuration theory is used as a lens to investigate how the structures embedded in a GDSS operate in ongoing quality teams. Before outlining the premises of adaptive structuration theory, we first explore GDSSs.

GROUP DECISION SUPPORT SYSTEMS

The fundamental goal of a GDSS is to support collaborative work activities such as idea creation, message exchange, project planning, document preparation, mutual product creation, and joint planning and decision making. Bostrom, Watson, and Kinney (1992), Johansen (1988), and Kraemer and King (1988) present extensive reviews of available and potential GDSSs and groupware. A wide variety of GDSS configurations are possible. Support may be offered for face-to-face meetings in a "decision room" and/or for dispersed groups of people meeting via computer or teleconference. In some cases members all meet at the same time, whereas in other cases GDSSs may be designed to support groups whose members log onto the system at different times and enter ideas for others to read later, that is, for asynchronous work. The ideal GDSS would probably support all of these possible types of "meetings," but most GDSSs target one or two situations.

The GDSS studied in this case, Software Aided Meeting Management (SAMM)[1], is designed to be used by groups meeting synchronously in a decision room. SAMM has a basic structure and features that are well-adapted to the tasks facing quality teams. SAMM, developed at the University of Minnesota, is intended to promote participative, democratic decision making in 3- to 16-person groups (DeSanctis, Sambamurthy, & Watson, 1987; Dickson, Poole & DeSanctis, 1992). Designed to be operated by the group itself, SAMM provides the following features to support group work (see Figure 12.1 for the overall configuration of SAMM): (a) agenda setting; (b) brainstorming; (c) a number of types of idea or solution evaluation methods, such as rating, ranking, and voting; (d) decision tools, such as stakeholder analysis (which is a strategic planning tool), multicriteria decision analysis (which helps groups analyze options by evaluating them against relevant criteria), and problem formulation (which helps groups define and explore problems they are trying to solve); (e) public and private messaging and options to send several preformulated messages; (f) a computerized scratchpad for making notes; and (g) facilities for storing records and minutes.

A menu-driven system, SAMM provides a group with a range of procedural control options: members can control the system themselves, or a facilitator or technician can help. SAMM is not intended to replace existing modes of group communication but rather is designed to support and encourage verbal and nonverbal interaction. Consequently, groups often use SAMM only at certain points during a meeting; typically, members work at SAMM for a while and then discuss the outputs on the public screen. The group assembles at a horseshoe-shaped conference table with a terminal and keyboard for each group member. Chairs swivel and have rolling feet, so users can move about comfortably to face one another. A large screen at the front of the room displays group information (such as vote tallies or idea lists generated during the meeting). Figure 12.2 shows the configuration of a SAMM decision room set up for a 10-person group.

---

[1]Software Aided Meeting Management (SAMM) is a copyright of the Regents of the University of Minnesota.

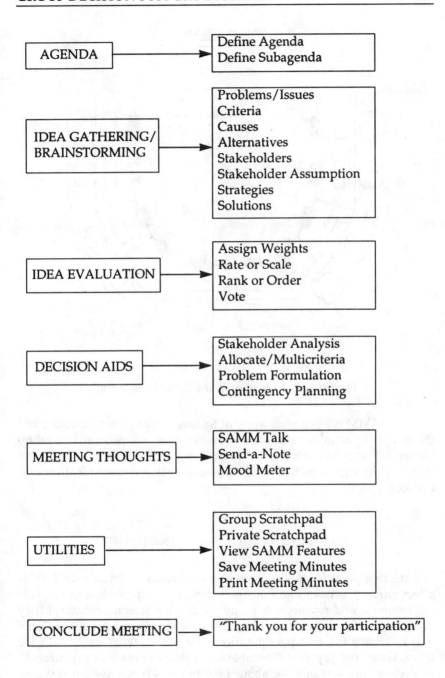

**Figure 12.1. Primary menu items in SAMM lead
to a series of underlying menus**

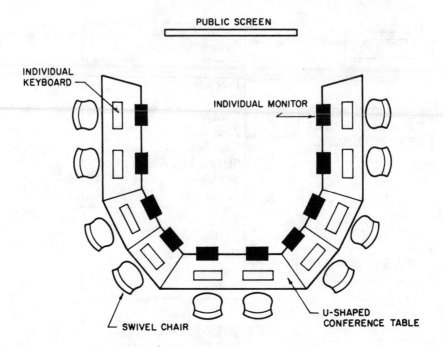

Figure 12.2. Layout of SAMM decision room

SAMM offers a wide array of features for groups to employ, and the range of possible applications is remarkable. Adaptive structuration theory helps us to compass this complexity by focusing on the central features through which GDSSs influence group communication and decision making.

ADAPTIVE STRUCTURATION THEORY

The starting point for this analysis seems obvious at first glance: GDSSs affect group processes and outcomes through the procedures (e.g., voting routines) and resources (e.g., public display screens, memory) they provide. Insofar as members use these procedures and rules, the GDSS will influence the group's operations. However, what exactly do we mean when we say that "members use procedures and resources?" Procedures are sets of rules about how to use various system features. For example, a voting procedure, designed to help groups express their views democratically, may consist of the following rules:

R1: Members should enter individual votes into the GDSS, which records these votes anonymously. They should remain silent while they think.

R2: Members may view their votes on the large screen by pressing the "view" button. They should wait until all members have entered their votes before viewing results, so that faster voters will not unduly influence slower ones.

R3: Members should discuss the votes tallied on the large screen to determine the reasons for favoring various options and possible compromises.

Several points can be made about a group that enacts this procedure. First, the group has chosen the procedure from among a repertoire of potential structures offered by the GDSS. Each group thus samples its own repertoire of procedures from those offered by the GDSS to create its own competency. Second, the rules can be followed exactly, or they can be "bent" in various ways. For instance, the group may ignore the second part of rule R2. If the group members do this, it may undermine the intent of the procedure because seeing others' votes prior to entering their own may put pressure on members to conform. Third, the violation of intent just noted is recognizable only because there is an overall philosophy uniting this set of rules—democratic expression.

Procedures and GDSS features embody what Giddens (1979) termed *structures*, rules and resources that actors use to generate, organize, and sustain social systems such as groups or organizations. A GDSS presents a group with an array of potential structures to draw down into its work. In our research (DeSanctis & Poole, in press; Poole & DeSanctis, 1990, 1992), we have distinguished two aspects of technological structures: their *spirit*, the general goals and attitudes the technology promotes (such as democratic decision making), and the specific *features* built into the system (such as anonymous input of ideas, or one vote per group member). The spirit is the principle of coherence that holds a set of rules and resources together, the general intent of the GDSS as reflected in its design, how it is presented and explained to groups, and how it is implemented. It is the "official line" regarding how to act when using the GDSS and how to interpret its features, and how to fill in gaps in procedure that are not specified explicitly. The features of a GDSS are designed to promote its spirit, but they are functionally independent and may be used in ways contrary to the spirit.

The process through which groups select, adapt, and develop their own working structures from among those on the GDSS is termed *structuration*. In general terms, structuration can be defined as the process by which systems are produced and reproduced through members' use of rules and resources (Giddens, 1979; Poole, Seibold, & McPhee, 1985). This definition is founded on several additional assumptions and distinctions. First, it assumes that structures are dualities: They are used to produce and reproduce the group system and to do the group's work, but the structures themselves are produced and reproduced through the group's activities. This means that structures have no reality independent of the social practices they constitute. Hence, when a group utilizes a GDSS's voting procedure, it is employing the rules that constitute the procedure to act, but—more than this—it is reminding itself that these rules exist, working out a way of using the rules, and perhaps creating a special version of them; in short, it is producing and reproducing its own version of the procedure for present and future use. This process is termed *appropriation of structures*. So it is really somewhat misleading to regard structures as static entities or to presume that the structural potential of a GDSS is equivalent to the structures that are used by the group. A voting feature does not, for all practical purposes, exist for a group if the group never employs it.

Central to structuration of GDSSs is the interplay between the spirit of the technology and the specific features members use. Any particular group develops its own reading of the spirit of the GDSS and this comprises the meaning of the GDSS to the group. This reading is influenced by how the system is explained to the group and by the group's sense of itself and its context. Hence, readings of the spirit of the GDSS may vary across groups within the same organization. A group's reading of the spirit of the GDSS determines its mode of appropriation of GDSS features. For example, if a group perceives that the GDSS is intended to speed up its decision processes, members might apply voting procedures in such a way that they omit rule R3 and rush on to their next agenda item after taking a vote.

In some cases, a group's reading of the spirit of the GDSS may not be consistent with the internal logic of the GDSS design or with how implementers present the GDSS. For example, the designers may have structured the GDSS as a vehicle for rational and careful decision making and the implementers may have presented it as such. However, assume that some members of a particular group are concerned that they are spending too much time in meetings; when they encounter the GDSS they might not notice the messages and cues reinforcing rationality and instead interpret them as a means of speeding up meetings. This group has thus developed its own particular reading of the spirit of the GDSS. Problems may arise, however, because this new reading is to some extent inconsistent with the structure of a system that is set up to support rational and careful decision making. This reading may create tensions between system capacities and the uses to which they are put.

For example, the GDSS may incorporate a feature allowing members to send private messages to each other, with the intent of allowing members to express doubts, share information, and otherwise dialogue with each other. However, in a group that regards the GDSS as a means of speeding up meetings, private messages may be used instead to pressure members to conform so that they can conclude the meeting quickly. Cases in which groups use the GDSS in ways inconsistent with the generally intended spirit are called ironic appropriations of the GDSS because they turn its structures in ways contradictory to its publicly intended spirit. It should be noted that not all ironic appropriations of GDSSs are harmful; some may actually be quite creative uses which designers and implementers simply did not foresee. For example, a group might use a public messaging feature to display the time left on a given agenda item, thus putting pressure on speakers to finish their discussion. Although this may violate the spirit of a rationally oriented GDSS to some extent, it may be an effective measure for groups that have to make speedy decisions—the resulting decision may be somewhat inferior to one that is discussed at length, but it might be "good enough" and enables the group to satisfy its deadline.

Structures provided by GDSSs are only part of the repertoire of structures a group employs. Members also bring other structures to bear; a member familiar with parliamentary procedure, for example, might try to combine it with a GDSS. Each group forms its particular amalgam of structural features which it employs in its practices. Giddens (1979) terms these appropriations of general social structures into concrete situations *modalities of structuration*. Here we simply call them "appropriations."

The process of structuration accounts for both stability and change of structures. Features are stable if the group appropriates them in a consistent way, reproducing them in similar form over time. Poole and DeSanctis (1990) discuss "stabilizing" appropriations, which are likely to promote the intended effects of a GDSS; they are characterized by use faithful to its spirit, high respect for and comfort with the technology, and a high level of consensus on use. This is the way in which designers generally assume the GDSS will be used. However, reproduction does not necessarily imply replication. Structures may change gradually, as in a group which, through a series of small, imperceptible stages, elevates one member to "system manager" of a GDSS that was designed originally to promote equal participation. They may also change when one structure is merged with another, such as when a group accustomed to parliamentary procedure uses a multipurpose GDSS to put Roberts' Rules of Order into practice. Structures might also be eliminated; for example, overuse of voting facilities may lead groups eventually to reject them.

The fact that structuring occurs in interaction implies that users may plan and control this process. However, their control is limited by other factors which shape structuration. The context in which the group operates places limitations on how technologies may be used. In particular, the group's task, internal group dynamics, and the amount of time pressure strongly influence how structures can by employed and, hence, how they are produced and reproduced. Users' level of knowledge and self-awareness about the technology and group processes also place limitations on what they can do and the degree to which they are able to control the structuring process. Only when a group has achieved functional autonomy and can operate the GDSS on its own can it strongly influence the course of structuration. This discussion highlights several things we might look for in studying the implementation of GDSSs in groups.

First, we would expect differences in the appropriation of GDSSs across groups, depending on such factors as internal group dynamics and external pressures on the groups, how the GDSS is introduced into the groups, and the larger organizational context in which the groups operate. Appropriations may vary in terms of: (a) which aspects of the GDSS's structural potential are realized; (b) the extent to which the group meshes GDSS structures with other structures; (c) the degree to which the group achieves functional autonomy with the GDSS; (d) the global reading of the GDSS's spirit; and (e) the stability of GDSS structures. Discovering the ways in which GDSS appropriations differ and the factors and processes which shape their structuration should help us to understand their impacts and better plan how to implement them successfully.

Second, there should be shifts in the appropriation of a GDSS over time. As a group applies GDSS structures to various tasks and experiences the consequences, it will adopt, adapt, or extinguish applications. GDSS structures will change as they are melded with other group structures, such as status hierarchies or standard operating procedures. Adoption of GDSS structures can foster the development of novel interpretive schemes and attitudes. These must be reconciled with the group's current interpretive schemes and attitudes, either through assimilation, change, or compartmentalization. Initially, groups may also depend heavily on facilitators or technical support people for advice on how to use the GDSS. In time, the group should achieve functional autonomy with the GDSS, controlling it and determining how to apply and adapt it. Analysis of how the group is set up for GDSS use and how it makes the transition into use should reveal crucial dynamics related to effective implementation.

THE TEAMS AND THE GDSS

The teams were part of an ongoing quality enhancement effort (QEE) implemented at Columbia Financial Enterprises[2], a large service organization. In common with many "quality circle" teams, these were cross-functional, cross-departmental, and cross-hierarchical (Kanter, 1983). Composed of between 5 and 10 volunteer members, the teams consisted of a diverse group of people from different units and levels at Columbia. The teams were charged with identifying and solving problems that reduced the quality of the agency's functioning and services and were expected to complete this task within one and a half years. The Quality Supervision Committee (QSC), composed of top managers, union officers, and staff members, made the final decisions as to whether the teams' solutions would be implemented. Team members were given time off from their normal jobs to participate, generally between two and eight hours per week. The teams utilized a specialized agenda of quality techniques created by the consultants who installed the QEE program and the head QEE facilitators. This agenda included many typical procedures, including formats to support problem definition, cause-effect analysis, and solution development. Team members were given training in group communication, team-building, and technical skills, such as survey design, quality measurement, and interpretive structural modeling. The teams were self-managing and were permitted to set up whatever leadership structure they deemed appropriate. A facilitator, specially trained in QEE procedures, was present at most meetings to help the team with the procedures and in its dealings with outside parties. The facilitator functioned as a liaison among the QEE head facilitators, the QSC, the team, and other organizational units.

The QEE teams faced many problems common to quality circle programs. Set up "parallel" to the existing bureaucracy, they experienced difficulties in legitimating themselves at Columbia. Members were often absent due to the demands of their principal jobs. Although the training package was excellent, many members were lacking in the skills necessary to run good meetings, organize a long-term project, and manage conflicts. The training sessions had presented too much material for members to assimilate in a short period of time. Moreover, the QEE procedures were new to most team members, and members often had difficulty applying them. Quite a few members were resistant to the QEE procedures, claiming that they were too difficult, took too much time, or were unnecessarily complex (Poole, 1991).

---

[2]The organization chooses to remain anonymous, and all references to it have been disguised.

In utilizing SAMM, the teams appropriate elements of its structural potential. The structural potential of SAMM is outlined in Table 12.1. The overall spirit of SAMM can be depicted as a set of general purposes that promote democratic, participative group meetings. Table 12.1 also shows the specific SAMM features which serve its general purposes.

To achieve the structural potential of SAMM, the teams have to use SAMM regularly and incorporate it into their work. Although the teams were supported by a facilitator and technical consultants, they were encouraged to take control of SAMM. Ideally, groups would incorporate SAMM into their day-to-day operations, using it when appropriate, until it became "second nature" to them, a tool like a flipchart or a written procedure.

RESEARCH PROCEDURES

To gain insight into the structuration of SAMM, we chose to compare groups which differed in: (a) the extent of their use of SAMM; (b) their overall evaluation of SAMM, as expressed during their meetings; and (c) the amount of progress they made toward their goals during the period of study, as judged by the administrators of the QEE program. This "backward" strategy of allowing outcomes to determine the groups studied is appropriate for illuminating differences in interaction processes that could produce differential outcomes. Four groups were chosen from a set of 12, based on their differences along these dimensions.

Table 12.1. Structural Potential of the SAMM GDSS

Structural Purposes	SAMM Features Serving Purpose
Empowerment and Self-control	SAMM manual; Unix-based design which lets members control use
Rational Procedure and Organization	Agenda; Decision aids, such as Stakeholder Analysis or Multicriteria Decision Analysis
Voice	Anonymous idea entry; Idea evaluation; Message-sending capacity
Focal Point	Agenda; Large screen display; Message-sending capacity
Self-reflection	Procedures for evaluating process (Quickpoll, Moodmeter); Agenda-setting

The meetings studied were sampled from an extensive set of videotapes. Unobtrusive videocameras in the SAMM room captured every meeting the groups held there. Because most groups met about twice a month, we had between 15 and 25 meetings per group to sample from at the time of the study. Team meeting time varied from about one hour to as much as six hours. Meetings were typically two hours long. Between four and six meetings spread over a 6- to 12-month period were sampled. We viewed the videotapes and made annotated notes about how the teams used SAMM, general group dynamics, the tasks the groups addressed, and other pertinent information. In addition, we interviewed members of the teams and the program administrators to fill out the picture of GDSS appropriation in each group.

ANALYSIS

General Observations

The four groups exhibited major differences in the degree and scope of SAMM use. Two groups developed functionally autonomous, stabilized appropriations of SAMM, whereas use in the other two was spotty and driven by outside facilitators. The development of functional autonomy seemed to derive from the degree to which the group was able to mesh SAMM with QEE procedures, which provided an institutionally legitimate anchor for SAMM, or with the group's meeting tasks, which showed SAMM's instrumental value.

Team 1. Team 1 used SAMM regularly during the five meetings we observed, which stretched over nine months. This team slowly but steadily made progress. It conducted focus groups with clients and sent out surveys to learn more about the problem and its "pain" (i.e., the cost to Columbia). By the fifth meeting, the group was attempting to redefine its problem due to difficulties in quantifying the "pain." For the most part, this group was well-organized; however, at times, it lacked a specific agenda and focus. The main problems facing the group were absenteeism and a tendency for lower status members to hold back from the discussion.

In two meetings SAMM use was light. In one of these, SAMM was used predominantly by one member of the team to send distracting messages and jokes. In the other, the group viewed items entered at an earlier meeting and recorded a preliminary problem statement which it planned to refine in subsequent meetings. In the other three meetings, the group used SAMM more extensively. The Idea Gathering feature was used to brainstorm about "the pain," and Idea Evaluation was invoked to narrow a list of potential problems from six to three and to prioritize results from the focus group interviews.

The use of SAMM by Team 1 seemed to vary according to how well members understood their task. When their goals were relatively concrete and it was clear to them how to proceed, they relied on SAMM. This was the case, for instance, when they were narrowing a list of problems. On the other hand, when the group's task was to "draft a problem statement," a less specific goal, the group appeared somewhat baffled as to how to use SAMM.

Team 1 attained a fair degree of functional autonomy with SAMM: Most members were able to use and understand SAMM, although the facilitators and the leader organized SAMM applications. When members had trouble with the menus, the leader helped them. Team 1 meshed SAMM with familiar QEE procedures fairly well. For the most part, the appropriation was a straightforward, one-on-one mapping in which SAMM was used like a flipchart to display ideas and tally evaluations. The group had problems mapping the unfamiliar procedure of writing a problem statement onto SAMM (there was a stepwise procedure for problem statement creation in the QEE reference manual, but the members did not use it). Throughout the period of observation, the group's use of SAMM increased. With the exception of one member, the group's comfort with SAMM also increased. Even though one person was unable to use SAMM without assistance, all members viewed SAMM positively and felt that it helped move the team forward.

Team 2. We observed four meetings of Team 2, spread over eight months. The team's charge was to develop corrective measures for revenue shortfalls in a specific department. The team spent a great deal of time trying to understand the technical details of the target department and the surrounding bureaucracy. Although the team was given some preliminary data about the nature of the revenue loss, they decided early on to gather further information. Initially, the team made good progress toward a definition of its problem, but then it ran into resistance from those from whom it was requesting information. After 10 months, the group still had not achieved a satisfactory problem definition. Morale had declined, and the group had entered a period of crisis as of the last observation; following this, the team finally obtained its data and moved ahead.

This was a highly organized team who followed a strict agenda and used parliamentary procedure. SAMM was used to enforce structure in the meetings, particularly through the agenda and voting procedures. The agenda for the next week was always entered at the end of each meeting and then printed for all members, and the next meeting began by displaying this agenda on SAMM's public screen. This group used a wide range of SAMM features, and its degree of use exhibited a good sense of what SAMM features were suited for. In the first two meetings, the group's goals were, respectively, to explore the perspectives of the various parties to the problem (for which it used stakeholder analysis and the group scratchpad for making notes) and to plan a presentation to the Quality Council (for which it used idea gathering and ranking, commenting, and file saving). The third and fourth meetings had no real goals, other than to share information and to vent frustrations at the blockage of the team's efforts; SAMM was used only for agenda setting and management.

Team 2 achieved functional autonomy with SAMM. Most members have some facility with the system, although one or two members and the facilitator organized system use. The team was fascinated by the details of SAMM use, such as how files were stored, how various SAMM modules were related, and how directories were managed. Very often they expressed more interest in the mechanics of SAMM use than in its particular role at that point of the meeting. For example, if a difficulty was encountered or a more complicated feature was invoked, it was not uncommon for several group members to stand up and look over the shoulder of the person using SAMM to watch and ask questions. Similarly, use of a SAMM feature led invariably to discussions about how the technology worked, "which buttons to push," and its advantages and disadvantages.

Concern with the mechanics of SAMM use resulted in an open, positive attitude toward the GDSS. This concern also helped members define a sense of SAMM's limitations and led to a temporary decline in usage as the team moved into more difficult stages of work. At later meetings, at which SAMM was used less, members commented that SAMM was too restrictive and wanted it to be more like a spreadsheet. It may be that in the face of nebulous political and access problems, constrained as it was by its own definitions of SAMM limitations, the group could find no way to map its tasks into SAMM features. Ironically, the same features of SAMM that the group had used earlier could have been used to list and discuss their roadblocks and to spark discussion about the group's mood and frustrations. However, members did not try to mold SAMM to fit their needs. When Team 2 had sufficient time and a more favorable environment, it was able to figure out how to use SAMM to its benefit, but faced with uncertainty, it had greater difficulty. Even when recognizing problems with SAMM, the team remained positive and open toward the system.

In later meetings after the ones included in this study, Team 2 surmounted its political problems and was able to get back on track. Use of SAMM picked up again, and members were quite active with the system during these meetings.

Team 3. We observed six meetings of Team 3, spaced over six months. The group spent the entire observational period defining its problem; in fact, it spent a year defining its problem, much longer than the benchmarks of the QEE recommend. In the last meeting we observed, the administrators of the QEE moved the group through to a final definition of its problem. In general, Team 3 was not organized; the group had trouble following agendas and seeing tasks through to a definite conclusion. There were many conflicts which were not acknowledged openly and, therefore, could not be dealt with. Members refused to agree with descriptions of the problem put forth by colleagues, but they would not examine the reasons for the disagreements or open themselves to others' points of view. Members stated their positions and held their ground.

When SAMM was first introduced, most members were quite enthusiastic because they saw it as an organizational tool. SAMM served that purpose well; the group began setting agendas at the end of each meeting and used SAMM to display and evaluate ideas. This was a simple appropriation of SAMM features which corresponded directly to group practices. However, there were some technical problems with the system in one meeting that caused frustration. At this point, some members remained very positive toward SAMM on the grounds of its potential, whereas others viewed SAMM as a source of delay and confusion. Initially, several members experimented with SAMM, but as pressure increased to agree on a problem statement, they spent less time with it. During the final meeting, the QEE administrators ran SAMM for the group and used it to direct and control the group. Thus, SAMM served to focus the group's attention during this meeting.

Team 3 never achieved functional autonomy with SAMM. Several members learned how to use the system, but they never learned how to adapt it to their specific tasks. Appropriation of SAMM never went past the obvious or banal; for example, one member used the projector to make shadow pictures on the screen. The group did not mesh the structures provided by either SAMM or the QEE into its operation. When the group used these structures, it was at the behest of a facilitator, who usually gave explicit instructions. In this particular group, SAMM seems to have been a resource to the administrators, which helped them overcome the group's problems with organization and conflict.

Team 4. Six meetings of Team 4 over a six-month period were observed. Like Team 3, this team spent the entire observational period attempting to define its problem. In general, the group was rather unfocused and inefficient and made little progress. There was a great deal of absenteeism, and when a quorum was present members had trouble accomplishing anything. Also like Team 3, this group had trouble seeing tasks through to conclusion and often revisited decisions made at previous meetings. Members had no long-term view of what the QEE process entailed and seldom applied QEE procedures. The group was also not very reflective: Members thought they were doing a good job and tended to attribute problems to other causes, such as facilitator absence or a lack of cooperation from other units.

Team 4 looked forward to the advent of SAMM enthusiastically, but after receiving training they did not have a meeting at which they could use SAMM for almost three months. They finally used SAMM, guided by a facilitator, to define people to be interviewed about the quality problem. The facilitator tried to adapt the stakeholder analysis task to do this, substituting "people to be interviewed" for stakeholders and "their concerns" for stakeholder assumptions. The operation of the system worked fine, but members were confused about the labels, in part because they did not understand the purposes of stakeholder analysis. Before the next meeting, when the interview was to be discussed again, a new version of SAMM was installed and the previous information was lost. Members were extremely critical of SAMM and, from this point on, their use of SAMM declined. (It should be noted that other teams had to re-enter information or wait for old information to be called up, but did not have this negative reaction.) Members tried to brainstorm ideas in a later meeting, but lost some ideas due to miskeys and system limitations, and this seemed to drive the final nail into the coffin.

Team 4 definitely did not achieve functional autonomy with SAMM. Members did not understand how to use the system nor did they appreciate its potential. This was due in part to technical problems, but it also stemmed from Team 4's inability or unwillingness to learn QEE and SAMM procedures unless prompted by its facilitator or leader. In general, the members adopted a rather reactive stance; they changed only when confronted with problems by their facilitator and generally avoided taking responsibility for their own progress. Basically, this group appropriated neither SAMM nor many of the QEE procedures. Actually, SAMM was appropriated in one sense—it was used as an excuse by the group when it had to account for its lack of progress. Both SAMM and the facilitators thus served as scapegoats for this group.

Synthesis

These brief summaries indicate differences in the degree to which SAMM's structural potentials were realized. Table 12.2 displays the degree to which the five potentials defined in Table 12.1 were realized by the four teams. Team 1 realized three structural potentials completely and one partially. SAMM served as a source of rational procedures and organization (several members commented that SAMM organized the group), a voice (several members commented that SAMM enhanced participation), and a focal point (the group, which often had rather low energy, became much more engaged while using SAMM). Team 1 also partially realized the empowerment potential of SAMM (members participated more when using SAMM, and the group had someone type for the member who could not type).

Team 2 realized all five SAMM potentials to at least some extent. SAMM served as a tool for empowerment (members talked about sharing control of SAMM at various points), a rational procedure and organizer, a voice (one member commented that he usually dominated meetings and was a little frustrated because SAMM allowed others to have input), a focal point (the leader emphasized this in an interview), and a source of self-reflection (members openly discussed how SAMM equalized participation and how the group should organize its work).

The other two teams, however, realized fewer of SAMM's potentials. In Team 3, SAMM served, in part, as a source of rational procedures (although when the group got into trouble it stopped turning to SAMM) and as a focal point. However, SAMM was not used as a tool for empowerment, self-reflection, or voice (although members used SAMM to vote, they rarely discussed the results and sometimes disregarded them). In Team 4, no SAMM potentials were realized and, in some cases, the group's work with SAMM structured it in ways antithetical to the poten-

Table 12.2. Structural Potential Achieved by Each Team

	Team 1	Team 2	Team 3	Team 4
Empowerment and Self-Control	Partial	Yes	No	No
Rational Procedures and Organization	Yes	Yes	Partial	No
Voice or Influence	Yes	Yes	No	No
Focal Point	Yes	Yes	Yes	No
Self-Reflection	No	Yes	No	No

tials. SAMM served as a focal point for the group's anger, but not for its attention. SAMM also made the group feel impotent, rather than powerful, and it served as an excuse the group used to avoid self-reflection.

Certainly the most robust of the structural potentials have SAMM as a focal point and as a rational procedure. These were realized in three out of four teams. The other potentials were much more fragile and depended on how the group handled SAMM.

Themes

There is a carryover of existing group dynamics and problems into the structuration of GDSSs. Unlike a special conference in which a group is taken to a special decision room out of its normal context and treated to a special agenda, when a group uses a GDSS on a day-to-day basis, it carries its problems and habits over into system use. The cases indicated that when a team had deep-seated problems, as did Team 4, they influenced SAMM appropriation. For example, avoidance of responsibility by Team 4 not only barred it from mastering SAMM, it led to the scapegoating of SAMM. Temporary setbacks also influenced GDSS appropriation. Team 2, which had a particularly difficult and frustrating project, was also unable to use SAMM to best effect because members were so overwhelmed in the last two meetings that they had no energy to figure out how to adapt SAMM to their tasks.

Effective group dynamics also carried over. In most meetings of Team 1 and in the first two meetings of Team 2, the desire for organization led to faithful and effective use of SAMM. Many studies of GDSSs and other new technologies presume that the technology will rearrange group dynamics and determine a new course for the group. This may well be the case for sessions that are planned and carefully orchestrated for special meetings and projects. However, our observations suggest that everyday use of a GDSS is conditioned more by the existing group structures and context than vice versa.

There were differences in how teams appropriated SAMM. Teams 1 and 2 developed fairly stable appropriations of SAMM. Both teams followed instructions carefully when they used SAMM features to list ideas and display ratings. This corresponded to a one-to-one mapping which moved their group activities wholecloth into SAMM. But there was a deeper, more skillful type of appropriation in which members engaged in problem solving and adapted SAMM features to nonobvious tasks. For example, the QEE administrators used stakeholder analysis to analyze interview requirements for Team 4. Although ultimately unsuccessful, the administrators' adaptation effectively restructured this feature

by adapting it to a different purpose. The stakeholder analysis module
was reinterpreted as a general contingency analysis module (which suggested an additional feature we have since added to SAMM). The QEE
administrators were quite proficient at moving beyond one-to-one map-
pings; this involved thinking in terms of general operations the features
were capable of, as well as decomposing SAMM features into individual
operations. For example, the QEE facilitators often used the agenda
module of SAMM for outlining, even though there was no general outlining capability in SAMM. Procedures are often thought of as templates
which are applied to predefined tasks. However, usually tasks are not
well understood at the outset. More often, our procedures are used to
define and shape tasks so we can deal with them. True facility with a
system requires this "deeper" type of appropriation, founded on superi-
or understanding.

Groups' general readings of the GDSS influence appropriations. We
mentioned previously the spirit of a GDSS as a general principle of
coherency which guides the use of various features. A group's reading
of a GDSS's spirit can be detected in the general meaning the system has
for members as reflected in their comments about the system during
meetings and in interviews. For Team 1, SAMM was a "problem solver,"
an "organizer," and a "secretary." Team 2 also thought of SAMM as an
"organizer," and during its first meeting the team referred to SAMM as
an "auditor." Team 3 saw SAMM as a source of structure. Team 4
believed that SAMM would solve all its problems, and members were
quite frustrated when SAMM took effort to learn and did not match
their tasks exactly. In addition, several members of Team 4 thought they
had to do "all their work" through SAMM and came to resent it. At the
same time, Team 4, which had many problems, viewed SAMM as a way
to demonstrate that it was a good group. Even when they were especially critical of SAMM, members of Team 4 said they wanted to use the system. (Although this group's feelings about SAMM were negative during
the meetings observed for this study, in three subsequent meetings they
used such SAMM features as stakeholder analysis successfully with the
help of their facilitator.)

The similarity in the meaning of SAMM for these groups is evident: Generally they viewed it as an organizer, emphasizing its capacity
to structure their group's work. This is an interpretation of SAMM's
spirit that we have noted among other users of the system (DeSanctis,
Snyder, & Poole, in press). The nature of work at Columbia Financial
Enterprises probably inclined the teams toward this reading of SAMM
because it required exegesis and interpretation of industry regulations
and legal requirements. Employees' inclinations to focus on detail car-

ried over into the QEE teams. Teams spent much time writing and interpreting charters and grasping the details of their problems and were less focused on the "big picture" in quality projects. This led them to underemphasize the features of SAMM designed to support emotional exchange, conflict management, and self-analysis of group activities. This may have been detrimental to the groups because they did not use SAMM to solve problems and build stronger teams.

The structuration of GDSSs occurs most strongly at key junctures during system use. Structuration of GDSSs does not always occur at the same rate. At key junctures—marked by events such as group crises, criticisms of the GDSS, success with the GDSS, and evaluation sessions—members engage in interchanges that determine the acceptance or rejection of the GDSS, how its structures are appropriated, and whether they are stabilized (Poole & DeSanctis, 1992). One obvious juncture is the group's first use of the GDSS, but there are also junctures at later points. We found definite evidence of junctures in two groups and a probable juncture in a third.

Team 4 tried to use SAMM and found it had not saved its work from a previous session. Members, never in firm control of the system, felt helpless to correct this. Later in the same meeting, the group used SAMM for brainstorming and lost some ideas due to a limitation in computer memory. Members became very negative and critical toward SAMM. This juncture started a bandwagon rejection of SAMM. At the next meeting when a member suggested using SAMM, she was met with a chorus of "No!". Later, members blamed the time they "wasted" on SAMM as a major cause of their group's failure.

However, SAMM navigated a critical juncture successfully in Team 2. Members were criticizing the system because its word processor did not wordwrap and because it was not as flexible as a spreadsheet. Throughout this period, other members mitigated this negativity by venturing that the group did not yet understand SAMM well enough and that they should study the operator's manual. At the end of the meeting, members remained basically positive about working further with SAMM. That we found these and other junctures in only a sample of meetings suggests their importance and ubiquity.

CONCLUSION

The purpose of this study was not to test hypotheses, but rather to describe the implementation of a GDSS in the ongoing work of self-managed teams, using the theory of adaptive structuration as a lens. Even though many of the teams at Columbia are enthusiastic about SAMM, have become dependent on it, and use it actively, the current analysis goes beyond general impressions to highlight particular successes and difficulties teams had with SAMM.

We found that the four groups appropriated the GDSS in quite different ways. Their uses varied from those promoted by the spirit of the technology to using the system as an excuse for nonperformance. Structuration appeared to occur most strongly at certain key junctures where the fate of the implementation hung in the balance. Moreover, existing group dynamics and external constraints appeared to be stronger determinants of whether the GDSS was structured into group work than did the technology itself. For example, groups lacking commitment or external support were less likely to initiate use of a GDSS than groups who functioned adequately.

Our analyses suggest three key determinants of the effectiveness of GDSS implementations. First, in order to realize the potential of a GDSS, groups must develop the ability to mesh GDSS structures with other structures, such as existing QEE procedures, and to match GDSS tools with tasks for which they are appropriate. Second, the general interpretation groups assign to the GDSS's spirit affects how they use it in their work. For example, groups who viewed the GDSS primarily as an organizer tended to emphasize its ability to structure their work and deemphasized its other capabilities. Third, the depth of understanding groups develop concerning the GDSS structures affects the way in which they are appropriated. Only with deep understanding could the groups adapt the system for broader purposes than those conceived originally by its designers.

What does this say to the practitioner who wants to maximize the possibilities for successful implementation of a GDSS? The first thing to bear in mind is that groups will change and adapt any system as they use it. It is important to monitor how groups apply the GDSS in ongoing work to determine whether it is being used properly and—just as important—whether dysfunctional unintended applications have emerged. In addition to numerous positive impacts, we also observed several ironic uses of SAMM that could have subverted QEE goals. Misuses of the GDSS are sometimes the result of purposeful actions by members who want to manipulate the group, but they may also result from the group's own inexperience with or misunderstanding of the GDSS.

Our observations showed that groups tended to learn how to use SAMM gradually. Facilitators often had to suggest how to apply SAMM, and teams achieved different levels of aptitude in matching SAMM tools to appropriate tasks. It took some time for teams to achieve functional autonomy with SAMM, and some teams never reached this point. The QEE coordinators found that it was best to introduce teams to a few basic features of SAMM at first and then to train them gradually in other tools as the need to use these tools arose. Successful implementation of a GDSS requires more than just an initial in-depth training session. There must be frequent refresher training, focused on applications of the GDSS to specific group problems. In addition, it is helpful to have support personnel to consult with groups concerning possible applications of the GDSS and to facilitate key meetings when new applications are being tried.

It is also important, however, to give groups sufficient leeway to experiment with the GDSS and to make it their own. Overcontrolling the GDSS or always providing facilitation encourages groups to remain dependent on support staff. Over the long run this could retard diffusion of the GDSS in the organization. Ideally, teams should attain functional autonomy with the GDSS so that they take control of it and adapt it to their specific needs. A team that has achieved functional autonomy might still work with a facilitator or support person from time to time, but the team should determine when and how this is done.

There is, then, a paradox inherent in implementing a GDSS. As groups achieve functional autonomy, the possibility of ironic appropriations and misuses of the GDSS increases, precisely because the groups have more leeway in using the system. Facilitators and support personnel can help insure that appropriations of the GDSS are consistent with its spirit, but they must tread lightly or they will foster dependency which ultimately may set back the implementation process. The movement toward functional autonomy is thus a halting one in which groups strike out on their own, develop confidence in some aspects of the GDSS, then depend on support staff to introduce other parts of the system, and then strike out again.

Another practical consideration is selection of the groups who will get to use the GDSS. It is important to select groups who have a high probability of benefiting from the technology. This is especially true in the initial stages of GDSS implementation because early failures may create a bad reputation for the GDSS and lead to termination of support for the program. Our analysis indicates that groups with serious preexisting problems do not fare well with SAMM. In general, GDSSs should be regarded as support systems and not as therapy for troubled groups. So, for the greatest chance of success, we should avoid groups at the low end of the scale and select those in the middle or upper range.

Group decision support systems and other groupware are among the most interesting and exciting communication technologies to emerge in recent years. They promise to change how organizations operate and to facilitate the move to team-based, participative organizations. It will be fascinating to see how these technologies develop in the coming years.

Epilogue

Cynthia Stohl, one of the leading scholars in the fields of organizational communication and small group communication, offers some observations about what we have learned from these case studies. She believes that these case studies teach us much about the process of facilitating bona fide groups in natural settings and the importance of studying such efforts. She also raises some thought-provoking questions about ethical issues and paradoxes that are involved in any group facilitation effort, offering examples from the studies in this volume to illustrate these points. Stohl thus provides some important ways of understanding the promises and the paradoxes of facilitating natural, bona fide groups that have been realized from these studies.

Facilitating Bona Fide Groups: Practice and Paradox

Cynthia Stohl
Purdue University

A common query upon completion of a scholarly book is, "So What?" What have I learned, what understandings have changed as a result of reading the text, what will I do differently, and/or what else do I want to know? This volume of case studies provides readers with a rich and provocative array of group facilitation techniques and data from research studies that suggest possibilities for action and questions for future research. After reading this text, it is clear that group facilitation is not a disembodied list of quick-fix techniques as popularized in "how to" books nor a set of clearly defined and articulated principles and methods. The authors explicate the intricate and interlaced texture of collaborative work with a common emphasis on the dynamic and processual qualities of social organization. Each chapter addresses organizing rather than organization, facilitating rather than facilitation.

As the cases in this volume illustrate, facilitating is composed of rich and varied communication activities. In the Introduction, Frey defines facilitation as any meeting technique, procedure, or practice that makes it easier for groups to interact and/or accomplish their goals. Facilitating activities may include, but are not limited to, the introduction of a new technology (e.g., GDSS or new formats for decision making) and/or the enhancement of old techniques (e.g., training for improved interaction management skills). Facilitation may be guided by outsiders (third-party interventions) and/or insiders (group members independently utilize new techniques). Facilitating may enhance pre-established structures and activities of a group, change the actual processes of the group, provide insight into group communication, and/or alter the dynamics of a larger interconnected system.

Whatever its form, the contributions in this volume provide strong evidence that facilitating is not merely about making a group better. *Facilitating involves fundamental changes in the way groups embed and are embedded in social systems.* All types of facilitation center on an essential question of group life: How are groups created and sustained in action? Putnam and Stohl (1990) use the term *bona fide groups* to embody the symbiotic relationship among individuals, groups, and larger social systems in which each contributes to the other's development and survival. Reading these case studies highlights the importance of recognizing and understanding the essential nature of bona fide groups; that is, the *permeable boundaries* of social systems, *interdependence with immediate context*, and the *multiple identities and group memberships* individuals bring to any group setting. What makes this volume unique, therefore, is that it explores the processes of facilitating bona fide groups.

Studying bona fide groups does not mean simply that the site of the facilitation is moved from the laboratory to the field. Changing the context or altering population samples without addressing the methodological and assumptive bases of facilitating would not address the dynamic, fluid, and complex array of actual group experiences. Rather, in each of these cases, operationalizations of effectiveness, identification of task requisites, and conceptualizations of relevant communication attempt to be congruent with the richness of the lived experience of the group in question—experiences marked by systemic embeddedness, permeable boundaries, interconnected activity, bounded rationality, and other nonrational constraints on task accomplishment.

Thus, what is compelling, I believe, about these case studies is not that the groups are located in the field, but that the authors address the multilevel complexity and interconnectedness of group experience. For example, to recognize explicitly that the 98% acceptance rate of team proposals is only related partially to the effectiveness of a facilitation and "due partly to management screening of inappropriate or redundant projects" (Felkins, p. 276) highlights issues of power, connectivity, and interdependence that are left out of most explications of facilitating teams.

Furthermore, in these cases, internal boundaries are not drawn neatly (nor should they be). Poole, DeSanctis, Kirsch, and Jackson use the term "ironic appropriations" to identify those cases in which groups use a facilitating mechanism in ways that are "contradictory to its publicly intended spirit" (p. 307). The GDSS studies comprise an outstanding exemplar of the ways in which groups carry over existing group dynamics and problems into the structuration of any facilitation. The connections Poole et al. make between the "contradictory" ways in which the GDSS structures are enacted and differences in the introduction of the facilitation, group's task, internal group dynamics, time pressures, and external demands are important and useful for understanding how and why facilitations of all sorts may not work "according to plan."

It is interesting to note that many of the cases in the book, besides highlighting the two essential characteristics of bona fide groups—permeable boundaries and interdependence with context (Putnam & Stohl, 1990)—blur the analytic and pragmatic distinctions between full-fledged and zero-history groups and naturally occurring and artificially created groups. In the studies of the focus groups by Kreps, Bormann, Bormann, and Harty, and Cragan and Shields, for example, individuals who did not have prior experience with each other were selected by the researchers/facilitators to be part of the group, there were few time pressures, and there was no commitment to future work with these group members (all part of the definition of full-fledged groups outlined by Bales & Strodtbeck, 1951). Yet, these bona fide groups are able to help solve real client-based problems. The facilitating processes are subject to the same constraints as groups that are considered traditionally to be full-fledged groups.

By illuminating facilitating activities in bona fide groups, ethical issues are also raised that have been, for the most part, unexamined by group facilitators (see Zorn & Rosenfeld, 1989). Programmatic efforts to help individuals and groups address large-scale social problems through systematic decision-making logics, attempts to promote dialogue in culturally diverse work environments, implementations of team approaches, and interventions designed to help focus group attention on particular messages and goals all reveal ethical dilemmas inherent in facilitating group processes.

Indeed, an underlying question embedded throughout these cases is: Who benefits from the facilitating efforts? Many of these cases raise ethical considerations that arise once a facilitation technique is formalized and becomes part of a commercial enterprise. Furthermore, facilitators and members of bona fide groups wear multiple hats and have multiple allegiances independent of who is sponsoring the facilitation efforts. Individuals simultaneously are members of multiple groups. Putnam (1989) refers to this overlapping membership as *psychological embeddedness*, which influences group commitment and divided loyalties. Facilitators and group members often have to make choices which privilege some interests over others. For example, the team approach has been recognized as a central control mechanism of management and the corporate elite (Parker & Slaughter, 1988). Even when not addressed explicitly, readers can sense the tensions of facilitators who must struggle with such issues as whether facilitating these groups helps or hinders workers' attempts to truly participate, what information known to the facilitator should be shared with the group, and so on.

Ethical questions pervade the narratives in this volume. Seibold carefully highlights how sensitivity to interpersonal, group, and organizational perspectives was necessary to gain trust and credibility for the facilitator. What should facilitators do, and what do they actually do, when these perspectives are mutually exclusive? Murphy identifies several limitations of a diversity workshop, not the least of which is that certain people are uncomfortable and untrusting of such a format and find the entire experience frustrating. When subtle discriminatory behavior is ongoing, should participation in a workshop be mandatory even when some people do not want to participate? Keltner's feedback facilitation techniques operate under the premise that individuals should check their messages "so that the *information transmitted* can be made more consistent with the *information received*" (p. 123). The iterative process of message feedback has profound implications for a subordinate who is "forced" by the facilitating mechanisms to inform a boss that she or he misses the point. Pearce and his colleagues respect the client's need for secrecy and the decision not to continue the facilitation. Underlying the systemic social constructionist approach is the ethical judgment that it is not the facilitator's place to say what is best for the client. Yet, aren't they doing precisely that when they engage in circular questioning and participate in "the orgy of hypothesizing" that "is not without rules, of course" (p. 100)?

Keyton also uncovers a common ethical dilemma when she identifies her disagreement with the senior resident regarding notification of the purpose of the feedback meeting. Should a facilitator go along with what he or she describes as "deceptive techniques?" Is the relationship between a facilitator and the group's members or the relationship with the management who is "allowing" the facilitation to take place the most critical part of the facilitation? Whose interests must take precedence? Only when researchers honestly discuss facilitating bona fide groups, as these authors do, can we begin to understand the complex ethical issues involved.

A most striking contribution to a conversation on ethics is raised by Broome when discussing group facilitating with the Comanche Tribe. Broome makes the point that:

> The holistic approach of IM [Interaction Management], its process orientation, and its ability to create a collaborative problem-solving environment are all compatible with Native American heritage. Thus, IM is potentially a valuable method that Tribes can use to confront the contemporary problems they face. (p. 48)

In these two brief sentences, Broome raises an ethical concern that rarely is discussed in the facilitation literature, perhaps because the issue only has relevance when we stop treating the group and facilitation as isolated entities and take into account the interconnectedness with communication activity outside the group. That is, does and/or should a facilitating process/technology match the prevailing cultural milieu in which the group (or at least some subset of the group) is interacting? Is it appropriate and/or ethical to use facilitating techniques that are inconsistent with social/cultural norms when we know that relationships within groups are overlapping, culturally instantiated, and permeate several arenas of activity? For example, training workers in a country of high power distance, where people accept power as part of society (see Hofstede, 1980), to comment in a group setting on managerial communication practices may have serious repercussions for the individuals in other settings. (See Stohl, 1993, for a discussion of cultural variability and its relationship to organizational participatory practices.) Even techniques as "simple" as brainstorming may be inappropriate in some cultural contexts. Clearly, ethical issues related to cultural relativity, parochialism, and cultural myopia are becoming more and more salient as organizations initiate facilitating efforts in a globalized workplace.

Taken together, these case studies develop a compelling argument for the need to continue our scholarly exploration of group facilitation from the perspective of bona fide groups. Small groups are becoming more central to all types of organizing, hence, there is an increasing reliance on facilitating activities in a diversity of contexts. Ironically, however, as Chilberg and others note, despite the strong evidence that many facilitating processes help groups become maximally effective, enable individuals to meet their needs, and improve intergroup communication, many groups do not accept nor incorporate these processes into their communication repertoire even when available.

By paying attention to the close association and interdependence among facilitating processes, permeable boundaries, and embedding contexts developed within these cases, three fundamental paradoxes emerge that can help us respond to the gap between knowledge of facilitating processes and actual adoption of the activities. I call these paradoxes: (a) the paradox of participation; (b) the paradox of power; and (c) the paradox of punctuation. The following section briefly identifies these paradoxes and concludes with the observation that in each circumstance, *resolution is impossible without reference to the tacit and explicit interfaces between groups and their environments.* In other words, it is the treatment and analysis of facilitation within the complex, dynamic, interwoven fabric of social affiliations that will allow researchers and practitioners to better understand and confront the constraints and potential of facilitating groups.

THE PARADOX OF PARTICIPATION

Throughout the facilitation literature, scholars and practitioners alike suggest that a necessary, but not sufficient, condition for effective facilitation is member commitment to the process. Indeed, an element of successful facilitation that is identified frequently is the joint participation of group members in the establishment of process norms that guide group interaction. As these studies of bona fide groups show, however, there is often an incompatibility between the goals of facilitation and the processes by which the facilitation is initiated. That is, facilitating processes are designed to increase the participation of all group members and to give all members a voice in the ongoing discussion, but typically they are designed and implemented without the participation of group members. This violates what scholars interested in sociotechnical systems call the "principle of compatibility," which states that the processes by which systems move toward an end must be compatible with the end that is desired (Emery & Trist, 1965). Thus, if the goal is a participatory system, the system must be designed in a participatory manner. Group facilitation techniques, like many organizational attempts at increasing worker participation, often become "things" the top tells the middle to do to the bottom (see Kanter, 1983). Separated from its larger historical and institutional context, a facilitation designed to increase participation may thus preclude the enactment of these goals by the very processes of design.

THE PARADOX OF POWER

An underlying and related tension in group facilitation is the notion that group empowerment comes from conforming to some external authority. As described in the first paradox, facilitations by definition comprise adherence to procedures and activities that are designed by individuals/groups external to the group itself. Groups, therefore, often resist facilitator attempts (activities intended to help the group become more powerful) in order to assert their own power. Ironically, this resistance often contributes to a group's sense of powerlessness and dependence on the facilitator: As group members fight against or oppose facilitating efforts, the group becomes less organized, members become frustrated, and positive contributions to the task decrease. It is important to note that the tensions surrounding power and control are experienced by facilitators as well. For example, Golembiewski and Blumberg (1977) described three paradoxical functions that facilitators must carry out: (a) functioning as an expert without projecting one's personal self; (b) functioning as both an outsider and an insider; and (c) maintaining a central role while helping the group to become independent of the facilitator. Because facilitation is never isolated from issues of power and dominance within the larger context, facilitating activities designed to empower groups are thus far more volatile (potentially threatening, co-opting, suspicious, and/or inept) than many facilitators acknowledge.

THE PARADOX OF PUNCTUATION

The third paradox is rooted in a primary goal of most facilitation attempts—making groups more effective and efficient. In the United States, efficiency is most often associated with saving time. Paradoxically, groups often perceive that facilitating processes take a great deal of time that is not related directly to the completion of critical tasks, and thus the facilitation is perceived to make the group less efficient, not more so. This punctuation of events (i.e., perceiving causal patterns and sequencing of behavioral events; Watzlawick, Beavin, & Jackson, 1967) makes a group resistant to the facilitating processes, thereby further increasing the time needed to master the facilitation techniques and separating the facilitation from "natural" group processes. In bona fide groups, there are often external time pressures as well as internal time demands derived from membership in other groups, conflicting individual commitments, political considerations, and so forth, that encourage groups to punctuate facilitating processes as a waste of time. This punctuation of events may even cause group members to become suspicious of the intent of the intervention. Group members unintentionally may sabotage their own success by punctuating communication sequences differently, leading the group, of course, to become less efficient. To paraphrase Watzlawick et al., the nature of the relationship between the group and the facilitation is contingent on the punctuation of communication sequences that take place within the facilitating process.

In conclusion, this volume of case studies presents the reader with a rich and textured view of group facilitation. The chapters draw our attention to the complex interplay among personal attitudes, group memberships, and the social contexts in which people find themselves. Perhaps most important, the culminating lesson from these case studies is that group facilitations are powerful techniques that have impact both in and outside the groups in which they are carried out. Even when the group finishes its task, when the facilitation is over and the group itself disbands, or when the facilitation has become so integrated into the group that it is no longer a parallel process but part of the group itself,

the residue of group facilitation lives on through social contacts, professional and personal relationships, and memberships in other groups. It
is our responsibility as scholars and practitioners to apply the most current research knowledge and our individual expertise to this important
area of communication practice so that the outcomes of facilitating fulfill
the great promise of the techniques of facilitation.

References

Ackoff, R. (1979). *Creating the corporate future.* New York: Wiley.

Alberts, H. (1992). *Acquisition: Past, present and future.* Paper presented at the meeting of the Institute of Management Sciences and Operations Research Society, Orlando, FL.

Albrecht, T.L. (1987). Communication and personal control in empowering organizations. In J. Anderson (Ed.), *Communication yearbook 11* (pp. 380-390). Newbury Park, CA: Sage.

Alderfer, C.P. (1972). *Human needs in organizational settings.* Glencoe, IL: Free Press.

Aldrich, H.E. (1979). *Organizations and environments.* Englewood Cliffs, NJ: Prentice Hall.

Allport, F.H. (1920). The influence of the group upon association and thought. *Journal of Experimental Psychology, 3,* 159-182.

Allport, G. (1954). *The nature of prejudice.* Reading, MA: Addison-Wesley.

Andersen, T. (Ed.). (1991). *The reflective team: Dialogues and dialogues about the dialogues.* New York: Norton.

Andersen, T. (1992). Reflections on reflecting with families. In S. McNamee & K. Gergen (Eds.), *Therapy as social construction* (pp. 54-68). London: Sage.

Annett, J. (1969). *Feedback and human behavior.* Baltimore: Penguin Books.

Argyris, C. (1982). *Reasoning, learning and action: Individual and organizational.* San Francisco: Jossey-Bass.

Argyris, C. (1991). Teaching smart people how to learn. *Harvard Business Review, 69*(3), 99-109.

Argyris, C., Putnam, R., & Smith, D.M. (1985). *Action science: Concepts, methods, and skills for research and intervention.* San Francisco: Jossey-Bass.

Argyris, C., & Schon, D.A. (1978). *Organizational learning: A theory of action perspective.* Reading, MA: Addison-Wesley.

Aronson, E., & Osheron, N. (1980). Cooperation, pro-social behavior and academic performance: Experiments in the desegregated classroom. In L. Bickman (Ed.), *Applied social psychology* (Vol. 1, pp. 163-

196). Beverly Hills, CA: Sage.

Ashby, W.R. (1958). Requisite variety and its implications for the control of complex systems. *Cybernetica, 1*(2), 1-17.

Ashford, S.J., & Cummings, L.L. (1983). Feedback as an individual resource: Personal strategies of creating information. *Organizational Behavior and Human Performance, 32,* 370-398.

Ashforth, B.E., & Mael, F. (1989). Social identity theory and the organization. *Academy of Management Review, 14,* 20-39.

Aubrey, C.A., & Felkins, P.K. (1988). *Teamwork: Involving people in quality and productivity improvement.* Milwaukee, WI: Quality Press & White Plains, NY: UNIPUB/Quality Resources.

Baburoglu, O.N. (1988). The vertical environment: The fifth in the Emery-Trist levels of organization. *Human Relations, 41,* 181-210.

Baird, A.C. (1927). *Public discussion and debate.* Boston: Ginn.

Bales, R.F. (1950). *Interaction process analysis.* Cambridge, MA: Addison-Wesley.

Bales, R.F. (1970). *Personality and interpersonal behavior.* New York: Holt, Rinehart & Winston.

Bales, R.F. (1985). The new field theory in social psychology. *International Journal of Small Group Research, 1,* 1-18.

Bales, R.F. (1988). *Overview of the SYMLOG system: Measuring and changing behavior in groups.* San Diego, CA: SYMLOG Consulting Group.

Bales, R.F., & Cohen, S.P. (1979). *SYMLOG: A system for the multiple level observation of groups.* New York: Free Press.

Bales, R.F., & Strodtbeck, F. (1951). Phases in group problem-solving. *Journal of Abnormal and Social Psychology, 46,* 485-495.

Barker, J.R. (1992). *The team makes the rules: Normative dynamics in the self-directed culture.* Unpublished manuscript, Department of Communication, University of Colorado, Boulder.

Barker, J.R., Melville, C., & Pacanowsky, M. (1992). *Self-directed work teams at XEL: Changes in communication practices during a program of cultural transformation.* Unpublished manuscript, Department of Communication, University of Colorado, Boulder.

Barnard, C.I. (1938). *The functions of the executive.* Cambridge, MA: Harvard University Press.

Barrett, W. (1978). *The illusion of technique.* Garden City, NY: Anchor Press/Doubleday.

Barton, W.A., Jr. (1926). The effect of group activity and individual effort in developing ability to solve problems in first year algebra. *Educational Administration and Supervision, 12,* 412-518.

Bateson, G. (1972). *Steps to an ecology of mind.* New York: Chandler.

Bateson, G. (1979). *Mind and nature: A necessary unity.* New York: Bantam.

Bauer, J., & Hout, T. (1988). Fast-cycle capability for competitive power.

Harvard Business Review, 66(6), 110-118.

Bayless, O.L. (1967). An alternate pattern for problem-solving discussion. *Journal of Communication, 17*, 188-197.

Benjamin, L.S. (1974). Structural analysis of social behavior. *Psychological Review, 81*, 392-425.

Benne, K.D. (1964). History of the play group in the laboratory setting. In L.P. Bradford, J.R. Gibb, & K.D. Beene (Eds.), *T-group theory and laboratory method: Innovation in re-education* (pp. 80-135). New York: John Wiley.

Bennett, W.L. (1979). Storytelling in criminal trials: A model of social judgment. *Quarterly Journal of Speech, 64*, 1-22.

Berger, C.R. (1979). Beyond initial interaction: Uncertainty, understanding and the development of interpersonal relationships. In H. Giles & R.N. St. Clair (Eds.), *Language and social psychology* (pp. 122-144). Oxford, England: Basil Blackwell.

Berger, C.R. (1986). Social cognition and intergroup communication. In W.B. Gudykunst (Ed.), *Intergroup communication* (pp. 51-61). London: Edward Arnold.

Berger, C.R., & Bradac, J. (1982). *Language and social knowledge: Uncertainty in interpersonal relationships.* London: Edward Arnold.

Berger, P.L., & Luckmann, T. (1966). *The social construction of reality: A treatise in the sociology of knowledge.* Garden City, NY: Doubleday.

Bergman, D.A., & Pantell, R.H. (1984). The art and science of medical decision making. *Journal of Pediatrics, 104*, 649-656.

Berteotti, C.R., & Seibold, D.R. (1994). Coordination and role definition problems in health care teams: A hospice case study. In L. R. Frey (Ed.), *Group communication in context: Studies of natural groups* (pp. 107-131). Hillsdale, NJ: Erlbaum.

Blake, R.R., & Mouton, J.S. (1968). *Corporate excellence through grid organization development.* Houston: Gulf.

Blake, R.R., & Mouton, J.S. (1978). *The new managerial grid.* Houston: Gulf.

Blake, R.R., & Mouton, J.S. (1985). *The managerial grid III: The key to leadership excellence.* Houston: Gulf.

Blumberg, A., & Golembiewski, R.T. (1976). *Learning and change in groups.* Harmondsworth, Middlesex, England: Penguin.

Boethius, S.B. (1987). The view from the middle: Perceiving patterns of interaction in middle management groups. *International Journal of Small Group Research, 3*, 1-15.

Bohm, D., & Edwards, M. (1991). *Changing consciousness.* San Francisco: HarperCollins.

Bolman, L.G., & Deal, T.E. (1991). *Reframing organizations: Artistry, choice and leadership.* San Francisco: Jossey-Bass.

Borgatta, E.F. (1960). Small group research. *Current Sociology, 9*, 173-272.

Borgatta, E., & Cottrell, L.S. (1955). On the classification of groups. *Sociometry, 18,* 665-678.

Borgatta, E., Cottrell, L.S., & Meyer, H.H. (1956). On the dimensions of group behavior. *Sociometry, 19,* 223-240.

Bormann, E.G. (1983). Symbolic convergence: Organizational communication and culture. In L. Putnam & M.E. Pacanowsky (Eds.), *Communication and organizations: An interpretive approach* (pp. 99-122). Beverly Hills, CA: Sage.

Bormann, E.G. (1985). Symbolic convergence theory: A communication formulation. *Journal of Communication, 35,* 128-138.

Bormann, E.G. (1989). *Communication theory.* Salem, WI: Sheffield.

Bormann, E.G. (1990). *Small group communication: Theory and practice* (3rd ed.). New York: HarperCollins.

Bormann, E.G., & Bormann, N.C. (1992). *Effective small group communication* (5th ed.). Minneapolis, MN: Burgess.

Bormann, E.G., Kroll, B.S., Watters, K., & McFarland, D. (1984). Rhetorical visions of committed voters in the 1980 presidential campaign: Fantasy theme analysis of a large sample survey. *Critical Studies in Mass Communication, 1,* 287-310.

Boscolo, L., Cecchin, G., Hoffman, L., & Penn, P. (1987). *Milan systemic family therapy: Conversation in theory and practice.* New York: Basic Books.

Bostrom, R., Watson, R.T., & Kinney, S. (Eds.). (1992). *Computer augmented teamwork: A guided tour.* New York: Van Nostrand Reinhold.

Bouchard, T.J. (1969). Personality, problem-solving procedure and performance in small groups. *Journal of Applied Psychological Monographs, 53*(1, part 2), 1-29.

Boulding, K. (1966). *The impact of the social sciences.* New Brunswick, NJ: Rutgers University Press.

Brand, N. (1992). Learning to use the mediation process—a guide for lawyers. *Arbitration Journal, 47*(4), 6-13.

Branham, R.J., & Pearce, W.B. (1985). Between text and context: Toward a rhetoric of contextual reconstruction. *Quarterly Journal of Speech, 71,* 19-36.

Brashers, D.E., Adkins, M., & Meyers, R.A. (1994). Argumentation and computer-mediated group decision making. In L.R. Frey (Ed.), *Group communication in context: Studies of natural groups* (pp. 263-282). Hillsdale, NJ: Erlbaum.

Breiger, R.L., & Ennis, J.G. (1979). Personae and social roles: The network structure of personality types in small groups. *Social Psychology Quarterly, 42,* 262-270.

Brenner, M. (1981). Patterns of social structure in the research interview. In M. Brenner (Ed.), *Social method and social life* (pp. 115-158). New York: Academic Press.

Briggs, C.I. (1986). *Learning how to ask: A sociolinguistic appraisal of the role of the interview in social science research.* Cambridge, England: Cambridge University Press.

Brilhart, J.K. (1966). An experimental comparison of three techniques for communicating a problem-solving pattern to members of a discussion group. *Speech Monographs, 33,* 169-177.

Brilhart, J.K., & Galanes, G.J. (1989). *Effective group discussion* (6th ed.). Dubuque, IA: Wm. C. Brown.

Brilhart, J.K., & Jochem, L.M. (1964). Effects of different patterns on outcomes of problem-solving discussion. *Journal of Applied Psychology, 48,* 175-179.

Brislin, R. (1981). *Cross cultural encounters: Face to face interaction.* Elmsford, NY: Pergamon.

Brislin, R. (1986). Prejudice and intergroup communication. In W. B. Gudykunst (Ed.), *Intergroup communication* (pp. 74-85). London: Edward Arnold.

Broome, B. (1983). The attraction paradigm revisited: Responses to dissimilar others. *Human Communication Research, 10,* 137-152.

Broome, B.J. (1993). Managing differences in conflict situations. In D. J. Sandole & H. van der Merwe (Eds.), *Conflict resolution theory and practice: Application and integration* (pp. 97-111). Manchester, England: Manchester University Press.

Broome, B.J., & Chen, M. (1992). Guidelines for computer-assisted group problem-solving: Meeting the challenges of complex issues. *Small Group Research, 23,* 216-236.

Broome, B.J., & Christakis, A.N. (1988). A culturally-sensitive approach to Tribal governance issue management. *International Journal of Intercultural Relations, 12,* 107-123.

Broome, B.J., & Cromer, I.L. (1991). Strategic planning for Tribal economic development: A culturally appropriate model for consensus building. *International Journal of Conflict Management, 2,* 217-234.

Broome, B.J., & Keever, D.B. (1989). Next generation group facilitation: Proposed principles. *Management Communication Quarterly, 3,* 107-127.

Brown, D.L. (1983). *Managing conflict at organizational interfaces.* Reading, MA: Addison-Wesley.

Burke, W.W. (1982). *Organization development: Principles and practices.* Glenview, IL: Scott, Foresman.

Burleson, B.R., Levine, B.J., & Samter, W. (1984). Decision-making procedure and decision quality. *Human Communication Research, 10,* 557-574.

Burns, T., & Stalker, G.M. (1968). *The management of innovation* (2nd ed.). London: Tavistock Publications.

Bush, R.R. (1981). Applied Q-methodology: An industry perspective. In J.F. Cragan & D.C. Shields (Eds.), *Applied communication research: A drama-*

tistic approach (pp. 367-371). Prospect Heights, IL: Waveland Press.

Carr, L.J. (1929). Experimental sociology: A preliminary note on theory and method. *Social Forces, 8*, 63-74.

Carter, L.R. (1954). Recording and evaluating the performance of individuals as members of small groups. *Personnel Psychology, 7*, 477-484.

Cattell, R.B., Saunders, D.R., & Stice, G.F. (1953). The dimensions of syntality in small groups: I. The neonate group. *Human Relations, 6*, 331-356.

Cecchin, G. (1987). Hypothesizing, circularity, and neutrality revisited: An invitation to curiosity. *Family Process, 26*, 405-414.

Cecchin, G. (1992). Constructing therapeutic possibilities. In S. McNamee & K. Gergen (Eds.), *Therapy as social construction* (pp. 86-95). London: Sage.

Cecchin, G., Lane, G., & Ray, W. (1992). *Irreverence: A strategy for therapists' survival*. London: Karnac.

Cecchin, G., & Stratton, P. (1991). Extending systemic consultation from families to management. *Human Systems, 2*, 3-14.

Cegala, D., Wall, V.D., Jr., & Rippey, G. (1987). An investigation of interaction involvement and the dimensions of SYMLOG: Perceived communication behavior of persons in task-oriented groups. *Central States Speech Journal, 38*, 81-93.

Chakiris, B.J. (1992). *Consultation skills workbook*. Chicago: B.J. Chakiris Corp.

Chakiris, B.J. (1993). *Human resource audit facilitation guide*. Chicago: B.J. Chakiris Corp.

Chilberg, J.C. (1989). A review of group process designs for facilitating communication in problem-solving groups. *Management Communication Quarterly, 3*, 51-70.

Christakis, A.N. (1985). High-technology participative design: The space-based laser. *Proceedings of the Society for General Systems Research, 2*, 925-933.

Christakis, A.N. (1987). Systems profile: The Club of Rome revisited. *Systems Research, 4*(1), 53-58.

Church, A.H., & Burke, W.W. (1993, Winter). What are the basic values of OD? *Academy of Management ODC Newsletter*, pp. 1-8.

Cissna, K.N. (1982). Editor's note: What is applied communication research? *Journal of Applied Communication Research, 10*, Editorial Statement.

Clement, D.A., & Frandsen, K.D. (1976). On conceptual and empirical treatments of feedback in communication. *Communication Monographs, 43*, 11-28.

Cleveland, H. (1973). The decision makers. *The Center Magazine, 6*(5), 9-18.

Cohen, A.M. (1961). Changing small group communication networks.

Journal of Communication, 11, 116-124, 128.

Cohen, A.M. (1962). Changing small group communication networks. *Administrative Science Quarterly, 6*, 443-462.

Coke, J.G., & Moore, C.M. (1981). Coping with a budgetary crisis: Helping a city council decide where expenditure cuts should be made. In S. W. Burks & J. F. Wolf (Eds.), *Building city council leadership skills: A casebook of models and methods* (pp. 72-85). Washington, DC: National League of Cities.

Collins, B.E., & Guetzkow, H. (1964). *A social psychology of group processes for decision making*. New York: Wiley & Sons.

Cook, S.W. (1984). Cooperative interaction in multiethnic contexts. In N. Miller & M. Brewer (Eds.), *Groups in contact: The psychology of desegregation* (pp. 97-114). New York: Academic Press.

Cooper, C.L. (Ed.). (1975). *Theories of group processes*. London: Wiley.

Cooper, C.L., & Mangham, I.L. (1971). *T-groups: A survey of research*. London: Wiley-Interscience.

Cooper, R., & Foster, M. (1971). Sociotechnical systems. *American Psychologist, 26*, 467-474.

Cordery, J.L., Mueller, W.S., & Smith, L.M. (1991). Attitudinal and behavioral effects of autonomous group work: A longitudinal field study. *Academy of Management Journal, 34*, 464-476.

Cotter, D., & Cragan, J.F. (1987, February). *The St. Louis Post Dispatch magazine focus group study* [Proprietary report to the editors of the *St. Louis Post Dispatch*]. St. Louis, MO: The Pulizter Company.

Cotter, J. (1983). *Designing organizations that work: An open sociotechnical systems perspective*. Cambridge, MA: J.J. Cotter & Associates.

Couch, C.J., Katovich, M.A., & Miller, D. (1987). The sorrowful tale of small groups research. In N. K. Denzin (Ed.), *Studies in symbolic interaction* (Vol. 8, pp. 159-180). Greenwich, CT: JAI Press.

Cragan, J.F., Dimiceli, D., Kingsley, E., Radtke, E., Steward, M., & Smith, C. (1992, September). *Fantasy themes and role emergence in the Jones v. ABC Oil Company mock jury simulations* [Proprietary report to John Doe and Associates]. Chicago, IL: John Doe and Associates. [Note: Identify Masked].

Cragan, J.F., & Shields, D.C. (Eds.). (1981). *Applied communication research: A dramatistic approach*. Prospect Heights, IL: Waveland Press.

Cragan, J.F., & Shields, D.C. (1992). The use of symbolic convergence theory in corporate strategic planning: A case study. *Journal of Applied Communication Research, 20*, 199-218.

Cragan, J.F., & Shields, D.C. (in press). *Symbolic theories in applied communication research: Bormann, Burke, and Fisher*. Cresskill, NJ: Hampton Press.

Cragan, J.F., & Wright, D.W. (1991). *Communication in small group discus-*

sions: An integrated approach. St. Paul, MN: West.

Craig, R.T. (1989). Communication as a practical discipline. In B. Dervin, L. Grossberg, B.J. O'Keefe, & E. Wartella (Eds.), *Rethinking communication: Volume 1. Paradigm issues* (pp. 97-122). Newbury Park, CA: Sage.

Cronen, V.E. (1990, November). *Coordinated management of meaning theory, circular questions, and the rhetoric of possibility.* Paper presented at the meeting of the Speech Communication Association, Chicago.

Cronen, V.E. (in press). Coordinated management of meaning: Practical theory for the complexities and contradictions of everyday life. In J. Siegfried (Ed.), *The status of common sense in psychology.* Norwood, NJ: Ablex.

Cronen, V.E., Johnson, K.M., & Lannamann, J.W. (1982). Paradoxes, double binds, and reflexive loops: An alternative theoretical perspective. *Family Process, 20,* 91-112.

Cronen, V.E., & Pearce, W.B. (1985). Toward an explanation of how the Milan approach works: An invitation to a systemic epistemology and the evolution of family systems. In D. Campbell & R. Draper (Eds.), *Applications of systemic family therapy: The Milan approach* (pp. 69-86). London: Grune and Stratton.

Cronen, V.E., & Pearce, W.B., & Tomm, K. (1985). A dialectical view of personal change. In K.J. Gergen & K.E. Davis (Eds.), *The social construction of the person* (pp. 203-224). New York: Springer-Verlag.

Cummings, T.G. (1978). Self-regulating work groups: A socio-technical synthesis. *Academy of Management Review, 3,* 625-634.

Cusella, L.P. (1980). The effect of feedback on intrinsic motivation: A propositional extension of cognitive evaluation theory from an organizational communication perspective. In D. Nimmo (Ed.), *Communication yearbook 4* (pp. 367-388). New Brunswick, NJ: Transaction Books.

Cushman, D.P., & Cahn, D.D., Jr. (1985). *Communication in interpersonal relationships.* Albany, NY: SUNY Press.

Cushman, D.P., & King, S.S. (1993). High-speed management: A revolution in organizational communication in the 1990s. In S. Deetz (Ed.), *Communication yearbook 16* (pp. 209-236). Newbury Park, CA: Sage.

Daft, R.L., & Huber, G.P. (1987). How organizations learn: A communication framework. *Research in the Sociology of Organizations, 3,* 1-16.

Daft, R.L., & Lengel, R.H. (1984). Information richness: A new approach to managerial behavior and organization design. In L.L. Cummings & B.M. Staw (Eds.), *Research in organizational behavior* (Vol. 6, pp. 191-233). Greeenwich, CT: JAI Press.

Dashiell, J.F. (1935). Experimental studies of the influence of social situations on the behavior of individual human adults. In C. Murchison

(Ed.), *Handbook of social psychology* (pp. 1097-1158). Worchester, MA: Clark University Press.

Davidow, W.H., & Malone, M.S. (1992). *The virtual corporation: Structuring and revitalizing the corporation for the 21st century.* New York: HarperCollins.

Davis, J.H. (1969). *Group performance.* Reading, MA: Addison-Wesley.

Deal, T.E., & Kennedy, A.A. (1982). *Corporate cultures: The rites and rituals of corporate life.* Reading, MA: Addison-Wesley.

Dean, J.W., Jr., Susman, G.I., & Porter, P.S. (1990). Technical, economic and political factors in advanced manufacturing technology implementation. *Journal of Engineering and Technology Management, 7*, 129-144.

Deetz, S.A. (1992). *Democracy in an age of corporate colonization.* Albany, NY: SUNY Press.

De Geus, A.P. (1988). Planning as learning. *Harvard Business Review, 66*(2), 70-74.

Delbeq, A.L., van de Ven, A.H., & Gustafson, D.H. (1975). *Group techniques for program planning: A guide to nominal group and Delphi processes.* Glenview, IL: Scott, Foresman.

Deming, W.E. (1986a). *Out of the crisis.* Cambridge: Massachusetts Institute of Technology, Center for Advanced Engineering Study.

Deming, W.E. (1986b). *Quality, productivity, and competitive position.* Cambridge: Massachusetts Institute of Technology, Center for Advanced Engineering Study.

Dennis, A.R., George, J.F., Giuseppe, L.M., Nunamaker, J.F., & Vogel, D.R. (1988). Information technology to support electronic meetings. *MIS Quarterly, 12*, 591-624.

DeSanctis, G., & Gallupe, B. (1985). Group decision support systems: A new frontier. *Data Base, 16*(2), 3-9.

DeSanctis, G., & Gallupe, R.B. (1987). A foundation for the study of group decision support systems. *Management Science, 33*, 589-609.

DeSanctis, G., & Poole, M.S. (in press). Capturing the complexity in advanced technology use: Adaptive structuration theory. *Organization Science.*

DeSanctis, G., Poole, M.S., Desharnais, G., & Lewis, H. (1991). Using computing to facilitate the quality improvement process: The IRS-Minnesota project. *Interfaces, 21*(6), 23-36.

DeSanctis, G., Sambamurthy, V., & Watson, R. (1987). Computer supported meetings: Building a research environment. *Large Scale Systems, 13*, 43-59.

DeSanctis, G., Snyder, J.R., & Poole, M.S. (in press). The meaning of the interface: A functional and holistic evaluation of a meeting software system. *Decision Support Systems.*

Des Jarlais, R.W. (1943). A measurement of participants' change of opinion during group discussion. *Speech Abstracts, 3,* 37.

Dewey, J. (1910). *How we think.* Boston: D. C. Heath.

Dickens, M., & Heffernan, M. (1949). Experimental research in group discussion. *Quarterly Journal of Speech, 35,* 23-29.

Dickson, G., Poole, M.S., & DeSanctis, G. (1992). An overview of the Minnesota GDSS research project and the SAMM system. In G.R. Wagner, R. Bostrom, R.T. Watson, & S. Kinney (Eds.), *Computer augmented teamwork: A guided tour* (pp. 163-180). New York: Van Nostrand Reinhold.

Dillon, P.C., Graham, W.K., & Aidells, A.L. (1972). Brainstorming on a "hot" problem: Effects of training and practice on individual and group performance. *Journal of Applied Psychology, 56,* 487-490.

Doyle, M., & Straus, D. (1976). *How to make meetings work: The new interaction method.* New York: Wyden Books.

Drucker, P.F. (1985). *Innovation and entrepreneurship.* New York: Harper & Row.

Duncan, R.B. (1972). Characteristics of organizational environments and perceived environmental uncertainty. *Administrative Science Quarterly, 20,* 313-327.

Dyer, W.G. (1988). *Team building: Issues and alternatives* (2nd ed.). Reading, MA: Addison-Wesley.

Elden, M. (1986). Sociotechnical systems ideas as public policy in Norway: Empowering participation through worker-managed change. *Journal of Applied Behavioral Science, 22,* 239-255.

Elliot, H.S. (1927). *The why and how of group discussion.* New York: Association Press.

Ellis, D.G. (1982, March). The shame of speech communication. *Spectra,* pp. 1-2.

Ellis, D.G. (1991). The oneness of opposites: Applied communication and theory. *Journal of Applied Communication Research, 19,* 116-122.

Elmes, M., & Wilemon, D. (1991). A field study of intergroup integration in technology-based organizations. *Journal of Engineering and Technology Management, 7,* 229-250.

Emerson, R.M. (1962). Power-dependence relations. *American Sociological Review, 27,* 31-40.

Emery, F.E. (1967). The next thirty years: Concepts, methods and applications. *Human Relations, 20,* 199-237.

Emery, F.E., & Trist, E. (1965). Socio-technical systems. In C. Churchman & M. Verhulst (Eds.), *Management science: Models and techniques* (Vol. 2, pp. 83-97). Oxford: Pergamon Press.

Erez, M. (1977). Feedback: A necessary condition for the goal-setting-performance relationship. *Journal of Applied Psychology, 62,* 624-627.

Farris, G.F. (1981). Groups and the informal organization. In R. Payne &

C. Cooper (Eds.), *Groups at work* (pp. 95-117). London: Wiley.

Feeg, R. (1988). Forum of the future of pediatric nursing: Looking toward the 21st century. *Pediatric Nursing, 14,* 393-396.

Felkins, P.K., Chakiris, B.J., & Chakiris, K.N. (1993). *Change consultation: A model for effective organizational performance.* White Plains, NY: Kraus Organization/Quality Resources.

Ferguson, M. (1980). *The aquarian conspiracy: Personal and social transformation in the 1980s.* Los Angeles: J.P. Tarcher.

Firestien, R.L. (1990). Effects of creative problem solving training on communication behavior in small groups. *Small Group Research, 21,* 507-521.

Fisher, K. (1986, Fall). Management roles in the implementation of participative management systems. *Human Resource Management,* pp. 7-14.

Fisher, K. (1993). *Leading self-directed work teams.* New York: McGraw-Hill.

Folger, J., Poole, M.S., & Stutman, R.K. (1993). *Working through conflict: Strategies for relationships, groups, and organizations* (2nd ed.). New York: HarperCollins.

Forgas, J.P. (1978). Social episodes and social structure in an academic setting: The social environment of an intact group. *Journal of Experimental Social Psychology, 14,* 434-448.

Forston, R.F. (1968). *The decision-making process in the American civil jury: A comparative methodological investigation.* Unpublished doctoral dissertation, University of Minnesota, Minneapolis.

Freeman, S., Littlejohn, S., & Pearce, W.B. (1992). Moral conflict and communication. *Western Journal of Communication, 56,* 311-329.

Frey, L.R. (1988, November). *Meeting the challenges posed during the 70s: A critical review of small group communication research during the 80s.* Paper presented at the meeting of the Speech Communication Association, New Orleans.

Frey L.R., O'Hair, D., & Kreps, G.L. (1990). Applied communication methodology. In D. O'Hair & G.L. Kreps (Eds.), *Applied communication theory and research* (pp. 23-56). Hillsdale, NJ: Erlbaum.

Frey, L.R. (in press-a). Remembering and "re-membering": A history of theory and research on communication and group decision-making. In R.Y. Hirokawa & M.S. Poole (Eds.), *Communication and group decision-making* (2nd ed.). Newbury Park, CA: Sage.

Frey, L.R. (in press-b). The naturalistic paradigm: Studying small groups in the post modern era. *Small Group Research.*

Frey, L.R., Botan, C.H., Friedman, P.G., & Kreps, G.L. (1991). *Investigating communication: An introduction to research methods.* Englewood Cliffs, NJ: Prentice Hall.

Frey, L.R., Botan, C.H., Friedman, P.G., & Kreps, G.L. (1992). *Interpreting communication research: A case study approach.* Englewood Cliffs, NJ: Prentice Hall.

Friedlander, F. (1976). OD reaches adolescence: An exploration of its underlying values. *Journal of Applied Behavioral Research, 12,* 7-21.

Friedman, P.G. (1989). Upstream facilitation: A proactive approach to managing problem-solving groups. *Management Communication Quarterly, 3,* 33-50.

Frost, P.J., Moore, L.F., Louis, M.R., Lundberg, C.C., & Martin, J. (1991). *Reframing organizational culture.* Newbury Park, CA: Sage.

Fulk, J., & Steinfield, C. (Eds.). (1990). *Organizations and communication technology.* Newbury Park, CA: Sage.

Furino, A. (Ed.). (1988). *Cooperation and competition in the global economy: Issues and strategies.* Cambridge, MA: Ballinger.

Galbraith, J.R. (1973). *Designing complex organizations.* Reading, MA: Addison-Wesley.

Geertz, C. (1973). *The interpretation of cultures.* New York: Basic Books.

Gibb, J.R. (1961). Defensive communication. *Journal of Communication, 11,* 141-148.

Gibb, J.R. (1962). *Factors producing defensive behavior within groups* [Final Technical Report, ONR Contract, NONr-3088 (00)]. Washington, DC: National Training Laboratories.

Gibb, J.R. (1964). Climate for trust formation. In L. P. Bradford, J. Gibb, & K.D. Benne (Eds.), *T-group theory and laboratory method: Innovation in re-education* (pp. 279-309). New York: Academic Press.

Giddens, A. (1979). *Central problems in social theory.* Berkeley: University of California Press.

Giddens, A. (1984). *The constitution of society: Outline of the theory of structuration.* Berkeley: University of California Press.

Goffman, E. (1974). *Frame analysis: An essay on the organization of experience.* Cambridge, MA: Harvard University Press.

Goldman, A. (1962). The group depth interview. *Journal of Marketing Research, 19,* 1-13.

Goldswig, S.R., & Cody, M.J. (1990). Legal communication: An introduction to rhetorical and communication theory perspectives. In D. O'Hair & G.L. Kreps (Eds.), *Applied communication theory and research* (pp. 245-267). Hillsdale, NJ: Erlbaum.

Golembiewski, R., & Blumberg, A. (Eds.). (1977). *Sensitivity training and the laboratory approach: Readings about concepts and applications* (3rd ed.). Itasca, IL: F.E. Peacock.

Goodman, G., & Esterly, G. (1988). *The talk book: The intimate science of communicating in close relationships.* Emmaus, PA: Rodale Press.

Gouran, D.S. (1982). *Making decisions in groups: Choices and consequences.* Glenview, IL: Scott, Foresman.

Green, S.G., & Mitchell, T.R. (1979). Attributional processes of leaders in leader-member relations. *Organizational Behavior and Human Performance, 23,* 429-458.

Greenbaum, T.L. (1988). *The practical handbook and guide to focus group research.* Lexington, MA: D. C. Heath.

Gudykunst, W.B. (1983). Uncertainty reduction and predictability of behavior in low and high context cultures: An exploratory study. *Communication Quarterly, 31,* 49-55.

Gudykunst, W.B. (Ed.). (1986). *Intergroup communication.* London: Edward Arnold.

Guetzkow, H., & Dill, W.R. (1957). Factors in the organizational development of task-oriented groups. *Sociomety, 20,* 175-204.

Guetzkow, H., & Somon, H.A. (1955). The impact of certain communication nets upon organization and performance in task-oriented groups. *Management Sciences, 1,* 233-250.

Gurnee, H. (1937). Maze learning in the collective situation. *Journal of Experimental Psychology, 11,* 348-368, 437-464.

Guzzo, R.A., Jette, R.D., & Katzell, R.A. (1985). The effects of psychologically based intervention programs on worker productivity: A meta-analysis. *Personnel Psychology, 38,* 275-291.

Haag, L.L. (1988, November). *The dramatistic-based focus group interview: A comparative analysis.* Paper presented at the meeting of the Speech Communication Association, New Orleans, LA.

Habermas, J. (1971). *Knowledge and human interests.* Boston: Beacon.

Hackman, J.R. (Ed.). (1990). *Groups that work (and those that don't): Creating conditions for effective teamwork.* San Francisco: Jossey-Bass.

Hackman, J.R., & Walton, R.E. (1986). Leading groups in organizations. In P. Goodman & Associates (Eds.), *Designing effective work groups* (pp. 72-119). San Francisco: Jossey-Bass.

Hall, J., & Williams, M. (1966). A comparison of decision-making performance in established and ad hoc groups. *Journal of Personal and Social Psychology, 3,* 214-222.

Handy, C. (1990). *The age of unreason.* Boston: Harvard Business School Press.

Harrison, R. (1965). *Cognitive models for interpersonal and group behavior: A theoretical framework for research.* Washington, DC: National Training Laboratories.

Harrison, T.M. (1982). Toward an ethical framework for communication consulting. *Journal of Applied Communication Research, 10,* 87-100.

Herbst, P.G. (1962). *Autonomous group functioning.* London: Tavistock Publications.

Herndon, S.L. (1993). Using focus group interviews for preliminary investigation. In S.L. Herndon & G.L. Kreps (Eds.), *Qualitative research: Applications in organizational communication* (pp. 39-46). Cresskill, NJ: Hampton Press.

Hersey, P., & Blanchard, K. (1975). A situational framework for determining appropriate leader behavior. In R.N. Cassel & R.L. Heichberger (Eds.), *Leadership development: Theory and practice* (pp. 126-155). North Quincy, MA: Christopher Publishing House.

Hill, G.W. (1982). Group versus individual performance: Are n+1 heads better than one? *Psychological Bulletin, 17*(3), 517-539.

Hiltz, S.R., & Turoff, M. (1978). *The network nation: Human communication via computer.* Reading, MA: Addison-Wesley.

Hirokawa, R.Y. (1980). A comparative analysis of communication patterns within effective and ineffective decision-making groups. *Communication Monographs, 47,* 312-321.

Hirokawa, R.Y. (1985). Decision procedures and decision-making performance: A test of a functional perspective. *Human Communication Research, 12,* 203-224.

Hirokawa, R.Y. (1990). The role of communication in group decision-making efficacy: A task-contingency perspective. *Small Group Research, 21,* 190-205.

Hirokawa, R.Y., & Gouran, D.S. (1989). Facilitation of group communication: A critique of prior research and an agenda for future research. *Management Communication Quarterly, 3,* 71-92.

Hirokawa, R.Y., Gouran, D.S., & Martz, A.E. (1988). Understanding the sources of faulty group decision making: A lesson from the Challenger disaster. *Small Group Behavior, 19,* 411-433.

Hirokawa, R.Y., Ice, R., & Cook, J. (1988). Preference for procedural order, discussion structure and group decision performance. *Communication Quarterly, 26,* 217-226.

Hirota, K. (1953). Group problem solving and communication. *Japanese Journal of Psychology, 24,* 176-177.

Hoffman, L.R. (1965). Group problem solving. In L. Berkowitz (Ed.), *Advances in experimental social psychology* (Vol. 2, pp. 99-132). New York: Academic Press.

Hofstede, G. (1980). *Culture's consequences: International differences in work-related values.* Beverly Hills, CA: Sage.

Hofstede, G. (1991). *Cultures and organizations: Software of the mind.* London: McGraw-Hill.

Hogg, M.A., & Abrams, D. (1988). *Social identifications: A social psychology of intergroup relations and group processes.* London: Routledge.

Howe, R.L. (1963). *The miracle of dialogue.* New York: Seabury Press.

Huber, G.P. (1984). Issues in the design of group decision support systems. *MIS Quarterly, 8,* 195-204.

Huseman, R.C., & Miles, E.W. (1988). Organizational communication in the information age: Implications of computer-based systems. *Journal of Management, 14,* 181-204.

Ichiyama, M.A., & Reddy, W.B. (1987). Assessment of small group dynamics: The SYMLOG system. In W.B. Reddy & C.C. Henderson, Jr. (Eds.), *Training theory and practice* (pp. 185-208). Arlington, VA: National Training Laboratories Institute.

Isenberg, D.J., & Ennis, J.G. (1981). Perceiving group members: A comparison of derived and imposed dimensions. *Journal of Personality and Social Psychology, 41,* 293-305.

Jablin, F.M. (1981). Cultivating imagination: Factors that enhance and inhibit creativity in brainstorming groups. *Human Communication Research, 7,* 245-258.

Janes, F.R. (1988). Interpretive structural modelling: A methodology for structuring complex issues. *Transactions of the Institute of Measurement and Control, 10*(3), 145-154.

Janis, I.L. (1972). *Victims of groupthink: A psychological study of foreign-policy decisions and fiascoes.* Boston: Houghton Mifflin.

Janis, I.L. (1982). *Groupthink: Psychological studies of policy decisions and fiascos* (2nd ed.). Boston: Houghton & Mifflin.

Janis, I.L. (1989). *Crucial decisions: Leadership in policymaking and crisis management.* New York: Free Press.

Janis, I.L., & Fleshbach, S. (1953). Effects of fear-arousing communication. *Journal of Abnormal and Social Psychology, 48,* 78-92.

Janis, I.L., & Mann, L. (1977). *Decision making: A psychological analysis of conflict, choice, and commitment.* New York: Free Press.

Jaques, E. (1986). The development of intellectual capability: A discussion of stratified systems theory. *Journal of Applied Behavioral Science, 22*(4), 361-383.

Jaques, E. (1990). In praise of hierarchy. *Harvard Business Review, 68*(1), 127-133.

Jarboe, S. (1988). A comparison of input-output, process-output, and input-process-output models of small group problem-solving effectiveness. *Communication Monographs, 55,* 121-142.

Jenness, A. (1932). The role of discussion in changing opinion regarding a matter of fact. *Journal of Abnormal and Social Psychology, 27,* 29-34, 279-296.

Jensen, A., & Chilberg, J. (1991). *Small group communication: Theory and practice.* Belmont, CA: Wadsworth.

Jessup, L.M., & Valacich, J.S. (Eds.). (1992). *Group support systems: New perspectives.* New York: Macmillan.

Johansen, R. (1988). *Groupware: Computer support for business teams.* New York: Free Press.

Johansen, R., Vallee, J., & Spengler, K. (1979). *Electronic meetings: Technical alternatives and social choices.* Reading, MA: Addison-Wesley.

Johnson, A. (1943). An experimental study in the analysis and measurement of reflective thinking. *Speech Monographs, 10,* 83-96.

Johnson, B.M. (1977). *The process of organizing.* Boston: Allyn & Bacon.

Johnston, W. (1987). *Workforce 2000.* Indianapolis, IN: Hudson Institute.

Jourard, S.M. (1971). *The transparent self.* New York: D. Van Nostrand.

Kanter, R.M. (1979). Power failure in management circuits. *Harvard Business Review, 57*(4), 67-75.

Kanter, R.M. (1983). *The changemasters: Innovation and entrepreneurship in the American corporation.* New York: Simon and Schuster.

Kapoor, S., Cragan, J., & Groves, J. (1992). Political diversity is alive in TV and newspaper rooms. *Communication Research Reports, 9,* 89-97.

Katzell, R.A., & Guzzo, R.A. (1983). Psychological approaches to worker productivity. *American Psychology, 38,* 468-472.

Keever, D.B. (1989, April). *Cultural complexities in the participative design of a computer-based organization information system.* Paper presented at the meeting of the International Conference on Support, Society and Culture: Mutual Uses of Cybernetics and Science, Amsterdam, The Netherlands.

Kelly, L., & Begnal, D.F. (1984). Group members' orientations toward decision processes. In G. M. Petelips & J. T. Wood (Eds.), *Emergent issues in human decision making* (pp. 63-79). Carbondale, IL: Southern Illinois University Press.

Kelly, L., & Duran, R.L. (1992). SYMLOG: Theory and measurement of small group interaction. In R.S. Cathcart & L.A. Samovar (Eds.), *Small group communication: A reader* (6th ed., pp. 39-52). Dubuque, IA: Wm. C. Brown.

Keltner, J. (1987). *Mediation: Toward a civilized system of dispute resolution.* Annandale, VA: Speech Communication Association.

Keltner, J.S. (1989). Facilitation: Catalyst for group problem solving. *Management Communication Quarterly, 3,* 8-32.

Keltner, J. (1992). Feedback and responding: Controlling and correcting our messages. In K.A. McCartney (Ed.), *Effective communication: The power of self in groups: Reading and resource book for the 22nd annual SAIC workshops.* Corvallis, OR: SAIC, Inc.

Keltner, J. (1994). *The management of struggle: Elements of dispute resolution through negotiation, mediation and arbitration* (pp. 197-214). Cresskill, NJ: Hampton Press.

Kemeny, J. (1980). Saving American democracy: The lesson of Three Mile Island. *Technology Review, 83*(7), 64-75.

Ketchum, L.D., & Trist, E. (1992). *All teams are not created equal: How employee empowerment really works.* Newbury Park, CA: Sage.

Kerr, E.B., & Hiltz, S.R. (1984). *Computer-mediated communication systems.*

New York: Academic Press.

Keyton, J., & Springston, J. (1990). Redefining cohesiveness in groups. *Small Group Research, 21*, 234-254.

Keyton, J., & Wall, V.D., Jr. (1989). SYMLOG: Theory and method for measuring group and organizational communication. *Management Communication Quarterly, 2*, 544-567.

Kilmann, R.H., & Thomas, K.W. (1978). Four perspectives on conflict management: An attributional framework for organizing descriptive and normative theory. *Academy of Management Review, 3*, 59-68.

Kinnear, T., & Taylor, J. (1983). *Marketing research: An applied approach.* New York: McGraw-Hill.

Klauss, R., & Bass, B. (1982). *Interpersonal communication in organizations.* New York: Academic Press.

Kochman, T. (1982). *Black and white: Styles in conflict.* Chicago: University of Chicago Press.

Koestler, A. (1967). *The ghost in the machine.* London: ARKANA.

Kraemer, K.L., & King, J.L. (1988). Computer-based systems for cooperative work and group decision making. *ACM Computing Surveys, 20*, 115-146.

Kreps, G.L. (1989). Reflexivity and internal public relations: The role of information in directing organizational development. In C. Botan & V. Hazelton (Eds.), *Public relations theory* (pp. 265-279). Hillsdale, NJ: Erlbaum.

Kreps, G.L. (1990). *Organizational communication: Theory and practice* (2nd ed.). White Plains, NY: Longman.

Kreps, G.L., Frey, L.R., & O'Hair, D. (1991). Applied communication research: Scholarship that can make a difference. *Journal of Applied Communication Research, 19*, 71-87.

Kressel, N.J. (1987). SYMLOG and behavior therapy: Pathway to expanding horizons. *Small Group Behavior, 18*, 420-436.

Krueger, R.A. (1988). *Focus groups: A practical guide for applied research.* Newbury Park, CA: Sage.

Lamm, H., & Trommsdorff, G. (1973). Group versus individual performance on tasks requiring ideational proficiency (brainstorming): A review. *European Journal of Social Psychology, 3*, 361-388.

Lanzetta, J.T., & Robey, T.B. (1956a). Effects of work-group structure and certain task variables on group performance. *Journal of Abnormal and Social Psychology, 53*, 307-314.

Lanzetta, J.T., & Robey, T.B. (1956b). Group performance as a function of work-distribution patterns and task load. *Sociometry, 19*, 95-104.

Larson, C.E. (1969). Forms of analysis and small group problem-solving. *Speech Monographs, 36*, 452-455.

Larson, C.E., & Gratz, R.D. (1970). Problem-solving discussion training and T-group training: An experimental comparison. *Speech Teacher, 19,* 54-57.

Laughlin, P.R., & Adamopoulous, J. (1980). Social combination process and individual learning for six-person cooperative groups on an intellectual task. *Journal of Personality and Social Psychology, 38,* 941-947.

Laughlin, P.R., & Jaccard, I.J. (1975). Social facilitation and observational learning of individuals and cooperative pairs. *Journal of Personality and Social Psychology, 32,* 873-879.

Lawler, E.E., III. (1986). *High involvement management.* San Francisco: Jossey-Bass.

Lawler, E.E., III. (1992). *The ultimate advantage: Creating the high-involvement organization.* San Francisco: Jossey-Bass.

Lawrence, P.R., & Lorsch, J.W. (1967). *Organization and environment: Managing differentiation and integration.* Homewood, IL: Richard D. Irvin.

Lawson, E.D. (1964a). Reinforced and non-reinforced four-man communication nets. *Psychological Reports, 14,* 287-296.

Lawson, E.D. (1964b). Reinforcement in group problem-solving with arithmetic problems. *Psychological Reports, 14,* 703-710.

Lawson, E.D. (1965). Change in communication nets, performance, and morale. *Human Relations, 18,* 139-147.

Leary, T. (1957). *Interpersonal diagnosis of personality: A functional theory and methodology for personality evaluation.* New York: Ronald Press.

Leathers, D.G. (1972). Quality of group communication as a determinant of group product. *Speech Monographs, 39,* 166-173.

Leavitt, H.J. (1951). Some effects of certain communication nets on group performance. *Journal of Abnormal and Social Psychology, 46,* 38-50.

Leavitt, H.J., & Mueller, R.A.H. (1951). Some effects of feedback on communication. *Human Relations, 4,* 401-410.

Lederman, L.C. (1990). Assessing educational effectiveness: The focus group interview as a technique for data collection. *Communication Education, 38,* 117-127.

Leppington, R. (1991). From constructivism to social constructionism and doing critical therapy. *Human Systems, 2,* 79-104.

Leventhal, H. (1967). Fear communication in the acceptance of preventive health practices. In R. L. Rosnow & E. J. Robinson (Eds.), *Experiments in persuasion* (pp. 168-192). New York: Academic Press.

Lewin, K. (1951). *Field theory in social science.* New York: Harper & Row.

Lewin, K. (1958). Group decisions and social change. In E. E. Maccoby, T. M. Newcomb, & E. L. Hartley, (Eds.), *Readings in social psychology* (3rd ed., pp. 197-211). New York: Holt.

Lewin, K., & Lippitt, R. (1938). An experimental approach to the study of autocracy and democracy: A preliminary note. *Sociometry, 1,* 292-300.

Lewin, K., Lippitt, R., & White, R.K. (1939). Patterns of aggressive behavior in experimentally created "social climates." *Journal of Social Psychology, 10,* 271-299.

Lewis, L.K., & Seibold, D.R. (1993). Innovation modification during intra-organizational adoption. *Academy of Management Review, 18,* 323-354.

Lieberman, M.A., Yalom, I.D., & Miles, M.B. (1973). *Encounter groups: First facts.* New York: Basic Books.

Likert, R. (1967). *The human organization.* New York: McGraw-Hill.

Lippitt, G.L. (1982). *Organizational renewal: A holistic approach to organizational development* (2nd ed.). Englewood Cliffs, NJ: Prentice Hall.

Lippitt, G., & Lippitt, R. (1986). *The consulting process in action* (2nd ed.). San Diego: University Associates.

Lippitt, R. (1939). Field theory and experiment in social psychology: Autocratic and democratic group atmosphere. *American Journal of Sociology, 45,* 26-49.

Lippitt, R. (1940). An experimental study of the effect of democratic and authoritarian group atmospheres. *University of Iowa Studies in Child Welfare, 16,* 43-195.

Lippitt, R., & White, R.K. (1952). An experimental study of leadership and group life. In G.E. Swanson, T.M. Newcomb, & E.L. Hartley (Eds.), *Readings in social psychology* (pp. 340-355). New York: Holt.

Litterst, J.K., & Ross, R.G. (1989, November). *Beyond the classroom: Discovery learning in a nonprofessional speech communication club.* Paper presented at the meeting of the Speech Communication Association, Chicago.

Littlejohn, S.W. (1983). *Theories of human communication* (2nd ed.). Belmont, CA: Wadsworth.

Lumsden, G., & Lumsden, D. (1993). *Communicating in groups and teams: Sharing leadership.* Belmont, CA: Wadsworth.

Lydecker, T.L. (1986). Focus group dynamics. *Association Management, 38*(3), 73-78.

Maidique, M., & Hayes, R. (1984, Winter). The art of high-technology management. *Sloan Management Review,* pp. 17-32.

Maier, N.R.F. (1970). *Problem solving and creativity in individuals and groups.* Belmont, CA: Brooks-Cole.

Malone, R. (1987, December). Global smart factory market. *Managing Automation,* pp. 24-26.

Manz, C.C., & Sims, H.P., Jr. (1982). The potentials for "groupthink" in autonomous work groups. *Human Relations, 35,* 773-784.

Manz, C.C., & Sims, H.P., Jr. (1984). Searching for the "unleader": Organizational member views on leading self-managed groups. *Human Relations, 37,* 409-424.

Marston, W.M. (1924). Studies in testimony. *Journal of Criminal Law & Criminology, 15,* 5-31.

Maturana, H. (1991). Maturana's basic notions. *Human Systems, 2*, 71-78.

McBurney, J.H., & Hance, K.G. (1939). *The principles and methods of discussion.* New York: Harper and Brothers.

McCafferty, M. (1988). *The next watch: Rhetorical visions of police officers.* Unpublished master's thesis, Illinois State University, Normal, IL.

McCafferty, M., & Vasquez, G. (1992, October). *Rhetorical visions of police academy graduates: A segmentation study* [Proprietary report submitted to the legal division, Police Academy]. Chicago, IL: Police Academy.

McCann, J.E., & Galbraith, J.R. (1981). Interdepartmental relations. In P.C. Nystrom & W.H. Starbuck (Eds.), *Handbook of organizational design* (Vol. 2, pp. 60-84). New York: Oxford University Press.

McDonald, P. (1990). *Group support technologies.* Cambridge, MA: United States Department of Transportation, Federal Aviation Administration.

McLeod, P.L., Liker, J.K., & Lobel, S.A. (1992). Process feedback in task groups: An application of goal setting. *Journal of Applied Behavioral Science, 28*, 15-41.

McWhinney, W. (1992). *Paths of change: Strategic choices for organizations and society.* Newbury Park, CA: Sage.

Meissner, M. (1969). *Technology and the worker: Technical demands and social processes in industry.* San Francisco: Chandler.

Merton, R.K. (1946). The focused interview. *American Journal of Sociology, 51*, 541-557.

Merton, R.K., Fiske, M., & Kendall, P.L. (1956). *The focused interview.* Glencoe, IL: Free Press.

Meyers, P.W., & Wilemon, D. (1989, June). Learning in new technology development teams. *Journal of Product Innovation Management*, pp. 79-88.

Miller, D.C. (1939). An experiment in the measurement of social interaction in group discussion. *American Sociological Review, 4*, 241-251.

Miller, G.A. (1956). The magical number seven, plus or minus two: Some limits on our capacity for processing information. *Psychology Review, 63*, 81-97.

Miller, G.R., & Fonts, N.E. (1979). *Videotape on trial: A view from the jury box.* Beverly Hills, CA: Sage.

Miller, G.R., Fonts, N.E., Boster, F.J., & Sunnafrank, M.J. (1983). Methodological issues in legal communication research: What can trial simulations tell us? *Communication Monographs, 50*, 33-46.

Mills, D.Q. (1993). *Rebirth of the corporation.* New York: Wiley.

Mills, P.K. (1983). Self-management: Its control and relationship to other organizational properties. *Academy of Management Review, 8*, 445-453.

Miner, F.C. (1984). Group versus individual decision making: An investigation of performance measures, decision strategies, and process losses/gains. *Organizational Behavior and Human Performance, 33,* 112-124.

Mintzberg, H. (1973). *The nature of managerial work.* New York: Harper and Row.

Mintzberg, H. (1989). *Mintzberg on management: Inside our strange world of organizations.* New York: Free Press.

Mirza, J. (1992). *Winning litigation the Mirza way.* Dearfield, IL: Clark-Boardment-Callaghan.

Moore, C.M. (1987). *Group techniques for idea building.* Newbury Park, CA: Sage.

Mortensen, C.D. (1966). Should the discussion group have an assigned leader? *Speech Teacher, 15,* 34-41.

Mosvick, R.K., & Nelson, R.B. (1987). *We've got to start meeting like this.* Glenview, IL: Scott-Foresman.

Mulder, M. (1960). Communication structure, decision structure and group performance. *Sociometry, 23,* 1-14.

Murrell, K., & Blanchard, D. (1986). *Facilitation manual for the organization simulation.* Chicago: B. J. Chakiris Corp.

Murrell, K., & Blanchard, D. (1992). OrgSim: Using an organizational simulation to create a "live" case. *Journal of Management Development, 11*(7), 67-76.

Nadler, D. (1979). The effects of feedback on task group behavior: A review of the experimental literature. *Organizational Behavior and Human Performance, 23,* 309-338.

Nadler, D.A., Gerstein, M.S., & Shaw, R.B. (1992). *Organizational architecture: Designs for changing organizations.* San Francisco: Jossey-Bass.

Nelson, W., Petelle, J.L., & Monroe, C. (1974). A revised strategy for idea generation in small group decision making. *Speech Teacher, 23,* 191-196.

Nemeth, C.J. (1986). Differential contributions of majority and minority influence. *Psychological Review, 93,* 23-32.

Nunamaker, J.F., Dennis, A.R., Valacich, J.S., Vogel, D.R., & George, J.F. (1991). Electronic meeting systems to support group work. *Communication of the ACM, 34*(7), 40-61.

Nutt, P. (1984). *Planning methods: For health and related organizations.* New York: Wiley.

Ogilvie, J.R., & Haslett, B. (1985). Communicating peer feedback in a task group. *Human Communication Research, 12,* 79-98.

O'Hair, D., & Kreps, G.L. (Eds.). (1990). *Applied communication theory and research.* Hillsdale, NJ: Erlbaum.

Olaniran, B.A., Friedrich, G.W., & VanGundy, A.B. (1992, May). *Computer-mediated communication in small group decisional stages.* Paper presented at the meeting of the International Communication

Association, Miami.

Ong, W.J. (1982). *Orality and literacy: The technologizing of the word.* London: Routledge.

Orsburn, J.D., Moran, L., Musselwhite, E., & Zender, J.H. (1990). *Self-directed work teams: The new American challenge.* Homewood, IL: Business One Irwin.

Osborn, A. (1957). *Applied imagination: Principles and procedures of creative thinking* (rev. ed.). New York: Scribner.

Pacanowsky, M. (1987). Communication in the empowering organization. In J. Anderson (Ed.), *Communication yearbook 11* (pp. 356-379). Newbury Park, CA: Sage.

Parker, M., & Slaughter, J. (1988). *Choosing sides: Unions and the team concept.* Boston: South End Press.

Parloff, M.B., & Handlon, J.H. (1964). The influence of criticalness on creative problem-solving in dyads. *Psychiatry, 27,* 17-27.

Pasmore, W.A. (1988). *Designing effective organizations: The sociotechnical systems perspective.* New York: Wiley.

Pearce, W.B., & Cronen, V.E. (1980). *Communication, action, and meaning: The construction of social realities.* New York: Praeger.

Pearce, W.B., McAdam, E., & Villar, E. (1992). "Not sufficiently systemic": An exercise in curiosity. *Human Systems, 3,* 75-87.

Pearson, A. (1988). Tough-minded ways to get innovative. *Harvard Business Review, 66*(3), 99-106.

Penn, P. (1982). Circular questioning. *Family Process, 21,* 267-280.

Pennings, J.M. (1987). Technological innovations in manufacturing. In J.M. Pennings & A. Buitendam (Eds.), *New technology as organizational innovation* (pp. 197-216). Cambridge, MA: Ballinger.

Perkins, A.D., Shaw, R.B., & Sutton, R.I. (1990). Summary: Human service teams. In J.R. Hackman (Ed.), *Groups that work (and those that don't): Creating conditions for effective teamwork* (pp. 349-357). San Francisco: Jossey-Bass.

Pessin, J., & Husband, R.W. (1933). Effects of social stimulation on human maze learning. *Journal of Abnormal and Social Psychology, 28,* 148-154.

Pfeiffer, W., & Jones, J. (1969-73). *A handbook of structured experiences for human relations training* (4 vols.). Iowa City, IA: University Associates.

Philipsen, G., Mulac, A., & Dietrich, D. (1979). The effect of social interaction on group idea generation. *Communication Monographs, 46,* 119-125.

Pinsonneault, A., & Kraemer, K. L. (1989). The impacts of technological support on groups: An assessment of the empirical research. *Decision Support Systems, 5,* 197-216.

Politser, P. (1981). Decision analysis and clinical judgment. *Medical*

Decision Making, 1, 361-389.

Polley, R.B., Hare, A.P., & Stone, P.J. (Eds.). (1988). *The SYMLOG practitioner: Applications of small group research.* New York: Praeger.

Pondy, L.R. (1967). Organizational conflict, concepts and models. *Administrative Science Quarterly, 12*, 296-320.

Poole, M.S. (1983). Decision development in small groups II: A study of multiple sequences in decision making. *Communication Monographs, 50*, 206-232.

Poole, M.S. (1985). Tasks and interaction sequences: A theory of coherence in group decision-making interaction. In R.L. Street & J.N. Cappella (Eds.), *Sequence and pattern in communicative behavior* (pp. 206-224). London: Edward Arnold.

Poole, M.S. (1991). Procedures for managing meetings: Social and technological innovation. In R.A. Swanson & B.O. Knapp (Eds.), *Innovative meeting management* (pp. 53-110). Austin, TX: 3M Meeting Management Institute.

Poole, M.S., & DeSanctis, G. (1990). Understanding the use of group decision support systems: The theory of adaptive structuration. In J. Fulk & C. Steinfield (Eds.), *Organizations and communication technology* (pp. 175-195). Newbury Park, CA: Sage.

Poole, M.S., & DeSanctis, G. (1992). Microlevel structuration in computer-supported decision-making groups. *Human Communication Research, 19*, 5-49.

Poole, M.S., & Doelger, J.A. (1986). Developmental processes in group decision-making. In R.Y. Hirokawa & M.S. Poole (Eds.), *Communication and group decision-making* (pp. 35-62). Newbury Park, CA: Sage.

Poole, M.S., & Hirokawa, R.Y. (1986). Communication and group decision-making: A critical assessment. In R.Y. Hirokawa & M.S. Poole (Eds.), *Communication and group decision-making* (pp. 15-31). Newbury Park, CA: Sage.

Poole, M.S., & Roth, J. (1989). Decision development in small groups IV: A typology of group decision paths. *Human Communication Research, 15*, 323-356.

Poole, M.S., Seibold, D.R., & McPhee, R.D. (1985). Group decision-making as a structurational process. *Quarterly Journal of Speech, 71*, 74-102.

Pozen, M.W., Lerner, D.J., D'Agostino, R.B., Belanger, A.J., & Buckley, S.A. (1982). Differential effects of experience on officers' admission diagnoses for patients with possible myocardialinfarction. *Medical Decision Making, 2*, 13-21.

Prince, G.M. (1970). *The practice of creativity.* New York: Harper & Row.

Pruitt, D.G. (1983). Experimental gaming and the goal/expectation hypothesis. In E. Volz (Ed.), *Small group interaction* (pp. 107-121).

New York: Wiley.

Pruitt, D.G., & Rubin, J.Z. (1986). *Social conflict: Escalation, statement and settlement*. New York: Random House.

Putnam, L.L. (1989). Perspective for research on group embeddedness in organizations. In S. King (Ed.), *Human communication as a field of study* (pp. 163-181). Albany, NY: SUNY Press.

Putnam, L.L., & Stohl, C. (1990). Bona fide groups: A reconceptualization of groups in context. *Communication Studies, 41*, 248-265.

Pyron, H.C. (1964). An experimental study of the role of reflective thinking in business and professional conferences and discussions. *Speech Monographs, 31*, 157-161.

Pyron, H.C., & Sharp, H., Jr. (1963). A quantitative study of reflective thinking and performance in problem-solving discussion. *Journal of Communication, 13*, 46-57.

Quick, J.D., Moorhead, G., Quick, J.C., Gerloff, E.A., Mattox, K.L., & Mullins, C. (1983). Decision-making emergency room residents: Preliminary observations and a decision model. *Journal of Medical Education, 58*, 117-125.

Reason, P., & Rowan, J. (Eds.). (1981). *Human inquiry: A sourcebook of new paradigm research*. New York: Wiley.

Reich, R. (1987). Entrepreneurship reconsidered: The team as hero. *Harvard Business Review, 65*(3), 77-83.

Renz, M.A., & Greg, J. (1988). Flaws in the decision-making process: Assessment of risk in the decision to launch flight F1-L. *Central States Speech Journal, 39*, 67-75.

Rice, A.K. (1958). *Productivity and social organization: The Ahmedabad experiments*. London: Tavistock Publications.

Rice, R.E., & Associates. (1984). *The new media: Communication, research, and technology*. Beverly Hills, CA: Sage.

Richards, I.A. (1951). Communication between men: The meaning of language. In H. von Foerster (Ed.), *Cybernetics: Circular causal and feedback mechanisms in biological and social systems. Transactions of the Eighth Conference, March 15-16, 1951* (pp. 45-91). New York: Josiah Macy, Jr. Foundation.

Rittel, H., & Webber, M. (1974). Dilemmas in a general theory of planning. *DMG-DRS Journal, 8*, 31-39.

Ritter, K. (1985). Drama and legal rhetoric: The perjury trials of Alger Hiss. *Western Journal of Speech Communication, 49*, 83-102.

Sacks, H.R., & Kurlantzick, L.S. (1988). *Missing witnesses, missing testimony, and missing theory*. Stoneham, MA: Butterworth Legal Publishers.

Sanbonmatsu, A. (1971). Darrow and Rorke's use of Burkean identification strategies in New York v. Gitlow, 1920. *Speech Monographs, 38*,

36-48.

Sato, T. (1979). Determination of hierarchical networks of instructional units using the ISM method. *Educational Technology Research, 3*, 67-75.

Schantz, D. (1986). The use of SYMLOG as a diagnostic tool in drug-related problems on the job. *International Journal of Small Group Research, 2*, 219-224.

Schein, E.H. (1958). *The development of organization in small problem-solving groups* [Final Report, Sloan Project No. 134]. Boston: Massachusetts Institute of Technology.

Schein, E.H. (1988). *Process consultation, Vol. 1: Its role in organization development* (2nd ed.). Reading, MA: Addison-Wesley.

Schneider, J.F., Schneider-Duker, M., & Becker-Beck, U. (1989). Sex roles and social behavior: On the relation between the Bem sex role inventory and the SYMLOG behavior rating scales. *Journal of Social Psychology, 129*, 471-479.

Schrage, M. (1990). *Shared minds: The new technologies of collaboration.* New York: Random House.

Schultz, B.L. (1992). Shifting to self-direction. *Target, 8*(3), 36-38.

Seibold, D.R. (1979). Making meetings more successful: Plans, formats and procedures for group problem-solving. *Journal of Business Communication, 16*, 3-20.

Seibold, D.R. (1986, May). *Process consultation and team building: Applying interpersonal and small group research.* Paper presented at the meeting of the International Communication Association, Chicago.

Seibold, D.R. (in press). Theoria and praxis: Reflections on means and ends in applied communication research. In K. E. Cissna (Ed.), *Applied communication in the 21st century.* Hillsdale, NJ: Erlbaum.

Seibold, D.R., Becker, M.R., Bradley, J.R., Deligiannis, P.P., Glaser, H.F., Heald, M.R., Holt, G.R., Lair, T.A., Mitra, A., Schenck, W.T., Steingard, D.S., & Sturgis, K.D. (1988). *"How are we doing?" Results of a survey assessing team management.* Unpublished report, University of Illinois, Department of Communication, Urbana-Champaign.

Seibold, D.R., & Contractor, N.S. (1992). Issues for a theory of high-speed management. In S. Deetz (Ed.), *Communication yearbook 16* (pp. 237-246). Newbury Park, CA: Sage.

Seibold, D.R., & Meyers, R.A. (1988, June). *What has group research done for us lately? An expanded view of "group research" and prospects for the future.* Paper presented at the meeting of the International Communication Association, New Orleans, LA.

Selvini Palazoli, M., Boscolo, L., Cecchin, G., & Prata, G. (1976). *Paradox and counterparadox.* New York: Aronson.

Selvini Palazoli, M., Boscolo, L., Cecchin, G., & Prata, G. (1980).

Hypothesizing—circularity—neutrality: Three guidelines for the conductor of the session. *Family Process, 19*, 3-12.

Senge, P.M. (1990). *The fifth discipline: The art & practice of the learning organization*. New York: Doubleday.

Sharp, H., Jr., & Millikin, J. (1964). Reflective thinking ability and the product of problem-solving discussion. *Speech Monographs, 31*, 124-127.

Shaw, M.E. (1932). Comparison of individuals and small groups in the rational solution of complex problems. *American Journal of Psychology, 44*, 491-504.

Shaw, M.E. (1954a). Some effects of problem complexity upon problem solution efficiency in different communication nets. *Journal of Experimental Psychology, 48*, 211-217.

Shaw, M.E. (1954b). Some effects of unequal distribution of information upon group performance in various communication nets. *Journal of Abnormal and Social Psychology, 49*, 547-553.

Shaw, M.E. (1981). *Group dynamics: The psychology of group behavior* (3rd ed.). New York: McGraw-Hill.

Shaw, M.E., & Rothschild, G.H. (1956). Some effects of prolonged experience in communication nets. *Journal of Abnormal and Social Psychology, 54*, 323-330.

Sheffield, A.D. (1926). *Creative discussion: A statement of method for leaders and members of discussion groups and conferences* (3rd ed.). New York: American Press.

Sherif, C.W., Sherif, M., & Nebergall, R.E. (1965). *Attitude and attitude change: The social judgment-involvement approach*. Philadelphia: W. B. Saunders.

Shields, D.C. (1981). Dramatistic communication based focus group interviews. In J.F. Cragan & D.C. Shields (Eds.), *Applied communication theory and research* (pp. 313-319). Prospect Heights, IL: Waveland Press.

Shields, D.C., & Cragan, J.F. (1971). *Justice and the jury: Issues and answers*. Cincinnati, OH: Campus Press.

Short, J., Williams, E., & Christie, B. (1976). *The social psychology of telecommunications*. New York: John Wiley.

Shotter, J. (1993). *Cultural politics of everyday life: Social constructionism, rhetoric, and knowing of the third kind*. Buffalo, NY: University of Toronto Press.

Simon, H.A. (1960). *The new science of management decisions*. New York: Harper & Row.

Simon, H.A. (1969). *The sciences of the artificial*. Cambridge, MA: MIT Press.

Simon, H.A. (1974). How big is a chunk? *Science, 183*, 482-488.

Simpson, R.H. (1938). *A study of those who influence and of those who are influenced in discussions* [Contributions to Education, No. 748]. New York: Columbia University, Teachers College, Bureau of

Publications.

Simpson, R.H. (1939). The effect of discussion on intra-group divergencies of judgment. *Quarterly Journal of Speech, 25,* 546-552.

Smith, M.J. (1982). *Persuasion and human action.* Belmont, CA: Wadsworth.

Solomon, M.J. (1981). Dimensions of interpersonal behavior: A convergent validation within a cognitive interactionist framework. *Journal of Personality, 49,* 15-26.

Sorensen, S. (1981, May). *Grouphate.* Paper presented at the meeting of the International Communication Association, Minneapolis.

Souder, W. (1987). *Managing new product innovations.* Lexington, MA: Lexington Books.

Spencer, W. (1990, Winter). Research to product: A major U.S. challenge. *California Management Review,* pp. 45-53.

Spich, R.S., & Keleman, K. (1985). Explicit norm structuring process: A strategy for managing task-group effectiveness. *Group & Organization Studies, 10,* 37-59.

Sproull, L., & Kiesler, S. (1991). *Connections: New ways of working in the networked organization.* Cambridge, MA: MIT Press.

Staley, C.C. (1990). Focus group research: The communication practitioner as marketing specialist. In D. O'Hair & G. L. Kreps (Eds.), *Applied communication theory and research* (pp. 185-201). Hillsdale, NJ: Erlbaum.

Staley, S.M., & Broome, B.J. (1993, November). *Managing cultural issues associated with technological change: Application of interactive design methodology in the automotive industry.* Paper presented at the meeting of the Speech Communication Association, Miami.

Steiner, I.D. (1972). *Group process and productivity.* New York: Academic Press.

Stewart, A. (1989). *Team entrepreneurship.* Newbury Park, CA: Sage.

Stewart, D.W., & Shamdasani, P.N. (1990). *Focus groups: Theory and practice.* Newbury Park, CA: Sage.

Stohl, C. (1993). European managers' interpretations of participation: A semantic network analysis. *Human Communication Research, 20,* 97-117.

SYMLOG Consulting Group. (1986). *The Bales report to your group.* San Diego: Author.

Tajfel, H. (1982). The social psychology of intergroup relations. *Annual Review of Psychology, 33,* 1-39.

Tannen, D. (1990). *You just don't understand: Women and men in conversation.* New York: William Morrow.

Taylor, A., Meyer, A., Rosegrant, T., & Samples, B.T. (1989). *Communicating* (5th ed.). Englewood Cliffs, NJ: Prentice Hall.

The payoff from teams. (1989, July 10). *Business Week,* p. 57.

Thompson, J.D. (1967). *Organizations in action*. New York: McGraw-Hill.

Thorndike, R.L. (1938a). The effect of discussion upon the correctness of group decisions, when the factor of majority influence is allowed for. *Journal of Social Psychology, 9*, 343-464.

Thorndike, R.L. (1938b). On what type of task will a group do well? *Journal of Abnormal Psychology, 33*, 409-413.

Timmons, W.M. (1939). *Decisions and attitudes as outcomes of the discussion of a social problem* [Contributions to Education, No. 777]. New York: Columbia University, Teachers College, Bureau of Publications.

Ting-Toomey, S.T. (1986). Interpersonal ties in intergroup communication. In W.B. Gudykunst (Ed.), *Intergroup communication* (pp. 114-126). London: Edward Arnold.

Tomm, C. (1985). Circular interviewing: A multifaceted clinical tool. In D. Campbell & R. Draper (Eds.), *Applications of systemic family therapy: The Milan approach* (pp. 33-45). London: Grune and Stratton.

Tompkins, P.K., & Cheney, G. (1985). Communication and unobtrusive control in organizations. In R. D. McPhee & P. K. Tompkins (Eds.), *Organizational communication: Traditional themes and new directions* (pp. 179-210). Newbury Park, CA: Sage.

Torrance, P.E. (1957). Function of expressed disagreement in small group processes. *Social Forces, 35*, 314-318.

Travis, L.E. (1925). The effect of a small audience upon eye-hand coordination. *Journal of Abnormal and Social Psychology, 20*, 142-146.

Travis, L.E. (1928). The influence of the group upon the stutter's speed in free association. *Journal of Abnormal and Social Psychology, 23*, 45-51.

Triplett, N. (1897). The dynamogenic factors in peacemaking and competition. *American Journal of Psychology, 9*, 507-533.

Trist, E.L. (1989). The assumption of ordinariness as a denial mechanism: Innovation and conflict in a coal mine. *Human Resource Management, 28*(2), 253-264.

Trist, E.L., Higgin, G.W., Murray, H., & Pollock, A.B. (1963). *Organizational choice*. London: Tavistock Publications.

Tuchman, B. (1965). Developmental sequences in small groups. *Psychological Bulletin, 63*, 384-399.

VanGundy, A.B. (1984). *Managing group creativity*. New York: AMACOM.

Varghese, R. (1982). Eriksonian personality variables and interpersonal behavior in groups. *Small Group Behavior, 13*, 133-149.

Versteeg, A. (1990). Self-directed work teams yield long-term benefits. *Journal of Business Strategy, 11*, 9-12.

Vogt, J.F., & Murrell, K.L. (1990). *Empowerment in organizations*. San Diego: University Associates.

Waagen, C. (1984). Agreement on procedure: A functional approach to consensus. In G. M Petelips & J. T. Wood (Eds.), *Emergent issues in human decision making* (pp. 80-93). Carbondale, IL: Southern Illinois University Press.

Wall, V.D., Jr., & Galanes, G. (1986). The SYMLOG dimensions and small group conflict. *Central States Speech Journal, 37,* 61-78.

Wallace, E., & Hoebel, E. A. (1986). *The Comanches: Lords of the south plains.* Norman: University of Oklahoma Press.

Walton, R.E. (1977). Work innovations at Topeka: After six years. *Journal of Applied Behavioral Science, 13,* 422-433.

Walton, R.E. (1985). From control to commitment: Transformation of workforce management strategies in the United States. In K.B. Clark, R.H. Hayes, & C. Lorez (Eds.), *The uneasy alliance: Managing the productivity-technology dilemma* (pp. 237-265). Boston: Harvard Business School Press.

Walton, R.E., & McKersie, R.A. (1965). *A behavioral theory of labor negotiations.* New York: McGraw-Hill.

Warfield, J.N. (1976). *Societal systems: Planning, policy and complexity.* New York: Wiley.

Warfield, J.N. (1982a). Interpretive structural modeling. In S. A. Olsen (Ed.), *Group planning and problem-solving methods in engineering* (pp. 155-201). New York: Wiley & Sons.

Warfield, J.N. (1982b). Organizations and systems learning. *General Systems, 27,* 5-74.

Warfield, J.N. (1986). Domain of science model: Evolution and design. *Proceedings of the Society for General Systems Research* (pp. H46-H59). Salinas, CA: Intersystems.

Warfield, J.N. (1990). *A science of generic design: Managing complexity through systems design.* Salinas, CA: Intersystems.

Waterman, R.H., Jr. (1990). *Autocracy: The power to change.* New York: W. W. Norton.

Watson, G.B. (1928). Do groups think more efficiently than individuals? *Journal of Abnormal and Social Psychology, 23,* 328-336.

Watzlawick, P., Beavin, J.H., & Jackson, D.D. (1967). *The pragmatics of human communication: A study of interactional patterns, pathologies, and paradoxes.* New York: Norton.

Weaver, R.L., II. (1971). Sensitivity training and effective group discussion. *Speech Teacher, 20,* 203-207.

Weick, K. (1979). *The social psychology of organizing* (2nd ed.). New York: Random House.

Weiner, N. (1954). *The human use of human beings: Cybernetics and society.* New York: Doubleday.

Weisbord, M.R. (1982). The cat in the hat breaks through: Reflections on OD's past, present, and future. In D.D. Warrick (Ed.), *Contemporary organization development: Current thinking and applications* (pp. 2-11).

Glenview, IL: Scott, Foresman.

Weisskopf-Joelson, E., & Eliseo, T.S. (1961). An experimental study of the effectiveness of brainstorming. *Journal of Applied Psychology, 45,* 45-49.

Wellins, R.S., Byham, W.C., & Wilson, J.M. (1991). *Empowered teams: Creating self-directed work groups that improve quality, productivity, and participation.* San Francisco: Jossey-Bass.

Wells, W. (1974). Group interviewing. In R. F. Ferber (Ed.), *Handbook of marketing research* (Vol. 2, pp. 133-146). New York: McGraw-Hill.

Weston, S.B., & English, H.B. (1926). The influence of the group on psychological test scores. *American Journal of Psychology, 37,* 600-601.

White, R.K., & Lippitt, R. (1960). *Autocracy and democracy.* New York: Harper.

Whyte, W.H. (1956). *The organization man.* New York: Doubleday Anchor.

Whyte, W.F. (Ed.). (1991). *Participatory action research.* Newbury Park, CA: Sage.

Whyte, W.F., & Whyte, K.K. (1988). *Making Mondragon: The growth and dynamics of the worker cooperative complex.* Ithaca, NY: ILR Press.

Wiggins, J.S. (1979). A psychological taxonomy of trait descriptive terms: The interpersonal domain. *Journal of Personality & Social Psychology, 17,* 395-412.

Wilson, G.L., Goodall, H.L., Jr., & Waagen, C.L. (1986). *Organizational communication.* New York: Harper & Row.

Wish, M., D'Andrade, R.G., & Goodnow, J.E., II. (1980). Dimensions of interpersonal communication: Correspondences between structures for speech acts bipolar scales. *Journal of Personality and Social Psychology, 39,* 848-860.

Wish, M., Deutsch, M., & Kaplan, S. J. (1976). Perceived dimensions of interpersonal relations. *Journal of Personality and Social Psychology, 33,* 409-420.

Wood, R., Hull, F., & Azumi, K. (1983). Evaluating quality circles: The American application. *California Management Review, 26,* 37-53.

Zammuto, T.F., & O'Connor, E.J. (1992). Gaining advanced manufacturing technologies' benefits: The roles of organization design and culture. *Academy of Management Review, 17,* 701-728.

Zander, A. (1982). *Making groups effective.* San Francisco: Jossey-Bass.

Zigurs, I., Poole, M.S., & DeSanctis, G.L. (1988). A study of influence in computer-mediated group decision making. *MIS Quarterly, 12,* 625-644.

Zorn, T., & Rosenfeld, L. (1989). Between a rock and a hard place: Ethical dilemmas in problem-solving group facilitation. *Management Communication Quarterly, 3,* 93-106.

Zuboff, S. (1988). *In the age of the smart machine: The future of work and power.* New York: Basic Books.

Author Index

Subject Index

DATE DUE
